# JOHN HEDGE(
## NEW MANUAL
## OF PHOTOGRAPHY

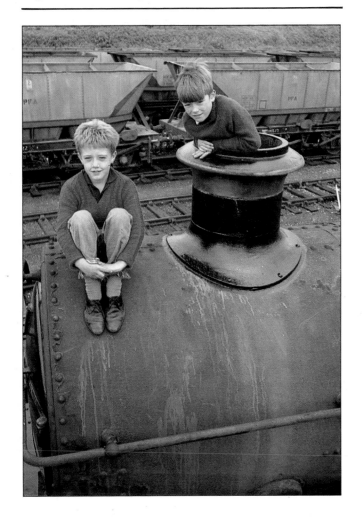

# JOHN HEDGECOE'S
# NEW MANUAL OF PHOTOGRAPHY

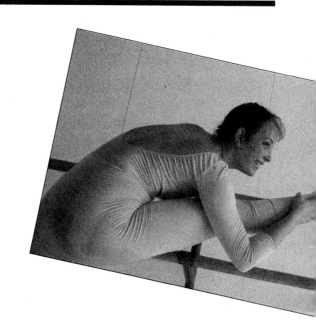

WEIDENFELD AND NICOLSON·LONDON

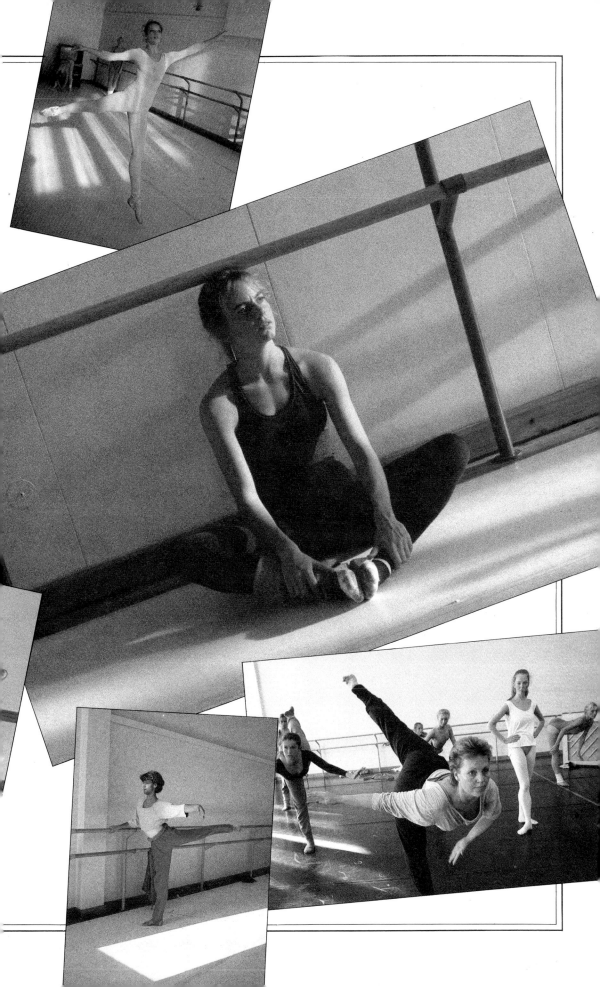

# CONTENTS

First published in 1986 by
George Weidenfeld & Nicolson Ltd
91 Clapham High Street,
London SW4 7TA

Filmset by
Text Filmsetters Ltd, London
Colour separations by
A. Mondadori, Verona
Printed and bound in Italy by
A. Mondadori, Verona

## Technical section

## Subject section

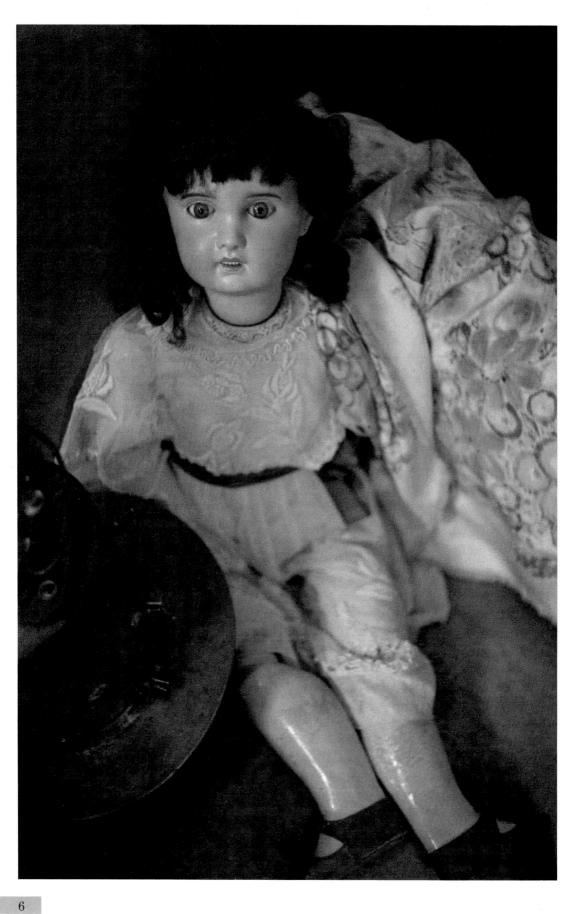

# INTRODUCTION

The aim of this book is to help the photographer to exploit his or her own ideas. I have tried to show how to do this – with full technical information and practical advice – and, at the same time, to demonstrate how even familiar subjects, approached with imagination and enthusiasm, can offer the chance to come up with new images.

The first section of the book explains the techniques and skills used in making pictures. None of them is complex and all are explained in terms that are easy to understand. Starting with a survey of the recent, exciting innovations in camera automation and the new generation of 35 mm SLR and compact models, this section covers all the practical aspects of photographic equipment and techniques: lens choice, exposure, lighting, focusing, composition, movement, colour, electronic flash, film, and filters.

Important though technical skill is, the camera is just the means by which a photographer expresses his creative vision. In the second part of this book, there are numerous examples that I hope will stimulate your imagination and trigger new ideas for pictures. Arranged thematically, this section explores the potential of many of the most popular photographic subjects, such as landscapes, the nude, portraits, sport, wildlife, and fashion. Making successful pictures means understanding what lies behind a subject's appeal, rather than just reacting intuitively. Analyse your reactions to a scene, deciding what is visually attractive and emotionally stimulating; which elements need emphasis and which should be ignored. It is the ideas behind the pictures that stimulate the senses and, after the initial impact, engage the imagination.

John Hedecoe

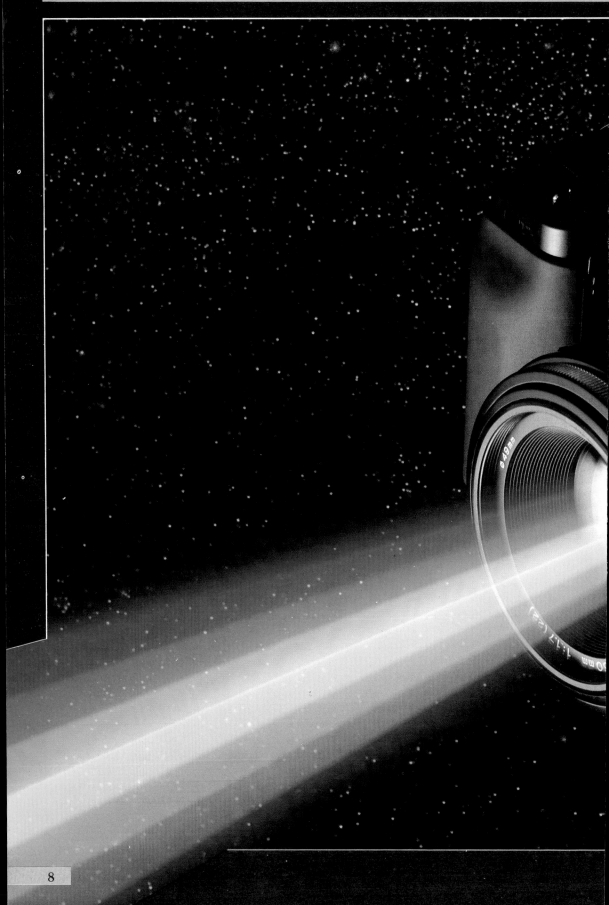

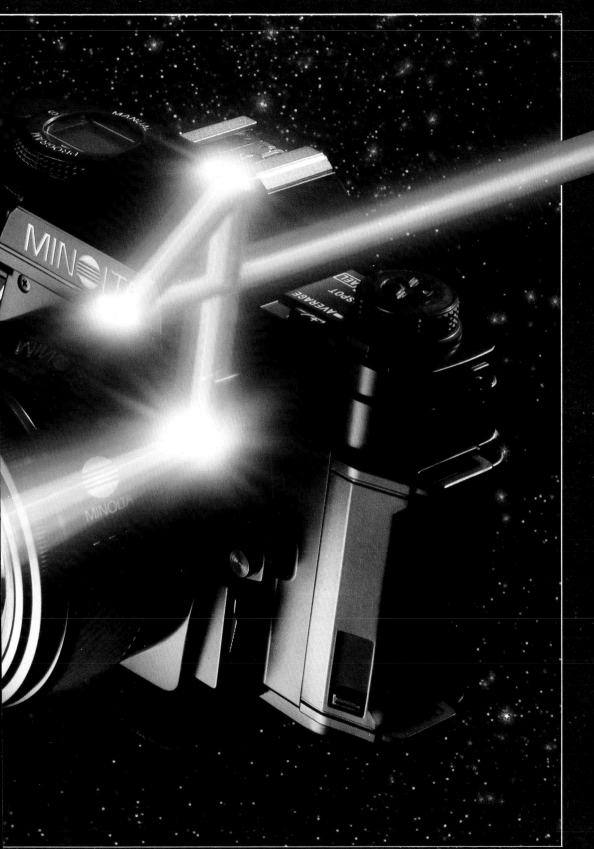

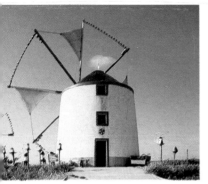

The camera of today is a highly computerized tool, incorporating some of the most advanced technology. The degree of sophistication is such that the modern 35 mm SLR can be set up to record at monthly intervals the changing seasons as they affect a landscape. These monthly exposures can be autofocused precisely, automatically metered and exposed, the exposure can be bracketed automatically, and all relevant data imprinted on each frame of film. Automation extends much further in fact, to film loading, film-speed setting, rewinding, selection of flash when needed, flash exposure, remote shutter release, remote exposure control, and the repertoire of automatic facilities is getting longer.

The most significant recent addition to automation is autofocusing. Compact cameras have had it for some time and, like autoexposure before, autofocus has been derided as a gimmick for the beginner. But new SLRs on the market that feature real-time, high-speed focusing systems housed in the camera rather than the lens are simply the first of a new breed that allow the photographer to focus faster and more

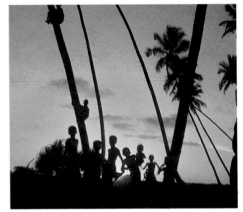

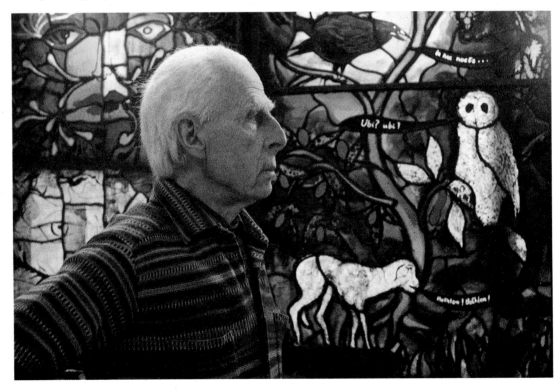

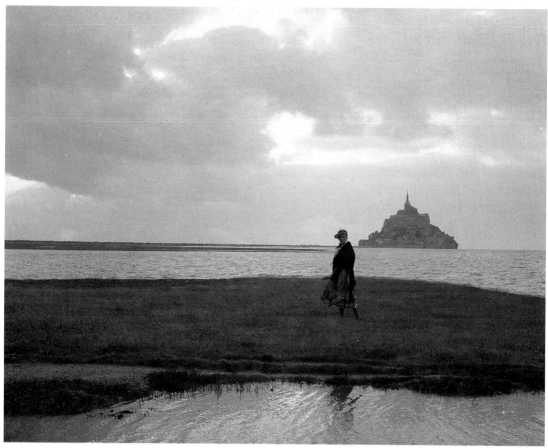

accurately than ever before. On the negative side autofocus systems still have failings, for there are situations when errors occur and not all cameras allow manual override or the locking of settings.

Autoexposure remains the most important modern development. Greeted with scepticism by the serious photographer who preferred total control over all the variables, by degrees automation has come a long way. Serious photographers, professionals among them, now regard semi-automatic exposure as helpful. Many have found that the sophistication of manual override and autoexposure locking gives greater control over setting than was ever possible with manual systems, allowing the fine tuning of image density in increments that are only just discernible to the human eye. In fact modern auto-exposure has, on sophisticated cameras, the ability to cope with all but a very few subjects, and fine-tune overrides are there to cope with the rest. This puts creative freedom in the hands of the photographer when it is wanted and minimizes the interference of technical problems.

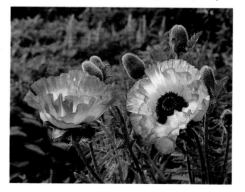

Advanced technology has enabled camera designers to incorporate autofocusing systems into the camera body. This has overcome the major problems of early, lens-based systems: excessive bulk, weight, and cost, coupled with clumsy handling. Integrated circuits and microchips control miniaturized motors guided by special focus sensors that 'see' through the taking lens. Response is rapid and accurate focus and refocus are almost instantaneous – all at the touch of a button. In fact, the newest cameras can keep up with a normal motordrive, to ensure that a moving subject is pin sharp in every shot. The advantages of this recent technological development are obvious, especially for photographers who have eyesight problems.

Subjects such as sport, wildlife, and children, as well as some scientific areas that feature rapid action all benefit from precise, real-time autofocusing. General disadvantages are the systems' reliance on battery power (although more advanced types have a manual override) increased bulk, and lenses that are 'slow' (have a relatively small maximum aperture). Focusing errors with modern contrast-comparing types are few providing there is enough ambient light. Infra-red types can be misled by glass in front of the subject or by focusing on strong foreground objects that are not the subject to be photographed.

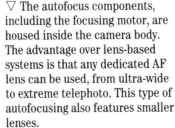

▽ The autofocus components, including the focusing motor, are housed inside the camera body. The advantage over lens-based systems is that any dedicated AF lens can be used, from ultra-wide to extreme telephoto. This type of autofocusing also features smaller lenses.

△ The scene is composed with the mirror at 45° (top picture) and the aperture fully open; pressing the shutter causes the mirror to rise (bottom picture), the taking aperture to be selected and the shutter to fire. After exposure the mirror returns and the aperture opens again.

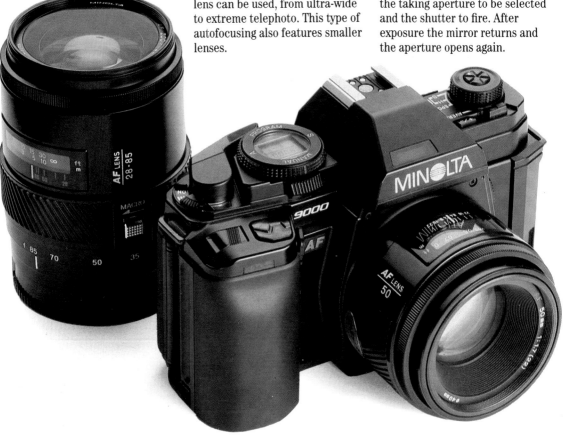

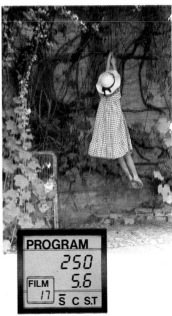

**PROGRAM**
*180*
**FILM** *9.5*
*18* $\overline{S}$ C S.T

**PROGRAM**
*750*
**FILM** *6.7*
*19* $\overline{S}$ C S.T

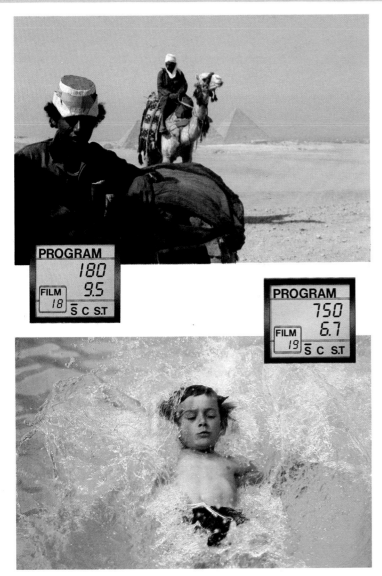

**PROGRAM**
*250*
**FILM** *5.6*
*17* $\overline{S}$ C S.T

With up-to-date, fully programmed exposure systems, the photographer can choose a programme that takes into account the type of lens being used. So, for wide-angle lenses, a programme that gives aperture setting priority over shutter speeds will be used. With moderate wide-angles, standard or short telephoto lenses, a programme offering a balance between aperture and shutter speeds can be selected. For telephoto lenses, faster speeds are important so a programme that prefers shutter speeds will be used. The latest versions select the right programme automatically, making the use of zooms with linked, fully programmed exposure a possibility.

Most cameras that boast autoexposure offer both semi-automatic and fully automated selection of aperture and shutter speed. Fully-automatic exposure systems set both the shutter speed and the aperture according to a pre-determined programme. Semi-automatic systems set one of these variables, the photographer sets the other. Both systems measure and select the exposure level, usually metering with a centre-weighted meter that biases the reading to the lower central part of the scene.

The main advantages of autoexposure systems are the ease with which they deliver 'correct' exposure and their speed of operation. The drawbacks are mainly related to subject failures and, with programmed exposure, selecting settings that do not take into account the type of photograph being made. Some modern programmed exposure systems feature one touch parameter modification and have wide, normal, and telephoto programmes to give the photographer even more precise exposure control. The latest, computer assisted autoexposure modes have a very high success rate, even with unusual subjects.

See also:
COMPACT CAMERAS pp16-17
CHOOSING EXPOSURE pp28-31
FOCUSING METHODS pp44-45

# 3 5 mm SLR CAMERAS

Electronic flash units are a compact and highly portable light source which, used properly, can give a variety of types of light, from balanced fill-in (to reduce contrast in daylight conditions) to soft or hard main light. There are many types of flash unit available, ranging from small, simple, camera-mounted guns to powerful and sophisticated professional systems that often incorporate two flash tubes – one main and one fill-in. Now that SLR cameras are offering flash-synchronization speeds of as fast as $1/250$ sec, the modern electronic flash has become a truly useful tool for the photographer.

Features that you would expect to find on a mid-range flash unit would include a guide number of about 30 in metres, automatic exposure measurement, manual override, multiple power settings, fast recycling for use with autowinders, fully-charged signal, a swivel head for bounced flash, wide-angle to telephoto coverage, off-camera capability, and accessories such as filters, a bounce reflector, and an external power pack. In the automatic-exposure mode, most models will confirm that correct exposure has been achieved with a visual and sometimes an audible signal. More complex units may also offer automatic TTL (through the lens) flash exposure with dedicated cameras, correct daylight-flash exposure balance, automatic zoom coverage, flash-assisted autofocus, mains AC inlet, and more power.

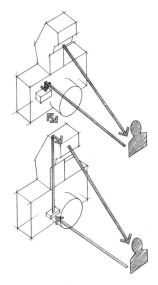

△ On some SLR cameras, an initial burst of LED light from the flash triggers the autofocus system to set correct focus, even in the dark.

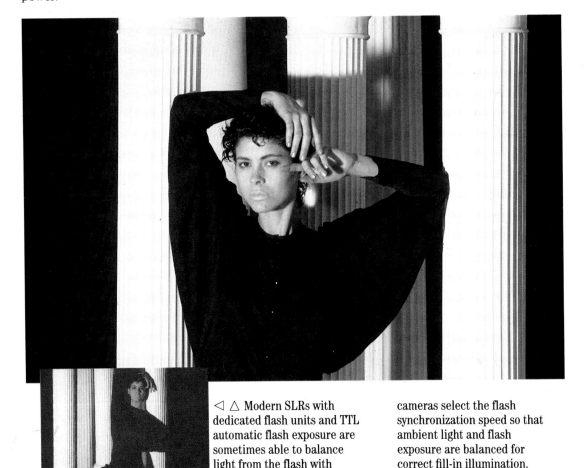

◁ △ Modern SLRs with dedicated flash units and TTL automatic flash exposure are sometimes able to balance light from the flash with ambient illumination. Some cameras select the flash synchronization speed so that ambient light and flash exposure are balanced for correct fill-in illumination.

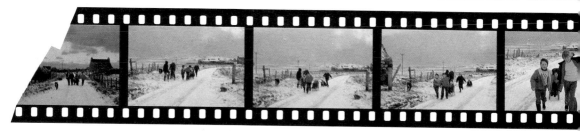

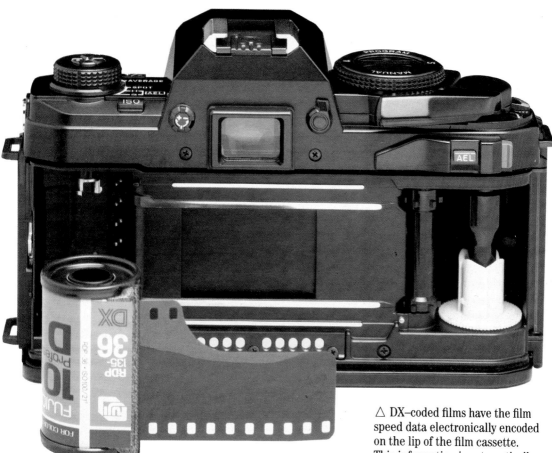

△ DX–coded films have the film speed data electronically encoded on the lip of the film cassette. This information is automatically read by the camera's DX contacts which are positioned on the inside edge of the film chamber and come into contact with the cassette as soon as it is loaded.

Film transport and handling have also benefited from new developments designed to simplify camera operation. One of the most irritating errors that photographers commonly commit is forgetting to adjust the film-speed setting when they load the camera. With the new DX coding, it should become a thing of the past. DX-coded films instruct the camera to set the correct ISO value automatically. Not all SLRs have this feature yet, but most new models will incorporate it. Other features new to SLRs with a built-in winder are automatic film advance to the first frame as soon as the back is closed, automatic film stop, with a signal to tell the photographer that the film is finished, and automatic rewind. Some cameras with autofocus have a dedicated motordrive that combines the automatic refocusing of each exposure with wind-on speeds of several frames per second.

See also:
COMPACT CAMERAS pp16-17
CHOOSING EXPOSURE pp28-31
FOCUSING METHODS pp44-45
SPORT & ACTION pp198-207

# COMPACT CAMERAS

Compact cameras are the smallest cameras using 35 mm film and are primarily designed for photographers who do not need the versatility provided by the SLR systems. Unlike the SLR, a compact does not have interchangeable lenses and the viewing system is quite separate from the lens. (A few sophisticated compacts take a limited range of interchangeable lenses.) However, sophisticated, modern compacts are quite capable of handling a wide range of subjects. Automation has been the compact manufacturers' main goal and from the moment the camera back is opened it starts – with DX-coded automatic film-speed setting, autowind to the first frame, autowind, autostop, autorewind, autoexposure, autoflash selection, autofill flash and, of course, autofocusing. Most models have little scope for overriding the automatic systems, which limits creative interpretation of exposure, perspective, focus, and framing. But the latest cameras are breaking new ground in this respect and provide autoexposure and focus locks, backlight compensation and built-in telephoto settings, usually of around 65 mm.

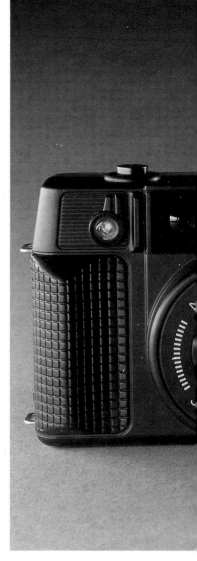

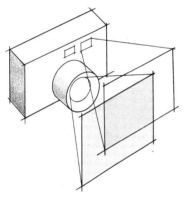

◁ ▽ The viewfinder on compact cameras is at one side of and slightly above the lens. The small difference in viewpoint between lens and viewfinder is not significant at normal distances but with close-ups it is enough to cause a framing error, known as parallax error. The diagram illustrates how parallax error is caused by this framing discrepancy. The top picture shows what appears in the viewfinder within the brightline frame and the bottom picture is what the lens actually records. To correct parallax error, make sure you use the parallax compensation marks, or reframe slightly high and to the left of the subject.

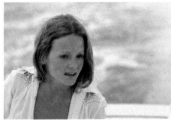

△ The camera pictured here is one of the most sophisticated models on the market today, but many, more modestly priced cameras share its main features, such as autofocusing and autoexposure. Modern compact cameras often have automated film-speed setting with DX-coded film, film loading, wind-on, rewind and stop, plus automatic flash operation. Some have extra features that may include a self-timer, limited exposure control and, in the case of this model, a data back for printing date and time on each picture.

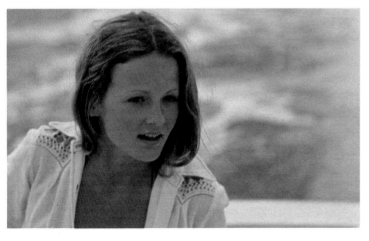

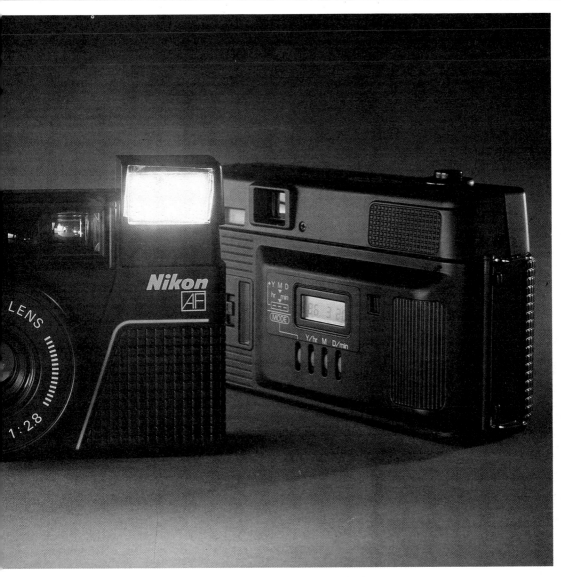

▷ The area covered by the lens is defined by the brightline frame (sometimes showing the corners only), with the parallax compensation marks near the top and also on one side if the finder is off-set. With autofocus models, the central focusing zone is indicated – here by two brackets – and a scale of symbols shows the distance focused on. Semi-automatic exposure cameras may also show the shutter speed or aperture selected for exposure. Fully programmed models often have 'correct' and 'out-of-exposure-range' indicators.

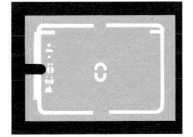

See also:
35 mm SLR CAMERAS pp 12-15
CHOOSING EXPOSURE pp28-31
STUDY IN MOSAIC pp238-239

# THE STANDARD LENS

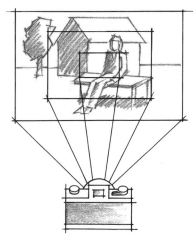

The 50 mm focal length was chosen as the standard lens because its angle of view approximates to the human field of vision and because it produces a natural perspective from normal distances. The standard lens for any particular format is approximately equal to the film format's diagonal. For the 6 × 6 roll film format it is 75-80 mm, while for the 5 × 4 format it is 150-200 mm.

The standard lens is the lens normally supplied with the camera body. It is an ideal focal length for the beginner to learn the fundamentals of photographic technique – focusing, framing, composition, and light metering – as well as for trying out new filters and lens attachments. When people first look through the viewfinder of a camera, they are often surprised that the normal view looks rather like a cut-out, with less included than they would expect. This is because the human eye actually scans a 180° field but only about 25 per cent in the centre is 'sharp'. The remainder is interpreted blur. This narrowing of sharp vision when compared to 50 mm framing means that the standard lens closely matches what we see of subjects in the near and middle distance, and it is best suited to that type of photography.

It is common for photographers to discard the 50 mm as they gain experience. This does not arise solely from a wish to explore new ground, but also because the standard lens is not ideally suited to two of our most popular subjects: landscapes and portraiture. Its real home ground is still-life, nature, architecture, and subjects that benefit from a selective viewpoint. As many modern standard lenses focus down to less than 50 cm, giving a magnification of about ×0.15, they are also very useful for close-up work. This role can be further developed by using extension tubes of a bellows unit.

Optical performance of standard lenses at normal distances is probably better than that of any equivalent lens at any aperture. This is because the design and construction of this lens type is less complex than some others and manufacturers place great importance on producing the best possible configuration. This makes the standard very useful for low-light work, where wide apertures may have to be used, and for throwing the background out of focus while keeping the subject sharp.

△ Angle of view, which is the amount of a scene included in the frame, varies with focal length. The diagram above illustrates the difference between a standard 50 mm lens's angle of view and those of two of the most popular 'second' lenses – a 135 mm telephoto and a 28 mm wide-angle. Their approximate angles of view are 45°, 20° and 75° respectively. The 45° angle of the 50 mm lens nearly matches the angle of view of human vision which is one of the reasons why it was adopted as the 'standard' for 35 mm photography. Other formats have different focal lengths as their standard lenses. Medium-format cameras generally have an 80 mm standard lens and 5 × 4 cameras use a 150 mm lens.

▷ A 35 mm SLR camera is part of a system and, although it is likely that you will buy only a 50 mm lens with the camera body, you will soon want to add other lenses. Two of the most versatile supplementary lenses are the 135 mm telephoto and the 28 mm wide-angle, shown here with the standard lens. The 135 mm lens and the 28 mm lens will allow you to tackle, respectively, sport and landscapes.

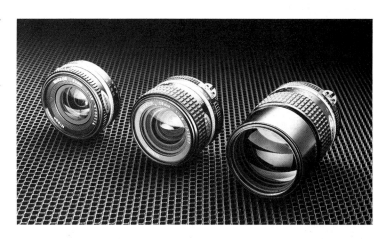

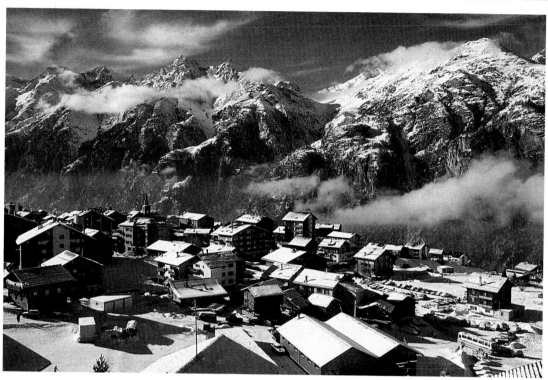

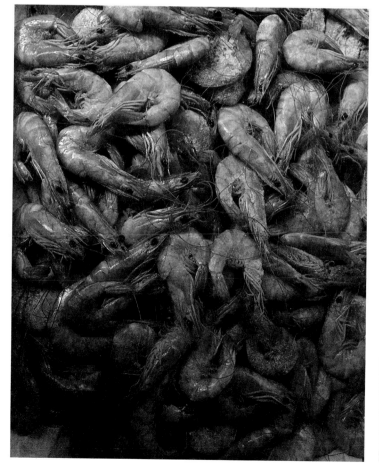

△ Novice photographers are often quick to discard the 50 mm lens, but, with more experience, they soon realize that it has many uses. With careful composition, it can be a good landscape lens, as with this Alpine scene.

*Pentax LX, 50 mm Ilford FP4 ISO 125, ¹/₂₅₀ sec, f16*

◁ The standard lens is especially useful for medium to close-up subjects, when its angle of view corresponds most closely to our own vision. It can also focus down to around 50 cm (20 in) for close-up details such as this bowl of shrimps.

*Pentax LX, 50 mm, Ilford FP4 ISO 125, ¹/₁₂₅ sec, f11*

See also:
35 mm SLR CAMERAS pp12-15
THE WIDE-ANGLE LENS pp20-21
THE TELEPHOTO LENS pp22-23

# THE WIDE-ANGLE LENS

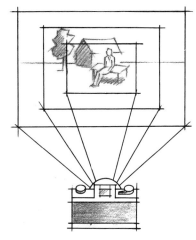

△ Wide-angle lenses range in focal length from about 14 mm to 40 mm, but most manufacturers offer a range that starts with a 35 mm lens and extends to 16 mm. The angles of view illustrated here include the coverage of 35 mm, 28 mm and 18 mm lenses. The angles of view for these lenses are 62°, 74° and 100°.

The wide-angle lens as we know it is a fairly young lens. Little more than a generation ago most photographers working with 35 mm cameras thought of the 35 mm lens as being 'the wide angle', and 28 mm lenses were a rarity. Perhaps even more surprising is the impact that the photograph's wide-angle vision has had on the way we see the world, art, and visual communication in general.

The wide-angle group of lenses in the 35 mm format extend from about 40 mm to 14 mm in focal length (fisheye lenses can be much shorter) and, as their name implies, they give a wider than normal field of view. For rollfilm cameras the range covers the focal lengths from 65 to 35 mm, and for the 5 × 4 format focal lengths from 135 to 65 mm. Within this range there are various groupings which come under a plethora of confusing headings – ultrawide, superwide, extrawide, moderate wide-angle, extreme wide-angle, and so on – none of which is definitive. Normally, for the 35 mm format, lenses described as moderate wide-angle fall within the 28 – 48 mm group, with those of shorter focal length being termed ultrawide. The most obvious effect of having a wider angle of view is that, from a given viewpoint, more is included within the frame as focal length decreases. This makes the wide-angle lens an obvious candidate for use in confined places or where a broad view is wanted from a close distance.

On the minus side, optical distortions – astigmatism and spherical, marginal, and chromatic aberrations – are more noticeable with shorter focal lengths, and wide-angle perspective becomes progressively steeper. These distortions, which increase towards the edge of the frame, are sometimes exploited to dramatize perspective and strengthen pictorial composition. Perspective in a photograph is created by compositional elements such as converging lines, decreasing scale, aerial haze, and colour.

By allowing the photographer to work close to a subject, yet to include as much of a scene as a longer lens would from farther away, wide-angle lenses make foreground objects loom large while distant objects appear miniaturized and recede. Converging lines are steep, scale is distorted, and near colour is emphasized. Many ultrawide lenses render straight lines at the frame edges as curves, and stretch objects into amusing distortions.

▷ Wide-angle lenses range from 35 mm to around 14 mm, their angle of view increasing as focal length decreases. The four lenses shown here are, from left to right, 35 mm, 28 mm, 24 mm, and 16 mm. The first two are regarded as moderate wide-angle lenses and serve the needs of most photographers looking for wider-than-standard coverage. The other two lenses are described as ultra-wide and are useful for landscape, documentary, and architectural work.

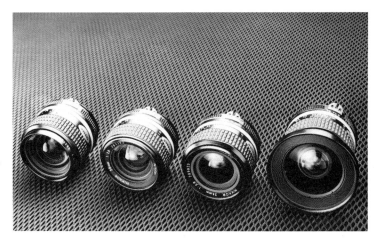

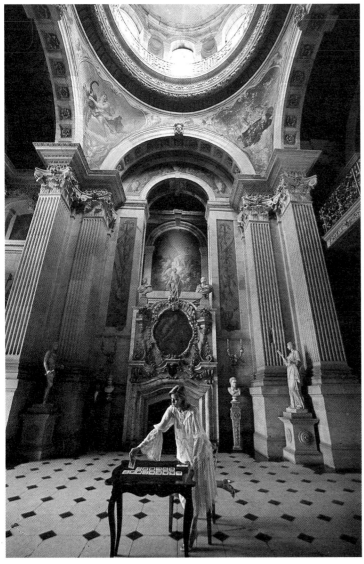

◁ In landscape photographs the perspective distortion of a wide-angle lens is not always apparent, but when a wide-angle lens is used with architectural subjects, where we expect to see parallel verticals, the distortion is obvious. Sometimes the effect can be exploited, as here, to suggest considerable space, but to keep the verticals straight, it is necessary to have the film plane parallel to them.

*Pentax LX, 24 mm, Kodak Ektachrome 64, ¹/₆₀ sec, f8*

▽ Wide-angle lenses are more likely to be affected by flare than lenses with a long focal length and need careful shading from light sources. Flare patterns, created by light reflecting off the iris diaphragm, are distinctive and form 'images' of the opening repeated across the picture.

*Pentax LX, 24 mm, Kodak Ektachrome 64, ¹/₂₅₀ sec, f8*

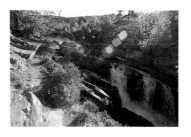

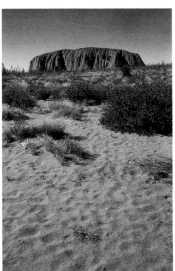

◁ A wide-angle lens has an inherently extensive depth of field so that, at any given aperture setting, it extends over a greater distance than longer focal length lenses. This makes the wide-angle especially useful for landscape photographs that include near foreground and distant detail that need to be recorded in sharp focus.

*Pentax LX, 28 mm, Kodak Kodachrome 64, ¹/₁₂₅ sec, f11*

See also:
THE STANDARD LENS pp18-19
THE TELEPHOTO LENS pp22-23
DEPTH OF FIELD pp40-41
VIEWPOINT AND SCALE pp48-49

# THE TELEPHOTO LENS

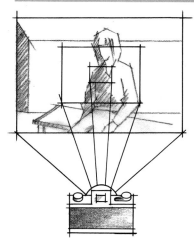

The telephoto lens lessens the gap between the photographer and a distant subject. It acts like a telescope, drawing the subject in and filling the frame to give a good-sized image. They are ideal for sports and action shots, and wildlife photography, when it is neither sensible nor safe to approach the subject closely, or for candid shots in which the photographer wants to avoid influencing the subject's behaviour. Short telephotos give tight framing of near subjects, creating an intimate view perfect for portraits.

In the 35 mm format, most systems offer telephoto lenses between 85 mm and 300 mm, and some include lenses of 1000 mm or even 2000 mm. For the 6×6 rollfilm format, short telephotos start at around 150 mm. In both formats the main characteristics are the same: magnification of subject, a narrow angle of view, a much reduced depth of field, and a flattening of perspective. As the focal length of the lens increases, these features became more noticeable. At the higher magnifications, the limited depth of field and exaggerated movement caused by camera shake can cause problems. Even with a 135 mm lens, an aperture of f32 is required to extend field depth from 10 metres to infinity, so precise focusing is essential with all telephoto work.

△ The angles of view for the 85 mm, 200 mm and 1000 mm focal lengths are illustrated here. Their respective angles of view are approximately 28°, 12°, and 3.5°, and they represent the extremes of most manufacturers' ranges of telephoto lenses, although there are telephotos of up to 2000 mm in focal length for specialist use.

Low contrast is often a problem with telephotos, since the lenses tend to pick up scattered UV and blue-wavelength light from the sky. A long lens hood and a UV filter help to combat this effect. To avoid camera shake, it is important to have a steady grip on the camera and, for high magnifications or longer exposures, a tripod is essential. Firing the shutter by cable release, with the mirror locked up, also helps to keep camera shake to a minimum.

The problem of the bulk and weight of extreme telephotos has been solved, to some extent, by the catadioptric telephoto lens, which uses an arrangement of mirrors and lenses to reduce barrel length. Mirror lenses are also very much lighter than conventional telephotos. But this system means that the lens aperture is unchangeable. New glass technology has improved the conventional telephoto. The chromatic aberration that was a serious drawback of older lenses has been almost eliminated. In fact, the latest short telephotos – from 85 mm to 150 mm – perform just as well as standard 50 mm lenses.

▷ For the keen photographer, a set of telephoto lenses spanning a range of 85–300 mm will be sufficient to cover most needs. The 85 mm lens – far right – is ideal for portraits, and some landscapes will benefit from its selective framing. The 135 mm lens – centre-right – offers wide maximum apertures and its compact styling makes it a versatile lens. Perspective flattening and a narrow field of view are more extreme with the 200 mm and 300 mm lenses – centre-left and left – which are ideal for distant subjects.

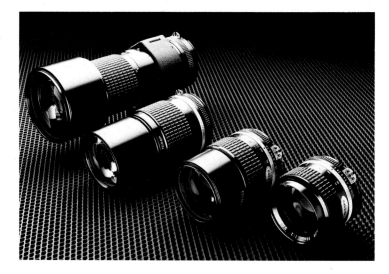

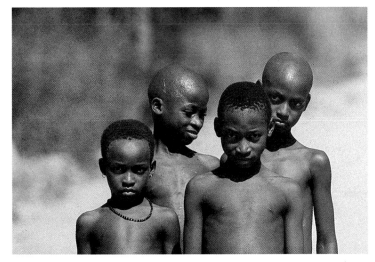

◁ The longer telephoto lenses, 200 mm and more, show progressively flattened perspective as focal length increases. This picture was made with a 350 mm lens and the perspective flattening creates the illusion that the two pairs of boys are standing almost on top of each other. In fact, a distance of several feet separates them. Long lenses have a shallow depth of field which can be used to throw the background out of focus.

*Pentax LX, 350 mm, Kodak Ektachrome 64, 1/500 sec, f8*

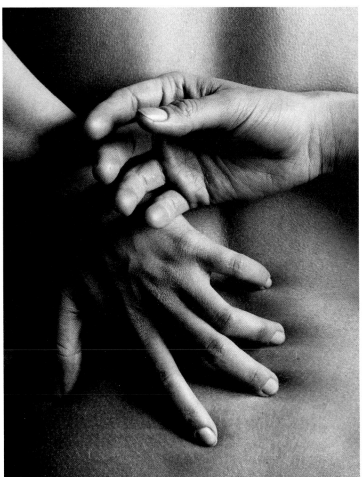

△ For a portrait study which fills a large part of the picture area, the best results are obtained by using a short telephoto. Perspective is flattened, making a more attractive picture, and a wide f-stop can be used to narrow depth of field and throw the background out of focus.

*Pentax LX, 85 mm, Kodak Ektachrome 64, 1/125 sec, f16*

△ Although close focusing with a telephoto lens does not extend into the macro range, very restricted areas of detail can be framed. Tightly cropped images, such as this pair of hands, have immediacy and impact.

*Hasselblad, 120 mm, Kodak Tri-X ISO 400, 1/250 sec, f11*

See also:
THE STANDARD LENS pp18-19
THE WIDE-ANGLE LENS pp20-21
DEPTH OF FIELD pp40-41
FILLING THE FRAME pp42-43

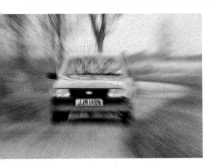

△ Changing focal length during a relatively long exposure creates fan-like streaks that emanate from the centre of the frame. For best results centre on a static image set against a background with highlights and strong shadow areas, mount the camera on a tripod and use an exposure of about ¼ sec.

*Pentax LX, 75-150 mm, Kodak Ektachrome 64, 1/15 sec, f22*

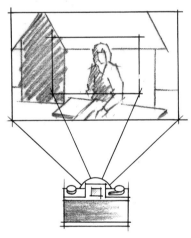

Zoom lenses have become enormously popular in recent years. They offer the photographer greater flexibility and convenience than traditional fixed-length lenses, allowing you to vary focal distance without having to change camera position. They give almost instant precise framing for a variety of situations, a great asset for in-camera cropping of transparencies.

Originally developed for movie cameras, zooms are now freely available for rollfilm formats and commonplace as attachments to 35 mm SLRs. In 35 mm format, there are many versions, covering a range of from about 24 mm to 600 mm, each suited to different types of photography. A modern zoom lens may have between ten and twenty glass elements, shifted along tracks under microprocessor control to produce different focal lengths. Probably the most popular are those that cover the standard lens or medium telephoto within their range – 35 mm to 80 mm, 75 mm to 150 mm, or 70 mm to 200 mm. These tend to be faster than more ambitious designs with higher zoom ratios (the ratio between longest and shortest focal length) and to display less distortion at the extreme settings. Good telephoto zooms made of low-dispersion glass perform as well, for most practical purposes, as fixed lenses of the equivalent focal length. The old prejudice that using a zoom meant losing quality is rapidly being undermined. A zoom is now a realistic alternative to having a selection of fixed focal-length lenses, dispensing with lens changing and minimizing missed shots. Experimentation is the key to discovering the capabilities of a zoom. Zoomed sequences, with separate exposures stepped down at different focal lengths, can be very effective. For simple shots, use the viewfinder at different ranges and then select the one you feel is most appropriate to the subject and setting to get the best composition.

Zoomed photographs are another technique specific to these lenses that you can exploit to creative effect. Zoom the lens as the exposure is taken to create an exploding image with streaks radiating from the centre, giving a dramatic sense of movement even to static subjects.

Different focal length zooms require different handling. The wide-angle zooms of shorter focal length introduce a strong sense of movement with just small lens changes, and image blur is more extreme towards the edge of the frame. Telephoto zooms offer more control and, given an isolated subject with strong local contrast, the results can be spectacular.

△ Zoom lenses are available in many different focal length configurations including quite extreme wide-angles – 21-35 mm – and telephotos – 400-600 mm. One of the most popular types, after the 80-200 mm, is the 35-80 mm telephoto zoom. In the diagram, its angle of view coverage from 62° to 25° is compared with the angle of view for the standard lens at 45° which this telephoto sometimes replaces.

▷ Some manufacturers offer a mid-range zoom, such as the 28-85 mm lens pictured here, as an alternative to the standard lens on a newly purchased camera body. This type of zoom, although initially more expensive than a standard lens, is very economical when compared with the cost of purchasing additional fixed focal length lenses.

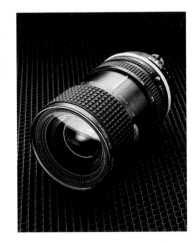

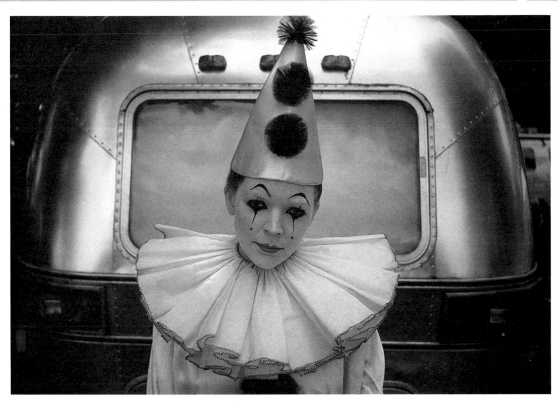

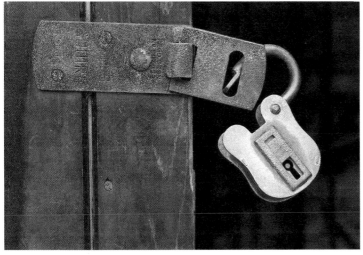

△ Zoom lenses are well-suited to in-camera cropping, so that the image fills the frame and can be composed precisely. This is invaluable if you use transparency film and do not intend to make enlargements from them, or for AV slides which can be shot as you want them to appear on the screen, without having to make selectively cropped duplicates.

*Pentax LX, 75-150 mm, Kodak Ektachrome 64, ¹/₆₀ sec, f8*

△ Many zoom lenses in the longer focal length ranges have a so-called 'macro' mode. The mode does not actually allow macro photography, but on switching to it, the optics are re-configured so that the shortest end of the zoom range is maintained. At the longest setting this allows you to make close-up photographs, such as here, that may be about ¼ life-size with some lenses.

*Pentax LX, 70-210 mm, Kodak Ektachrome 64, ¹/₃₀ sec, f11*

See also:
THE STANDARD LENS pp18-19
THE WIDE-ANGLE LENS pp20-21
THE TELEPHOTO LENS pp22-23
BLURRING MOVEMENT pp62-63

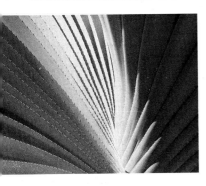

For general photography, the lenses we have already looked at (see pp.18-25) will produce excellent results. They have been designed to be as versatile as possible, but there are times when their specifications are too restricted. Unusual picture requirements, such as extreme close-ups, extraordinary angles of view and the manipulation of perspective, require specially designed lenses.

Among the most important are macro lenses, perspective control or shift lenses, mirror lenses and fisheye lenses. Of these, macro lenses are probably the most useful for general photography. They were originally designed for specialist macro – that is, life-sized photography – in the field of medicine, but recent designs perform extremely well at normal distances. This makes them very versatile, with the ability to focus down to a few centimetres, produce about half-life-sized images, and then refocus to infinity at a touch. There are focal lengths for 35 mm cameras from 50 mm to 200 mm that behave just as any other lens, plus wide-angle versions, usually between 20 mm and 35 mm, for use with bellows focusing. Many photographers now use the macro as their 'standard' lens.

△ Macro lenses are probably the most versatile lenses available to the photographer, particularly the 50 mm and 90/100 mm versions. These focal lengths are in constant use for general photography but the macro facility allows you to make one-quarter or half-life-sized images without the need to use extension tubes. Their only drawback is their speed – usually f2.8 or f4 – which is relatively slow compared with that of a normal lens.

*Pentax LX, 50 mm macro, Kodak Ektachrome 200, 1/125 sec, f11*

Shift lenses have been designed to overcome the architectural photographer's commonest problem, that of keeping verticals straight when taking pictures from ground level. With a normal lens and the camera facing upwards to include the top of the building, the structure's sides converge in a steep, unnatural perspective. With a shift lens, the camera back can be kept parallel to the building and the lens is shifted up to include the top in exactly the same way as the rising front movement of technical cameras. This keeps the verticals straight. Shift lenses can also be used to exaggerate convergence by moving the lens down to steepen perspective; this is ideal for landscapes. In fact, shift lenses have many other uses which result from their ability to shift their coverage from straight ahead to one side.

Although mirror lenses are really no more than telephoto lenses, their 'catadioptric' design puts them in the 'special' group.

▷ Four of the most widely-used special lenses are the shift lens, the mirror lens, the fisheye and the macro. Shift lenses are wide-angle optics designed to control converging verticals in architectural pictures. A mirror lens's compact size is a product of combining mirrors and glass elements in its construction. The fisheye lens produces a circular image and has an angle of view of at least 180°. Macro lenses are designed for extreme close-up work but make versatile general-purpose lenses too.

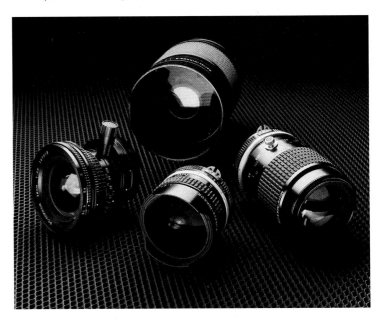

Because the light path is folded by mirrors, the lens can be much smaller than a conventional lens. This advantage of convenience and size is counterbalanced by two disadvantages: their fixed aperture – slow by normal standards – and their fragility.

Fisheye lenses with their extreme coverage of anything up to 360° have specific technical and scientific uses, but it is their drastic distorting effect that attracts the general photographer. Surroundings are swept back in a steep circle, near objects recede, horizons become hump-backed or dished, squares become spherical and circles stretch to ellipses. It is a special-effects lens and therefore needs to be used sparingly.

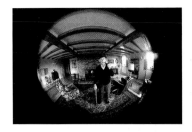

△ The distorted image in this picture is typical of the fisheye lens. Fisheye lenses have a wide coverage and practically infinite depth of field, which makes focusing unnecessary.

*Pentax LX, 16 mm, Kodak Ektachrome 64, ¹/₃₀ sec, f5.6*

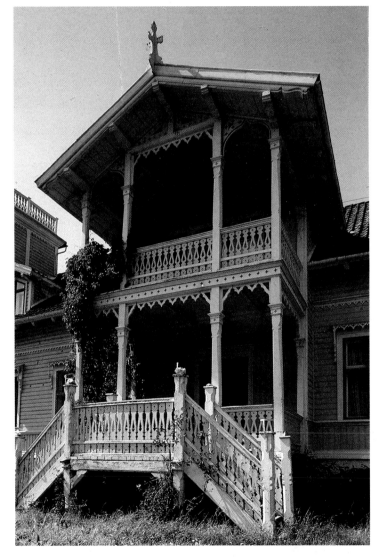

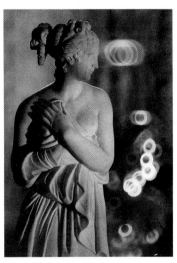

△ A mirror lens has advantages of size and weight over conventional telephoto designs but there are disadvantages: the fixed aperture, the brightness fall-off, and the characteristic doughnut-shaped highlights.

*Pentax LX, 500 mm mirror, Kodak Ektachrome 200, ¹/₁₀₀₀ sec, f8*

△ Shift lenses give the SLR camera some ability to imitate the extensive rising front of large format technical cameras. Normally a camera is tilted up to include the top of a tall building, which causes the vertical lines to converge. With a shift lens, the camera is kept level and the lens is shifted.

*Pentax LX, 28 mm shift, 8mm vertical shift, Kodak Kodachrome 64, ¹/₁₂₅ sec, f16*

See also:
THE STANDARD LENS pp18-19
THE WIDE-ANGLE LENS pp20-21
THE TELEPHOTO LENS pp22-23
THE VERSATILE LENS pp196-197

# CHOOSING EXPOSURE

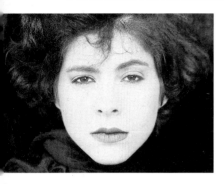

The quality of light recorded in a photograph – its exposure – is one of the major factors contributing to its overall success. It is in understanding and judging exposure that the art and science of photography most closely meet.

In general, a photographer tries to capture detail in all areas of a subject, whether brightly lit or cast in shadow. Overexposure produces a washed-out looking image, with detail lost in bright areas; underexposed images are dark and shadowed areas are indistinct. Although both under- and overexposure can be used creatively to enhance mood in a photograph, a balance is usually sought – a 'correct' exposure that reveals acceptable detail in all parts of the image.

Deciding on the exposure to use depends upon knowing how much light is falling upon the subject. The camera's light meter gives an indication of this. The amount of this light entering the camera is determined by the shutter speed and aperture setting chosen. Finally, the exposure will depend on the sensitivity to light of the film and its exposure latitude – the range of brightness over which it will still record an acceptable image.

△ ▷ Overexposure must be carefully executed or too much tone and detail will be lost and the image will have an unattractive, washed-out appearance. In the portrait above, a hint of light tone has been left in the girl's face and the overexposure lifts her from the dark background. Using underexposure (right) is more straightforward, since the eye more readily accepts the darker enriched tones. Here the darkened shadow areas contrast well with the highlights and help to strengthen atmosphere.

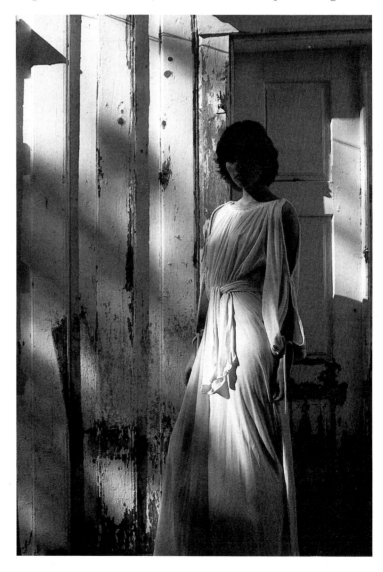

Determining the quality of light in a scene can be difficult. One area may be particularly bright, while the rest falls in dark shadow – the white walls of a house in a forest setting, for example. Most light meters, including the TTL (through-the-lens) meters built into SLRs, tend to give an averaged reading of the whole scene. (TTL meters operate regardless of lens attachments, with the exception of some colour filters.) This works well enough for most purposes, but is not dependable for unusual conditions. It is a good practice to assess the light quality of each scene for yourself, for not only does this prepare you for difficulties when they arise, but it also means that you look at the scene more closely. Take shots at different exposures – ½-1 stop apart – and compare the results.

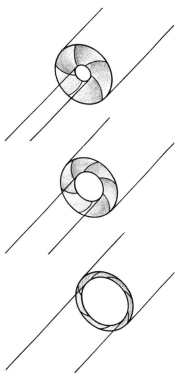

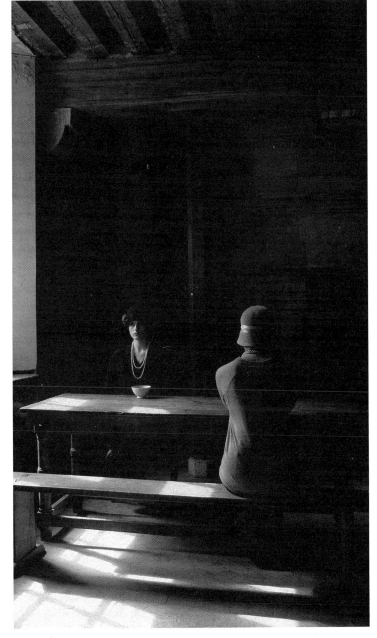

△ Increasing the size of the aperture increases exposure by letting more light into the camera. All lenses set to the same aperture transmit the same amount of light.

◁ All films have a limited range of brightness over which they will record detail. In a scene such as this, detail in highlight or shadow areas may be lost if a mid-range exposure is set. Take readings from the lightest and darkest parts of the scene. If the difference between these is greater than four stops, detail will be lost in transparencies; if greater than seven stops, detail will be lost on colour negative film, too.

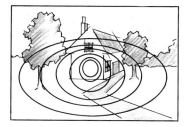

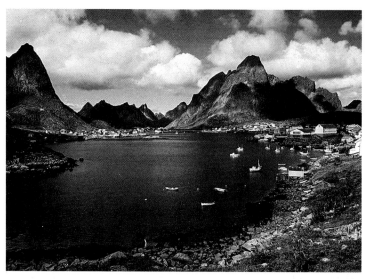

△ ▷ Centre-weighted metering is featured in most SLRs. The term refers to the bias given to the central and lower parts of the frame, with less importance progressively being given to outlying areas. This arrangement prevents undue influence from the sky, and, provided the important areas of the composition are placed centrally, as in this landscape, and there are no disproportionate areas of light and dark, most subjects will be correctly exposed.

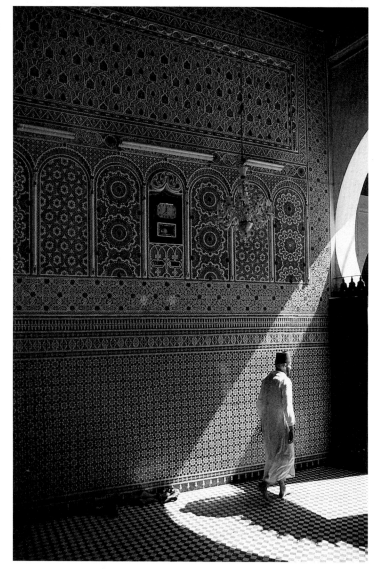

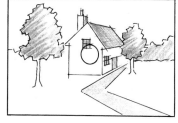

△ ▷ Spot-metering is restricted to a narrow, central circle in order to give very precise readings of a small area. The area is marked on the focusing screen and, with a 50 mm lens, the angle of coverage may be restricted to 2°. So you can estimate exposure by reading from small areas of important details within the scene, such as this figure caught in a shaft of strong sunlight.

Most photographers take a number of readings from the light meter before deciding, with the result they want in mind, what exposure to set. If the mid-tones of a composition are important, then an average of high, low, and mid-tone readings gives a more accurate estimate than an overall reading. To favour shadow detail, base the exposure on an average between mid-tone and shadow; to enrich highlights, use a reading based on the average between mid-tone and highlight areas.

Take into account local conditions, such as patches of snow or areas of reflective materials, and remember that a small change in camera angle can alter the exposure, especially when you are taking back-lit shots.

Sometimes it is not possible to approach closely enough to take high- and low-light readings without other parts of the scene influencing the result. Here, a spot-meter is useful. Spot-meters have a narrow field of view with an angle of between one and ten degrees. In TTL systems that have a spot-metering mode, this area is indicated by a circle on the focusing screen. Fitting a telephoto lens to an SLR in effect converts the camera so that it gives a spot-meter reading. In some cases even spot-metering is not possible. If an incident reading can be obtained, this is the best solution, but a reading from a mid-tone object – many photographers use the palm of the hand – held in shadow or in light, depending, of course, on the light that is falling on the subject, will give you a reading you can work with.

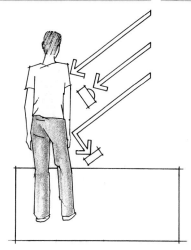

△ Meter readings measure the light reflected off the subject. Incident readings are taken with the meter pointing toward the camera, the cell covered with a white diffusing cone to reduce intensity.

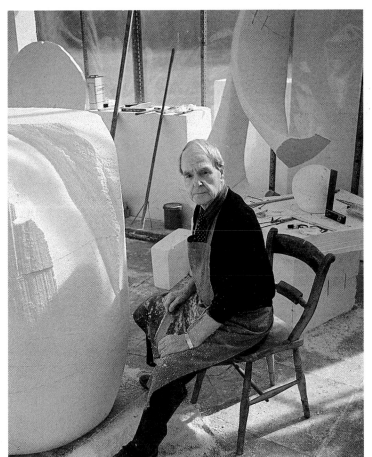

◁ Averaged reading meters will be misleading if the subject contains large light or dark areas because the meter assumes the subject is an overall, mid-tone grey. With dark subjects, the meter will indicate a setting to lighten it to grey, resulting in overexposure. In a bright subject, as illustrated here, the meter will indicate a setting to darken it to mid-tone grey, resulting in underexposure. The photographer has to recognize these potential errors and compensate, in this case by overriding the meter and giving an extra ⅔ stop exposure.

See also:
LIGHT AND CONTRAST pp 32-33
USING BACKLIGHT pp34-35
COLOUR INTENSITY pp70-71
LIGHT AS SUBJECT pp138-155

# LIGHT AND CONTRAST

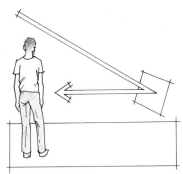

△ Contrast can be controlled by using a reflector to bounce light back into the shadows. Use a matte white or crumpled foil surface so that the reflected light is soft and does not make a second set of shadows. The reflector should be placed opposite the light source.

Technically speaking, light is merely a visible form of energy that activates the creation of a photographic image out of a dull grey emulsion. For the photographer, it is the emotive properties of light – its intrinsic qualities and associated moods – that are important. Understanding their significance and knowing how to exploit them are essential steps on the way to photographic success.

Contrast is one aspect of light that has a profound effect on mood. Clearly defined dark shadows against brilliant highlights make an image dynamic and create a sense of drama. Open shadows with subtle detail harmonizing with soft highlights create a calmer, more contemplative atmosphere. Lighting contrast means the difference between the intensity of light falling on the bright areas and that falling on the dark areas of the scene, so it has a direct effect on subject contrast. Subject contrast is the difference between the brightness levels of the darkest part and brightest part of a scene. The wider the difference, the greater the contrast and tonal range of the scene. Directional light that throws distinct shadows increases overall contrast; diffuse light that creates indistinct shadows lessens contrast. Generally, pictures with good contrast work better than

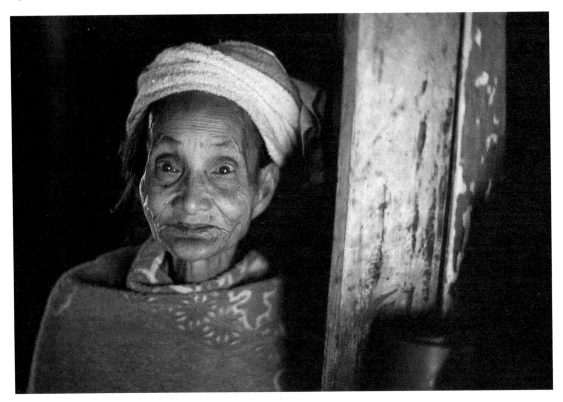

△ The predominance of dark and very rich tones in this portrait is typical of the low-key approach. The eye is drawn to emphasized highlights, which concentrate the attention on the woman's face. Successful low-key pictures frequently have a limited area of highlight and mid-tone balanced by a larger mass of shadow.

*Pentax LX, 50 mm, Kodak Ektachrome 64, 1/30 sec, f4*

those that lack it. This is not because low contrast is not acceptable, but because making a successful low-contrast picture can be difficult. The result can often look flat, an expanse of tonal desolation.

An exception is the high-key image. High-key pictures are low in contrast, but the tones are all light, colour is diluted, and any richness is restricted to very small areas. An airy, delicate atmosphere is the aim of high-key work and it can be applied to many subjects. Frontal light is best kept very soft and should be combined with overexposure of up to two stops, depending on the subject. With back-lit subjects, expose for the shadows. If the subject is dark or rich in colour, some extra exposure might be needed. Low-key is the opposite. Here, rich, dark tones and strong colours predominate. Many subjects are suitable for this dramatic treatment but remember that, with portraits, the lit areas will relentlessly expose every blemish and wrinkle. Highlights must also contain good colour to create an intense and more dramatic mood, so exposure is based on them rather than on mid or shadow tones. Directional light is often best for low-key pictures, especially if its coverage is limited, but excessive contrast should be avoided by means of slight underexposure.

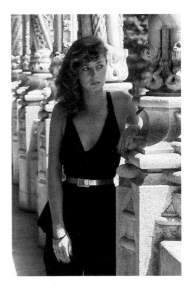

△ In this picture, subject tones range from the black of the girl's dress to the light sand colour of the stonework. Even in the soft light of an overcast day the contrast would be high, but the strong lighting contrast of direct sunlight, in combination with the subject contrast, exceeds the brightness range that the film is able to record.

*Pentax LX, 85 mm, Kodak Ektachrome 64, ¹/₁₂₅ sec, f8*

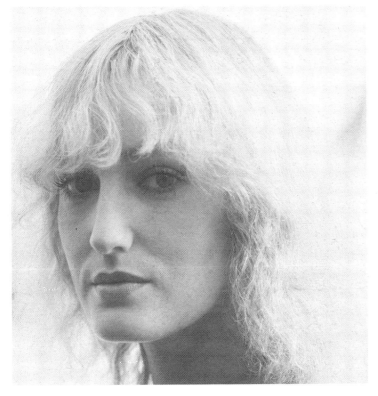

△ Strong backlighting has been combined with totally diffused frontlighting to evoke a light, romantic mood. This has been enhanced by deliberate overexposure to create a high-key image. All the tones in the portrait are pale, from the girl's lips to the burnt-out highlights in her hair, and add to the soft and airy atmosphere.

*Pentax LX, 85 mm, Kodak Ektachrome 64, ¹/₆₀ sec, f8*

See also:
CHOOSING EXPOSURE pp28-31
USING BACKLIGHT pp34-35
COLOUR INTENSITY pp70-71
LIGHT AS SUBJECT pp138-155

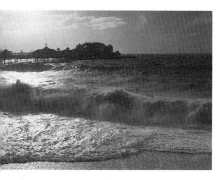

The old advice to photographers to keep the sun behind their shoulder produces photographs with well-lit subjects. Results tend to be predictable in style with a rather similar 'look', but exposure problems are kept to a minimum. But there are times when it is far more effective to have the sun – or the light source – behind the subject. The outline of the subject is dramatically revealed and this technique works well with simple shapes. Colour is much reduced, further emphasizing the outline.

With the camera pointed towards the light, dramatic shadows and highlights form pleasing patterns of contrast, adding energy and impact to the image. This form of illumination is called backlighting, and it brings with it some technical problems which need careful handling. Estimating the best exposure is tricky. The extreme brightness range almost always exceeds the film's latitude, so that the photographer has to accept some loss of detail and, because the incoming light produces brilliant highlights, the meter will indicate much less exposure than will actually be required.

Most autoexposure systems can be overridden to give one or two stops extra exposure, so that some mid-tone and shadow detail is recorded. Alternatively, a close-up reading can be taken off an important mid-tone area and the autoexposure system

△ Exposing for the bright highlights in this picture has rendered the Palace Pier stretching out into the sea at Brighton as a graphic silhouette, with a dramatic contrast between light and shadow.

*Pentax LX, 35 mm, Kodak Ektachrome 64, $^1/_{125}$ sec, f11*

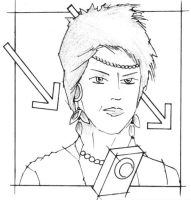

◁ An overall meter reading of a back-lit subject will result in underexposure and loss of detail in the important shadow areas. It is best to take a close-up reading, as shown, so that the bright light from behind the subject does not influence the result.

▽ The attractive rim-light around this model's outline helps to separate her from the background. This is a very useful effect of backlight. The exposure was based on the skin tones of her face, so that her back-lit hair has become overexposed, and fine detail is burnt out.

*Pentax LX, 85 mm, Kodak Ektachrome 64, $^1/_{125}$ sec, f5.6*

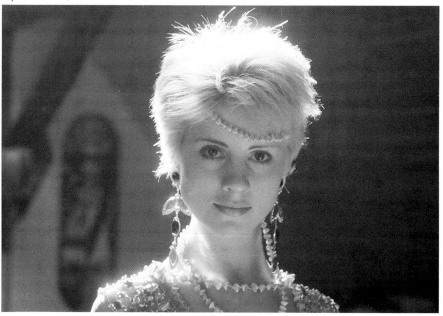

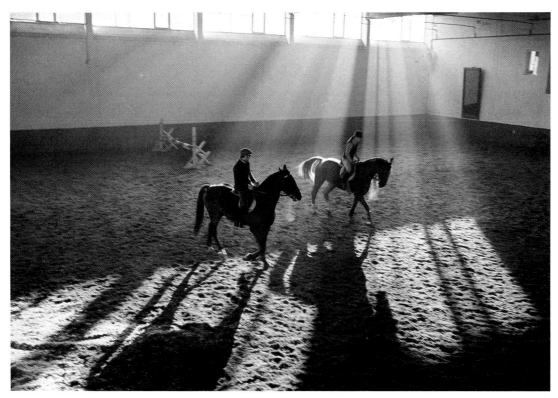

△ Backlight in early morning and evening is characterized by its clear tones and long shadows. This early morning shot taken in a riding school captured the atmosphere of that time, the exposure being balanced to record the tone in both the highlights and the shadow. Dust thrown up by exercising horses has picked up the shafts of sunlight, which have become an important part of the composition.

*Pentax LX, 35 mm, Kodak Ektachrome 200, 1/60 sec, f8*

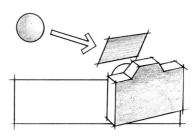

locked or set manually. Whichever way you estimate exposure, you must decide which of the highlight, mid-tone, or shadow areas are most important, because losing detail in one or more areas will create quite different moods in the picture.

If the colour and texture of the highlights are to be retained, then much of the subject will be recorded in silhouette. But should you want to have detail in the subject, you will find instead that the rim-lit areas bleach out, creating a softer mood. With care, it is also possible to reduce lighting contrast by using reflectors or weak flash to fill in the shadows. If you are using black and white film you can overexpose slightly and then shorten the development of the film, which will lower contrast.

Shooting into the light can also lead to problems with flare. Loss of contrast, reduced colour saturation, and diaphragm flare patterns can all combine to ruin an image. Good lens shading is the answer. When your lens hood is insufficiently deep, you can often use your hand, a notebook, or a piece of card to shield the lens from direct light. Sometimes it is possible to place the camera in a shadow thrown by a convenient tree or part of a building.

△ Lens hoods are very often too short to be of much use in shielding the lens from direct light. Your hand or a piece of card held away from the lens is a very good alternative but you must check to see that it does not appear in the shot. Mounting the camera on a tripod leaves you free to check that a shadow is cast over the front of the lens.

See also:
CHOOSING EXPOSURE pp28-31
LIGHT AND CONTRAST pp32-33
COLOUR INTENSITY pp70-71
LIGHT AS SUBJECT pp138-155

# S O F T   A N D   H A R D   L I G H T

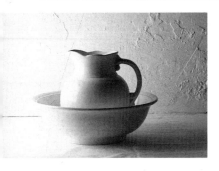

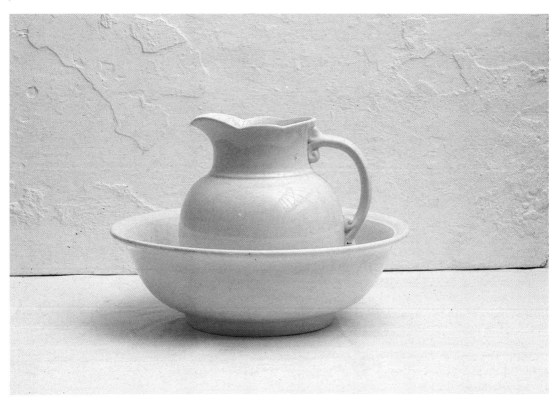

△ ▽ The still-life above has been shot under semi-diffused lighting, while the one below has been shot under diffused lighting. Semi-diffused light has a directional quality and throws a distinct shadow. Subject form and depth have been emphasized by the tonal gradation, which describes the roundness and the background surface. The diffused-light picture has indistinct shadows and an even luminosity that gently reveals form and subdues texture.

*Pentax LX, 50 mm, Kodak Ektachrome 160 Tungsten, ½ sec, f11*

Light is fundamental to all photography – the whole process of taking a photograph depends on light and the results are largely dependent on its qualities. All photographers therefore need to understand the moods, qualities, and uses that can be made of light. It is important to appreciate how light can change and what effects different lighting has on the surroundings. Most people are aware of light intensity – whether it is dim or bright – and can estimate lighting direction. But intensity and direction are just two of a number of characteristics of light that determine the success or otherwise of a photograph.

Gauging the hardness or softness of light is very important to the photographer. Hard light typically gives strong shadows with hard edges. Subject outlines tend to be well-defined, and the whole effect is one of harsh contrast and drama. In soft light the shadows are less well-defined, and even disappear entirely when the light becomes extremely soft. Overall shape and form are revealed, and the contrast between dark and light is subdued to create a restful mood. In daylight photography, direct sunlight gives hard lighting, while soft lighting is produced by an overcast sky or when cloud covers the sun.

In general terms, the softness or hardness of the lighting is determined by the size of the light source in relation to the subject. A comparatively small light source will give hard light, while a comparatively large source will give soft light. When the sun is in a clear sky it is a small source, giving hard directional light, but when a cloud passes in front of the sun, the cloud itself becomes the light source. The cloud is a larger light source in relation to the observer, and the light is softer. Taken to an extreme, when the cloud covers the whole sky, the light comes from one huge, very even light source, the diffuse light causing

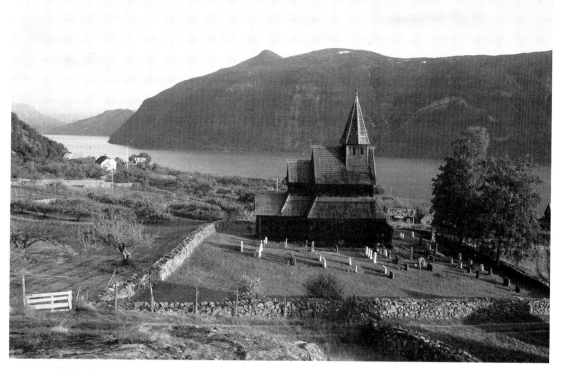

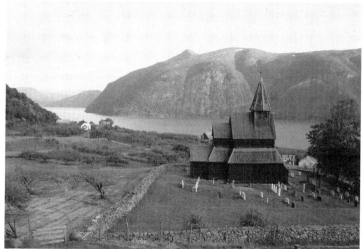

△ ◁ **Early evening sun throws long, distinct shadows, a characteristic of a hard light source, top.** Each tree, wall, and building is given extra depth and is lifted from the background by contrasting shadows against highlights. In the second picture, left, a cloud has passed over the sun, bathing the landscape in diffused light. Without the shadows and bright highlights, the picture has less depth and little textural quality, making the scene appear flat.

*Pentax LX, 85 mm, Kodak Ektachrome 64, 1/250 sec, f8*

*Pentax LX, 85 mm, Kodak Ektachrome 64, 1/250 sec, f8*

quite indistinct shadows. In light-toned surroundings lighting becomes omnidirectional – in other words, the light reflected from below almost matches the light from above – and shadows can no longer be seen.

A common mistake is to confuse a softening in light quality with a drop in intensity, or to assume that a bright light source is necessarily a hard one. This is not true – light from the sun is no harder than light from the much dimmer moon, as pictures taken in pure moonlight will show. Shadows are just as strong. In fact, the best way of determing the hardness or softness of light is to take a close look at the edges of shadows, and observe how deep they are compared with directly lit areas. You can then decide

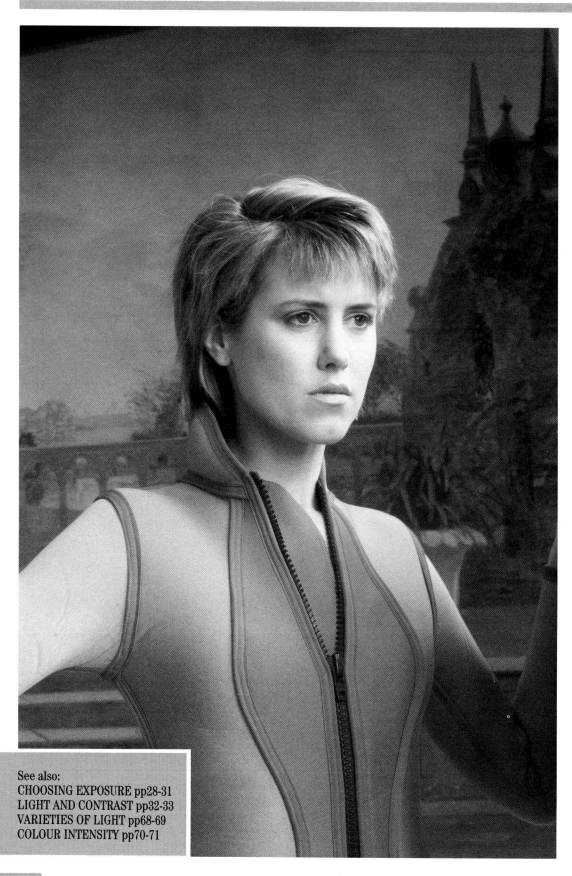

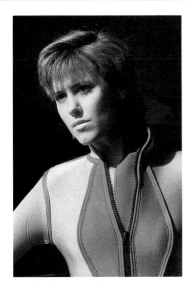

whether the lighting quality suits the subject or not.

In general terms, hard light with its hard-edge shadows is best for subjects that have strong simple shapes or brilliant colour. Texture will be revealed by hard directional light that skims across the surface to create a myriad of contrasting highlights and shadows. In larger forms, the shadows can be used as part of the composition, where they make their own strong lines and shapes. But there are times when shadows can dominate or confuse, and so diminish the impact of a picture, so this type of lighting needs to be handled carefully.

Lighting direction is of vital importance and needs careful attention. The almost shadowless illumination of soft lighting with its low contrast and subtle effect on composition is much more forgiving. Its main drawback is that over-use will lead to a feeling of sameness in your pictures, even if you are photographing a wide range of subjects. Soft light creates a soft mood, it is gentle in atmosphere and favours overall form because the light wraps itself around objects to give delicate modelling, while subduing texture and revealing detail. Colour is muted and there are no extremes of light and dark. Soft lighting allows the photographer a greater choice of viewpoints, which can be of help when a subject is moving or has a complex or potentially confusing pattern of shape and surface texture.

Half-way between hard and soft illumination is semi-diffuse, or soft directional light, where the direction of the light is still very apparent but the shadows cast have less obvious edges. Form is still complemented by shadow shape, but there is less contrast, and colour is not so vibrant as with hard light. Semi-diffuse lighting is ideal for giving a strong sense of reality.

◁ △ The portrait, top, made in hard directional light shows strong shadows and highlights on the model's face, the impact of the photograph being moody and dramatic. The second portrait, left, was shot in semi-diffuse light. The shadows cast have less obvious edges, but the direction of the light is still apparent. The mood is gentle and the form and texture of the model's face and skin are more subtly revealed.

*Top: Pentax LX, 85 mm, Kodak Ektachrome 64, ¹/₁₂₅ sec, f8*

*Left: Pentax LX, 85 mm, Kodak Ektachrome 64, ¹/₆₀ sec, f8*

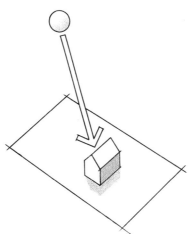

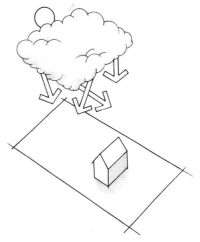

△ Hard light is characteristic of a relatively small source of light such as the sun, a bare light bulb, open flash, or a candle flame. Directional light travels in straight lines and objects in its path block light from an area immediately behind them, forming hard-edged shadows that correspond with their outlines.

△ Soft or diffuse light is the product of a large light source such as sunlight filtering through cloud, window light through net curtains, or reflected illumination in an area of shade. The light is not directional but is scattered and reaches the subject from a wider area, resulting in lighter shadows with softer edges.

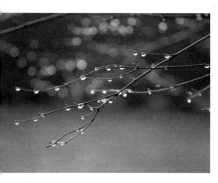

△ Very shallow depth of field can be used to throw a background out of focus, making the main subject stand out dramatically.

Depth of field is used to control the overall impression of sharpness in a picture. The term means the distance between the nearest and farthest points in a scene that show acceptably sharp focus. The key word is 'acceptably', for although depth of field is measured in finite terms and is shown as such on most lenses, it is really a subjective assessment. The extent of sharp focus varies according to three factors – the aperture selected, the focal length of the lens, and the focus setting. Depth of field extends about one third in front of and two thirds behind the point of true focus. Controlling depth of field can have a dramatic effect on composition, particularly with subjects containing both near and distant objects. A shallow depth of field throws a background out of focus, making the main subject stand out. Subjects that have little dimensional depth, such as the façades of buildings or landscapes that concentrate on very distant views, show very little visual change as depth of field is altered. Aperture selection is the principal depth of field control, and small apertures – those with large f numbers such as f22 – give extensive depth of field, while large apertures – those with small f numbers, such as f2.8 – limit depth of field.

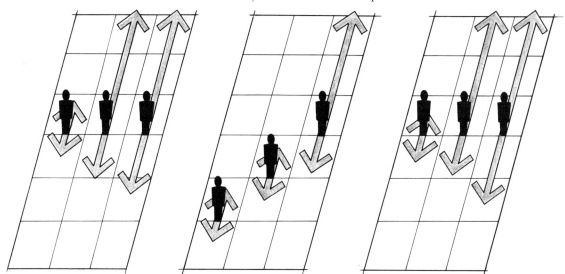

△ **Lens aperture**
Changing the aperture is the prime means of altering depth of field. This diagram shows how, at the wide aperture of f2, the band of acceptable sharpness is narrowest, but as smaller apertures are selected – f8 and f16 – sharpness, and therefore depth of field, extends further both in front of and behind the point of true focus.

△ **Point of focus**
The point of focus also affects the extent of depth of field. With a constant f-stop setting it can be seen that depth of field is greatest with distant focus settings, and smallest with near focus settings.

△ **Focal length**
Depth of field is affected by focal length. At the same focus and aperture settings, different focal length lenses give different amounts of depth of field. Wide-angle lenses have the most extensive depth of field at a given setting, while long focus lenses give the shallowest.

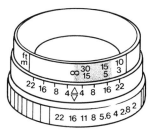

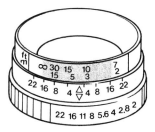

## △ Hyperfocal distance

With photographs that need extensive depth of field, such as a landscape with important features both near and far away, the best approach is not to focus on infinity, but to focus on a nearer point, placed at the so-called hyperfocal distance. This setting gives the maximum possible depth of field. To find the hyperfocal distance, first set the lens to infinity, then, using the depth-of-field scale on the lens barrel, note the near point of the depth of field. In this case, at f16, the near point is 4 m (13 ft). Focus the lens to 4 m (13 ft) and the depth of field will reach from just over 2 m (6½ ft) to infinity. The hyperfocal distance changes as the aperture is varied, and according to the focal length of the chosen lens.

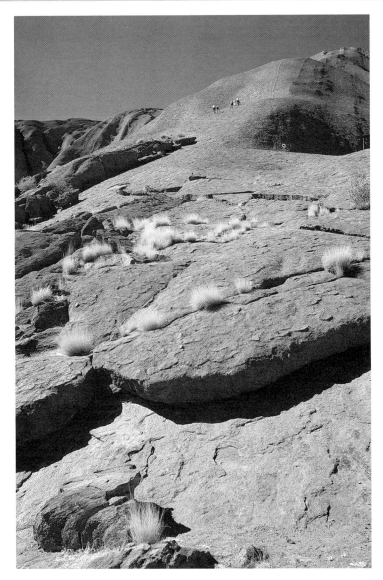

△ This landscape at Ayers Rock in Australia was taken by setting the wide-angle lens to a small aperture and focusing on the hyperfocal distance.

*Pentax LX, 24 mm, Kodak Ektachrome 64, 1/250 sec, f16*

▷ Using a long lens and a wide aperture has restricted the depth of field to a narrow band that just includes the speeding figure.

*Pentax LX, 400 mm, Kodak Ektachrome 200, 1/1000 sec, f5.6*

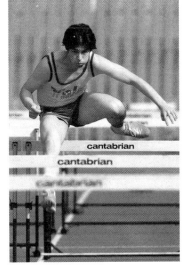

See also:
THE STANDARD LENS pp18-19
THE WIDE-ANGLE LENS pp20-21
THE TELEPHOTO LENS pp22-23
FOCUSING METHODS pp44-45

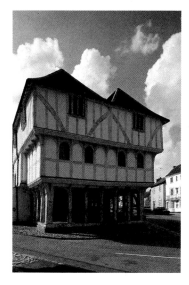

△ A wide-angle lens can be used to isolate a subject by moving in very close to exclude any surrounding distracting elements. In this picture of the Guildhall in Thaxted, Essex, the wide angle of view of a 28 mm shift lens provides enough coverage to include the whole building, but exclude the surrounding buildings.

*Pentax LX, 28 mm shift, Kodak Ektachrome 64, ¹/₆₀ sec, f5.6*

▷ Small subjects need to be given special emphasis if they are to stand out. In this picture the telephoto lens used was set to a wide aperture to restrict depth of field. Both foreground and background are blurred, in complete contrast to the boy's critically focused head.

*Pentax LX, 135 mm, Kodak Ektachrome 200, ¹/₅₀₀ sec, f4*

See also:
THE WIDE-ANGLE LENS pp20-21
THE TELEPHOTO LENS pp22-23
DEPTH OF FIELD pp40-41
BLURRING MOVEMENT pp62-63

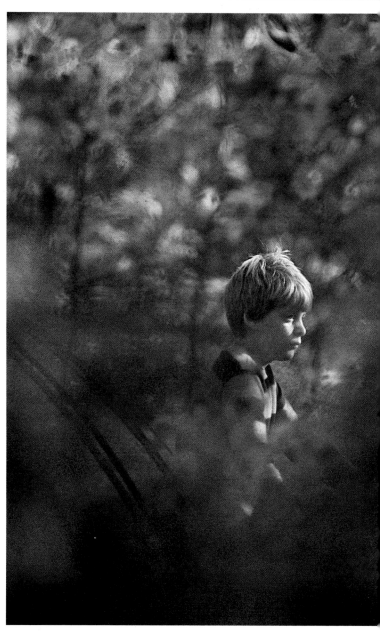

The camera is an indiscriminate observer, never differentiating between what is visually important and what is not. As a result, there are many times when a photograph disappoints us when we compare it with our memory of the scene. One common fault is that the subject of the picture is often too small, blending with the background, and is surrounded by distracting details that went unnoticed at the time of exposure.

The best way around the problem is to fill the frame with the subject. The importance of a subject is closely linked to its size relative to other objects within the picture, and to the overall size of the image. Small subjects seem unimportant, while large ones seem important. The subject size does, however, need to be balanced within the constraints of the composition. Often a subject can be made more important simply by fitting a longer

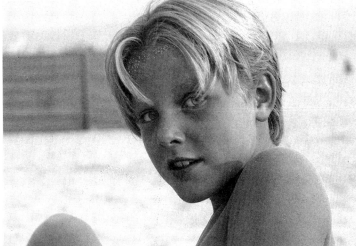

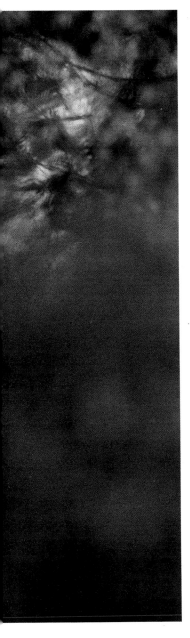

△ Complicated background detail is often distracting and can confuse the outline of the main subject. The background here has been reduced to a blur by moving in close and selecting a wide aperture. Use the camera's stop-down preview to check the effect before exposing.

*Pentax LX, 85 mm, Kodak Ektachrome 64, ¹/₅₀₀ sec, f4*

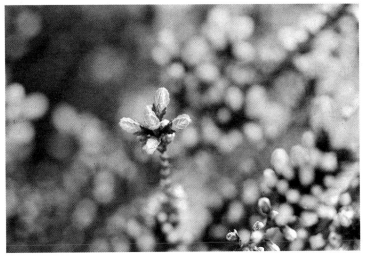

△ Subjects stand out in macro photographs because the depth of field is extremely limited.

*Pentax LX, 100 mm macro, Kodak Ektachrome 64, autoexposure, f5.6*

lens or moving nearer. Moving in close has the advantage that distracting surroundings can be restricted or excluded altogether. Usually a moderate wide-angle is the best lens to use; its wider field of view allows the photographer to get near enough to cut out unwanted detail and still include the most important part of the scene.

Sometimes it is not possible to isolate the subject in this way. The answer then is to use selective focusing, restricting depth of field to the subject plane so that the subject stands out, sharply focused against a blurred background. It follows that the narrower the depth of field, the more pronounced the effect. Therefore, wide apertures and telephoto lenses give the best effects. Results have even greater impact if the subject is relatively close to the camera.

# FOCUSING METHODS

Not all camera lenses are capable of being focused. Miniature format and compact cameras are often equipped with fixed-focus lenses designed with sufficient depth of field to render both near and far objects in focus, although they are somewhat restricted for close-up work. This compromise is well suited to photographers who are not too concerned with the aesthetics of an image, but not to those who want control over focus and the ability to emphasize certain parts of an image. The serious photographer will want a manual or autofocus lens. Probably best of all is an autofocus camera that allows you to make the focus setting and then the lens position can be locked so that the camera can be moved for better composition.

On an SLR the focus is monitored on the focusing screen, which is placed at the same distance from the optical centre of the lens as the film plane. Many SLR manufacturers offer several different types of screen, although the one most often fitted as standard is the split image/microprism type, which will work with a large range of lenses and subject matter. Specialized screens include the microprism spot for use with wide-angle lenses, and the all-matte screen, which is used with telephoto lenses and in close-up photograpy. Keeping focus with a manual lens is not easy, especially when the subject is racing towards you.

But there are ways of dramatically increasing your chances of maintaining correct focus. The most important of these is to familiarize yourself with the lens's rate of focus change as subjects come towards you. Another technique is to focus on a spot on the ground that you expect the subject to pass over. Frame the subject before it reaches the spot and start panning before triggering the shutter as the subject passes the preselected position. This is an especially useful technique for sports photography. A similar approach is useful for candid pictures when it is important not to attract the attention of your subject by aiming the camera and focusing before making the exposure. Simply prefocus on a dummy subject at a similar distance and recompose to include the real one. With luck, your intentions will be obscured and a true candid portrait will result. Of course, if you have an autofocus camera the same result can be achieved without having to resort to prefocusing.

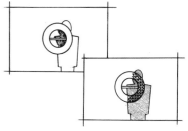

△ Most 35 mm SLRs have a split-image/microprism collar arrangement on a ground-glass screen as their standard focus screen. Out-of-focus subjects appear blurred on the ground glass and vertical lines that cut across the split-image zone in the centre are offset, while the microprism collar appears to shimmer.

▽ Autofocus cameras have a viewfinder display to indicate when the subject is correctly focused. Details vary from camera to camera but most also offer manual focusing.

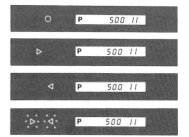

▷ With fast-moving subjects such as this running fox the problems of keeping focus are great, particularly so here, because the subject is close. This is because the focusing ring has to be moved a great deal more for an equivalent change in focus setting than would be needed for distant subjects.

*Leica, 105 mm, Kodak Ektachrome 200, 1/60 sec, f16*

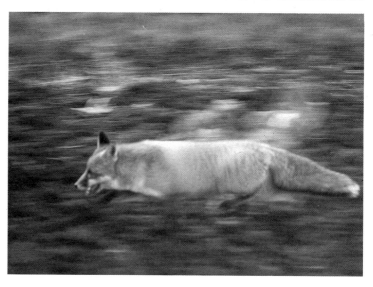

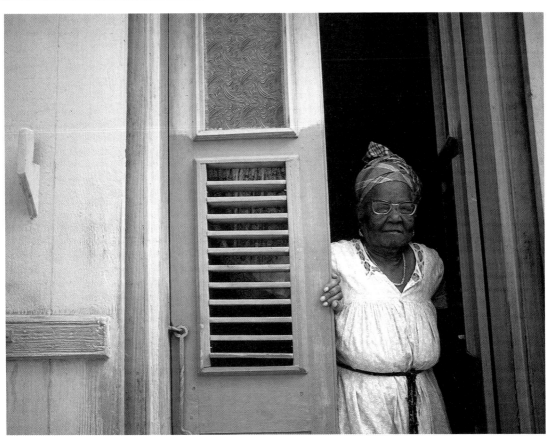

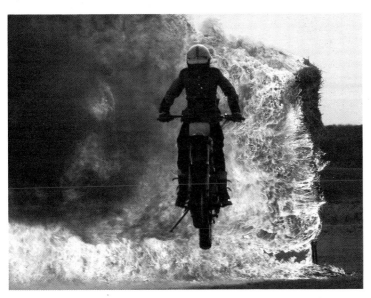

△ Prefocusing is a technique that is invaluable for making natural-looking candid pictures. To avoid attracting the attention of this lady before being ready to shoot, the lens was focused on another doorway at a similar distance but out of sight. It was then just a matter of turning round and tripping the shutter.

*Pentax LX, 70-150 mm, Kodak Ektachrome 64, autoexposure, f8*

△ A motorcycle stuntman hurtling out of a sea of flame is not easy to focus on unless your camera has a rapid-response autofocus system. One approach is to prefocus on the ground over which the bike will fly, and then release the shutter just before it gets there. This requires precise timing and accurate anticipation.

*Pentax LX, 400 mm, Kodak Ektachrome 200, 1/1000 sec, f11*

See also:
35 mm SLR CAMERAS pp12-15
COMPACT CAMERAS pp16-17
THE TELEPHOTO LENS pp22-23
DEPTH OF FIELD pp40-41

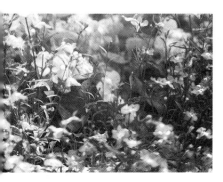

Soft focus is one of the most successful techniques for conveying an atmosphere of romance and mystery. It is a very popular technique for advertising such products as scent, bath oils, wine and chocolates, where it is often used to evoke an atmosphere of nostalgia and fantasy. The commonest way of creating a controlled soft image – as opposed to the unpredictable and seldom attractive softness produced by camera shake or poor focusing – is by using a special filter or lens attachment that diffuses fine detail. There are many types, some with a mottled surface pattern and others with bubbles in them, or with circular lines engraved in one surface or frosted coating. It is difficult, if not impossible, to tell which type has been used in a particular picture. Some manufacturers make their soft-focus attachments in varying strengths.

△ A fog filter has brought about the delicate and misty atmosphere in this picture. Fog filters are graded in varying strengths, the weaker ones producing the more attractive results. Their main effect is to reduce contrast and slightly soften detail.

*Pentax LX, 50 mm, Kodak Ektachrome 64, $^1\!/_{125}$ sec, f11*

Diffusion filters also affect the resolving power of prime lenses. They have a clear area in the centre so that part of the image is still sharp and contrasts with the softened area. These filters have the added advantage of making it possible to vary the amount of soft-focus by varying the lens aperture.

Subjects that respond well to soft-focus treatment are often high-key, have high contrast, and are well lit. Backlight can also enhance the effect, and where the background is dark, the spreading highlights may form a glowing halo-like outline. Strong soft-focus images are characterized by spreading highlights, slightly blurred detail, lowered contrast, and decreased colour saturation. Therefore, old or simple lenses, if you can find them, often make ideal soft-focus optics. You can make a soft-focus lens by attaching a magnifying glass to an extension tube or set of bellows. Inexpensive plastic magnifying glasses often produce interesting chromatic aberrations in the form of rainbow patterns.

▽ Vaseline smeared around the edges of a clear haze filter was used to produce the soft-focus effects in both of these photographs. The clear central area of the filter causes the better definition in the centre of the pictures, which is made more obvious at small apertures.

*Pentax LX, 50 mm, Kodak Ektachrome 64, $^1\!/_{60}$ sec, f11*

If you do lots of soft-focus photography, you might consider buying a purpose-built soft-focus lens. These are designed with partially-corrected optics and a perforated disc built into the lens. At wider apertures, very soft results can be achieved, but if you stop down, the softness is decreased. Other methods of producing softness include shooting through gauze, fine mesh, or stockings, breathing on a cold filter, or spreading petroleum jelly on a clear filter.

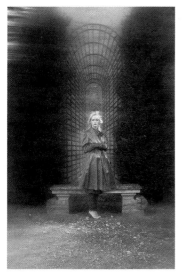

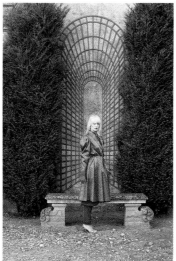

▷ Soft-focus filters are available in a variety of strengths, their effect on the image differing subtly. The filter used for this romantic nude study had a mottled surface which tends to soften definition yet retain image contrast. The effects are not altered by selecting different apertures.

*Pentax LX, 50 mm, Kodak Ektachrome 64, $^1\!/_{60}$ sec, f16*

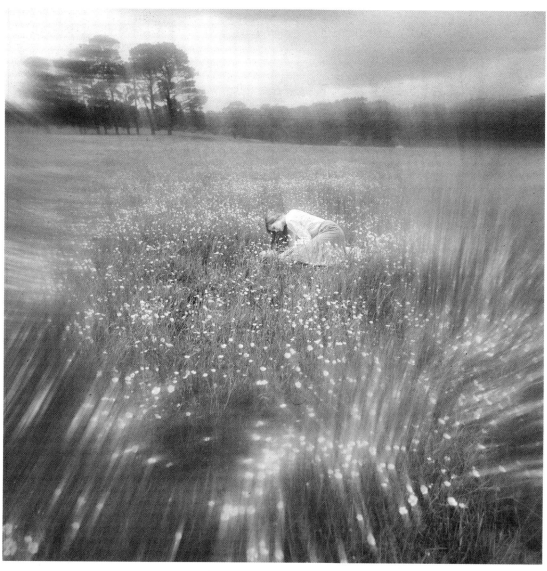

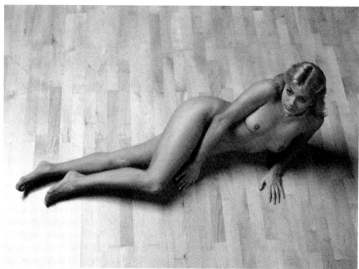

△ The results from using Vaseline on the lens are unique, and its use can be tailored to specific needs. Dramatic blurring of the image at the edges is reduced towards the centre, so that the girl is quite sharp.

*Hasselblad, 80 mm, Kodak Ektachrome 200, ¹/₁₂₅ sec, f8*

See also:
BLURRING MOVEMENT pp62-63
SPECIAL FILTERS pp82-85
FANTASY FIGURES pp264-265

# VIEWPOINT AND SCALE

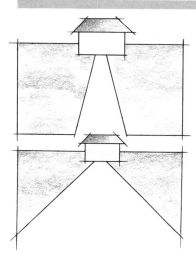

△ With a conventional lens (top), light converges gradually on the aperture. Using a wide-angle lens (bottom), the convergence is steeper, so that distant objects appear smaller and true perspective is distorted.

Composing a picture involves making aesthetic decisions. The first choice is one of viewpoint, which determines what is contained in the photograph and, by selection, gives the subject its significance. Viewpoint also has a profound effect on the relationship between the viewer and the subject. Most cameras have eye-level viewfinders, so the normal approach is to take most photographs from this viewpoint. This works with some material, but adopting a more original viewpoint will more often than not improve the picture. Low viewpoints are the most dramatic. Looking up at the subject increases its stature and strength, and can accentuate contrast – an excellent way to dramatize a symmetrical composition. Using a low viewpoint in conjunction with vertical framing emphasizes the effect.

Adopting a high viewpoint lets the viewer look down on the scene, putting him in a position of superiority. Subject stature is diminished and the picture elements are often abstracted, so that pattern and line predominate over depth and contrast. Often, the overall effect is to increase the sense of tranquillity.

Changing the viewing distance is also a useful device. Move in closer for a more intimate view. The effect is to simplify the image and isolate the subject from distracting surroundings. Straightforward images from a close viewpoint are easy to read and put the viewer into a close relationship with the subject. Conversely, the distant view will put the subject in context with

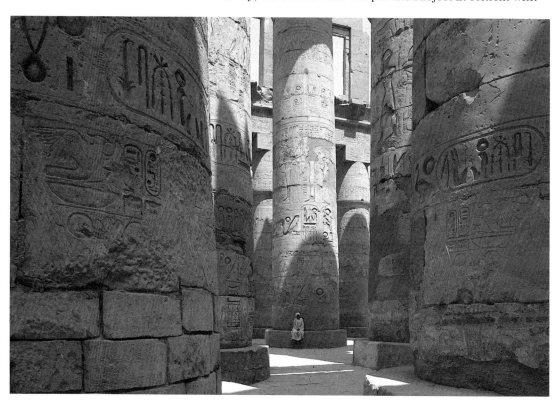

△ Without the human figure there would be no sense of scale in this photograph of Egyptian ruins. In addition, the feeling of depth is increased by having one column close to the camera and others in the distance.

*Pentax LX, 28 mm, Kodak Ektachrome 64, 1/60 sec, f16*

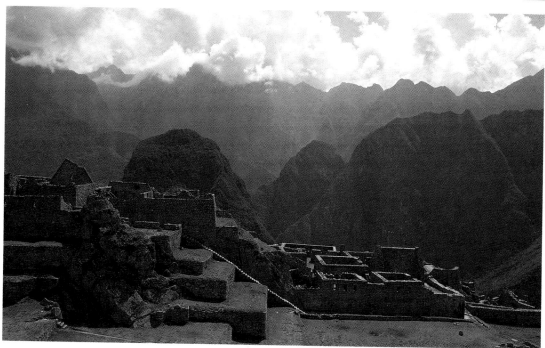

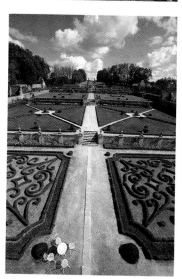

△ The contrast between the pale elements in the distance and the darker tones of the foreground adds to the sense of depth in this landscape.

*Pentax LX, 28 mm, Kodak Kodachrome 64, ¹/₂₅₀ sec, f8*

▷ Linear perspective is increased by clear-cut outlines, aerial perspective, and diminishing size, an effect added to by the use of a wide-angle lens.

*Pentax LX, 15 mm, Kodak Ektachrome 64, ¹/₁₂₅ sec, f11*

its environment or relate it to other, lesser points of interest. Distance can also give extra significance by including elements that emphasize scale and perspective.

A picture is given its sense of depth by the way that objects appear to diminish in size as they get farther away. A large figure in a landscape appears closer than a small one, a short telegraph pole, for example, appearing more distant that a tall one. But these clues to scale are read in conjunction with other indicators of depth such as linear and aerial perspective. Linear perspective is the apparent convergence of parallel lines in a photograph as they recede into the distance. It is one of the strongest ways of implying depth and works best when the subject has strong outlines. But remember that perspective can be distorted by the lens that you use – with wide-angle lenses of 28 mm or less, objects in the foreground appear much closer and those in the background more distant. Pulling the foreground up close using a wide-angle lens can add depth to a composition.

Aerial perspective results in the lightening of tonal values caused by haze and an increase in distance. It can be very effective in landscape photography, especially when a dramatic sense of scale is produced by the inclusion of a figure in the foreground. But scale can be exploited in other ways than contrasting the size of familiar subjects. You can compose the shot so that objects are both close to and far from the camera.

See also:
THE WIDE-ANGLE LENS pp20-21
THE TELEPHOTO LENS pp22-23
COMPOSING THE SHOT pp52-53
LINEAR PERSPECTIVE pp224-225

# FRAMING THE SUBJECT

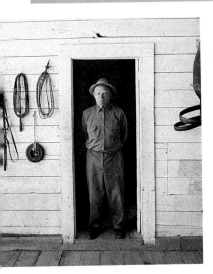

△ The combination of several framing devices in this portrait of an American horse owner serves to echo his solid stance. The square format suggests stability and placing him in a centrally framed doorway concentrates the attention on his figure. On a smaller scale, his face is framed by the hat and his light skin stands out against the darkness of the interior.

*Pentax LX, 50 mm, Kodak Ektachrome 64, ¹/₆₀ sec, f11*

Framing is one of the photographers's principal compositional aids, serving to concentrate the viewer's attention on the picture. Anyone who picks up a camera for the first time is immediately aware of the viewfinder's impact on the frame; it is a window on the world, hiding from view all that lies outside its boundaries. The photographer has at his disposal a very effective compositional device in the viewfinder and the film format.

Film formats are square or rectangular. It is generally accepted that a rectangular picture shape holds more interest because it evokes a feeling of tension and energy, whereas the square format is more static and more limited in scope. The landscape – that is, horizontal – format produces a feeling of tranquillity and space, while a portrait – that is, vertical – format tends to convey a feeling of strength.

The 35 mm rectangle, with its ratio of 2:3 is quite elongated, and a tempting shape into which to fit images. The danger is that all your photographs will have the same 'look' if they aren't cropped in some way. Cropping is also particularly important if you are using the 6 × 6 cm format, as it enables you to overcome the constraints of the square. Overcoming the common habit of letting the camera format lead you into framing a shot is not always easy, and even experienced photographers will often adhere to the landscape format, neglecting the portrait alternative.

You can also create frames within the picture area to emphasize or strengthen the overall format, but it is not necessary to echo the rectangular format in order to reinforce its impact; they can contrast in shape but still add clarity. Generally, strong geometry works well – for example, placing the subject in the cusp of a V or using a circle, such as a wide-brimmed hat, to frame a face.

The placing of the subject within the frame has a profound effect on compositional balance. Many artists instinctively put the centre of interest approximately one-third of the way into the frame from any side. The 'rule of thirds' is a useful device and is well worth following at times. Horizons respond well to this treatment, particularly in the portrait format, and it is often successful with figure studies. But the key to success is to experiment. Like any rules, those of composition are not inflexible and are made to be broken, and many successful images have the subject placed dead centre.

▷ When there are strong diagonal lines in a picture their impact is strengthened if they are framed so that they enter from a corner. In this picture the bridge and horizon line meet where two imaginary lines drawn one-third in from the bottom and right sides would intersect.

*Pentax LX, 28 mm, Kodak Ektachrome 64, ¹/₁₂₅ sec, f8*

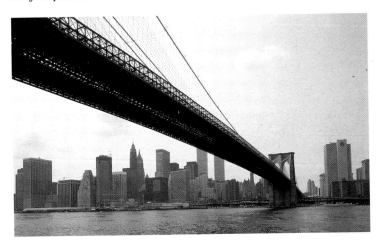

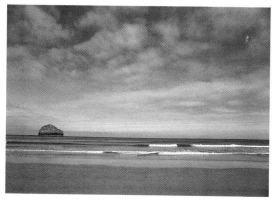

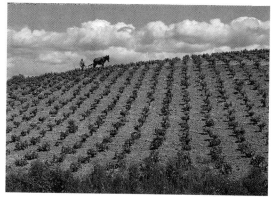

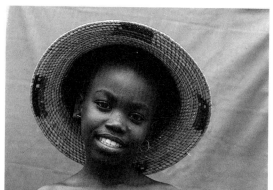

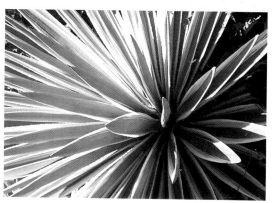

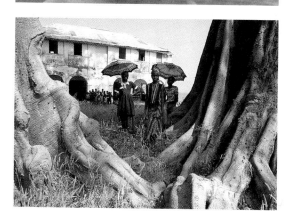

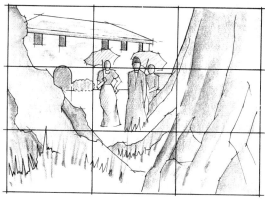

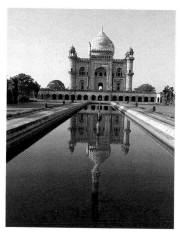

The pictures on this page illustrate several of the basic guidelines to composition, but remember that these aren't hard-and-fast laws that impose a straitjacket on your creativity, but should be thought of as a basis from which to start. Placing horizon lines near the top or bottom of the frame is more dynamic than placing them centrally. Using strong shapes as frames concentrates attention on the subject, while dividing the frame into thirds, then arranging the composition to coincide with the divisions helps pictorial balance. Try tracing the diagram and then overlaying it on each of these pictures to see the 'rule of thirds' at work.

See also:
FILLING THE FRAME pp42-43
COMPOSING THE SHOT pp52-53
CAPTURING MOVEMENT pp60-61
ADVANCED COMPOSITION pp208-227

# COMPOSING THE SHOT

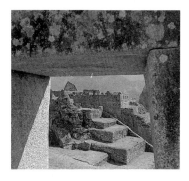

△ Although this picture of Inca ruins in Peru demonstrates framing that uses a strong foreground shape, there is a subtler compositional device at work – that of false attachment. The tone and texture of the stone archway imply that a close-up view of the distant ramparts would reveal the same features.

*Pentax LX, 50 mm, Kodak Kodachrome 64, 1/125 sec, f8*

See also:
FILLING THE FRAME pp42-43
FRAMING THE SUBJECT pp50-51
CAPTURING MOVEMENT pp60-61

Strong pictures rely, to varying degrees, on the use of compositional devices to help give the image structure and a centre of interest that stands out from its surroundings. You need to decide what is the best way to present the image, what is the major element and where the emphasis should be, and then what devices will achieve this. Devices of this type can include several different elements in the one photograph – a dash of colour that adds impact, for example, or a false relationship between a foreground object and a distant subject, or even a combination of colour, framing, and perspective.

Colour is one of the strongest aids to composition; we are very aware of it and our response to different tones and hues is almost instinctive and often associated with strong emotion. Reds, oranges, yellows, and browns are warm, assertive colours that 'come forward' in a composition. Violets, blues, and greens, on the other hand, are cool and restful colours that seem to 'recede' into the background. Compositions that make use of colour contrast between the centre of interest and its surroundings are endowed with extra dramatic emphasis. But great impact can also be achieved with quite subdued colour, providing that there is a definite break or contrast.

Shape and line are two further powerful aids to composition. A common fault in many pictures is that there is no centre of interest or that there are too many and the eye is reluctant to travel to, and then stay in, one place. Shapes within the picture itself can be used to frame the subject, but it is best if they have an obvious connection – a doorway into a room, for example. Distinctive shapes arranged at significant points in the picture can be used to encourage the eye of the viewer to travel through the composition, sometimes to a centre of interest, but always without creating a division of interest. Again, shapes that are related to each other either symbolically or physically tend to work best together.

Many scenes can be photographed to create areas of similar tone and shape that attract our attention. Bear in mind, however, that strong tonal contrasts attract the eye more readily than an area of similar tones and, in this way, it is possible to draw attention to small objects by placing them against a larger mass of contrasting tone.

Lines leading to an important element within the scene are useful aids to composition, and their effect can be doubled if they enter from a corner of the frame rather than the side. But there must be a centre of interest, otherwise the viewer will be led up to a visual anticlimax.

Two other compositional devices that can be used to good effect are juxtaposition and false attachment. These are similar in many ways and their strength lies in the camera's ability to take an element out of context and to present it as a complete image. False attachments occur when one element in a scene is placed against a quite separate one in a way that connects them – a portrait with a tree or lamppost seeming to grow out of the head is a common mistake, but a similar deliberate arrangement of a figure with its background could imply that your subject is supporting an impossibly heavy boulder. Similarly, juxtaposed elements can be presented in such a way as to imply a relationship that does not necessarily exist, either to create humour or to distort reality. Such is the power of composition.

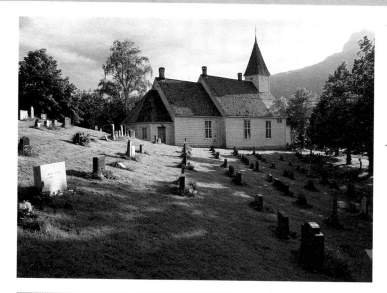

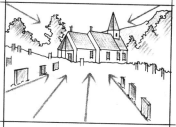

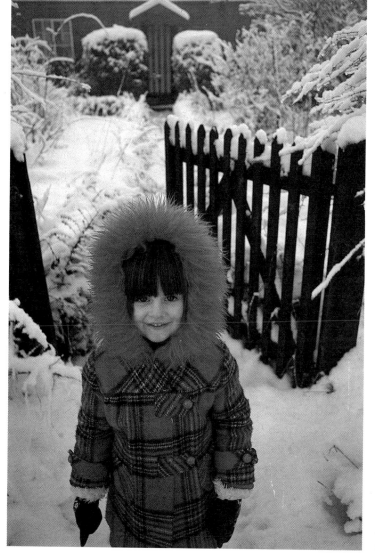

◁ △ Lead-in lines do not have to be physically continuous. They can take the form of a series of similar-shaped or related objects that diminish in size as they approach the subject of the composition. In this picture, taken in Norway, the rows of headstones and the trees form strong lead-in lines that draw the eye to the church.

*Pentax LX, 28 mm, Kodak Ektachrome 64, 1/125 sec, f11*

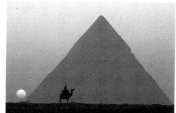

△ Strong shapes and tonal balance are powerful elements in composition. Here, the scale of the dark camel rider and the foreground are perfectly balanced by the pale mass of the pyramid.

*Pentax LX, 135 mm, Kodak Ektachrome 64, 1/60 sec, f8*

◁ The dark coat in this shot is given added impact because the eye tends to enlarge small areas of strong, assertive tone when these are seen against a contrasting ground. This, and cropping part of her figure, projects the girl forward.

*Pentax LX, 35 mm, Kodak Kodachrome 64, 1/250 sec, f11*

# BLACK AND WHITE

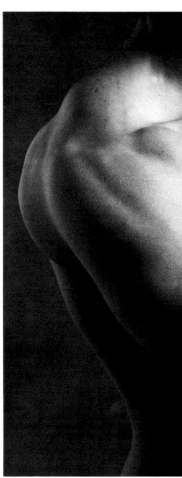

Many experienced photographers prefer working in black and white. This is probably because the medium has a graphic quality that is more interpretative and less rooted in the real world than is colour photography. Black and white also lends itself to image manipulation, allowing the photographer great creative freedom. But in order to gain this freedom, the photographer needs to invest in a darkroom in addition to his camera equipment. Treating black and white film like colour negative film, and sending it to a commercial laboratory rarely produces results that do justice to the process.

Composition in black and white follows the same guidelines as for colour. Light is the most vital element; its character and mood will have a profound effect on the atmosphere as well as image contrast. Subject qualities such as shape, form, line, pattern, texture, and tone all play crucial roles in image structure, but perhaps surprisingly, colours have to be taken into account, as they affect the tonal balance of the picture. Tonal balance can suggest different moods – predominantly pale tones suggest a light sunlit atmosphere, and tend to give the image an ethereal quality, whereas large areas of dark tones or black can lead to a sombre atmosphere and a sense of drama. Contrast also affects mood. Pictures containing bright and dark tones next to each other heighten the sense of drama, adding energy, but pictures containing similar, more subtle tones create a quiet, harmonious impression.

The choice of film will have an important influence on the final image. There are many different types on the market from ultra-fine grained graphic films which produce only blacks and whites, to highly sensitive, grainy films with panchromatic response, which produce a full range of tones. There are some special black and white films, designed for specific uses, such as medical photography.

▷ This picture was shot on high-speed film and shows the obvious granular pattern typical of this film type. It breaks up fine detail, especially in the mid-grey tones, but can introduce a pleasing textural effect with the right subject and create a moody atmosphere.

*Hasselblad, 500 mm, Kodak Tri-X, ¹/₂₅₀ sec, f16*

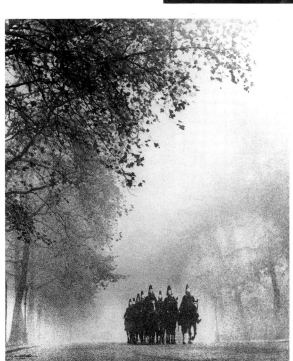

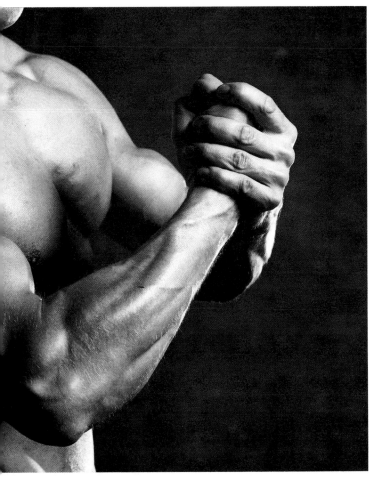

◁ In a black and white image tone plays an important compositional role. In this picture the three-dimensional form of the man's torso is largely expressed in terms of tonal variation. Soft, directional light has revealed skin texture without losing detail in highlight and shadow areas.

*Hasselblad, 120 mm, Kodak Tri-X, flash, f16*

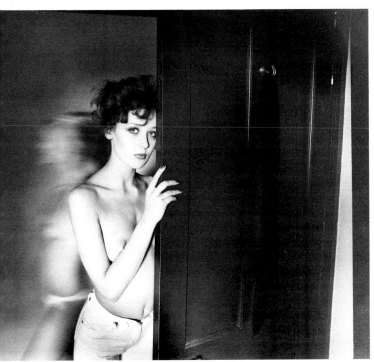

◁ Fine-grained films of slow speed are ideal for subjects that have delicate textural qualities and large areas of even tone where grain is most noticeable. They are also sharper than fast films and can be enlarged to a greater extent without a severe loss in image quality.

*Pentax LX, 50 mm, Ilford FP4, ISO 100, 1/30 sec, f8*

# BLACK AND WHITE

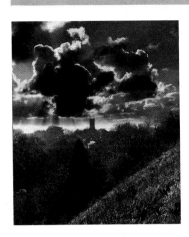

◁ This landscape conveys a mood of sombre drama. The main image is dark-toned, the scattering of light areas contrasting strongly with the deep greys and blacks. The low-key effect has been enhanced by using a red filter, which darkened the blue sky. Exposing for the mid-tone areas has restricted detail to the lighter parts of the image.

*Hasselblad, 150 mm, Kodak Tri-X, ISO 400, ¹/₂₅₀ sec, f11*

▷ Tonal distribution in a black and white picture is largely responsible for the overall mood. In this landscape the range is restricted to mid to light greys, suggesting a tranquil atmosphere. Contrasting objects – the dark cow, trees, and the ruin with its splash of sun – are given extra emphasis and attract the eye's attention.

*Hasselblad, 150 mm, Kodak Tri-X, ISO 400, ¹/₂₅₀ sec, f11, yellow filter*

There are also two fundamentally different types of process, producing chemically different images. The conventional image is formed from silver halide crystals – examples are Ilford FP4, Kodak Tri-X, and Agfapan 25. Newer films, such as Ilford XP-1 and Agfapan Vario XL, use a dye-based chromogenic process similar to the colour negative process. Chromogenic black and white films have two important advantages. Because the dye has a finer chemical structure than the silver in conventional film, enlargements have finer resolution. Secondly, successful prints can still be made from excessively under- or overexposed film.

Broadly speaking, conventional black and white film follows the simple guideline that slow speed films – those that have low sensitivity to light – such as Kodak Technical Pan ISO 25 have fine grain, enhanced sharpness and high contrast, while fast films – those that have high sensitivity to light – such as Kodak Tri-X ISO 400 have coarse grain, moderate sharpness, and a long tonal range. Chromogenic films are almost grainless, have good sharpness, and a long tonal range. They also have a wide sensitivity range which, in effect, gives them a variable speed rating of ISO 100-800.

Choosing the most suitable film is largely a matter of personal preference, because results are affected by so many variables such as the subject qualities, lighting, exposure, processing, and printing. Becoming expert at controlling these variables is all part of learning black and white photography. For beginners, good general purpose films are the faster types such as Kodak Tri-X, Agfapan 400 and Ilford XP-1. For more critical work Ilford FP4 (ISO 125), Agfapan 100, and Ilford XP-1 are good choices, the latter being especially suited to portraiture, owing to its characteristic roundness of tone. In the studio, small formats benefit from high-resolution films such as Agfapan 25 and Kodak Technical Pan (ISO 25), but their slow speed may be a handicap.

A technically perfect negative, produced from an appropriate film type is only a starting point from which to make a print. It is up to the printer to make a picture that instantly communicates a powerful sense of mood, be it dark and menacing, light and airy, mysterious and unearthly, or stark and real. There is no need to try and reproduce all the subject tones in the print. In some ways that approach can stifle creativity, leading to predictable and rather clinical results that fail to communicate your own deeper feelings and impressions.

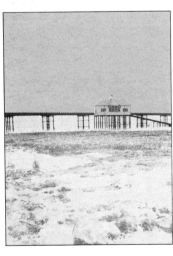

△ Delicate tones of pale grey and white predominate in this high-key landscape giving it a lightness which is reflected in the way that the pier seems to float. The effect is largely achieved at the printing stage by underexposing the paper. The negative was normally exposed and contains a full range of tones.

*Rolleiflex, 80 mm, Ilford FP3, ¹/₂₅₀ sec, f11*

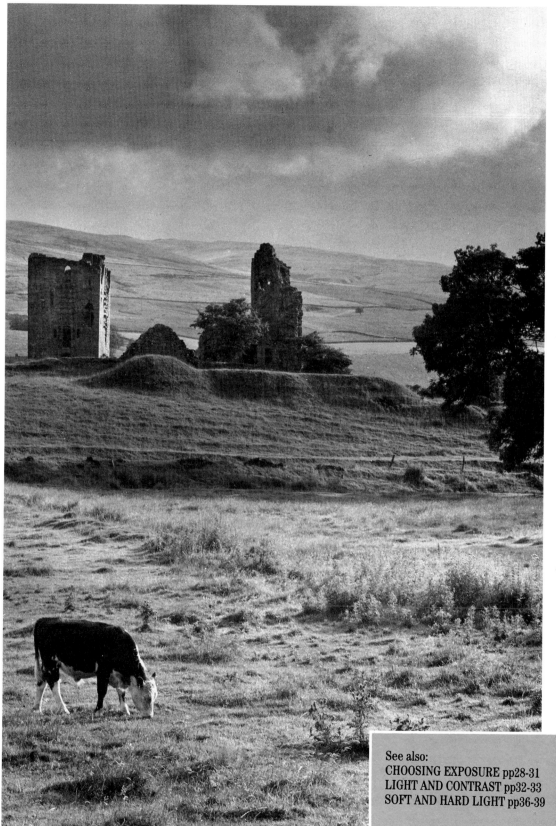

See also:
CHOOSING EXPOSURE pp28-31
LIGHT AND CONTRAST pp32-33
SOFT AND HARD LIGHT pp36-39

# PATTERN AND DETAIL

Pattern, texture, detail, and form can be used as main or supporting elements of a picture. Recognizing their presence, whether they occur in the natural world, a man-made environment or a meeting of the two, and deciding how they can be used to best effect is an essential part of the photographer's skill.

We tend to ignore the more subtle features of the world around us such as the rhythm of terraced rooftops, the texture of the granite facings used on modern office blocks, or the abstract pattern of wood veneer. It is only when a photograph presents one of them, captured and framed for us to study in detail, that we appreciate its visual delights.

The eye is very sensitive to repeated shape, colour and form, and the brain discerns patterns in the flimsiest of visual information. Since pattern is therefore a powerful visual element, most photographs are stronger for its inclusion. The pattern itself need not be very graphic. In fact, strong patterns need to be treated with care and circumspection because they can easily overpower the main image, while a single, repeated pattern will usually become boring unless it is interrupted, includes some slight variation or is balanced by other patterns within the picture. A second important consideration with repeated elements is rhythm within the repeat. Pictures that contain forms and patterns suggestive of flow and rhythm generated by the placing of elements are easy to read and instantly pleasing. The best examples may even have a harmonious and appealing quality like that of orchestral music.

Texture is often confused with pattern. However, texture in a photograph shows a subject's tactile qualities, conveying an impression of what it would be like to touch. Obviously, a photographic representation cannot be touched, so it is solely the way the photograph appears that must carry the suggestion. Texture is strongly evoked by tonal contrast, and sharpness of focus is essential to its impact. It is also a valuable supplement to other information in a picture, and, because our sense of touch has many associated memories, texture can be used to suggest abstract concepts such as sensuality, security, exhilaration, and the passage of time.

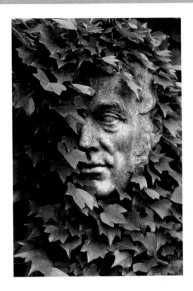

△ Patterns are to be found everywhere; some are man-made, others – like these ivy leaves – are natural. Unrelieved patterns can be monotonous and it is often a break that creates the visual impact. In this picture the stone face is emphasized by the surrounding leaves, but their pattern effect is strengthened by the face's presence.

*Pentax LX, 85 mm, Kodak Ektachrome 64, 1/30 sec, f11*

▷ Although this study of piled rope lacks a structured design it nevertheless has a strong pattern that is composed almost entirely of lines. Curved lines in a composition suggest a natural rhythm that can be reinforced if they flow into each other in a harmonious way. The soft, directional light of hazy sun provides enough tactile information to suggest texture without throwing a mass of confusing shadows.

*Pentax LX, 50 mm, Kodak Ektachrome 64, 1/125 sec, f11*

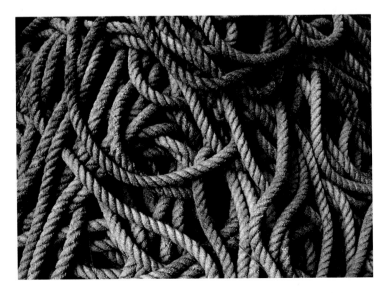

Detail and abstraction are two visual qualities that can be used to provide an element of surprise, giving a new angle on even a well-worn subject. Close-up details reveal hidden textures and shapes not normally visible to the eye or elements that are usually lost in distracting surroundings. The value of detail in pictures lies in providing an unusual view or in taking a subject out of context to enhance impact. Abstraction depends on interpreting form and tone as a strong design or pattern, which themselves can become a major element in the image. Often, good abstract images are very simple, and have an obvious uncomplicated structure that is based on, for example, geometric or natural forms.

▽ This landscape illustrates how abstraction, which is the most important image element here, can be used without obscuring the subject's identity. A simple repetition of horizontal lines and tonal steps introduces a natural rhythm and encourages the eye to scan the picture easily and pleasurably.

*Pentax LX, 135 mm, Kodak Ektachrome 64, 1/125 sec, f8*

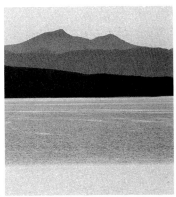

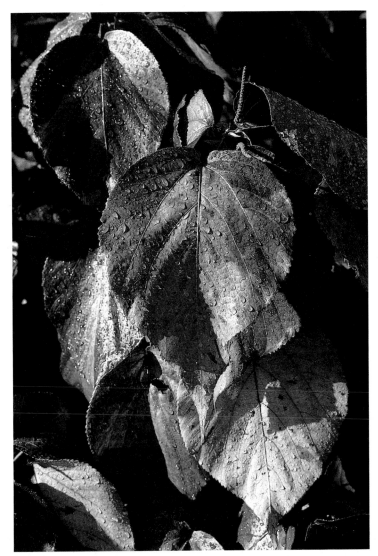

△ Pictures of detail direct our attention to subjects that are usually ignored. This shot of dew-laden leaves in autumn sunlight reveals strong textural qualities: the wetness of water droplets and the smooth, leathery feel of freshly fallen leaves.

*Pentax LX, 50 mm macro, Kodak Ektachrome 64, 1/30 sec, f11*

See also:
SOFT AND HARD LIGHT pp36-39
SHADOW DESIGNS pp144-145
LIGHT ON WATER pp136-137

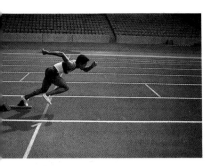

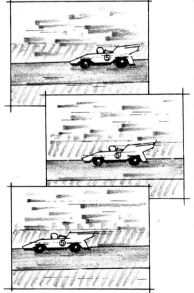

△ Action shots that feature people derive much of their impact from body angle and facial expression: things that are constantly and rapidly changing. Good timing and a keen sense of the precise moment when all elements are perfectly balanced are essential qualities for the action photographer. Notice how this shot an an athlete just off the starting blocks is framed and his body, full of newly released energy, has been frozen by use of a fast shutter speed.

*Pentax LX, 300 mm, Kodak Ektachrome 200, ¹/₅₀₀ sec, f8*

Photography, and particularly still photography, is an ideal medium for capturing moments in time and giving them significance. This is especially true of action photography, where timing and movement are vital elements in making powerful images. There are four basic ways of conveying a sense of movement: composition, freezing action, panning to create a blurred background, and controlled blur.

Although capturing movement of film usually demands instant reactions and a keen sense of timing, a strong sense of motion can also be communicated by the overall composition. Compositional aids such as strong contrasts, diagonal lines, oblique angles, low viewpoints, steep perspective, and a dramatic sense of scale are all devices used to add drama and impact. The effect is enhanced if the subject embodies energy and dynamism. Framing the action correctly so that the direction of travel is implied by imbalance and space is a simple technique employed by sports photographers. A centrally placed figure suggests balance, stability, and rest. Framing the same figure to one side suggests that he is about to move forwards across the shot or that he has already moved across and is about to leave it. Moreover, if the picture is composed so that the subject is positioned at an angle to the frame's axis, the sense of movement that is already implied is strengthened still further.

Freezing action for maximum sharpness can capture movement that is too fast for the eye to see clearly. Pole-vaulters in mid-air, speeding cyclists, a goalkeeper leaping for the ball, a bird in flight are all examples of high-speed action that only the camera can freeze as a clear image. Sometimes, there is a moment when movement changes direction – for example, the split second when a basketball player's leap changes from ascent to descent – and the action slows momentarily. This 'peak' is an ideal time to freeze movement, but you need to be able to anticipate it and release the shutter just before it happens. Fast shutter speeds, from ¹/₁₂₅ sec up to ¹/₂₀₀₀ sec, or even faster, are necessary. Many SLR cameras are capable of this, providing there is sufficient light and a fast film is used. Practical constraints often dictate the use of a wide aperture, but this is a mixed blessing because a sharply imaged subject might be lost against an equally sharp background.

◁ The three diagrams illustrate how framing the action affects the sense of movement implied. In the first frame, the compositional imbalance of the space in front of the car as it enters the shot implies that the car will travel through it, creating a sense of movement. In the second frame, the car is centrally placed and the structure is static and indecisive. The third frame, with the car just about to leave the shot, is similar in effect to the first but the movement implied is that already completed by the car across the frame.

▷ The split second when movement changes direction and action slows is known as 'peak of the action'. It is an ideal moment to freeze movement, but is sometimes hard to anticipate. In this picture the girl is at the highest point of her leap out of the water. Her action and the drops of water are sharply imaged by the brief exposure of electronic flash – something in the order of ¹/₅₀₀ sec to ¹/₁₀,₀₀₀ sec.

*Pentax LX, 85 mm, Kodak Ektachrome 200, X-sync, f8*

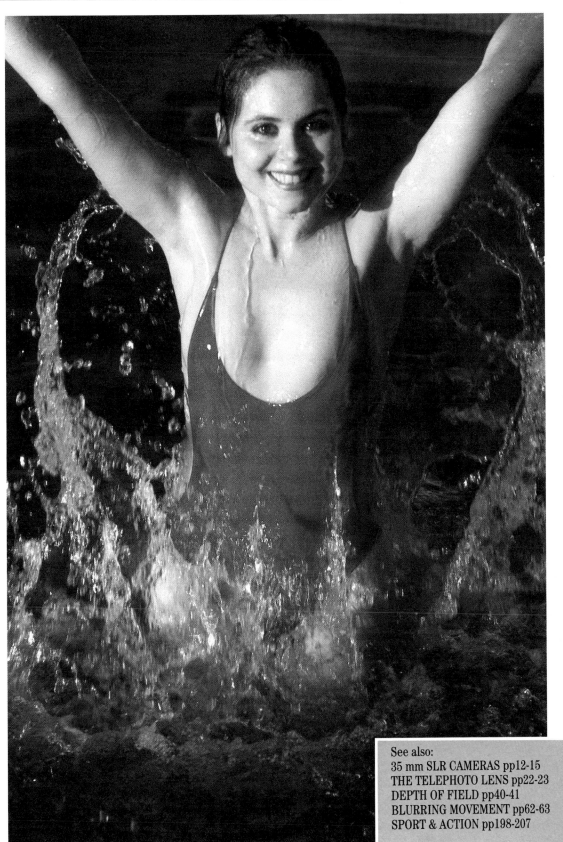

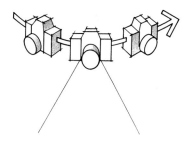

△ Panning is the technique of following a moving subject with the camera and then releasing the shutter during the pan, as illustrated in the diagram. It is important to continue the pan after releasing the shutter, as stopping will cause the camera to jerk, thus spoiling the image.

An alternative technique for creating a soft background is to pan the camera. This involves following a subject with the camera; the movement blurs the background but preserves subject sharpness. This is because the camera movement keeps the subject more or less stationary in relation to the film, while the scene behind rushes past, shadows and highlights creating streaks. Our eyes do exactly the same thing when following the ball in a football or tennis match but we are not aware of the blurred background because our attention is focused on the ball. Panning has the same effect in that, besides conveying a strong sense of movement, it focuses attention on the subject as being the single area of sharpness. Panning is a skill that requires practice. Mounting the camera on a tripod with a swivel head will help for subjects travelling along a pre-determined path. It is important to pan, release the shutter and then continue with the pan, rather than pan, release the shutter and then stop. Stopping will almost certainly cause you to jerk the shutter and thus ruin the image. With practice, the sequence can be carried out hand-held in one, fluid motion and quite slow shutter speeds can be employed, depending on the path of the subject. A motordrive or autowinder is a great help for getting the maximum number of images in any one pass and their use will reduce the likelihood of camera shake, which can also spoil the image.

Even slower speeds than those needed for panning can be used to create a deliberately blurred background as a more abstract interpretation of movement. Panning a cantering horse requires a

▷ In this picture the shutter was released when the group was sideways-on, the slow shutter speed creating blurred streaks in the background and giving a strong sense of movement. The subjects' feet are blurred because they move faster individually than the rest of their bodies and in different planes of movement.

*Pentax MX, 85 mm, Kodak Tri-X, ISO 400, ¹/₃₀ sec, f16*

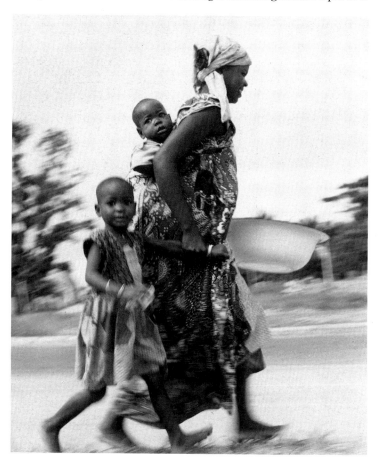

shutter speed of about $\frac{1}{125}$ sec to get sharp images, but if the shutter speed is reduced to $\frac{1}{30}$ sec or less, the combined effects of camera shake, pan and the horse's erratic motion will create an exciting swirl of colour and tone against a rushing backdrop. The effects are hard to visualize and many exposures will not live up to expectations, so it is best to take plenty of pictures. Deliberate blurring works well when the subject contrasts with the background – a white dove against a dark hillside, for example – and a strong sensation of motion can still be conveyed with speeds as slow as $\frac{1}{15}$ to $\frac{1}{4}$ of a second.

With all these techniques, the single, most important factor for capturing movement on film is the moment of exposure. A fraction too late or too early in firing the shutter and the impact is lost – an expression changes, muscles relax, an action peak passes. Many sports, such as athletics, racing, diving and judo, involve prolonged periods of waiting around interspersed with sudden bursts of intense activity. Knowing when these bursts of intense activity are going to occur and being ready to capture them is vital to success.

▽ Movement is a powerful compositional element in communicating drama. If the subject is relatively static, as was the case with this speaker, moving the camera during the exposure causes the image to streak. The degree of streaking depends on the shutter speed and the extent of displacement of the camera. The man's taut expression combined with the blurred streaks of tone have created an image with a powerful and dramatic impact that truly reflects the dynamism of the personality.

*Pentax LX, 135 mm, Kodak Tri-X, ISO 400, $\frac{1}{30}$ sec, f16*

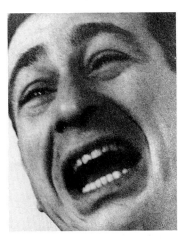

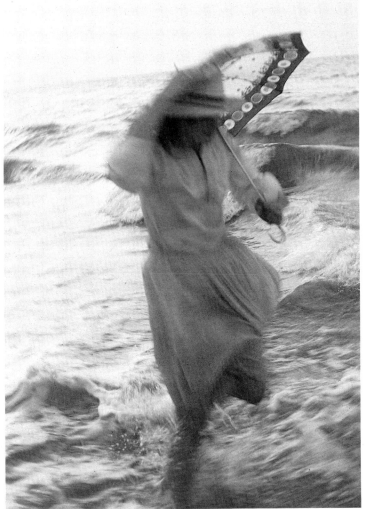

◁ Controlled blur using a slow shutter speed is an evocative way of conveying motion. Often it creates exciting swirls of colour and tone, as with this picture of a girl running along the beach at the edge of the sea.

*Pentax LX, 35 mm, Kodak Ektachrome 200, autoexposure, f8*

See also:
35 mm SLR CAMERAS pp12-15
THE TELEPHOTO LENS pp22-23
DEPTH OF FIELD pp40-41
CAPTURING MOVEMENT pp60-61
SPORT & ACTION pp198-207

# ACTION SEQUENCES

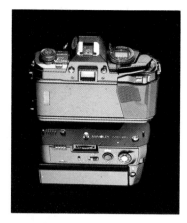

△ A separate motordrive can be fitted to some cameras which do not have one built-in. It can achieve rates of up to five or six frames per second. Gears and contacts are connected through the camera base.

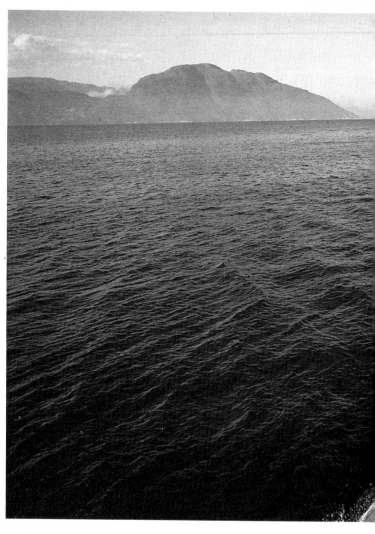

See also:
35 mm SLR CAMERAS pp12-15
PORTRAIT STORY pp172-175
SPLITTING IMAGES pp212-215

Movement at a specific moment of time can be described in a single frame, but one frame is too restricted adequately to describe change over a period of time. However, two, three, or more shots, taken in sequence, can be used to illustrate change over periods ranging from a fraction of a second to years. A sequence may cover the few seconds when a water droplet explodes on impact with the ground or many years in the life cycle of a tree. Photographic sequences allow us to see a world where time and change are artificially stretched or compressed into convenient parcels.

In fact, any roll of exposed film could be described as a sequence in that it shows pictures taken in succession, reflecting the order in which you worked and your progression from one subject to the next. Rolls taken on holiday are sequences of your travels, the events you enjoyed, the places you visited, and the sights you saw. They are narrative sequences, the theme really being a form of story. In fact, any sequence is, in essence, a story, providing the link between the pictures is maintained. This link may be abstract, as would be the case if the viewpoint remained static, or it may be contained within the pictures, if they concentrate on one subject.

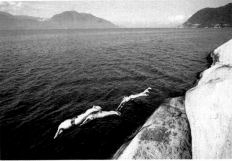

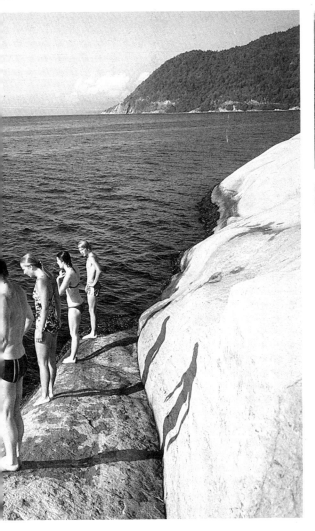

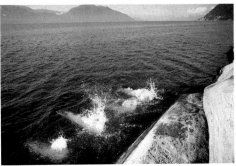

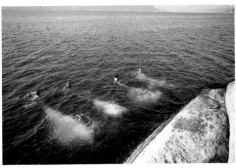

A variation on sequence photography is time-lapse photography, whereby changes in a subject are recorded in relation to elapsed time. The scientific approach is to take pictures at fixed intervals that may vary from milliseconds to years, depending on the subject and rate of change. Accuracy and precision are essential for scientific research but, for pictorial work, visual impact is as important as the subject and its changes, so the best pictures may not be separated by precisely the same interval of time. For clarity, the viewpoint should remain static so that changes are obvious from frame to frame. Time-lapse sequences over a long time span, such as a landscape through the seasons, will show wide variations in the quality, direction and intensity of light unless you take care when you make each exposure. High-speed time-lapse has its own problems. Use of a motordrive with fast recycling flash can achieve rates of up to five or six frames per second – sufficient to cover action cycles of about one to five seconds. More specialist equipment includes stroboscopic flash units which give rapid pulses of light while the camera shutter is left open, and high-speed cameras, with continuously running film and a rotating prism to act as the shutter, that can record at rates exceeding 10,000 frames per second.

△ One aspect of sequence photography is its ability to analyze movements or changes that are too quick for the eye to see clearly or too prolonged for us to appreciate as one action. In this sequence of two couples diving into an inviting blue sea, the complete action took a couple of seconds, but it is neatly divided into four, separate instants of time.

*Pentax LX, 50 mm, Kodak Ektachrome 64, autoexposure, f8*

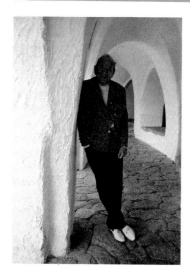

△ Colour photographers have to take into account not only tone but the characteristics of colours when composing photographs. If shot in black and white, this portrait of Noel Coward would show a good range of tones, with mid-tone values applying to the jacket and face. In colour, the scarlet has a striking effect on composition, immediately seizing the attention and ensuring that the figure is dominant.

*Leicaflex, 35 mm, Kodak Ektachrome 200, 1/250 sec, f8*

▷ We associate certain colours, particularly blue, green, and grey with coldness, since they tend to recede. In this picture of Brooklyn Bridge, New York, colour is restricted to blues and steely greys, making the atmosphere seem cold, remote, and bleak.

*Pentax LX, 35 mm, Kodak Ektachrome 200, 1/250 sec, f11*

Colour gives the photographer a rich and varied palette with which to add depth and create mood, accent, and drama. Colour photography is complex and the photographer has to understand and appreciate colour relationships, take them into account, and then exploit them to strengthen the image. For example, in the portrait of Noel Coward (left), the eye is immediately drawn to the brilliant red jacket, ensuring that the figure is the dominant element in the composition. Colour is what gives the shot its impact. Moreover, there are times when colour not only helps the subject, but is the subject itself.

In black and white photography, grey looks darkest against a white ground and lightest against a black one; colours have similar contrast effects. Mood and atmosphere may be evoked by the predominance of 'warm' or 'cool' colours in a picture. The inclusion of bright, vibrant colour will add drama, excitement, and energy, whereas subtle, harmonizing tones suggest tranquillity. Used with control and a good understanding of its special qualities, colour adds a further dimension to many pictures.

Colour film is available in two main types: colour transparency and colour negative. Transparency film – also called slide or reversal film – produces positive colour images directly from the exposed film through processing. The positive images are viewed with transmitted light either on a light box or a hand viewer or by being projected on to a screen. Image and colour quality in this film type are unsurpassed. It is cost effective in terms of price per shot and is the preferred choice of professionals, unless many prints are required. (Prints can be made, using paper capable of producing a positive from a positive, providing the subject contrast is not too harsh and that the colour has been rendered accurately in the original transparency.) Some of the most popular brands are Fujichrome 100, Kodachrome 64, Kodak Ektachrome 64, and Scotch (3M) 1000.

Colour negative or print film is the better choice for photographers who want to make colour prints. As with black and white work, the exposed film is an intermediate stage from which prints are made. The processing allows a great deal of manipulation so that errors in exposure, extreme brightness ranges and odd colour casts can be compensated for in the print making process. Top brand names include Agfacolor, Fujicolor, Kodacolor, and Scotch (3M).

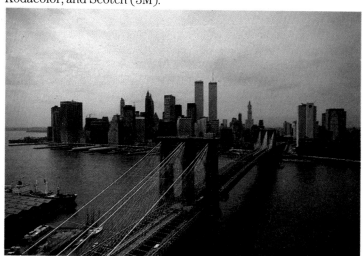

Film speed is also an important factor in film choice because the image is affected by the emulsion's sensitivity and structure. Slow films, such as Ektachrome 64 and Fujichrome 50D, are extremely sharp, have very fine grain, good colour saturation, and moderate contrast. Fast colour films, such as Fujichrome P1600 and Kodacolor VR 1000, cannot match the maximum speed of black and white film. Even so, grain is obtrusive and interferes with detail, while colour saturation is moderate and contrast high.

▽ The heat and light of summer is associated with warm colours. The red and yellow in this image seem warm and evoke a sense of intimacy and well-being.

*Pentax LX, 50 mm, Kodak Kodachrome 64, ¹/₅₀₀ sec, f8*

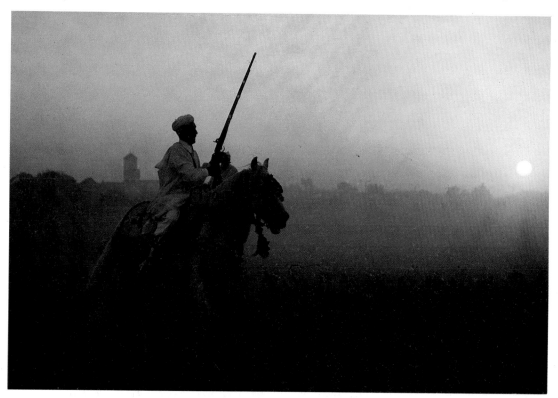

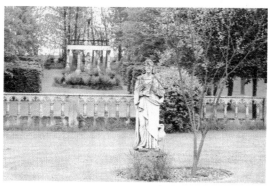
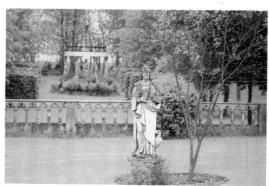

△ These landscapes have been shot on the fastest (right) and slowest (left) E6-process transparency film – Fujichrome P1600 D and Fujichrome 50D – to show the qualities affected by film speed: grain, sharpness, colour balance, and contrast.

*Pentax LX, 85 mm, Fujichrome 50D, ¹/₆₀ sec, f8*

*Pentax LX, 85 mm, Fujichrome P1600 D, ¹/₂₅₀ sec, f22*

See also:
VARIETIES OF LIGHT pp68-69
COLOUR INTENSITY pp70-71
COLOUR FILTERS pp72-73
EXPLOITING FILM pp80-81

# VARIETIES OF LIGHT

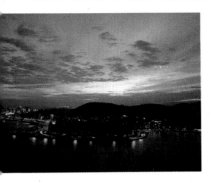

The earth's atmosphere envelops the globe and acts like a filter, modifying the colour and the intensity of the sunlight passing through it. This is because the air is laden with minute particles of dust and water vapour, which tend to scatter light rays as they pass through. The degree of scattering depends on the position of the sun relative to the earth – at sunset and sunrise, for example, light has to travel much farther through the atmosphere than at midday, and so the scattering is greater. The short wavelengths (blues) are scattered most easily by the particles in the atmosphere and this causes the characteristic reds and oranges of dawn and dusk. At midday, the distribution of colour wavelengths is more even.

To the photographer, the changes in the quality of the light with the passing of the day can be likened to an artist's palette of colours. Each hour offers subtly different hues and contrasts. Before the sun rises, when the air is cool and moist, the clarity of the atmosphere favours the yellowish light characteristic of dawn. The bright sky overhead lightens shadows with a delicate, bright glow that minimizes harsh contrasts in a way unique to sunrise. In these early minutes, light changes rapidly, so stay alert. Clouds are picked out in crimson against a golden backdrop and, as the sun climbs, their richness turns to rose and then, finally, to the palest yellow before taking on the familiar white of daytime. Early morning light, like that of evening, throws long shadows, lighting the landscape so that every shape and form is depicted in sharp relief. But the clarity of the air and the unique light give dawn a quality quite different from that of dusk.

At midday in summer, if the sun is shining from a clear sky, the light will be as pure in colour as it will ever be. Daylight film is balanced to record accurately colours in this light, which is why they appear at their most brilliant and saturated. Noonday photographs are characterized by a stark contrast that is likely to result in a loss of detail in both the bright highlights and in the deep shadows. These striking black shadows are short because the sun is directly overhead, and they can be included as part of the composition. But, be warned: their colouring may appear cold and it is advisable to use an 81A or UV filter.

Evening brings a return of low, texture-enhancing light that throws long, strident shadows over warm patches of a sunlit scene. Evening sun is redder than light at dawn, since the dust-laden atmosphere absorbs all the short, cool-coloured wavelengths of light. When the sun finally sets, a beautiful, soft illumination bathes the landscape. The sky will still be bright for some time, and photographs taken at dusk can give the impression of a well-detailed night scene.

△ Just minutes after the sun has dropped below the horizon, the light takes on a special quality that lasts for only a little while. This cityscape photograph has captured the fleeting light of the sun as its last rays bathe the highest clouds in a rich golden and rosy glow. Below, in the darkening city, street lamps create a scattering of brightly coloured pinpoints of light and there is just enough ambient light from the twilight sky to pick out the boats in the harbour and details of the shoreline.

*Pentax LX, 50 mm, Kodak Ektachrome 64, 1 sec, f11*

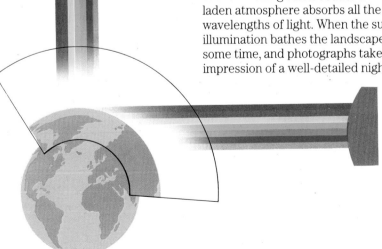

◁ At midday, the sun is directly overhead and its rays travel their shortest route through the atmosphere. At sunrise and sunset, the rays have to pass through more of the atmosphere, losing the shorter, bluer wavelengths on the way, and leaving the reds and oranges to colour the land and sky.

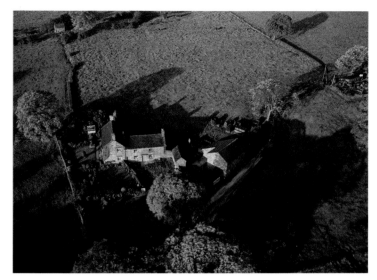

◁ The beautiful shadows that reach out across the land are a feature of the low, early morning sun. The air in the early hours is often crisp and clear, and so the sunlight is golden in quality – rather than the orange-red it will be in the evening – and the shadows, illuminated by the brightening sky above, hold just a hint of the blue that will dominate the rest of the day.

*Pentax LX, 35 mm, Kodak Ektachrome 64, $^1/_{125}$ sec, f8*

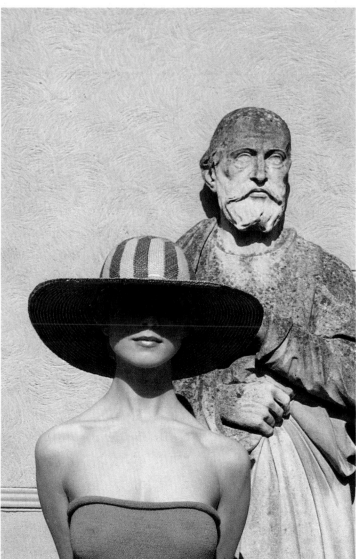

◁ Light can be extremely bright at midday. When the sun is at its zenith, shadows are short, dark, and imposing. Intense sunlight can cause glare and destroy detail in lighter parts of the picture. This portrait illustrates the quality of noonday sun on a summer's day in England. Colours are very accurate, but the stark contrasts can be eye-piercing in their intensity.

*Pentax LX, 85 mm, Kodak Ektachrome 64, $^1/_{250}$ sec, f8*

See also:
LIGHT AND CONTRAST pp32-33
SOFT AND HARD LIGHT pp36-39
ELECTRONIC FLASH pp74-77
TUNGSTEN LIGHTING pp78-79

# COLOUR INTENSITY

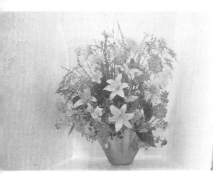

△ Warm, muted colours predominate in this simple still life study of flowers. The tonal range is limited to lighter colours from mid-grey to white – making this a high-key image – but the shot still contains colour. The misty effect is produced by using a soft, overhead light and fitting a diffuser and fog filter to the lens.

*Pentax LX, 85 mm, Scotch (3M) 100, 1/250 sec, f8*

▷ The bright yellow and red stripes of the balloon are strong and vibrant, but their impact is strengthened by the contrast with the deep blue sky. A touch of black provides a forceful counterpoint. Hard, bright sunlight and an exposure set to favour the highlights has ensured that these exciting colours are fully saturated.

*Pentax LX, 135 mm, Kodak Ektachrome 64, 1/250 sec, f11*

Colour has a profound effect on a picture's mood. Bold, striking colours are eye-catching and energetic; pastel tones suggest harmony and invite the eye to explore the photograph at leisure. Understanding and controlling colour so that it can be enriched or muted to achieve the desired mood is an essential part of the photographer's skill.

Vibrant colours can form the dominant element in a photograph's composition. Strong colour contrasts intensify the impact of different tones, especially if there are just one or two pairs set against each other. Colour pairs that have the most contrast are complementaries – blue-yellow, green-magenta, and red-cyan – but any warm colour placed next to a cool one will add impact. A similar effect is achieved when a photograph is largely composed of one bold colour with small areas of black, grey, or white as a neutral counterpoint.

Colours can be manipulated and strengthened by appropriate choice of exposure, film, lighting, and filters. Exposure plays an important role in manipulating colour. If you are using colour transparency film, you must avoid underexposure, as this will desaturate colour. However, many photographers increase colour contrast by underexposing slightly – usually by 1/3 to 1 stop. But remember, if you are using colour negative film, the reverse is true: colour contrast can be increased by overexposing, but subjects with a wide brightness range may lose colour in the highlights if overexposure is extreme. Precise exposure control is crucial, so a separate light meter with an incident-light attachment is recommended.

Lighting quality can also be exploited to enhance colour. Notice how the colour quality of, for example, a familiar building, changes in the sunlight at different times of the day. With landscapes, the clear air produced after heavy rain allows distant

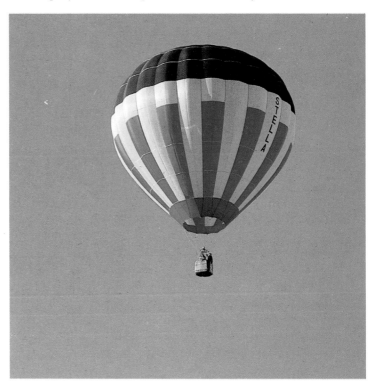

colour to record with extra clarity, and the wet surfaces also deepen the colour balance. Hard, strong light – typical of noonday summer sun – is ideal for giving emphasis to bold colour, and any desaturation caused by glare from reflections or heat haze can be reduced by using a polarizing filter.

If, on the other hand, you wish to evoke a poignant or romantic atmosphere, you should aim to use soft, muted colours. Harmony is suggested by pastel colours of similar tones and hues. Soft, diffuse light is ideal for recording subdued colour, and slight overexposure – about ⅓ to 1 stop – of the transparency will dilute it further to enhance the effect even more. It is also possible to mimic the softening effect of mist by using a fog or diffusing filter over the lens, or by using as the prime lens a cheap plastic magnifying glass fitted to extension rings or bellows.

▽ It can be argued that monochromatic subjects are just as effective in black and white as in colour but, as this portrait shows, large areas of neutral tone bring out any slight colour tints that are present – here, in the girl's skin and hair – making them much more effective.

*Pentax LX, 85 mm, Kodak Ektachrome 64, ¹/₂₅₀ sec, f8*

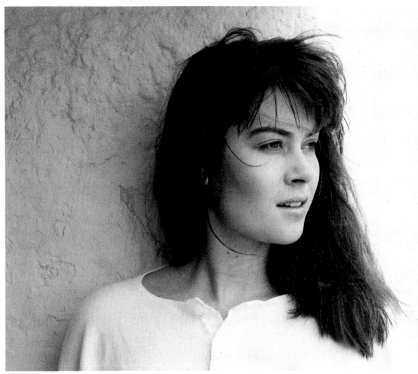

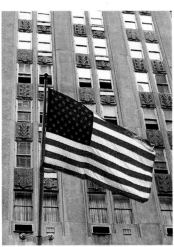

◁ Set against a neutral field of grey concrete, the bold colours and stripes of the American flag seize the viewer's attention. The close viewpoint and framing strengthen the effect of the intense colour and strong design.

*Pentax LX, 135 mm, Kodak Ektachrome 64, ¹/₂₅₀ sec, f11*

See also:
SOFT AND HARD LIGHT pp36-39
COLOUR FILM CHOICE pp66-67
VARIETIES OF LIGHT p68-69
COLOUR FILTERS pp72-73

# COLOUR FILTERS

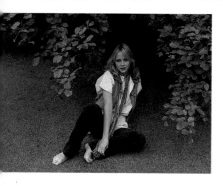

Colour film rarely shows true colour balance except under very controlled conditions, while excessively contrasty conditions may lead to loss of detail in the highlights and/or shadows. A good knowledge of the non-effects colour filters available, and their use, will help you to counteract these deficiencies.

The UV or 'haze' filter – ranging from almost clear to yellowish in colour – is probably the most popular of all filters, and is used in landscape work to reduce the density of the distant haze caused by ultraviolet light. Skylight filters also absorb UV light, but their pinkish tint helps reduce the blue cast that sometimes colours shadow areas.

The polarizing (PL) filter helps increase colour saturation under certain conditions. Light from the open sky or reflected from non-metallic surfaces is polarized. The filter is used by rotating it in its mount until incoming polarized light is stopped from reaching the film, and consequently colour saturation is increased in those areas.

Colour-balancing filters are used to fine-tune the colour of light to match the requirements of the film. Warm coloured 81 and 85 series and cool coloured 80 and 82 series filters are available in closely spaced ranges for balancing daylight and tungsten film in various lighting conditions. Neutral density (ND) filters are generally used with fast film to reduce light intensity, so that wide apertures or slow shutter speeds may be used. Graduated grey filters are effective when you want to decrease the contrast between the bright and dark parts of the image.

△ On a sunny day, light in the shade comes mostly from blue sky and is much 'cooler' in colour than the summer sunlight that daylight films are balanced for. This causes a blue cast which is quite unpleasant, but it can be corrected by using an 81A or 81B filter (below). The same filters can be used for 'warming up' light on a cloudy day.

*Pentax LX, 85 mm, Kodak Ektachrome 64, $1/125$ sec, f8*

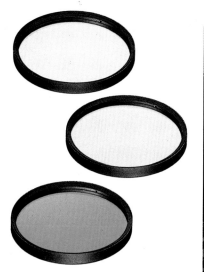

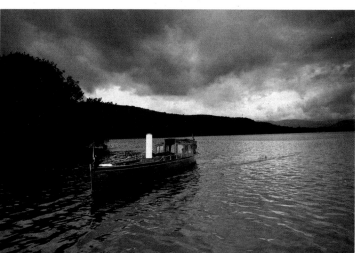

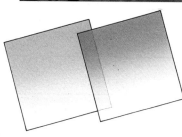

△ Grey graduated half-colour filters, (left), are used for balancing exposure between light and dark parts of an image. Square filters, held in a special mount, can be raised or lowered to cover the correct part of the image.

*Pentax LX, 28 mm, Kodak Ektachrome 64, $1/125$ sec, f8*

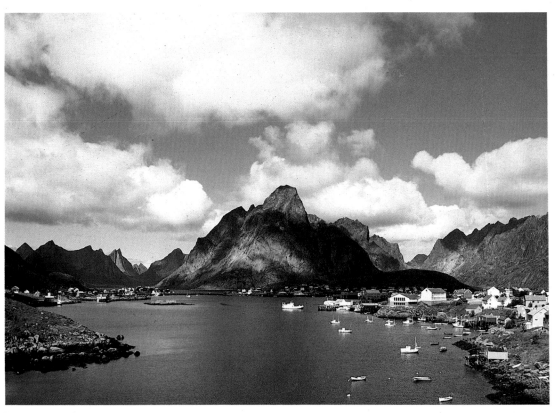

△ A polarizing filter can be used to increase colour saturation in blue skies. Here, it also balances the brightness of the sky with the rest of the picture.

*Pentax LX, 28 mm, Kodak Ektachrome 64, ¹/125 sec, f8*

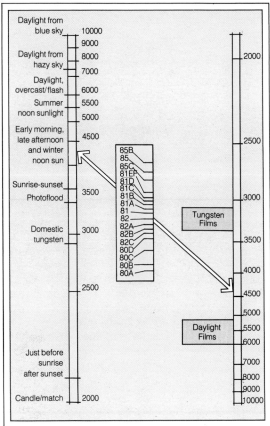

◁ The table shows the correct filter to use in different lighting conditions. Just hold a straight edge from the film scale on the right to the colour temperature scale on the left. The filter to use is indicated by the point at which the central scale and the straight edge intersect.

See also:
SPECIAL FILTERS pp82-85
STUDIO SILHOUETTES pp248-249
COLOURED LIGHT pp252-253

# ELECTRONIC FLASH

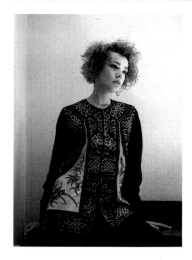

△ Studio flash systems are most often used to emulate daylight, which normally comes from above and slightly to one side, is neutral in colour and can be anything from direct to omnidirectional. This portrait has a look of natural light and this is the best guide to the successful use of flash. It was lit using a silver umbrella attachment.

*Pentax LX, 85 mm, Kodak Ektachrome 64, X-sync, f11*

Electronic flash is the most widely used artificial light source in photography. Its accurate colour, versatility, portability and power, plus the vast range of accessories available to modify its output are attributes not shared by tungsten or quartz-halogen sources. Electronic flash can be divided into two main groups: flashguns and studio flash.

Flashguns are small and portable. The more powerful types have sufficient output to cope with a wide range of tasks from lighting shadows as a fill-in to providing the main light and they have, therefore, become indispensable accessories. Electronic flash units give a very brief pulse of light – about $\frac{1}{1000}$ sec or less with flashguns and $\frac{1}{250}$-$\frac{1}{1000}$ sec with studio units – that discharges from a gas-filled tube. A straw-coloured coating ensures that the colour temperature of the light matches daylight film. Most SLRs are fitted with a focal plane shutter that has to be fully open before the flash fires. This only occurs at the X-sync speed or at speeds slower than $\frac{1}{250}$ sec, depending on the camera. Bladed shutters can usually be set to any speed for flash synchronization.

The simplest flashguns are pocket-sized, clip on to the camera's hot-shoe and have a fixed, low output. Exposure is calculated manually according to subject distance. More sophisticated units can vary output in steps – usually full, $\frac{1}{2}$, $\frac{1}{4}$, $\frac{1}{8}$ etc. – have computerized autoexposure that quenches the tube when a sensor has detected sufficient light for exposure, fast recycling times and additional features, such as a 'zoom' head to alter the width of the light beam to match the angle of view with different lenses, fill-in flash and a host of accessories for softening, bouncing and colouring the output. The power output of the most expensive and versatile units equals that of a small studio flash. Exposure is calculated using the camera's own autoexposure system which balances flash output with ambient light. In some sophisticated cameras the flash is used in conjunction with the autofocus in poor light. The flash sends out an exploratory beam to determine the focal distance. A second beam illuminates the subject.

One of the major disadvantages of flashguns is the lack of a modelling light, so you have to rely on experience to visualize the effects. Studio flash units are usually powered from A/C mains and incorporate a tungsten lamp so that lighting can be previewed. Photographers mostly use studio flash as a substitute

▷ Two of the most useful studio flash accessories are a diffuser (right) and an umbrella reflector (left). The diffuser, which can be a soft box, a cotton umbrella or a screen, is translucent and the light is softened by passing through it. The reflector has a silvered inside surface for maximum efficiency and the light output is a broad beam of semi-directional light.

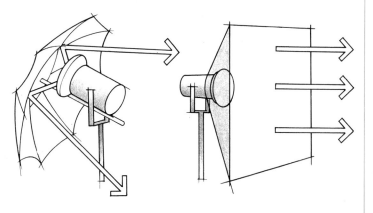

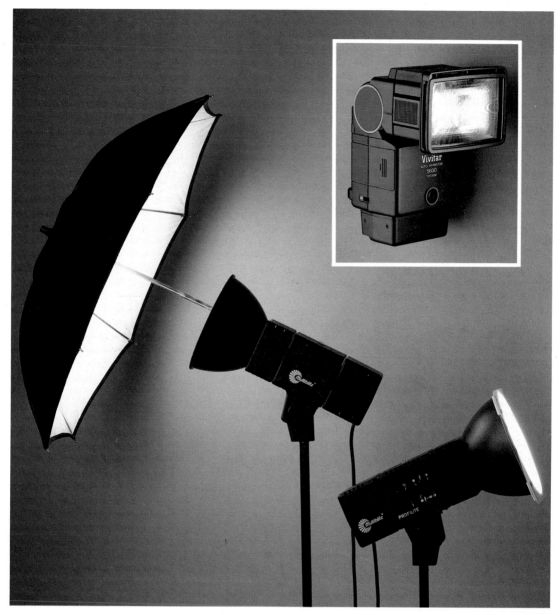

for daylight, so units have to be sufficiently powerful to allow slow film and small f-stops to be used. Most professionals use two or three flash units at a time. Only one unit is linked directly to the camera by means of a synchronization cord; the others are simultaneously triggered by light-detecting cells called slave units.

There are numerous accessories available to alter lighting quality. Chief among these are standard reflectors, umbrella reflectors and diffusers. Standard reflectors give a concentrated beam of hard light, much like a flashgun. An umbrella reflector is larger and produces a flood of semi-hard light. A diffuser, which is placed in front of the flash, softens the light. Unlike the smaller flashgun, studio flash systems have no autoexposure facilities and a hand held flash meter has to be used to calculate exposure.

One of the most useful functions of the small electronic flash

△ Electronic flash can be divided into two main groups. Flashguns (inset) are small, portable and usually mounted on the camera. Studio flash (main picture) is quite separate from the camera and is mains powered.

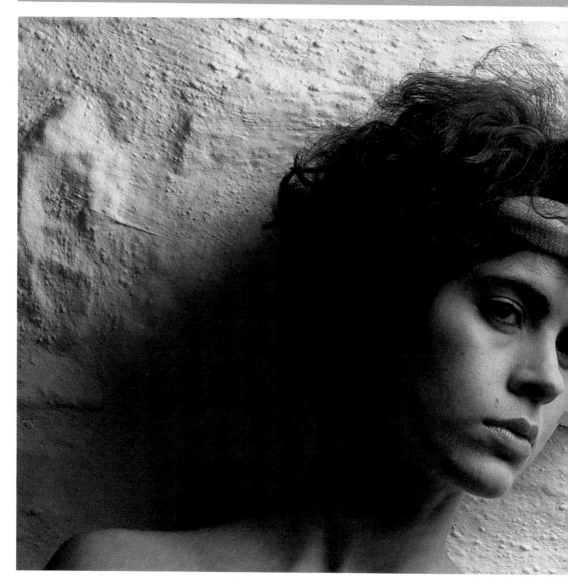

△ Directional light from a flash unit is too hard for portraits and the narrow coverage of most flashguns can lead to the subject being spotlit in a surrounding darkness. Bouncing flash off a convenient white or pale coloured ceiling gives a soft flattering illumination with sufficient coverage to light up the surroundings. When you are shooting colour, the reflecting surface must be neutral or the light will be tinted, producing a colour cast.

*Pentax LX, 85 mm, Kodak Ektachrome 64, X-sync, f11*

unit is to lighten dark areas when the ambient light is hard and throws deep, ugly shadows. Two common situations are outdoor portraits in bright sun and interiors where the brightness range from outside to inside is too extreme. For fill-in flash outdoors – sometimes known as syncro-sun flash – the unit is mounted on the camera. Just enough flash to lighten the shadows is needed; this is usually about two stops less than the ambient light exposure. To estimate fill-in flash exposure, use the manual calculator on the flash unit to find the normal f-stop setting for the subject distance. Stop down by a further two stops and then set the shutter speed to give the correct exposure for ambient light at that f-stop. If this is faster than the X-sync speed, cover the flash with one layer of white tissue for every halving of the shutter speed. A similar technique is used to balance outdoor light with interior illumination, but, for a natural-looking exposure balance, the view outside should be overexposed by about one stop and the interior adjacent to the window underexposed by one or two stops. For more convincing interior lighting, soften

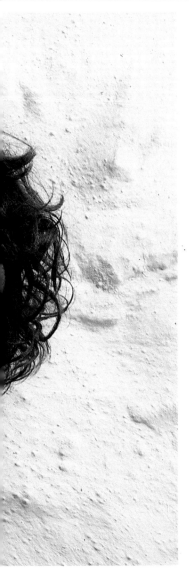

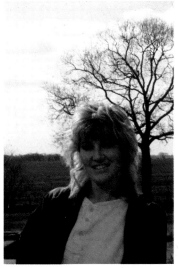

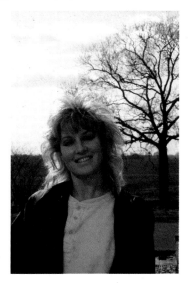

△ Fill-in flash is used for lightening shadow areas when the difference between them and the highlights is too extreme for the film to record detail in both. Ambient light exposure is kept normal, but the flash exposure is calculated to be about two stops less to keep the overall balance natural.

*Pentax LX, 85 mm, Kodak Ektachrome 64, sec, f8*

*Pentax LX, 85 mm, Kodak Ektachrome 64, X-sync, f8*

▷ Guide numbers (on film instructions sheets, film cartons etc.) are easy to use to determine exposure. Divide the guide number by the flash-to-subject distance in feet to give the aperture (f stop). Here, the guide number is 80 and the distance is 10 ft, giving f8.

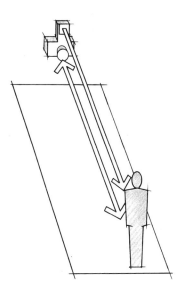

and broaden the flashgun's light by bouncing it off a pale toned wall or ceiling. If you are shooting colour, use a wall or ceiling in a neutral shade. Bounce flash is also a flattering light for portraits, compared with direct flash. In any case, direct flash causes 'red-eye' unless the unit is held away from the camera lens. (If the flash is close to the camera lens and the camera is aimed directly at the subject's face, the beam of light illuminates the retina at the back of the eyes. This makes the pupils appear red, rather than black in the image.) If there is no modelling light to ensure that the flash is being directed on to the subject, remember that the angle of incident flash on the deflecting surface will equal the angle of reflection. Autoexposure units will still function correctly, providing the sensor faces the subject.

A good approximate calculation when bouncing light off a white surface is to allow an extra stop for light loss; but remember that the subject distance is the length of the entire light path not simply the shorter, direct distance from the flashgun to the subject.

See also:
35 mm SLR CAMERAS pp12-15
SOFT AND HARD LIGHT pp36-39
TUNGSTEN LIGHTING pp78-79

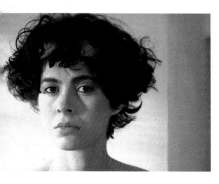

△ The warm colouring of tungsten lighting, when used with daylight-balanced film, can be exploited to tint cool shadows with a warm glow that is very effective for portraits. The main light for the girl's face was from a window; the shadow side was lit by a 500 W tungsten light.

*Pentax LX, 85 mm, Kodak Ektachrome 64, ¹/₁₂₅ sec, f8*

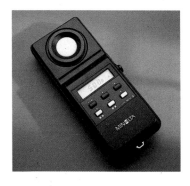

△ Colour meters are sometimes used by professionals who work in many different indoor locations and need an accurate assessment of colour temperature.

Tungsten lighting and flash are the two alternatives to using natural light. Although electronic flash has largely replaced tungsten in most photographers' studios, tungsten is far from defunct – a complex tungsten lighting set-up is far cheaper than studio flash. Tungsten is a continuous light source rather than a single pulse of intense light, it has a colour temperature of 3200K, and generates a great deal of heat – enough to make models perspire and feel very uncomfortable and some still-life and natural subjects wilt or dry up.

The beauty of tungsten lighting is that it behaves much the same way as natural lighting. It is easy to see how lighting direction and intensity affect the picture, and how shadows fall. The lamps themselves are relatively simple, consisting of little more than a bulb, a reflector, and a stand. The standard set-up is a 500 W bulb with a parabolic reflector, and gives a hard, directional beam that can be softened by fitting a wire scrim diffuser over its front. A larger shallow reflector known as a floodlight produces a broader, less directional light similar to that obtained from a flash umbrella. If you wish to gain more directional control over the lighting you can use spotlight attachments with a Fresnel lens to focus the beam, or clip-on 'barn doors' that act like blinkers, and restrict light spread. If you need extremely hard illumination, you can fit a spotlight with a 1000 W bulb.

Used with daylight film, tungsten lighting gives a warm cast, rather like that found at sunset. You can exploit this 'fault' to warm up cool interiors and shadows. If you want proper colour balance you need a colour-correction filter such as an 80B. You can put the filters over either the lights or the camera lens. Alternatively, you can use tungsten balanced film and correct it for daylight with an 85B filter. In some ways this is a better compromise because tungsten film is designed to cope with the long exposures associated with tungsten lighting and the loss of speed due to the 85B's filter factor is less important in bright daylight. The ability to cope with long exposures and the film's relatively high speed – from about ISO 150 to 640 – together make tungsten film ideal for interiors. Even in very orange domestic lighting you only need use a relatively weak 82C or 82B filter.

If you have an interior lit by fluorescent tubes, you will find that any uncorrected colour film yields a strong greenish-yellow cast. Many filter manufacturers make standard correction filters – for daylight film these are deep magenta, but they will only correct properly for one type of tube, the so-called 'cool white'. The only way of correcting the imbalance accurately is to find out the make and type of tube (warm white, warm white deluxe, cool white deluxe etc) and then make trial exposures with a range of correction gels. Use the table below as a rough guide to filtration values, or try using CC30M or CC30R filters.

**Filtration values for fluorescent light**

|  | Lamp | Day | White | Warm white deluxe | Warm White | Cool white deluxe |
|---|---|---|---|---|---|---|
| Daylight | 40M+30Y | 20C+30M | 40C+30M | 60C+30M | 30M | 30C+20M |
| Tungsten | 30M+10Y +85B | 40M+40Y | 30M+20Y | 10Y | 50M+60Y | 10M+30Y |

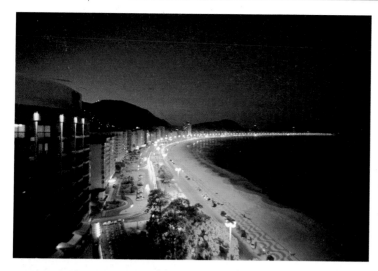

◁ The weak ambient light of evening has coloured the areas outside the warm pool of domestic light a cool blue because tungsten-balanced film has been used. By contrast, the low colour temperature of the caravan lights has created a slight orange cast, producing an atmosphere of warmth and comfort beneath the awning.

*Pentax LX, 135 mm, Kodak Ektachrome 160 Tungsten, 1/30 sec, f8*

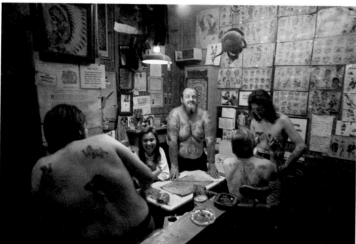

◁ Fluorescent lights generally produce a greenish-yellow cast, as here, but the exact colour is hard to predict. When this lighting is mixed with other types, it is a compromise, but, as a general guide, use daylight film and correct for the fluorescent light unless it is by far the weakest light source.

*Leica, 21 mm, Kodak Ektachrome 200, 1/8 sec, f4*

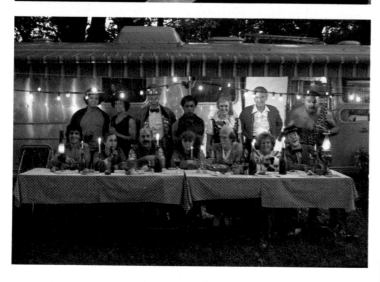

◁ Sodium and mercury-vapour lamps are mainly used for street lighting, sports stadiums, and large industrial interiors. They are hard to correct because their light is frequently limited to one or two colours: yellow in the case of sodium, and green or green and blue with mercury.

*Pentax LX, 50 mm, Kodak Ektachrome 200, 1 sec, f8*

See also:
CHOOSING EXPOSURE pp28-31
SOFT AND HARD LIGHT pp36-39
ELECTRONIC FLASH pp74-77

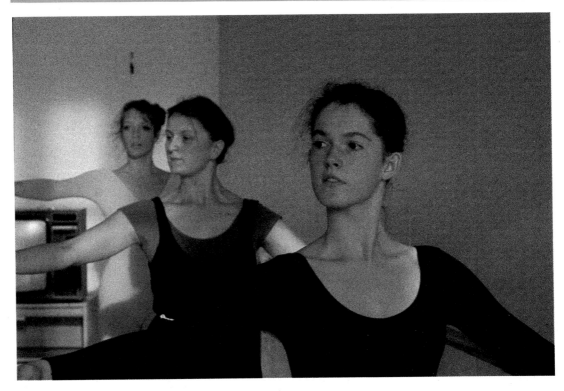

△ High-speed colour film has very coarse grain which overlays the image with a gravel-like texture. Some, such as Fujichrome P1600 D and Scotch (3M) 1000, have grain patterns that are attractive in their own right and that can be used to alter the textural qualities of smooth surfaces, as with the skin of this model. Fast colour films such as these – and Polachrome 35 mm – have a very high contrast and are best used in soft light.

*Pentax LX, 35 mm, Scotch (3M) 1000, ¹/₂₅₀ sec, f11*

Every photographer is aware that the word photography means drawing with light. In the same way that a painter understands and manipulates pigments, the photographer uses light to create the desired mood and atmosphere in his pictures. But we tend to forget that the film itself, on which the image is formed, can be exploited for its own qualities in order to strengthen the impact of a picture.

Every film – colour or black and white – has unique characteristics differentiating it from others that are nominally similar. This is especially noticeable with colour transparency film; each type uses slightly different dyes resulting in small variations in colouring. For example, Kodak Ektachrome has a cool colour balance that is especially marked in overcast conditions, and yet this apparent drawback can be used to intensify the colouring of blue flowers in soft light. Fujichrome has a warm bias that can be used to enhance skin tones in portraits. This type of exploitation is common on an everyday level, but for special effects we may turn to more unusual film. Very high-speed emulsions, such as Scotch (3M) 1000 and Fujichrome P1600 D (the fastest film on the market at present), are inherently grainy, forming a pattern that textures the image. The much slower Polachrome 35 mm instant film also has a marked grain structure, but one which is quite different. These effects can be used to add texture to normally smooth surfaces or to break up fine detail, such as leaves on a distant tree. Alternatively, part of the image can be massively enlarged to reveal the individual colours of grains in each dye layer that recalls the *pointillist* technique of painting.

Special films, such as Kodak Infra-red, Polaroid Polagraph, and Kodalith, can be used straight to produce unnatural tones or tints by virtue of their response to light and colour. Pictorial use of

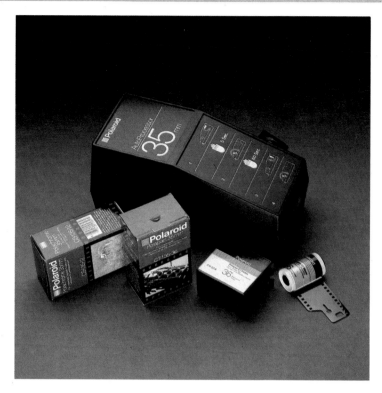

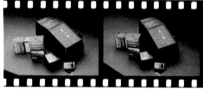

▷ ▽ Polaroid instant 35 mm transparency films – Polachrome, Polapan and Polagraph – are developed in a daylight processor to yield a filmstrip of dry images in less than three minutes. The Polachrome, in particular, has a unique image quality which is a result of the way the colour image is made up.

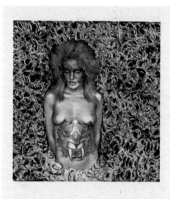

these emulsions has to be experimental because many have no stated ISO rating and the effects of different light sources, filters, and so on are not fully catalogued.

Some standard emulsions, such as Polaroid 600 Series print films, can be manipulated in various ways to distort tone and colour and create bizarre images. Heat, cold, emulsion stripping, physical manipulation, processing in the wrong chemistry, and even straight push-processing to an extreme, can all be used in very simple ways to manipulate the film and to create fresh, exciting and unique images.

△ Polaroid 600 Series film is amenable to manipulation immediately after the print has been ejected from the camera. The swirling pattern was made by moving the emulsion around with the rounded end of a pencil.

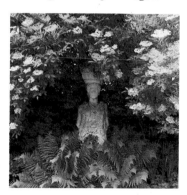

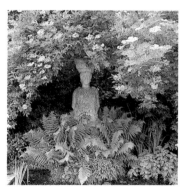

△ The bizarre colouring in this image has been produced by shooting on colour infra-red film. Practical experience is the only way to have full control over its effects. Using green, yellow, or orange filters will alter the colour range. Note the difference between this IR shot and the normal view also shown.

*Pentax LX, 50 mm, Kodak Ektachrome Infra-red, 1/250 sec, f8, yellow filter*

See also:
COLOUR FILM CHOICE pp66-67
COLOUR FILTERS pp72-73
SPECIAL FILTERS pp82-85
SPLITTING IMAGES pp212-215

# S P E C I A L   F I L T E R S

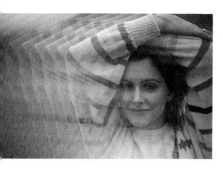

△ This image relies on a multi-image filter. The right side of the filter is clear, so that a normal image is recorded but the left side has six facets to create the repeating pattern.

▷ The irregular and uneven surface of the diffusing filter has softened sharpness and spread the highlights in this picture. Contrast is also reduced, which helps to create a romantic mood.

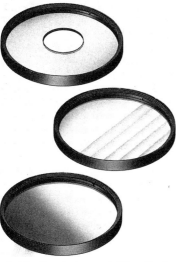

△ The fog centre-spot filter (top) mimics the effect of fog, with a clear area in the centre. Each facet of the parallel multiple prism filter (centre) forms an image; the repeated images giving a sense of movement to static subjects. The diffusing filter (bottom) is ideal for creating a romantic mood in portraits and landscapes.

Filters for special effects vary from the subtle to the extravagant but, used with care, they can transform a mundane or dull subject into an exciting and expressive image. Filters have been in use from the earliest days of photography, when photographers made their own to suit particular images, but now many manufacturers make filter systems to create a wide range of effects.

Probably the most useful special-effects filters are those that do not have a pronounced effect on the photograph. Filters that produce eye-catching results are best reserved for occasional use because, as with fisheye or extreme telephoto lenses, the effect tends to swamp the image and become tedious if employed too frequently. When using many special attachments it is important to judge what the effect will be at the taking aperture, as well as to check how the results will vary with different focal lengths, and to adjust the exposure as necessary.

Some of the simplest effects filters are colour filters. Strong colours work best with bright, contrasting subjects that can easily take on the filter's hue, while pale filters work well for tinting scenes to emphasize mood, softening the image and adding a

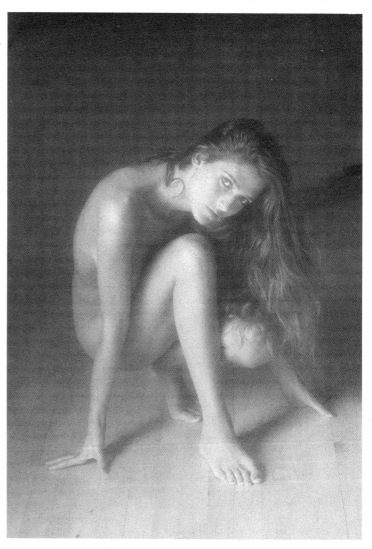

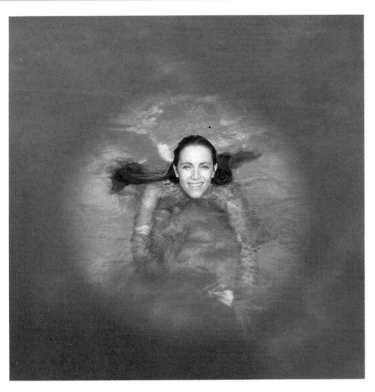

◁ Variously known as soft-spot or fog centre-spot this filter has a smoky-coloured area around a clear centre. The size of the clear part varies according to the lens and aperture used.

▽ Square filters in attachment holders allow the photographer to position any 'half-effect' filter to suit the subject and composition. Here a parallel multi-image filter has been placed to affect just the top margin of the shot.

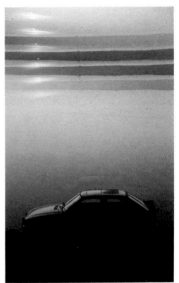

sense of warmth to the composition. There are also multiple-colour filters – often featuring two or three contrasting colours – that can be used to create fantasy images.

Sharp-edged half-coloured filters are for tinting one half of the image only, and are commonly used for reducing contrast between bright and dark areas, between the sky and the foreground in landscape photographs, for example. The disadvantage with these filters is that the cut-off between the clear and coloured areas is very marked, especially when used with wide-angle lenses and at small apertures. If this is a problem, the answer may be graduated filters, which have a gradual change in density from deep tint to clear.

There are many subjects that are enhanced by soft-focus techniques. The diffusing filter is one of the simplest ways of achieving this effect. It is either etched with fine lines, or has a mottled surface, to break up fine definition and spread highlights into shadow areas. As well as creating soft-focus, they are ideal for taking the edge off harsh contrast, for example when taking portraits under bright sunlight. There are versions, called centre-spots, which leave a central area clear. Some add colour to the diffused area as well. Other variations on the centre-spot arrangement are non-diffusing colour, fog effect, and close-up. As with most lens attachments, the effects vary according to the focal length of the lens and the taking aperture. The longer the lens, the larger and less well-defined the central area. Stopping-down makes the edges more defined.

Overall, fog filters, which have a milky appearance, do not reduce sharpness as much as diffusion attachments, but they scatter highlights more, and reduce the contrast in much the same way as real mist. They are most effective when used for close-up to middle distance shots.

Point sources of light can be dramatized by fitting a cross-screen or starburst filter, which creates a pattern of rays. These filters are engraved with a set of fine lines and the light from a point source flares out along them, with the result that, where the rays intersect, a star is formed. The filter can be rotated so that the rays can be placed to suit the composition. Starburst filters are ideal for glittering night scenes, the theatre, and funfairs, as well as for adding impact with the sun.

Diffraction filters are etched with extremely fine lines which split light into its component colours, forming small rainbows. Different etching patterns form different rainbow patterns – patterns in straight lines, multi-coloured discs, and radiating rainbow spokes, for example.

Multi-prism or multi-image lenses are used to repeat the subject within a single frame and often evoke a sense of movement. There are many different types, but two of the most popular produce multiple images either in a circular pattern or arranged in a straight line. The effects of all these filters are emphasized if the subject is given a dark background.

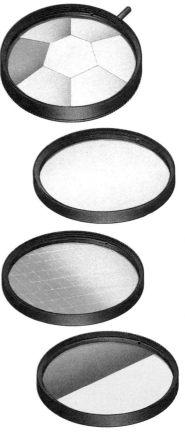

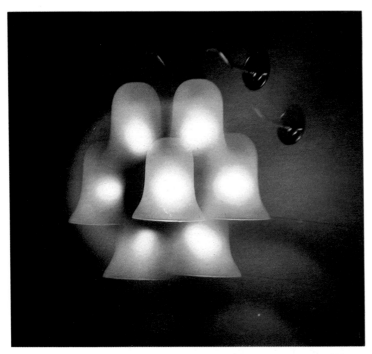

△ Top: multiple image filter; second: diffraction filter; third: starburst filter; bottom: dual magenta/yellow filter.

◁ A seven-faceted multi-image filter was used to repeat the lamps around a central image. The filter has six facets arranged about one in the centre.

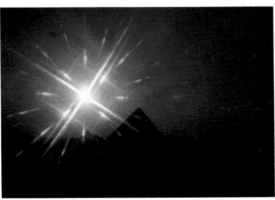

◁ Combining filters can give exciting results. To emphasize the effect of the coloured rays, this picture of the pyramids was taken with a 16-point diffraction filter combined with a 4-star cross-screen filter.

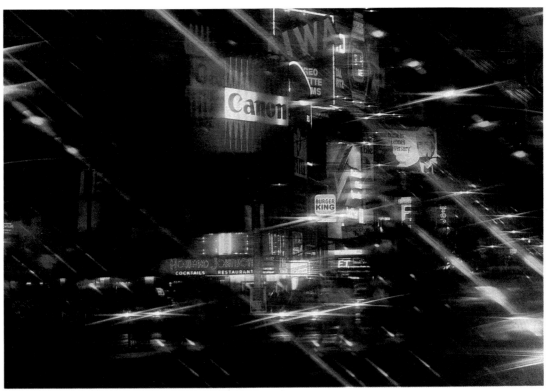

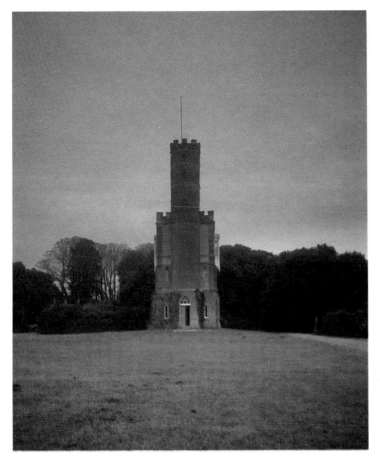

△ Night scenes with plenty of bright point sources of light are ideal for exploiting the effects of a diffraction filter. This picture was made with a linear diffraction attachment.

◁ Dual- or tri-coloured filters can create eye-catching pictures but have to used sparingly. Usually, contrasting colours are used, such as red/blue, orange/green, or yellow/pink, as shown here.

See also:
COLOUR FILTERS pp72-73
MULTIPLE IMAGES pp86-87
STUDIO SILHOUETTES pp248-249
COLOURED LIGHT pp252-253

# MULTIPLE IMAGES

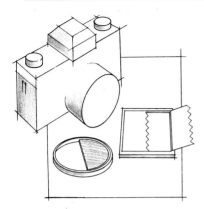

Photography is an extremely versatile medium that is often called upon to do no more than make an accurate record of an event or an object. But there is no reason to limit yourself to this kind of image, for there are many ways of distorting or manipulating reality, modifying the camera's role as an impartial observer.

One of the most effective kinds of image distortion is multiple-imaging. Pictures of this kind are easy to produce in-camera, and can strike the viewer with their strange abstractions and vivid imagery. The exploration of another dimension in photography gives you the opportunity to exercise your creative freedom in an unusual way. Multiple images on separate frames are the simplest to take: there are no technical problems with balancing exposure levels and keeping the film from moving between shots. Even with few techical considerations, successful multiple images need planning, and the relative positions of picture elements within each frame need to be noted and then shot according to an arranged sequence. The final result may be a simple pairing to create mirror images or a whole film laid down in strips.

Exposing several shots on one frame in register can be difficult with SLRs unless they have a multiple-exposure button. With many shots it is possible to make multiple exposures by holding

△ ▷ A double mask, above, lets you make two 'half' exposures on one frame. Two quite different images can be combined in this way or, as here, the mask can be used to create an amusing double situation. It was shot with the camera mounted on a tripod and the first exposure made with the mask covering the right half. The girl disrobed and moved to the other end of the bench, the camera shutter was reset using the multiple-exposure button and the mask turned through 180° before making the second exposure.

*Pentax LX, 50 mm, Kodak Tri-X ISO 400, 1/60 sec, f16*

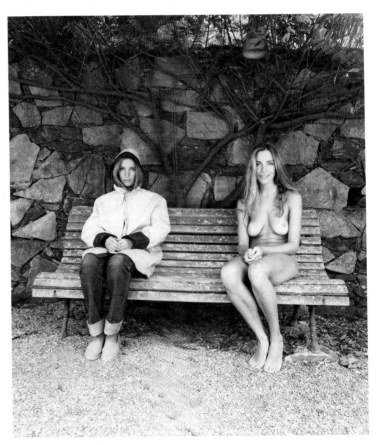

the film under tension with the rewind knob, pressing the rewind button, and winding on. If you are lucky, the frame will remain in register, but it is possible to produce effective images even if you are unable to guarantee good registration. Visualizing is even more important if you are making multiple exposures on one frame. Try to limit the total number of exposures, because areas of image overlap will become progressively lighter and eventually burn out. Ideally, dark parts of one exposure should form the background for light parts of another. (Planning is easiest with a sketch.) TTL readings should not need modification unless there are substantial areas of light- or mid-tone overlap, when you will need only half to a quarter of the indicated exposure. For accurate registration you might find that it is necessary to mark the film leader as shown in the diagram, expose the whole roll, rewind and reload using the marker as a guide for exact positioning of the leader.

The basic technique of multiple exposure can be just the starting point for experiments. You can try changing viewpoint, varying scale by using a zoom lens or changing fixed-focus lenses, colour by using filters, and focus by using diffusers, blur or de-focusing. Fitting a double mask in front of the lens will allow you to expose one half of the frame at a time to create double images.

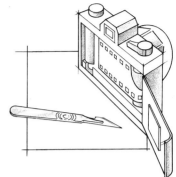

△ You can ensure proper registration for multiple exposures by marking the film gate with a notch or a waterproof pen opposite the end of the film when you first load it. Expose the film, rewind and then reload, positioning the mark carefully.

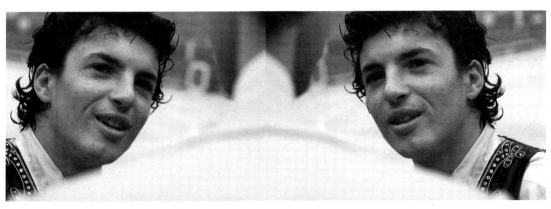

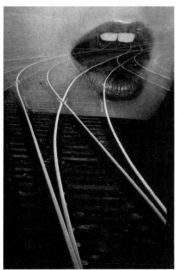

◁ When making double exposures, ensure that the bright parts of one image are overlapped with the dark parts of the other. The simplest method is to use the multiple-exposure button which disengages the wind-on mechanism while the shutter is reset. Alternatively, you can take up film slack by gently rewinding before exposing, make the first exposure, hold in the rewind button, reset the shutter, and make the second exposure.

*Portrait: Pentax LX, 50 mm, Kodak Ektachrome 64, ¹/₂₅ sec, f11*

*Railway: Pentax LX, 28 mm, Kodak Ektachrome 64, ¹/₁₂₅ sec, f11*

△ Multiple images can be built up with separately exposed frames of film to create bizarre and amusing mosaics, montages, and mirror images, as here. Planning the overall design from the outset is essential for convincing results.

*Pentax LX, 28 mm. Kodak Ektachrome 64, ¹/₆₀ sec, f11*

See also:
ACTION SQUENCES pp64-65
SPECIAL FILTERS pp82-85
SPLITTING IMAGES pp212-215

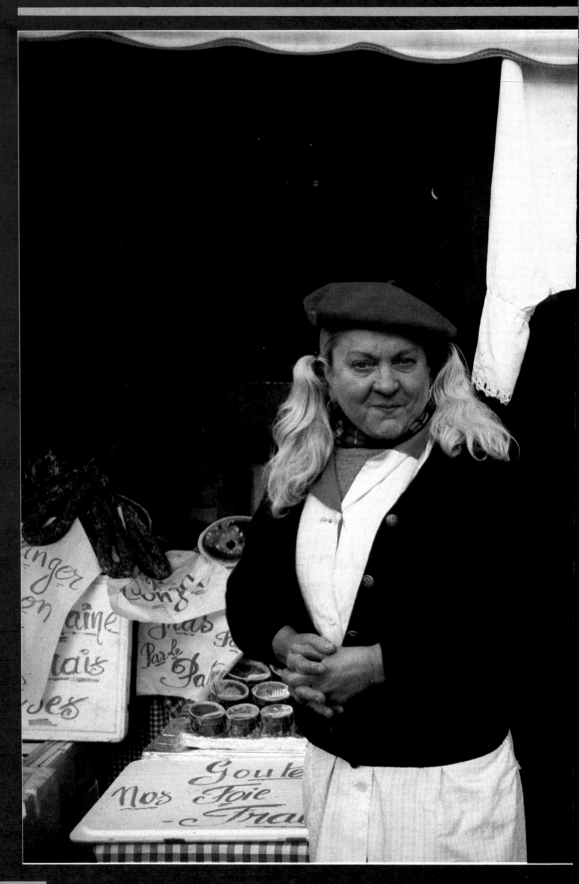

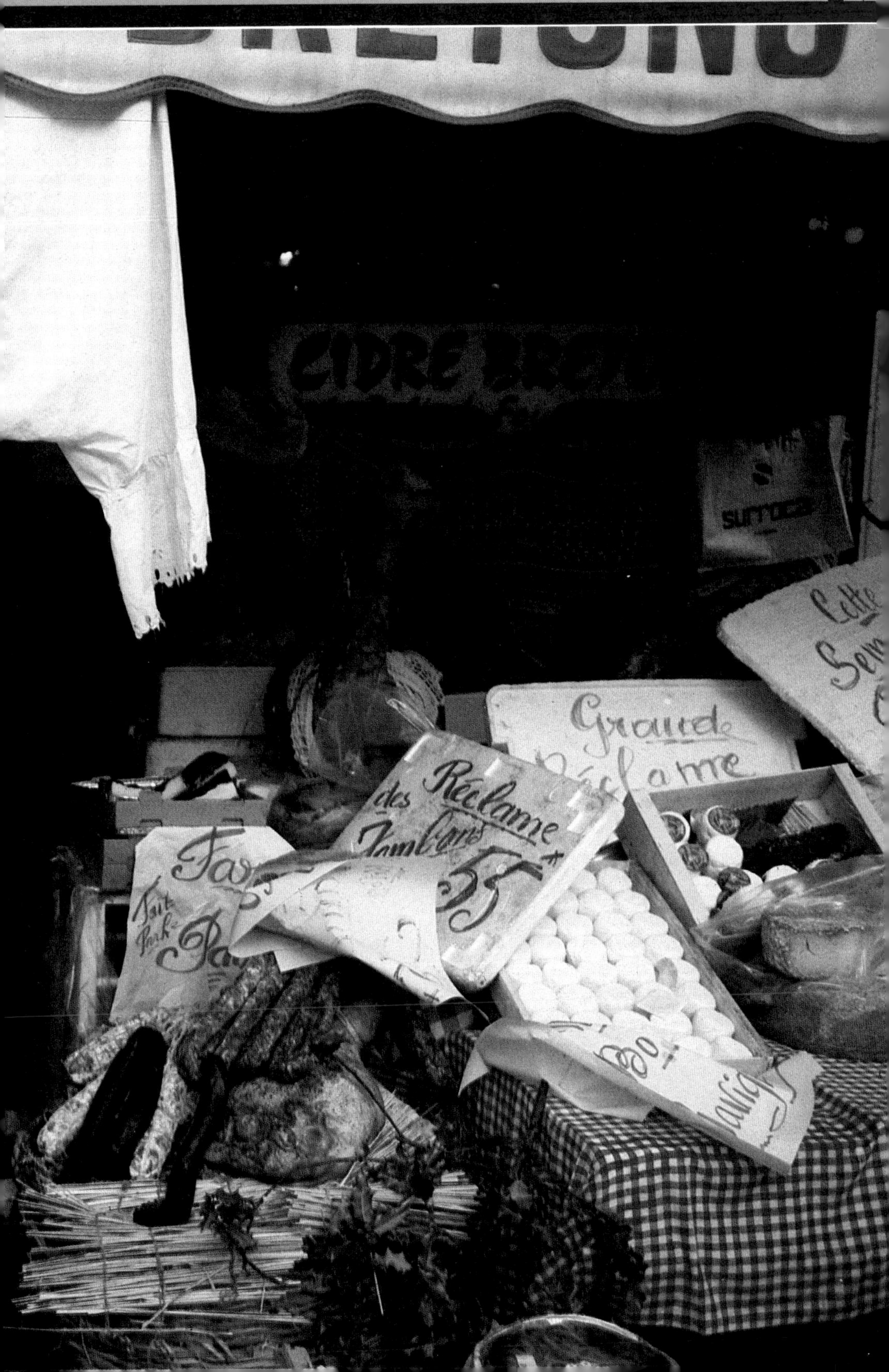
Grande Réclame
des Réclame Jambons
55

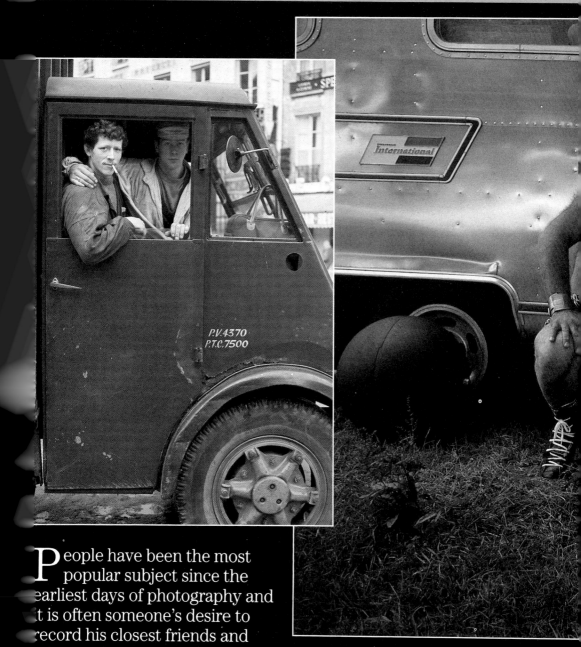

P eople have been the most
    popular subject since the
earliest days of photography and
it is often someone's desire to
record his closest friends and
relatives that is the catalyst for his future development of photographic
expertise. Frequently, it is the relationship that people have with their
environment that becomes the main subject of the photograph, although
it is a sad fact that many photographers only exploit the situation if it is
unusual – for example, when they are travelling away from home. In fact,
those whom we know well offer the best opportunities to make truly
good portraits that capture the essence of a personality, as it is essential

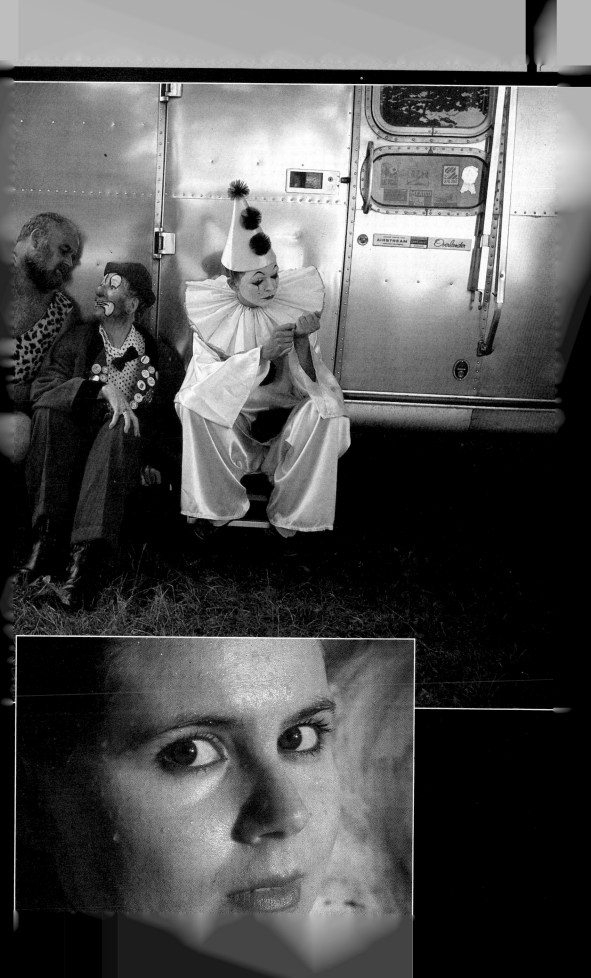

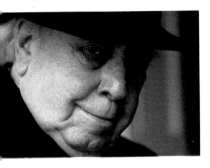

△ A tilted hat and sloping collar frame novelist J B Priestley's wry expression. The angles emphasize the modelling in the face and add interest themselves.

*Pentax LX, 100 mm macro, Kodak Ektachrome 200, 1/30 sec, f16*

▷The subject's direct gaze, hidden by dark glasses, gives this portrait of artist Graham Sutherland a sinister air.

*Leicaflex, 90 mm macro, Kodak Ektachrome 64, 1/250 sec, f8*

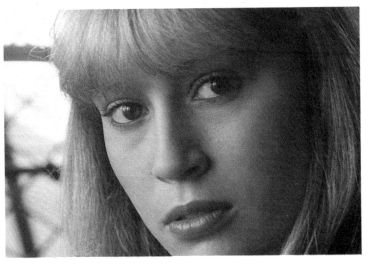

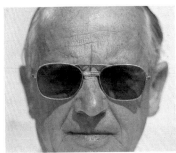

△ Soft colouring and gentle winter sunlight help to create the delicate harmony of this portrait. A romantic impression is conveyed by the gently inclined head and thoughtful expression.

*Pentax LX, 135 mm, Scotch (3M) 1000, 1/60 sec, f16*

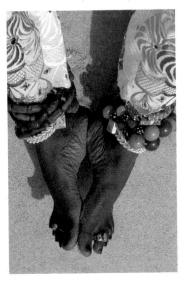

△ This woman used her feet to display her jewellery for sale. Although her wares were striking in themselves, it was the method of display that gave the picture its eloquence.

*Pentax LX, 85 mm, Kodak Ektachrome 64, 1/250 sec, f8*

The face is the most expressive part of the body and pictures which concentrate on it usually contain both intimacy and impact. The viewer is given a rare chance of seeing in detail the nuance of expression and gaze, so it is not surprising that close-ups can reveal a person in a frank way. Isolating the face can make people appear younger, by excluding tell-tale signs of age, such as grey hair or a wrinkled neck, but any blemishes on the skin will be exaggerated. This factor is naturally of considerable importance when the aim is to make a flattering portrait. Softer lighting and even the use of a soft-focus technique may be required to produce the right effect.

Making successful close-ups demands careful technique. Normally, they should be very sharp, and to achieve this critical focusing and an adequate depth of field are required. With portraits it is particularly important to have the eyes sharply focused. A portrait with blurred eyes will not work, because people depend on the eyes to read a person's expression. But portraits in which the eyes are hidden, or those in which the eyes are averted, may have an added sense of mystery.

After the face, the other most important close-up features in portrait studies are the hands and feet. Like the face, the hands reflect the age and suggest the experience of the person. They can be tiny and perfectly formed, like those of a baby, or they can be clear and soft-skinned like those of a young woman, or they can be gnarled and tanned by a lifetime's toil. As with any portrait, background and setting can add a great deal to the image, and making close-ups of hands, feet and other details can often help to relax a person before a full-figure picture is taken.

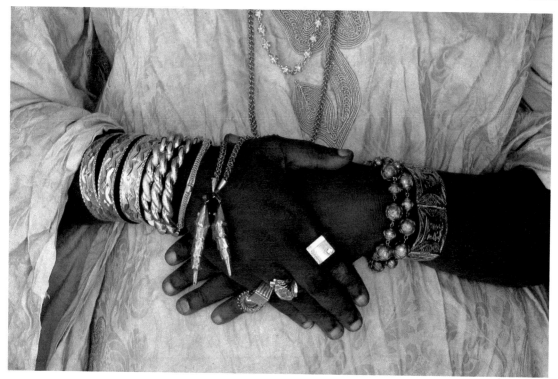

△ The native women of Gambia display their wealth in gold bracelets and bangles of which they are rightly proud. This woman welcomed the chance to exhibit her most prized possessions for the benefit of the photographer.

*Pentax LX, 135 mm, Kodak Ektachrome 64, 1/250 sec, f8*

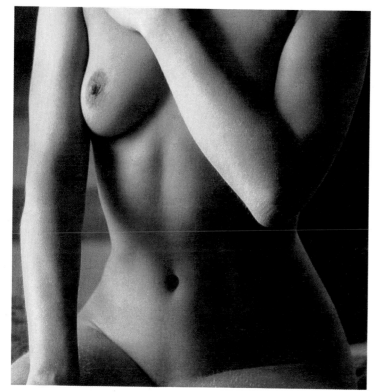

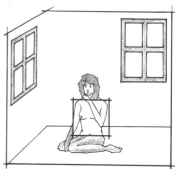

△ Bright side-light from a window gives good modelling, while a second small window behind provides a slight rim-light (see diagram, above right).

*Pentax LX, 135 mm, Kodak, Ektachrome 200, 1/60 sec, f16*

See also:
SOFT AND HARD LIGHT pp36-39
SOFT FOCUSING pp46-47
THE VERSATILE LENS pp196-197

# THE DIRECT APPROACH

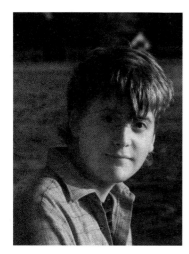

△ Photographs made the instant a child turns and notices your presence have the greatest chance of capturing a totally natural but direct look. In this picture, the rich light from the early-evening sun has highlighted the features of the boy's face.

*Pentax LX, 150 mm, Scotch (3M) 1000, 1/125 sec, f8*

▷ A three or four year old's face may reveal a wide-eyed innocence that makes a powerful portrait in close-up. It is best photographed in soft, diffused light that complements the delicate texture of a young child's skin and the rounded features reminiscent of babyhood. Photograph: Julia Hedgecoe.

*Pentax LX, 135mm, Kodak Tri-X, 1/125 sec, f5.6*

A direct approach to making children's portraits does not necessarily involve posing them in any formal sense. In fact, it is hardly in keeping with their true nature and they deserve a much more sympathetic treatment than the clichéd school-portrait style – 'head and shoulders, smile please' – beloved of commercial studios. Any portrait should be much more than a mere physical likeness and, with children, the photographer should aim to portray an essential facet of their characters in such a way as to capture a little of everyone's memory of childhood days. It might seem a difficult task and certainly the subject requires the same degree of serious consideration and attention to detail as any other. However, children tend to be much more natural and relaxed in front of the camera than adults and are not conditioned by years of posing for pictures. Their ideas of how they want to be presented to the world change by the minute and indeed many are oblivious to such concepts. As a result, the chances of getting a true likeness are great. Portrait settings, such as gardens, bedrooms, and playgrounds, are often preferred by both children and parents to the sterile background of a studio. A child's playroom, for example, is conducive to creating a suitable atmosphere. Such settings also make it easier for the photographer to relax the subject, chat to him about something he finds interesting, and engage him in activities likely to provide good picture opportunities.

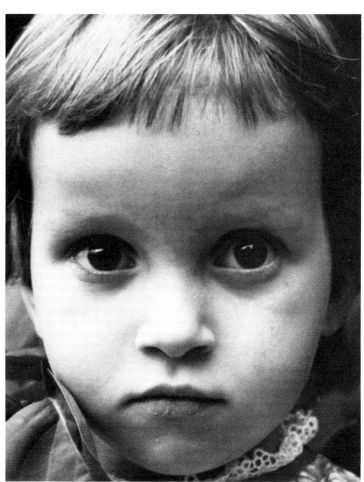

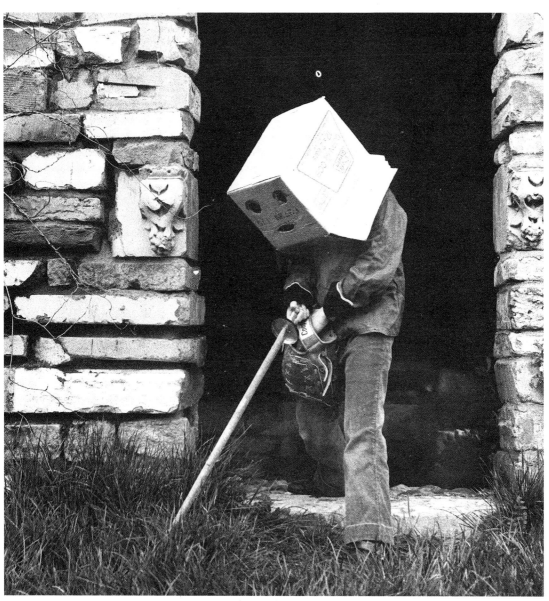

▷ A toddler's span of attention rarely extends beyond a few minutes. Their interest in the session soon evaporates and it is pointless to try and coerce them into posing for more pictures. This shot expressively illustrates the end of one such session. In these situations, you have to bow to the child's wishes and hope that the short time available is sufficient to capture a worthwhile picture.

*Pentax LX, 135 mm, Kodak Ektachrome 64, ¹/₁₂₅ sec, f8*

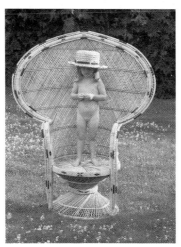

△ Good opportunities often arise when the subject has momentarily forgotten the camera. Here the boy's wayward armour kept getting the better of him.

*Hasselblad, 80 mm, Kodak Tri-X, ¹/₆₀ sec, f11*

See also:
SOFT AND HARD LIGHT pp36-39
BLACK AND WHITE pp54-57
GARDEN SETTINGS pp114-115

# PORTRAIT GROUPS

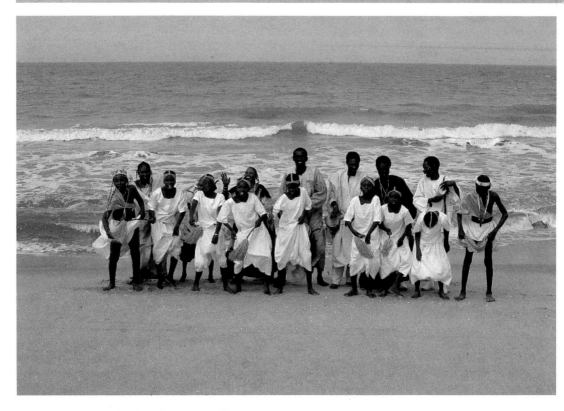

△ This group of native Gambian dancers on a West African beach was rehearsing under the guidance of their director. A chance encounter produced an animated picture that captured the mood of the moment.

*Pentax LX, 85 mm, Kodak Ektachrome 64, 1/250 sec, f8*

Many people buy cameras to enable them to record family events and occasions. Even for professionals, the essential problems of photographing groups of people remain the same. The aim is to produce a result that is not only pleasing to the photographer (and, perhaps, the picture editor), but to the people involved too. To achieve this, care must be taken with every detail – lighting, the setting, positioning and direction – so that the session can proceed with the minimum of fuss and the maximum of enjoyment.

With formally posed groups, it is important to have a clear view of every individual; it is always a disappointment afterwards if anyone finds himself wholly or partially obscured. Although it is seldom attractive, the rank-upon-rank arrangement is often the easiest, especially for large numbers of, say, 20 or more, and so is often fitting for groups such as sports teams, clubs, and societies. To avoid totally predictable results, vary the usual procedure of standing the tallest individuals at the back and the shortest at the front, by, for example, having some people standing on chairs at the back. You can also pose the gathering in a curve, with the ends towards the camera, to break the monotony of the line. A few well chosen props can add interest too. To avoid confusion, arrange each person's position beforehand, have ready any props, and use a tripod to fix the camera position so that you are free to move around.

Although informally posed groups give the photographer a chance to make more interesting pictures, they still need the same care taken over arrangements. There is often a group hierarchy and, though it does not necessarily mean putting the most important person at the front, he or she usually wants to be prominent in some way.

▷ Another chance encounter in Africa – this time with a solitary girl on her hammock – evolved into a group shot. As news of the event spread, children were collected to form a background. The girl's relationship to the group and dominance of the picture is retained by the choice of lens and viewpoint and by controlling the focus.

*Pentax LX, 28 mm, Kodak Ektachrome 200, 1/60 sec, f8*

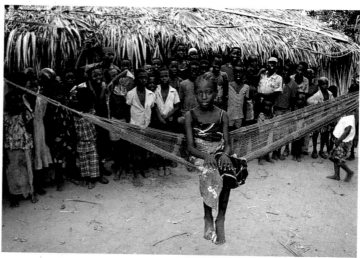

▷ A common sight at London events is the Pearly Kings and Queens and their children. These Pearly Princesses were posed against a simple but brightly coloured background, as a counterpoint to their ornate black and white costumes. The self-conscious poses of the older girls contrast with the shy, retiring pose of their little sister.

*Pentax LX, 50 mm, Kodak Ektachrome 64, 1/250 sec, f8*

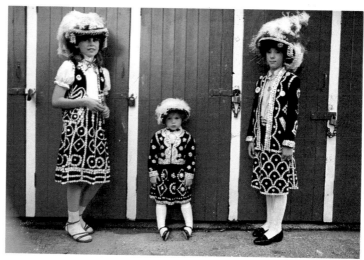

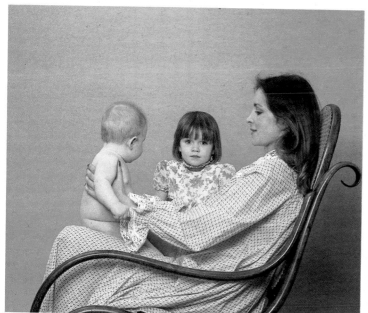

◁ For family portraits in the studio, a soft, even light is ideal. Keeping the attention of young children is not always necessary, and insisting on a particular pose can cause upsets and tension that ruin the results.

*Hasselblad, 80 mm, Kodak Ektachrome 64, 1/250 sec, f8*

See also:
USING BACKLIGHT pp34-35
SOFT AND HARD LIGHT pp36-39
WEDDING ALBUM pp158-161

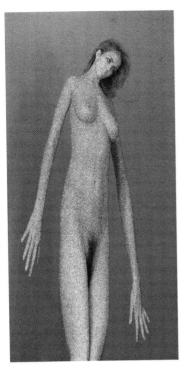

△ Most people are familiar with the distorted reflections seen in a fairground 'Hall of Mirrors' and the same effects can be achieved by bending plastic mirrors. Nudes make interesting distorted images which can be extreme or as subtle as you like, depending on the flexibility of the mirror, and it is possible to create shapes reminiscent of modern figure sculpture where emphasis and form are used to create impact.

*Pentax LX, 85 mm, Scotch (3M) 640 Tungsten, 1/30 sec, f8*

A reflection in a mirror is always a source of interest when included in a photograph. Mirrors have a strange and almost mystical fascination and add an extra dimension and lend an element of mystery and ambiguity when the subject of the reflection is not included in the composition.

Plastic mirrors have opened up new possibilities for the photographer. Not only are they light and portable, but they are unbreakable and therefore quite safe. There are no handling problems when it comes to using large mirrors and a great deal of fun can be had by distorting reflections to create bizarre and surreal images. Large mirrors also make ideal reflectors and, because of their high reflectivity, can be used as a second light source. Placing mirrors within the picture calls for careful positioning of all elements and of the camera. It is also important to focus on the reflected image and not on the mirror's surface. If the subject is in view you will need to use a very small aperture to give sufficient depth of field.

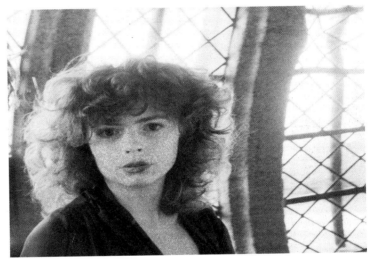

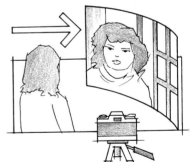

△ ▷ Plastic mirrors can be used in ways that do not shock or surprise the viewer with bizarre distortions. Slightly bending a mirror can subtly alter the shape of a face or figure in ways that are both flattering and intriguing. In this picture, the camera and model were positioned in front of and facing away from a window. The model looked into a plastic mirror that was curved into a concave shape. The camera was then focused on the reflected scene, as shown in the diagram.

*Pentax LX, 85 mm, Kodak Ektachrome 200, 1/250 sec, f11*

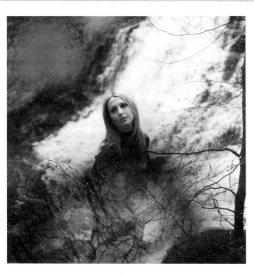

◁ The original intention was to portray this girl in the romantic setting of a secluded waterfall, but the image seemed too cluttered and needed extra impact. A small plastic mirror provided the solution. Placed very close to the lens, which was set to a wide aperture to ensure that the mirror surface was out of focus, the reflection surrounded the girl in an ethereal flow of water.

*Hasselblad, 60 mm, Kodak Ektachrome 64, $^1/_{125}$ sec, f4*

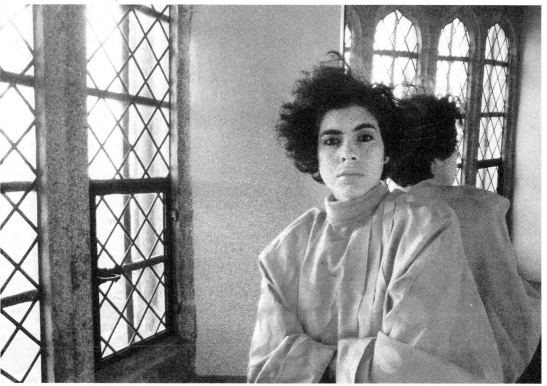

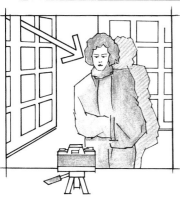

◁ △ This portrait was composed so that the only window provided a rich side light against a background of a blank white wall. To relieve the monotony, a mirror was used to cover part of the wall and introduce a second area of interest.

*Pentax LX, 85 mm, Kodak Ektachrome 200, $^1/_{30}$ sec, f16*

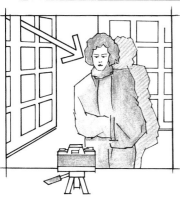

See also:
DEPTH OF FIELD pp40-41
FOCUSING METHODS pp44-45
REFLECTED IMAGES pp146-147
MIRRORED IMAGES pp280-281

# PATTERN AND PORTRAIT

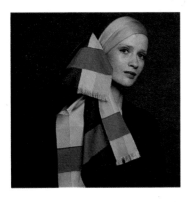

△ The colour and pattern of the scarf are what first attracts the eye, which is then drawn to the face. Dressing the model in dark clothes and using a dark background have isolated the scarf and the face, their colours striking a bold contrast. Flash with a reflective umbrella provided the soft light.

*Hasselblad, 80 mm, Kodak Ektachrome 64, f16*

Patterns are a good way of strengthening a portrait, either as a background or as a complementary feature. Background patterns are viewed as a setting and therefore need careful handling, otherwise they will overwhelm the subject. It is like selecting wallpaper for a room: one has to live with the choice. Portraits of people dressed in pastel colours, or where a contemplative atmosphere is required, need a harmonizing pattern of complementary colours and rhythm. To inject drama and energy into portraits of, say, children or creative people, bright colours and a vibrant pattern can be used effectively, as long as a sense of balance and proportion is maintained. Balance depends largely on matching the background to the subject. As the background to a portrait, pattern can be used in a variety of ways. It can lead the eye to the person, either by isolating him or her, or by echoing a colour, shape, or design featured in his or her figure. Pattern can also provide a counterpoint, where its colour, design, and scale contrast with the subject and strengthen the overall impact. Pattern lends an element of design to a portrait and experimentation can lead to fresh and exciting results.

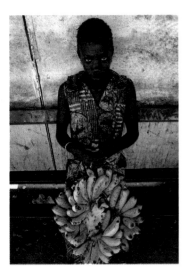

△ In an African marketplace there were dozens of children selling fruit, but this girl's arrangement of her wares caught the eye at once. The circle of bananas provided a pattern rich in colour, shape, and texture.

*Pentax LX, 35 mm, Kodak Ektachrome 200, 1/30 sec, f11*

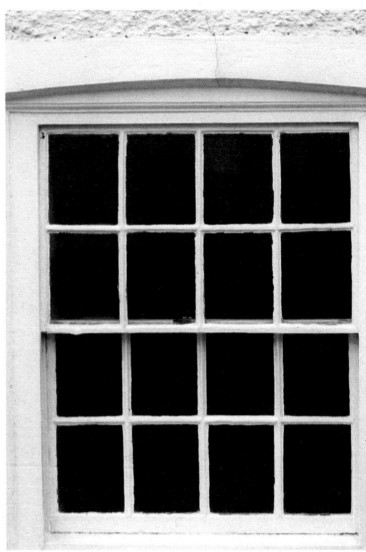

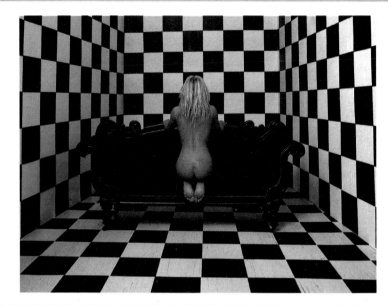

◁ This shot was one of a series experimenting with a nude against a powerful geometric setting. Although there was a contrast both in form and colour, the model was lost until the dark sofa provided local background.

*Hasselblad, 80 mm, Kodak Ektachrome 200, $^1/_{30}$ sec, f16*

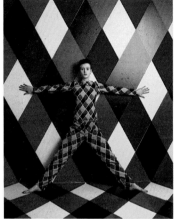

△ The design of the harlequin suit inspired the background for this picture. Different degrees of balance could be achieved by moving the girl away from the pattern, but here the intention was to emphasize the backdrop.

*Hasselblad, 80 mm, Kodak Ektachrome 64, f16*

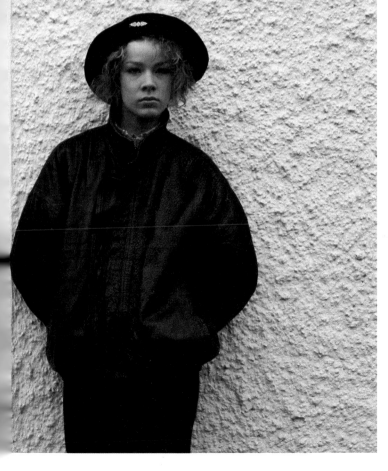

◁ Another image where pattern is a crucial part of the composition. The regular squares of the dark window provide a strong counterpoint to the less symmetrical shape of the girl.

*Pentax LX, 50 mm, Kodak Ektachrome 200, $^1/_{30}$ sec, f8*

See also:
SOFT AND HARD LIGHT pp36-39
PATTERN AND DETAIL pp58-59
BEHIND THE SCENES pp112-113

# POSED PORTRAITS

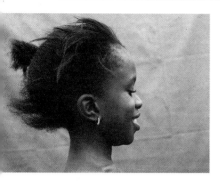

△ If you are staying in one place, it is simple to set up an outdoor 'studio' and take a series of posed portraits.

*Pentax LX, 100 mm macro, Kodak Ektachrome 64, 1/125 sec, f8*

Children are always rewarding subjects for the camera and, in the more remote parts of the world, our interest in them is often matched by their fascination with the magic of photography. These pictures were taken in Gambia, where children appeared, apparently from nowhere, and crowded around the camera as soon as it was taken from its case. This avid interest in a stranger's every move and an irresistible urge to pose as soon as the equipment appears makes it almost impossible to take candid shots. The only alternative is to exploit the circumstances, direct the children's poses, and hope to maintain a degree of control. Enlisting the aid of one or two little helpers is a great benefit; they can communicate your wishes to other members of the group and maintain some semblance of order, leaving you slightly freer to concentrate on the photography. If one or two youngsters catch your eye as being particularly good portrait subjects, keep it to yourself at first and take a selection of group pictures to ensure that everyone has had a chance to be included. Then, with the help of your young assistants, approach the individuals.

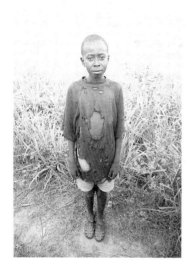

△ Wordlessly this boy pointed to the camera and stood to attention. His proud stance and unwavering gaze seem quite at odds with his tattered shirt. Overexposure by one stop revealed skin texture.

*Pentax LX, 28 mm, Kodak Ektachrome 64, 1/60 sec, f8*

▷ The intention was to photograph one child, but this group quickly assembled, waiting for a turn in front of the lens.

*Pentax LX, 28 mm, Kodak Ektachrome 64, 1/125 sec, f11*

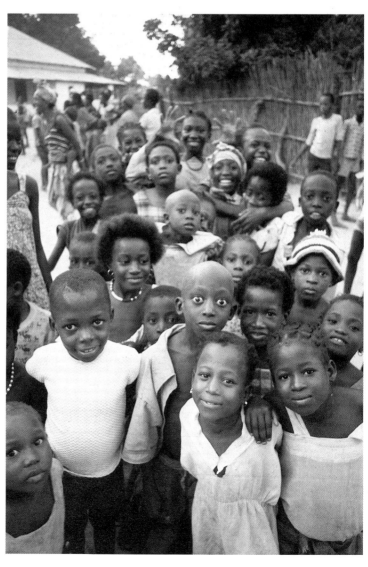

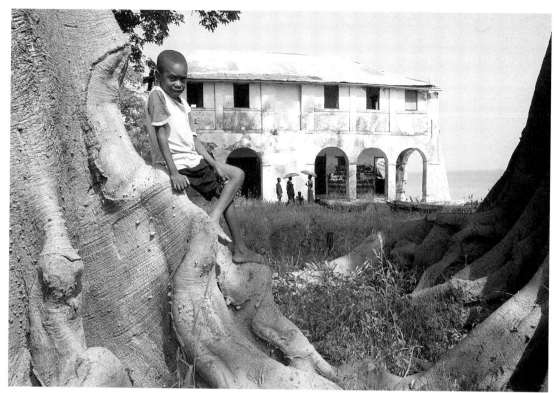

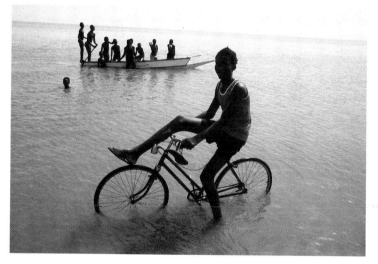

△ While this building was being photographed and the shot composed with the tree trunks either side as a framing device, a boy perched on one to watch. His intrusion has added an extra, human element that gives the picture increased interest and greater impact.

*Pentax LX, 28 mm, Kodak Ektachrome 64, 1/125 sec, f11*

△ This picture also came about largely as a result of a child's curiosity about the picture-taking process. This time the boat and its crew were the subject, drawing him into the shot. A change of viewpoint to balance the two picture elements within the frame was all that was needed before setting the exposure to render them as silhouettes.

*Pentax LX, 28 mm, Kodak Ektachrome 64, 1/125 sec, f11*

See also:
FILLING THE FRAME pp42-43
FRAMING THE SUBJECT pp50-51
COMPOSING THE SHOT pp52-53
THE DIRECT APPROACH pp94-95

# THE SIMPLE SETTING

Portraits of people taken in their own environments are greatly improved by selecting a background which reflects the subject. Backgrounds contribute in different ways but the most important is to provide a contrasting backdrop which adds to our knowledge of the sitter. The balance between subject and setting, which is particularly important with this kind of picture, is determined by the placing of the person in relation to the camera and background, taking into consideration colour contrast and lighting. People framed towards the centre and near to the camera dominate their setting, whereas people placed well into the room and framed off-centre become more a part of their environment. Bright, contrasting clothes draw the attention of the eye. If the room is dimly lit, localized lighting can be used to highlight a person's face or figure.

▷ For this portrait of a tea planter's wife, no arranging was necessary. With obvious pride and self-assurance she sat in the centre of the picture and looked straight at the camera.

*Pentax LX, 28 mm, Kodak Ektachrome 200, 1/60 sec, f11*

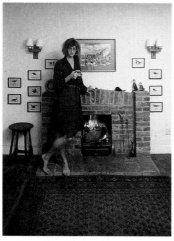 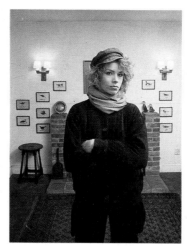

◁ In the first of these photographs, taken in an English country cottage, the room and girl are of equal importance and the picture is as much a portrait of the room as of the girl. The second picture illustrates the change in relationship between subject and background when the former is positioned close to the camera. Light was bounced off the ceiling from two photoflood lamps.

*Pentax LX, 28 mm, Kodak Ektachrome 160 Tungsten, 1/30 sec, f8*

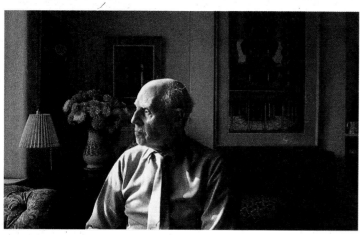 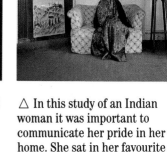

△ Tonal contrast through careful lighting is another way of selecting a balance between subject and background. In this shot of artist Edward Bawden, a shaft of sunlight spotlighted him.

*Pentax LX, 28 mm, Kodak Ektachrome 200, 1/60 sec, f11*

△ In this study of an Indian woman it was important to communicate her pride in her home. She sat in her favourite chair and the picture was framed to include much of the room.

*Pentax LX, 28 mm, Kodak Ektachrome 200, 1/30 sec, f8*

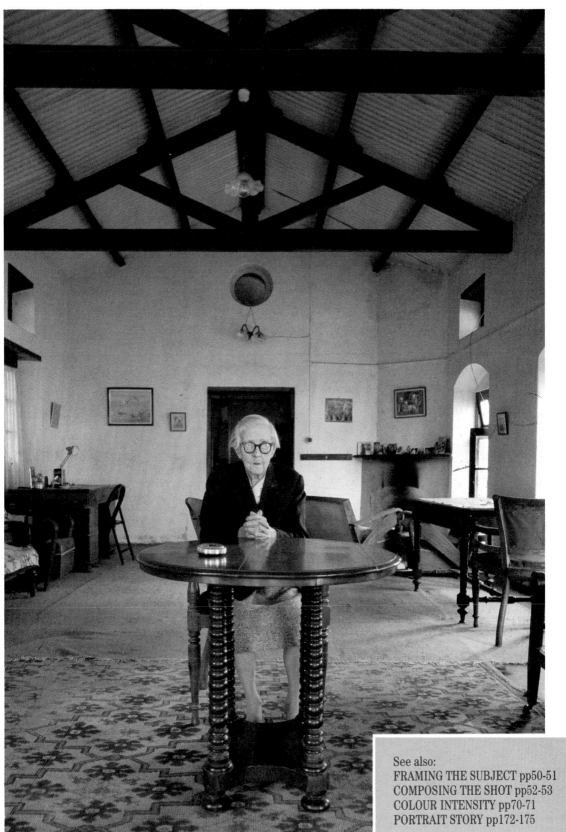

See also:
FRAMING THE SUBJECT pp50-51
COMPOSING THE SHOT pp52-53
COLOUR INTENSITY pp70-71
PORTRAIT STORY pp172-175

It is always a problem to keep your work fresh and lively when you attempt to tackle the same subject time and time again. For professionals the problem is even more acute, for if their work doesn't contain a flow of new ideas they will go out of business. Gimmicky filters, coloured gels, and distorting optics are the easy way out, but they are not always appropriate and can become repetitive. Presenting a subject in a realistic but unique way takes far more creative flair.

One approach is to approach the subject from an unusual viewpoint. Portraits, in particular, can be given fresh impetus when taken from an unusual angle. Naturally, you'll need the cooperation of the sitter, and you may need to persuade your model that he or she will not look ridiculous. For this reason, it's probably best to start your experiments with family and friends.

▷ Simply posing the girls with their heads upside down made these pictures quite different from conventional portraits, even though the features are not distorted and are clearly visible. But a visual puzzle is presented to the viewer and the temptation is always to turn the image upside down. But even when you do, the orientation remains disturbing.

*Pentax LX, 28 mm, Kodak Ektachrome 200, ¹/₁₅ sec, f16*

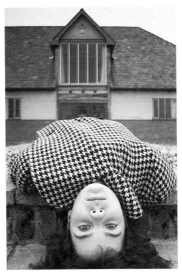

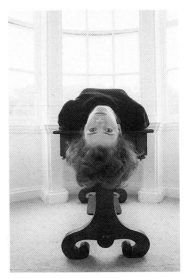

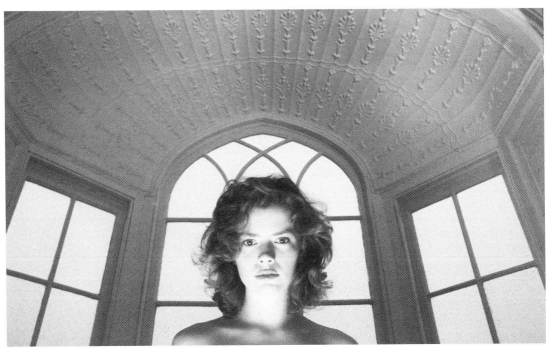

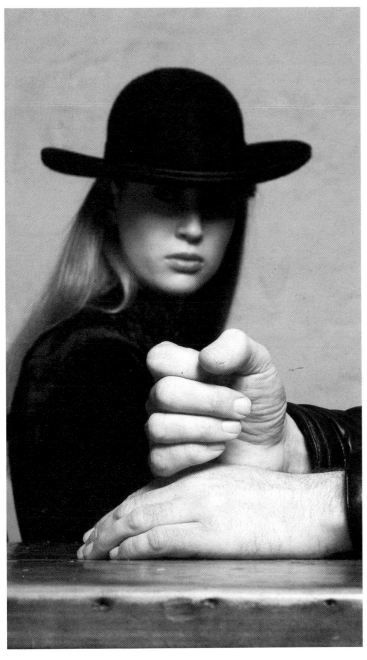

◁ A low viewpoint close to the hands has emphasized the element of mystery conveyed by their juxtaposition with the girl's face. Hands are an expressive subject in themselves, but their impact has been sharpened by the disproportionate sense of scale and by the posing of a clenched fist that echoes the outline of the girl's chin. The scene was lit by studio flash with umbrella reflectors, directed to throw a shadow over the model's eyes.

*Hasselblad, 60 mm, Kodak Ektachrome 200, ¹/₁₂₅ sec, f22*

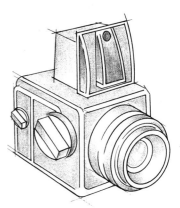

△ Medium-format cameras that use 120 or 220 rollfilm share some of the ease of handling of a 35 mm SLR camera but they offer the benefits of a much larger picture area.

◁ This window bay provided an attractive background but, from a normal height, the view outside proved too distracting. An answer to the problem was found by standing the model on a set of steps and taking the shot from below. A wide-angle lens was used to include the ceiling and to exaggerate the odd perspective created by a low viewpoint. The unreal atmosphere was further strengthened by providing tungsten foot-lighting and shooting on tungsten-balanced film to give the sky a cooler tone.

*Pentax LX, 24 mm, Kodak Ektachrome 160 Tungsten, ¹/₃₀ sec, f8*

See also:
VIEWPOINT AND SCALE pp48-49
FRAMING THE SUBJECT pp50-51
COMPOSING THE SHOT pp52-53

▽ In order to bounce flash off a ceiling or wall, it is necessary to aim it so that the angle of incidence is the same as the angle between the wall or the ceiling and the subject.

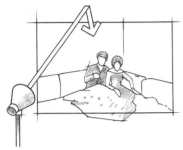

Backgrounds are more than something that just happens to be behind the subject of a portrait – they are part of the portrait. An effective background should contribute something to the picture, even if it is in the simple role of providing an unobtrusive setting, so the photographer must take care in selecting it. Exciting and exotic backgrounds are an unusual element in portrait pictures, although they can overpower the subject. If interior shots require flash lighting, remember to bounce the flash to avoid glare.

Frequently, creative and energetic personalities will have stylish and original decor in their homes. Country houses and castles often contain some of the best interiors, while modern corporate buildings, hotels, motels, and nightclubs sometimes feature unusual interior design. Many can be used as photographic settings for a fee, an acknowledgement, or in exchange for useful pictures.

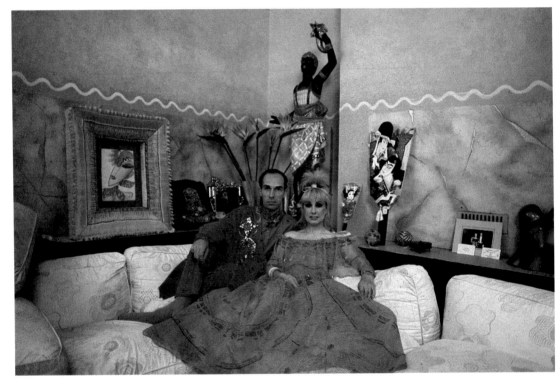

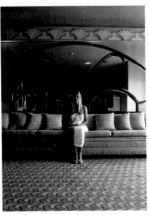

◁ Art deco design in a Brazilian hotel provided the setting for this picture. It was taken on the spur of the moment, after eating in the hotel restaurant, but the existing light was a little harsh.

*Pentax LX, 50 mm, Kodak Ektachrome 200, $^1\!/_{125}$ sec, f11*

△ Exotic settings can lead you into traps when you use bounced flash, since reflecting the light off colourful surfaces can give it a colour cast. Fortunately, in this picture of fashion designer Zandra Rhodes and artist Andrew Logan, the ceiling was white, but had it been tinted, the solution would have been to bounce the flash off white paper.

*Pentax LX, 28 mm, Kodak Ektachrome 200, $^1\!/_{60}$ sec, f16*

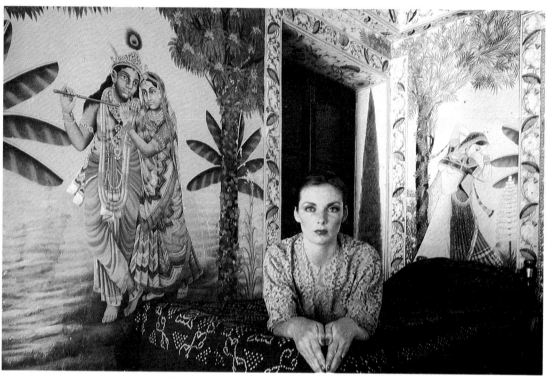

△ Sometimes the decor contains very strong designs, as in this hotel suite in Udaipur in India. The photographer then has to set the subject against a contrasting background and encourage him or her to adopt a strong enough pose to counterbalance the effect of the decor.

*Pentax LX, 28 mm, Kodak Ektachrome 200, 1/30 sec, f11*

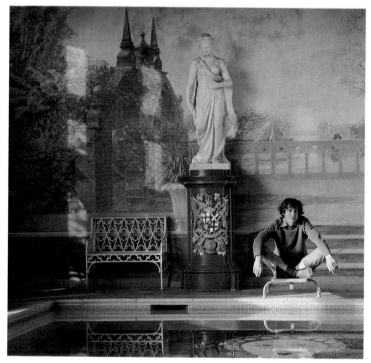

△ The natural light from an overcast day was too flat for this portrait of author Tom Chitty, making him blend in with the background. A flash, fired through french doors from the left, added a touch of 'sun' and modelling, separating him from the mural.

*Hasselblad, 80 mm, Kodak Ektachrome 64, 1/125 sec, f8*

See also:
FRAMING THE SUBJECT pp50-51
COMPOSING THE SHOT pp52-53
ELECTRONIC FLASH pp74-77

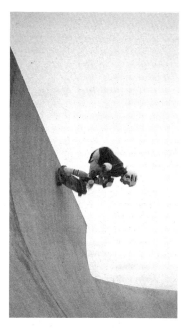

Children are ever-changing, ever-expressive subjects for the photographer, rarely remaining the same for more than a few minutes at a time. Their vitality is one of their most endearing characteristics, but it does cause problems when making pictures, whether candid or posed. The best approach has more in common with sport and wildlife photography than with straightforward portraiture. Exuberant children at play are rarely predictable, rushing madly about at one moment and stopping suddenly at the next. The photographer can be left with a bewildering choice of subject matter, with little or no time for making conscious decisions about framing and composition.

Indoors, the best light is bounced electronic flash that softly lights the whole room. Flash exposures are extremely short – down to as little $\frac{1}{30,000}$ sec in some flash units – and boisterous action shots, such as pillow fights, present no problems, as the soft, overall illumination allows you to change your viewpoint without having to change the lighting.

Outdoors, diffused directional light is best. It is strong enough to bring out the bright colours that children like to wear without casting distinct and heavy shadows. There is enough light to use fast shutter speeds and yet stop down to increase depth of field.

△ High-speed activities, such as skateboarding, are not always as difficult to capture on film as they may at first appear. Here, the skateboarder followed a regular path and all that was necessary was to pre-set focus and exposure, wait for his approach, then shoot at the appropriate moment. Skilled activities that take nerve and determination often attract extrovert characters who are more than willing to perform their most daring stunts for the camera.

*Pentax LX, 135 mm, Kodak Ektachrome 200, ¹/₁₀₀₀ sec, f8*

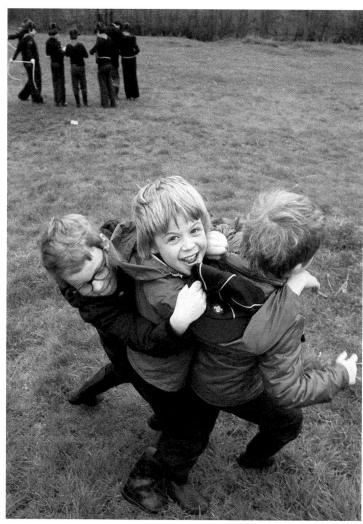

▷ In the background, a group of cub scouts attentively surround their leader who is teaching them how to tie knots. By complete contrast, a precocious trio of noisy young tearaways let off steam for the benefit of the camera.

*Pentax LX, 28 mm, Kodak Ektachrome 200, ¹/₆₀ sec, f16*

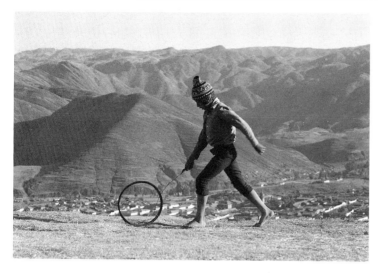

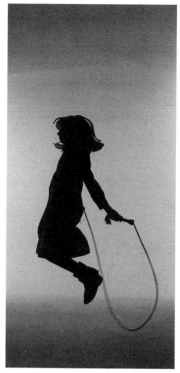

△ High above Cuzco in the Peruvian Andes, a boy trots along playing with a homemade hoop and stick. He is clearly outlined against the backdrop of the barren mountain range that is his homeland. In any photograph of a child it is important to try to capture that magical, elusive, and innocent quality that we call the spirit of childhood.

*Pentax LX, 85 mm, Kodak Kodachrome 64, ¹/₂₅₀ sec, f16*

△ This picture is one of a series depicting children's games, made as silhouettes in the studio. For this skipping picture, a shutter speed was selected that would freeze all motion in the girl but give a touch of blur on the rope, providing a sense of movement.

*Pentax LX, 50 mm, Kodak Ektachrome 160 Tungsten, ¹/₂₅₀ sec, f8*

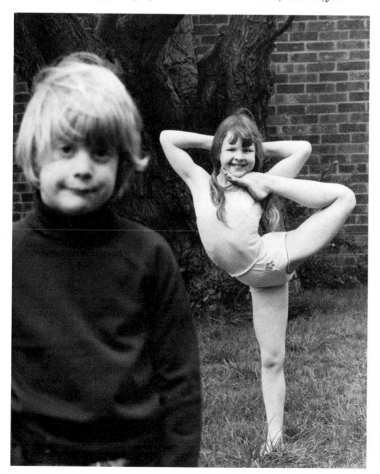

◁ Child prodigies not only amaze adults, but their abilities are sometimes regarded by their peers as beyond belief, as here, when the boy chanced on this extraordinary acrobatic feat.

*Hasselblad, 80 mm, Kodak Tri-X ISO 400, ¹/₂₅₀ sec, f8*

See also:
FOCUSING METHODS pp44-45
CAPTURING MOVEMENT pp60-61
THE DIRECT APPROACH pp94-95

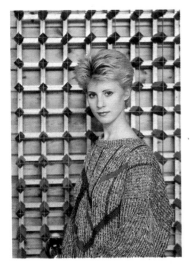

△ Empty wine racks in a cellar create a rigidly symmetrical background of squares against which the face is clearly seen.

*Pentax LX, 150 mm, Kodak Ektachrome 200, 1/60 sec, f8*

▷ A wall of filing cabinets form the background, their colour and pattern harmonizing with the soft, winter sunlight. The inclined head and odd darker drawer interrupt the strict symmetry.

*Pentax LX, 135 mm, Kodak Ektachrome 200, 1/250 sec, f11*

▷ A strongly patterned carpet produced too brilliant a contrast with the girl's leotard. In order to mute the colours of the carpet, a board was placed between the carpet and the light source – a window. The girl was lit by uninterrupted window light.

*Pentax LX, 85 mm, Kodak Ektachrome 200, 1/250 sec, f8*

While the studio provides a controlled environment where the background is constructed to suit the portrait, there are times when ready-made backgrounds encourage the photographer to experiment. Then the photographer is inspired to choose appropriate props, to select a model, and to decide on the lighting to be used. This may appear to be creating a portrait around the least important part of the picture but backgrounds are a vital element and this way you won't find that you've created an unsuitable one. Such an approach often casts the background as an element that underlines the importance of the subject.

The background can serve as a contrasting backdrop, or one that harmonizes with the general atmosphere or mood. A dark background will highlight a brightly dressed person, a textured one will emphasize a smooth skin, a blue background will accentuate a tanned complexion. Shape can also be used to provide contrast. The curved outline of a figure is set off effectively by an angular background. Harmony can be enhanced by, for example, echoing a shape in the subject's pose with one in the background or by matching colour and tone. By selecting the background carefully before shooting, the photographer can avoid the very common pitfall of using one which does not complement and enhance its subject.

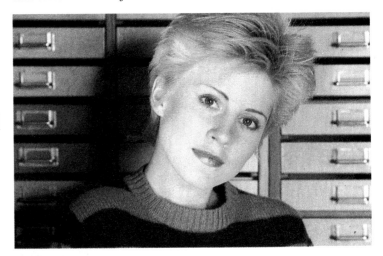

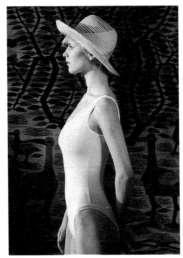

▷ A set of bedsprings hanging in an outhouse provided the background here. Their shape echoes the curly hair of the girl.

*Pentax LX, 135 mm, Kodak Ektachrome 200, 1/60 sec, f16*

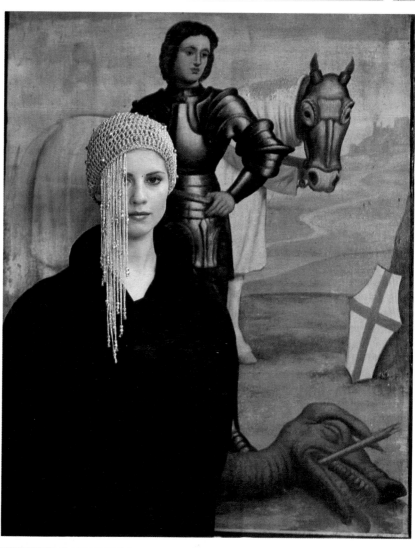

△ Occasionally, unusual and
striking backgrounds are to hand,
like this George & Dragon pub
sign. Originally, the model was
dressed in bright clothing,
but black proved to be more
appropriate to the mood.

*Hasselblad, 150 mm, Kodak
Ektachrome 200, ¹/₆₀ sec, f11*

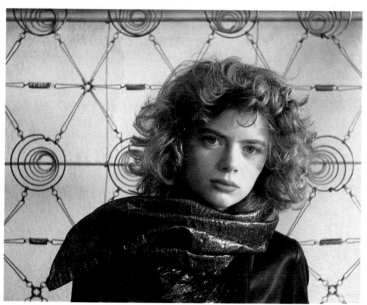

See also:
FRAMING THE SUBJECT pp50-51
COMPOSING THE SHOT pp52-53
PATTERN AND PORTRAIT pp100-101

# GARDEN SETTINGS

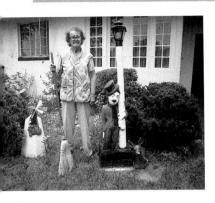

△ Garden gnomes are popular in many parts of the world and these novel designs are part of a collection that inhabits a garden in Long Island, New York. Like many gardeners and collectors of these 'little folk', this lady was very proud of her pieces.

*Pentax LX, 50 mm, Kodak Ektachrome 200, ¹/₁₂₅ sec, f8*

▷ The garden was the obvious setting for this portrait of Father Simplicity, a master gardener who practised his craft in an English monastery. His produce has been arranged with a good sense of design and the strength of the composition is enhanced by the positioning of the mass of flowers in the foreground. It is evident from his expression that he is justly proud of his produce.

*Hasselblad, 60 mm, Kodak Ektachrome 200, ¹/₁₂₅ sec, f16*

Gardens are created to be enjoyed. They are places of rest and relaxation where people can simply enjoy the smell and beauty of the surroundings, or can stroll, play games, or have picnics. As well as being places of recreation, gardens are also a source of pleasure for their owners. A great deal of time and energy is invested in the creation of beautiful gardens, and photographers should not miss the opportunity of using them as settings or as subjects in their own right.

A garden may be seen as a natural studio offering a wide variety of backgrounds and a selection of fine settings to suit almost any mood. A large garden, planted with large shrubs and trees, provides a range of different lighting moods from the warm, atmospheric light of evening to bright sunlight.

Owners and gardeners will often allow the photographer to use a small area – especially early or late in the day, when there are no other visitors – for a portrait session or for a wedding group. The results are likely to be more exciting than the more conventional churchyard and register office pictures. Many professional photographers regularly make use of public and private gardens as colourful backdrops for fashion and advertising, often at little or no cost.

A white reflector such as a sheet or a large piece of cardboard is very useful. So, too, is a tripod for the camera. If you use a garden setting sensibly you will find that you will not require any other special equipment.

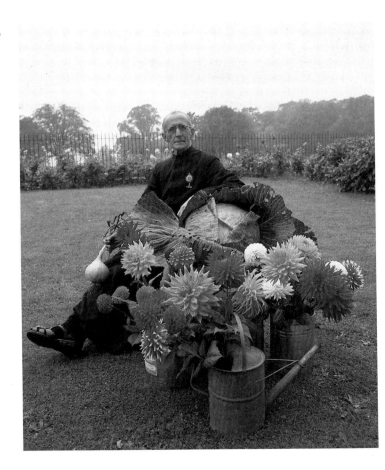

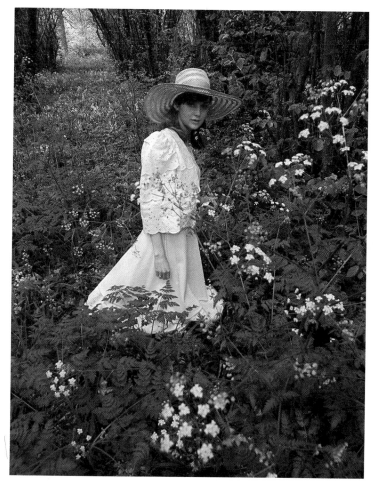

◁ Many large gardens contain semi-wild woodland areas which are ideal for romantic portraits and fashion pictures. For professional or lengthy portrait sessions it is always wise to seek permission, which is usually given gladly. The best time of year is mid-spring to early summer, when flowering is at its peak, the vegetation is lush, and the heady atmosphere of the new year's growth is at its height.

*Pentax LX, 28 mm, Kodak Ektachrome 64, ¹/₆₀ sec, f11*

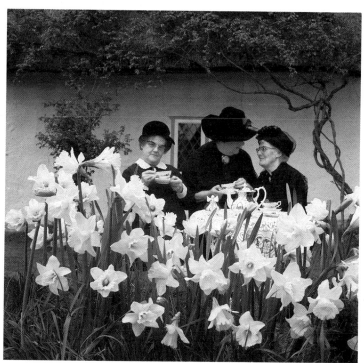

◁ A time-honoured English tradition is to take afternoon tea in the garden, a tradition that is the subject of this picture shot for a magazine feature. Early spring daffodils make a fine foreground with their especially 'English' quality, and the elderly ladies chattering over cups of tea create perfectly the peaceful, genteel atmosphere.

*Hasselblad, 60 mm, Kodak Ektachrome 200, ¹/₁₂₅ sec, f16*

See also:
LIGHT AND CONTRAST pp32-33
VIEWPOINT AND SCALE pp48-49
COMPOSING THE SHOT pp52-53

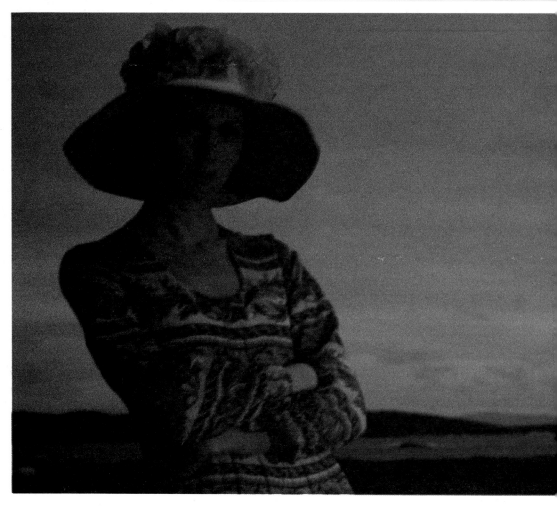

△ For this moody and romantic picture it was necessary to balance three exposures: the ambient light of evening, the car headlamps and the torchlight on the girl. In fact, several combinations and variations were tried, including the use of a second car's headlamps deflected on to the girl via a small mirror. But this subdued picture captured the right atmosphere. The use of tungsten film retained the warmth of the artificial lights, which contrasts well with the cool rendition of the sky.

*Hasselblad, 80 mm, Kodak Ektachrome 160 Tungsten, ¼ sec, f16*

A good torch is a useful light source for photography. It may be used as a main light to recreate the harsh, melodramatic illumination found in pantomime and old-fashioned theatre; it can produce soft, warm fill-in light without the fuss of setting up reflectors and studio flash; or its light can be included in the picture as part of the composition.

Until recently, photography by torchlight was made difficult by troublesome considerations such as the need for long exposures, which lead to reciprocity failure. But advances in technology have brought faster lenses, faster and finer-grained film, and reliable exposures from automatic cameras, quite apart from more powerful and compact torches. If you own a good compact camera, it's virtually a matter of pressing the shutter button, switching on the torch, and letting the camera sort out the exposure. But for pictures with the added atmosphere of the ambient glow of twilight, torchlight and natural light have to be balanced properly.

If you have a selenium-cell exposure meter in your camera you will find that it is slow in responding to low light levels, and, if this is the case, a hand-held CdS meter is useful for estimating exposures. When balancing torchlight with the much more powerful light from a flash, you can use slower speeds than the X-sync speed with focal-plane shutters.

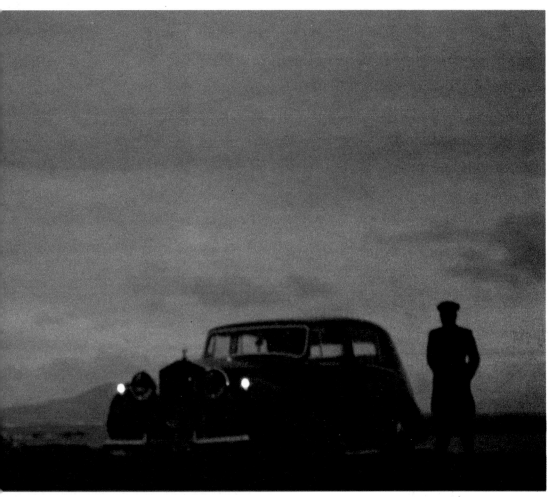

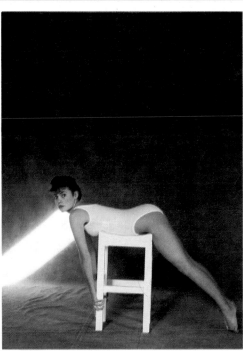

◁ The eye seizes on the light in this picture before it explores the rest of the image. The dazzling streak of white was made by reflecting the beam of a handheld stormlight off a tall mirror on to the background, as if with a spotlight. The model was lit by balanced studio flash.

*Hasselblad, 80 mm, Kodak Ektachrome 200, ⅛ sec, f11*

See also:
CHOOSING EXPOSURE pp28-31
VARIETIES OF LIGHT pp68-69
TUNGSTEN LIGHTING pp78-79

# INSTANT IMAGES

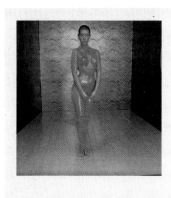

△ Strong colours can be introduced by fitting filters over the camera lens. For this shot a blue 85B filter was used.

With Polaroid instant-picture cameras such as the Supercolor 600 Series or the older Autofocus 660, the finished print appears within seconds. The way the image appears never fails to delight, involving everybody in the picture-taking process. As well as providing instantaneous fun, these cameras can be used for another, perhaps more serious, purpose. Many professionals find them invaluable as an instant check that all the elements for a studio session are correctly balanced before shooting begins, thus avoiding expensive and time-consuming errors and a possible re-shoot later.

The cameras are simple to use, but the very simplicity of the system's operation invites carelessness. Often backgrounds are overlooked, lighting not finely adjusted, props left out, or pictures shot indiscriminately. The cameras lack the sophisticated features such as viewfinder accuracy, exact exposure control, and sensitivity to subject brightness that many SLR users take for granted, but the advantages of the medium often outweigh the disadvantages. Polaroid prints offer no scope for cropping, so the image has to be carefully composed to fill the frame, but other unique forms of image manipulation can make Polaroid preferable to conventional film.

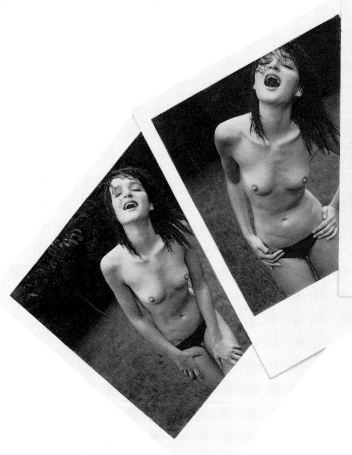

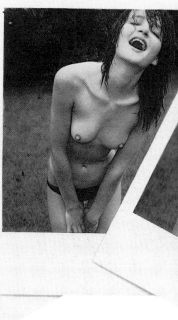

△ Polaroid prints taken originally for reference or experimental shots sometimes have potential as sequences. Each successive exposure was made from a higher viewpoint. In good light these prints give strong tones that can be enhanced by warming the film beforehand.

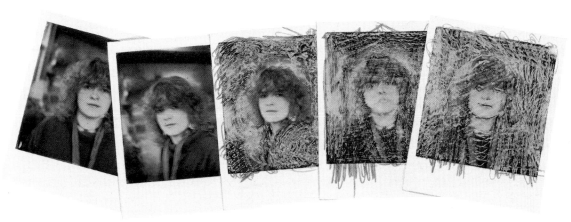

△ These pictures were taken in low light. The first two in the sequence suffer from softness caused by camera shake. In the other prints the background has been manipulated by moving the emulsion with a spoon handle immediately after the image became visible. The final picture in the series has also been drawn on with a ball-point pen, to enhance the effect.

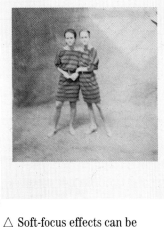

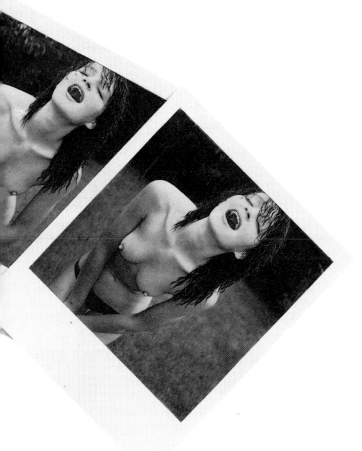

△ Soft-focus effects can be achieved by conventional means – filters, gauze, and Vaseline – or you can fool the ultrasonic autofocus system by shooting through a sheet of glass. The camera then focuses on the glass, not the subject beyond, the degree of softness depending on the relative positions of camera, glass, and subject. The slight double imaging and diffusion combine to create an atmosphere of nostalgia and romanticism.

See also:
ACTION SEQUENCES pp64-65
EXPLOITING FILM pp80-81
SPECIAL FILTERS pp82-85
MULTIPLE IMAGES pp86-87

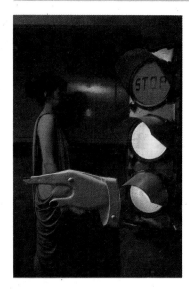

The weak light from a torch may seem an unlikely source of illumination for photography. The light beam covers a very small area, usually too small for most subjects, and the weakness of the light precludes using a diffuser to increase coverage. The solution is to play the beam over the subject during a long exposure. A moving light source such as this produces soft and, if care is taken, even illumination.

The technique is called 'painting with light', and has many possible variations. For example, you can paint from one viewpoint, giving the effect of one large lamp, or you can move the torch about outside the camera's field of view to produce almost shadowless light throughout the frame. Another approach is to include the moving lamp in the composition in order to create brilliant streams and bands of light.

△ The warm torchlight on the girl provides a dim glow that is in keeping with the shadowy mood of the picture.

*Pentax LX, 50 mm, Kodak Ektachrome 160 Tungsten, 8 sec, f22*

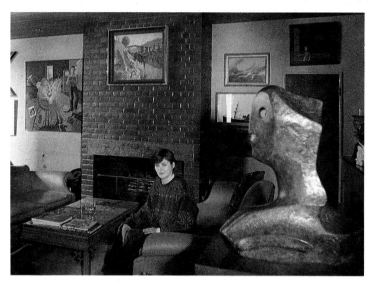

△ The multi-coloured streak of light was created by covering a fluorescent tube with green, yellow, and red gels. The model is lying on a table which, like the background, is covered with black velveteen. The main exposure was with flash, with the shutter held open, and the lamp was moved at walking pace.

*Hasselblad, 80 mm, Kodak Ektachrome 64, 20 sec, f11*

▷The effect of a large soft-light source on the girl's face was achieved by moving a torch during the exposure. Tungsten film has enhanced the blue of the evening sky to contrast with the yellowish glow of the torchlight.

*Pentax LX, 28 mm shift, Scotch (3M) 640 T, 6 sec, f22*

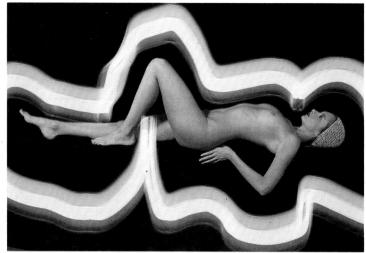

△ A single window lit this spacious room, leaving large areas of dense shadow, so a hand torch was used carefully to fill the shadows with soft light.

*Pentax LX, 28 mm, Kodak Ektachrome 160 Tungsten, 6 sec, f22*

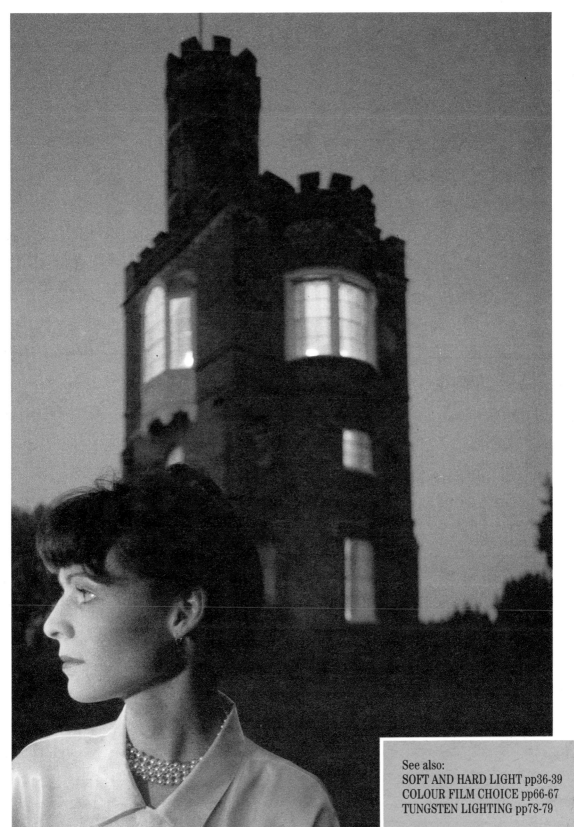

See also:
SOFT AND HARD LIGHT pp36-39
COLOUR FILM CHOICE pp66-67
TUNGSTEN LIGHTING pp78-79

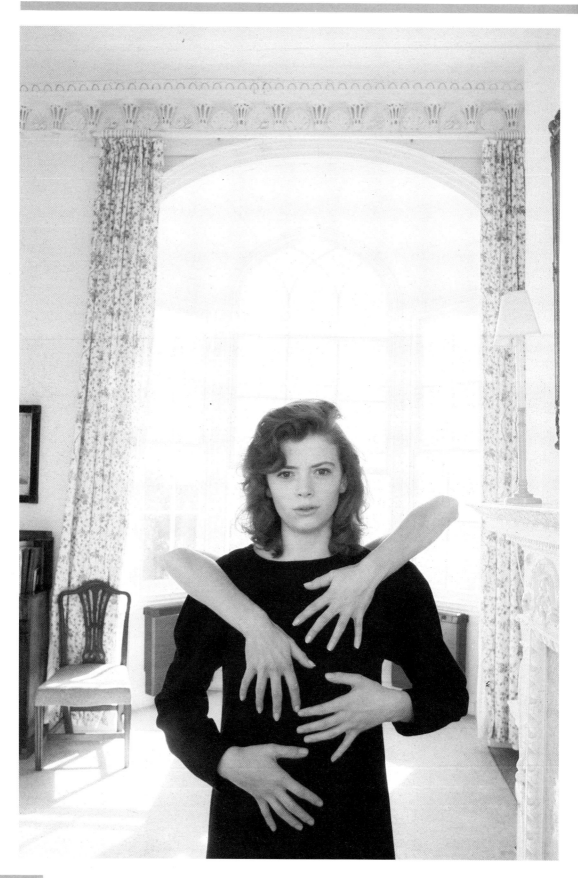

Most of us approach photographing friends and relations with a sense of fun, the intention being to present people in a lighthearted atmosphere. We can take conventional portraits a step further and exploit our friends' willingness to participate in making images that are both amusing and intriguing. Humour in photographs can catch the attention, but it takes a little more to keep it – in short, a degree of thought-provoking puzzlement. This can be achieved in several different ways – by striking composition, by odd framing, or by unconventional poses. These may result from the peculiar postures that people adopt naturally – for example, people will make use of an armchair in ways never envisaged by the designer – or from deliberate, more imaginative poses that create greater impact.

◁ With more than one model, it is possible to combine parts of their bodies and design extraordinary poses. To isolate and emphasize the hands, the model wore a black tracksuit top and the shot was slightly overexposed to lighten skin tones and burn out distractions.

*Pentax LX, 28 mm, Kodak Ektachrome 200, ¹/₆₀ sec, f11*

▽ All that was needed to simplify the setting for this picture of a ballet student practising steps for a modern dance routine was the removal of a chair. Keep alert for interesting environments – making use of them and putting your subject in odd places can lead to some fascinating and eye-catching shots.

*Pentax LX, 28 mm, Kodak Ektachrome 200, ¹/₆₀ sec, f8*

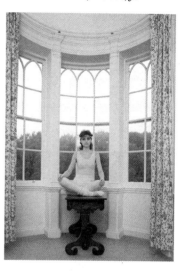

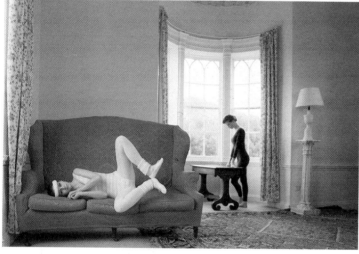

◁ The continuing ballet rehearsal provided many opportunities to explore different poses and inter-relationships. The impact of this picture is in the two separate but complementary centres of interest, the sense of scale and depth, and the position of the two figures.

*Pentax LX, 28 mm, Kodak Ektachrome 200, ¹/₆₀ sec, f8*

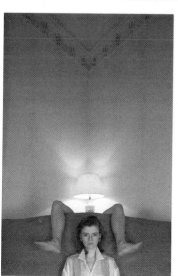

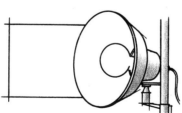

◁ △ A straightforward portrait was intended, but the ideas sparked off by previous pictures suggested a more creative approach. A tungsten flood (above) was balanced to the power of the tablelamp.

*Pentax LX, 28 mm, Scotch (3M) 640T, ¹/₃₀ sec, f8*

See also:
COLOUR INTENSITY pp70-71
TUNGSTEN LIGHTING pp78-79
DESIGN WITH FIGURES pp124-125

# DESIGN WITH FIGURES

▽ In these two photographs, the quality of the light has lent a mellow illumination to the models' faces. In the shot immediately below, the red dress brings the girls closer to us, for emphasis, but the result could still be improved on. In the accompanying shot a more exciting arrangement has been found that makes much more use of the environment.

The man is smaller this time but his effect on the design is far greater. The exposures were based on the flesh tones and the lens was opened up by a half a stop to retain detail in the black clothing.

*Hasselblad, 60 mm, Kodak Ektachrome 200, 1/15 sec, f11*

The reasons why a picture works are complex, but good design is undoubtedly a fundamental element in its success. Without it, the photographs below would constitute a straightforward but uninspired record of a portrait group. However, design has given the viewer an extra insight into the feelings and emotions being communicated. It is essential that from the outset you understand and isolate what stimulates you in the subject, and, just as important, identify those elements that you do not like. The latter can then be excluded.

Photographing several friends together is a good way to start the exploration of composition with figures. Being relaxed in each other's company dispels any feeling of awkwardness and, when you work as a group, ideas usually abound. With three or four people the combinations of arrangement and poses are endless, and the results are as varied as they are numerous. If the group are young, creative people – as these were – then the session is likely to prove even more exciting and productive. Changes of clothing will add an extra dimension to the proceedings but try not to overdo it as too much choice can be a hindrance. Choose a setting which will complement the subjects without dominating them, since the background is as much a part of the image's design as the subjects themselves.

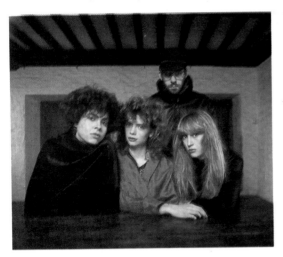

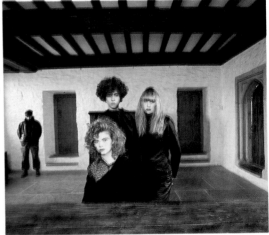

▷ For this shot, each model was carefully positioned to include all the elements and make maximum use of the background. The drama is heightened by balancing the tension and energy of the girl's brightly coloured legs with the other forms in the shot. The contrast of the available light – which comes from a window to the left and behind the camera as well as from the window in the background – has been balanced with reflectors.

*Pentax LX, 28 mm, Kodak Ektachrome 200, 1/30 sec, f16*

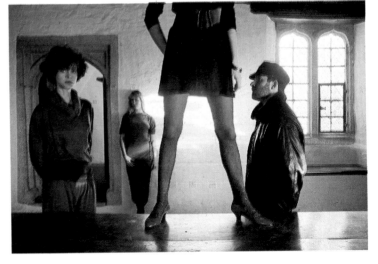

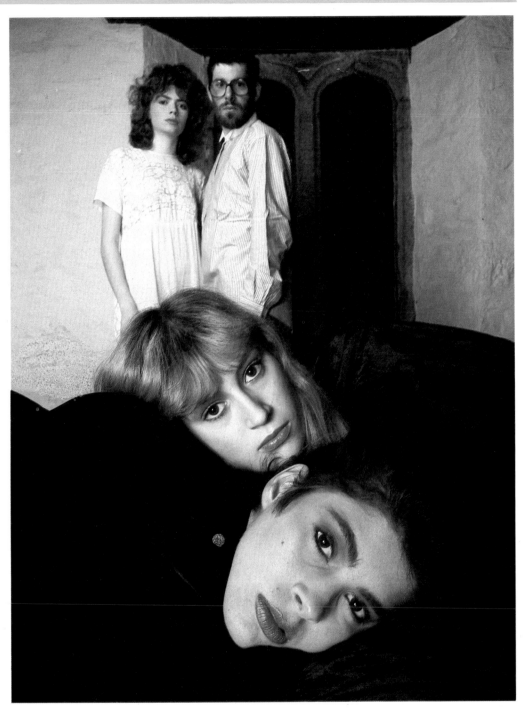

△As the session progressed, stronger ideas on design and mood evolved. This proved to be one of the most powerful images of the series. A change of clothing and of viewpoint, and the careful placing of the figures – those in the background are over 2 m (6 ft) away – all add to the feeling of depth. This was further stressed by the perspective drawing of the wide-angle lens used at close range and the pale faces contrasting with the dark clothing.

*Hasselblad, 60 mm, Kodak Ektachrome 200, ¼ sec, f22*

See also:
THE WIDE-ANGLE LENS pp20-21
VIEWPOINT AND SCALE pp48-49
COMPOSING THE SHOT pp52-53
UNUSUAL POSES pp122-123

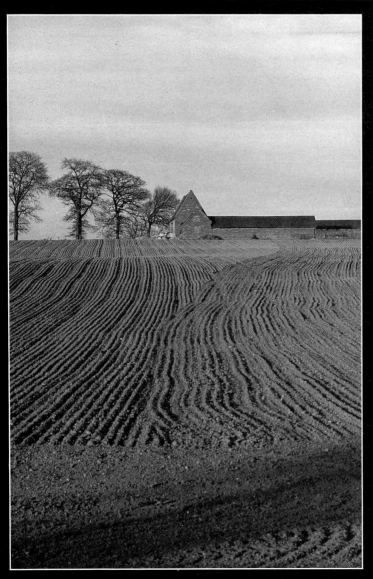
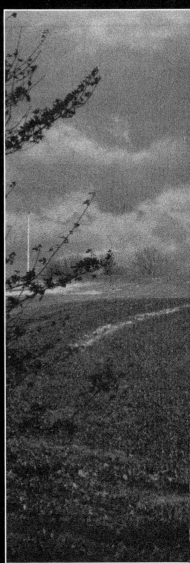

L andscape is a challenging subject. It is not easy to select a single, telling image from the mass of different visual impressions of any one scene. A landscape photograph may be a traditional vista that describes a sense of great space and the quality of changing light; equally, the same scene may provide countless, intimate close-ups of rocks and plants with images rich in texture and detail. Whatever approach you favour – representational, where the image is an accurate depiction of a scene or interpretative, where atmosphere takes precedence over physical likeness – the chief attributes of the landscape photographer are keen eyes, and an intuitive sense of composition.

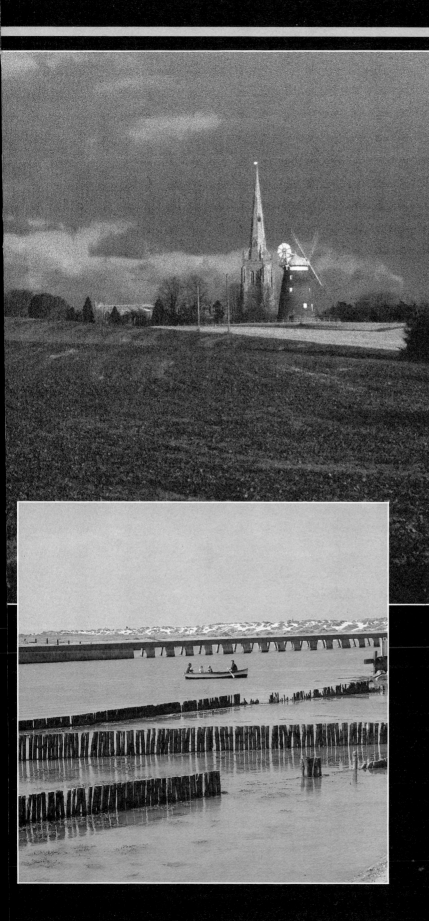

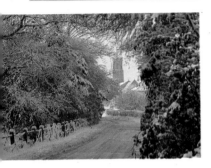

△ The effect of sunlight on snow evokes a special emotional response in the viewer. Exposure must be exact to capture the sense of freshness and tranquillity.

*Pentax LX, 28 mm, Kodak Ektachrome 64, 1/125 sec, f16*

L andscape is one of the most challenging types of photography, mainly because the photographer is reliant on the vagaries of the weather when trying to capture the essential qualities of the scene. What, on one day, may appear as a dull and uninteresting ploughed field, can be transformed the next into an exciting pattern of textured soil. Such dramatic changes in mood depend too on the quality of light – its colour, intensity, and direction. Frequent storms and strong winds bring with them fast-changing light and a wide repertoire of moods. Heavy cloud from approaching showers brings about a sense of foreboding. Bright, hard light from clearing skies throws strong shadows and produces a fresh, crisp atmosphere. Misty mornings soften contrast, the water-laden air scattering the light, obscuring detail, and muting colour to create an air of tranquillity. Snow, mist, rain, fog, heat haze, clear air – all have unique properties that contribute to the mood of a landscape at any given time. Often you may discover a scene which you feel has strong photographic possibilities, only to be disappointed that the results are not quite what you had hoped. It may require several different visits in different weather conditions before you can capture a successful, expressive image.

▷ The bolt of lightning in this picture was captured by fixing the camera to a tripod, fitting a neutral density filter to the lens, and directing the camera towards the area where previous flashes had occurred. The filter, combined with a small aperture and the use of slow film, allowed an exposure long enough to include the lightning flash and to turn the rain into mist.

*Pentax LX, 85 mm, Kodak Ektachrome 64, ×2 ND, 4 sec, f32*

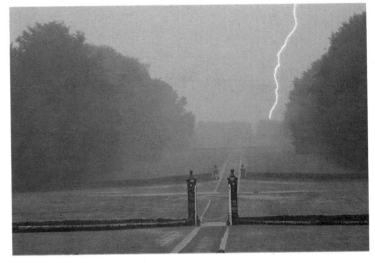

▷ This landscape in Norway gradually changed under the influence of evening light from a cool, crisp mountain scene into one of warmth and tranquillity. The distant mountains, which were a wall of black rock in semi-silhouette, are now full of detail and soft colour. The impressive sense of scale and depth is a result of strong aerial perspective, where the tonal values become progressively weaker with increased distance.

*Pentax LX, 85 mm, Kodak Ektachrome 64, 1/60 sec, f11*

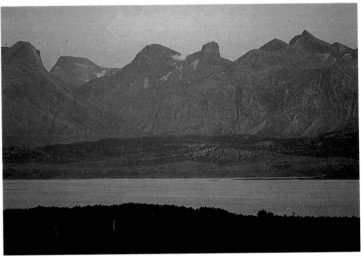

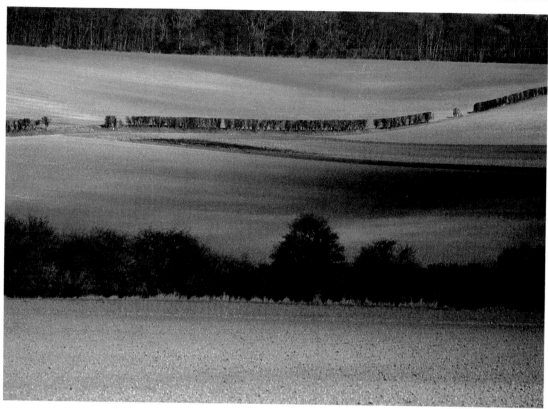

▽ Moonlight creates a characteristic atmosphere that is not easy to capture on film. This is largely because, although we expect to see a soft, cool luminosity, moonlight is in fact much the same as sunlight. Also, long exposures lead to colour shifts that lead to unconvincing rendition of night-time scenes, so the best time to make natural-looking moonlight pictures is in late twilight, when exposures can be shorter and the sky is still blue. The full moon, the cottage with a welcoming light, and the snow on the ground, all help to create a convincing atmosphere in this classically simple composition.

*Pentax LX, 50 mm, Kodak Ektachrome 64, 1 sec, f6.3*

△ Under uniform light these East Anglian fields appeared uninteresting. But, with broken cloud cover, the pattern of diffuse light and shade complemented the gentle undulations of the land and suggested this simple landscape shot. The pattern and shape of the silhouetted hedgerows interrupt the plainness of the monochromatic fields and constitute an essential part of the composition.

*Pentax LX, 85 mm, Kodak Ektachrome 200, 1/250 sec, f11*

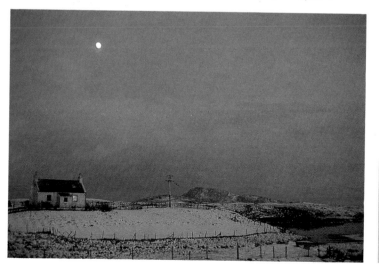

See also:
SOFT AND HARD LIGHT pp36-39
VARIETIES OF LIGHT pp68-69
COLOUR INTENSITY pp70-71
COLOUR FILTERS pp72-73

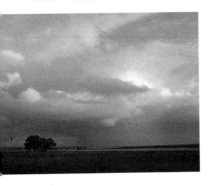

△ A storm gathers over the flat landscape of Lincolnshire. The contrasting play of shape and tone is a momentary event, and so there was no time to attend to the niceties of composition.

*Pentax LX, 35 mm, Kodak Ektachrome 64, ¹/₁₂₅ sec, f11*

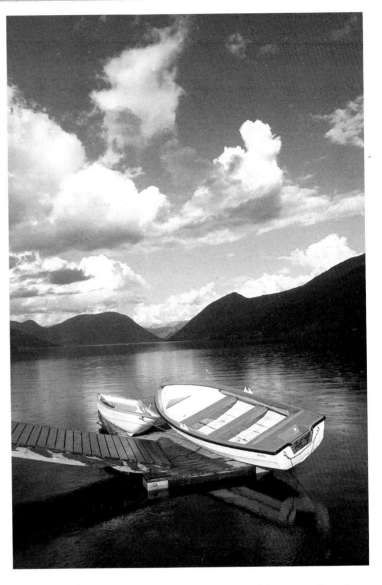

▷ Crisp Scandinavian air has an unreal quality that allows us to see for miles. This characteristic effect has emphasized the airy perspective of the Norwegian fjord seen here.

*Pentax LX, 28 mm, Kodak Ektachrome 64, ¹/₁₂₅ sec, f11*

Considering that clouds are made up of nothing more than tiny transparent water droplets, they exert a powerful influence on any land- or seascape. Many pictures would be lifeless without the relief of a few white wisps in an otherwise blank sky. Clouds come in many different guises, but are most often in a constant state of flux, their mutations providing a wealth of subject matter. Because each water droplet refracts the sun's rays, clouds can create a dazzling array of light effects that colour the land below. In black and white photographs cloudscapes can be dramatized by using a red, orange, or yellow filter to darken the blue of the sky and increase the tonal contrast within the cloud mass. Red tends to cause extreme darkening, so yellow and orange are most useful. With colour film, a polarizing filter will enrich blue skies, the impression being strongest away from the sun, while a half-coloured neutral density (ND) filter can reduce the level of contrast between sky and land so that detail in both will be recorded. Most useful are the 0.3 and 0.6 NDs, because the exposure difference may be as much as four stops.

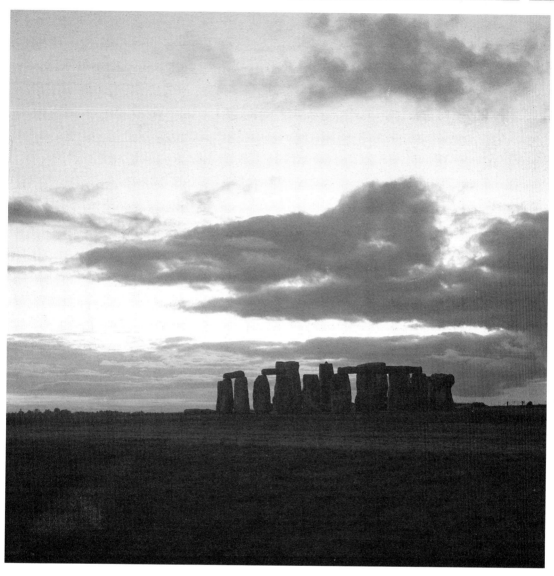

△ The ancient religious site of Stonehenge in the middle of Salisbury Plain is silhouetted against a pale sky. The clouds, too, are in partial silhouette, which strengthens the mood, their cool grey creating a tonal counterpoint to the pallid sky.

*Rolleiflex 6×6, 80 mm, Kodak Ektachrome 64, 1/250 sec, f11*

When framing the picture, it is important to achieve a balance between the compositional weight of the sky and that of the land or sea below. A straightforward fifty-fifty division seldom works well – the effect is too well-ordered and contrived. A greater sense of drama can be injected into a composition by adopting extremes – for example, by showing very little land beneath a vaulting mass of cloud and sky, shot with a wide lens to increase the effect. The nature of the landscape is also important: flat, empty countryside such as that found in East Anglia calls for a different treatment from mountainous scenes, where cloud-masses and hills constantly interact and contrast with one another.

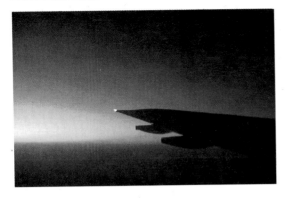

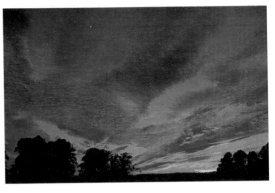

△ Sunrise over the top of a cloud mass is a sight familiar to air travellers. Often, the colour display is varied and dramatic. Photography through an aircraft window is not conducive to high-quality images, so settle for bold colour and shape and check interior reflections.

△ Lit from below, the clouds of late-summer sunrises provide a unique display of vivid colour. Taken in New Hampshire at first light, this shot illustrates the advantages of being an early riser. The air is cleaner at dawn, giving colours a clarity not seen at sunset.

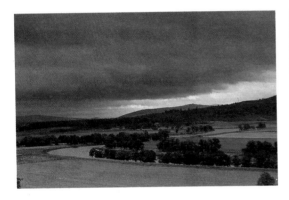

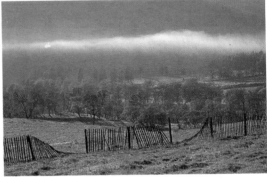

△ These storm clouds over the Scottish Lowlands seem to compress the light and deepen the colour. Summer storms often provide dramatic light effects.

△ Early morning rays of sunlight sidelight this strip of cloud in the sky over the Welsh Marches, lending a penetrating luminosity to the scene.

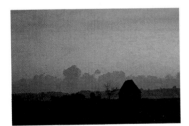

△ Twilight has tinted the low cloud a delicate shade of purple and the wispy altocumulus a vibrant shade of cerise.

▷ A Hebridean shepherd is silhouetted against a clearing sky, forming a counterpoint to the airy cloud-masses.

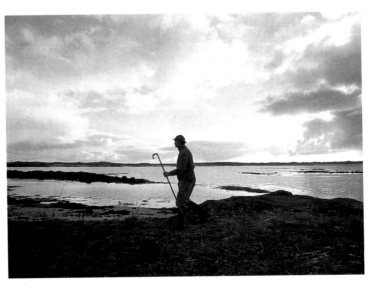

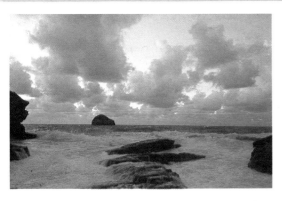

△ Scurrying cumulus at dawn heralds the start of a showery day off the North Cornish coast. The darker clouds set against a bright sky increase the sense of space and perspective.

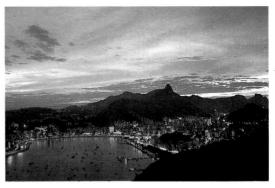

△ Dusk over Rio de Janeiro. Cool water and green street lights offer a strange, artificial colour mix that is heightened by the muted pastels of the sky.

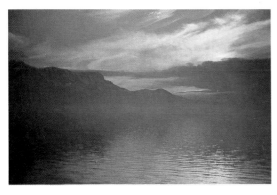

△ Lake Geneva in a mystical, opalescent light. High cirrocumulus – formed of ice crystals – is lit from beneath by a setting sun and throws its bright reflection across the lake's surface. Land, air, and water blend in an ephemeral combination.

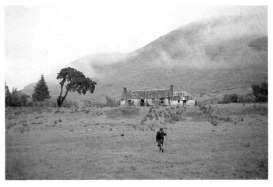

△ In the Highlands of Scotland, low cloud over high ground acts like a studio light tent, giving a soft, even light of great delicacy. The cool tones deepen the impression of isolation.

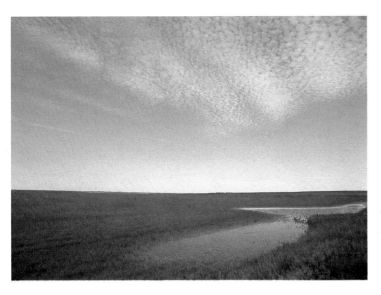

◁ Rippled altocumulus often gives rise to vivid cloudscapes of great beauty. These are pictured above the head of the Thames in Gloucestershire, their forms looking as if they have been created by a painter.

See also:
CHOOSING EXPOSURE pp28-31
VARIETIES OF LIGHT pp68-69
COLOUR INTENSITY pp70-71
COLOUR FILTERS pp72-73

# FLEETING LIGHT

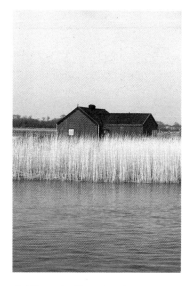

The ways in which light affects a landscape vary enormously, from the subtle to the dramatic. At dawn and at sunset, the speed of the sun's ascent and descent can transform the lighting quality in minutes – altering its colour, intensity, and direction – so the photographer must be acutely aware of the changes. Shortly before or after storms, when cloud cover is broken and the wind still strong, fast-moving patches of light pass across the scene, illuminating small areas as they travel. Light intensity fluctuates – wildly, if the sun bursts through – varying from soft to hard, and subtly altering colour.

In such situations landscape photography is not the tranquil art some believe it to be. The photographer has to be alert, anticipating how the light will play on the land, being aware of the changing formations of cloud patterns, and gauging wind speed to judge the exact moment when the picture elements come together. Timing is as crucial to producing good results in this field of photography as it is in the more obvious disciplines required to take sports and action pictures.

△ The soft, directional sunlight broke through the cloud for this picture of a scene on the Norfolk Broads, but it lasted only a minute or two, highlighting the golden reeds.

*Pentax LX, 85 mm, Kodak Ektachrome 64, $^1/_{125}$ sec, f8*

▷ Towards the end of an overcast day in Morocco, the sun broke through just long enough to bathe the landscape in warm light.

*Pentax LX, 50 mm, Kodak Ektachrome 64, $^1/_{125}$ sec, f8*

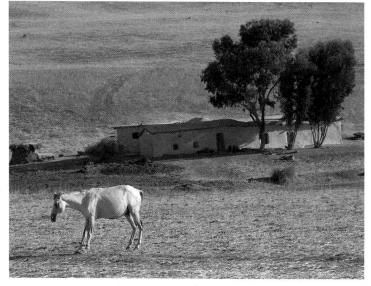

▷ Turbulent mountain air frequently leads to stormy skies with briskly moving clouds that create a fast-changing play of light and shade on the land below. Mood and atmosphere can alter by the minute, creating many different opportunities for good pictures. Try to judge when the shifting play of the elements makes the best shots. Stay and watch carefully, be prepared to make many exposures, and exercise fine judgements in timing.

*Pentax LX, 100 mm, Kodak Ektachrome 64, $^1/_{250}$ sec, f8*

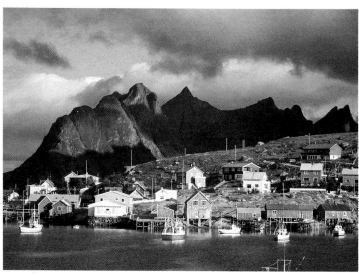

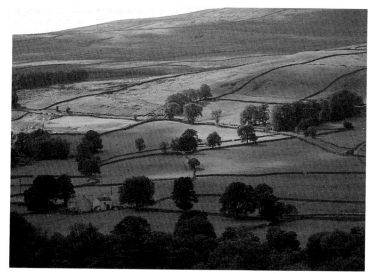

◁ Low cloud scudding across the uplands of Northern England laid a constantly changing pattern of subtle light and tone over the land. To make a success of this type of picture it is important to wait for a pleasing balance between light and shade before making the exposure. Sometimes this entails discomfort and patience.

*Pentax LX, 135 mm, Kodak Ektachrome 200, 1/125 sec, f8*

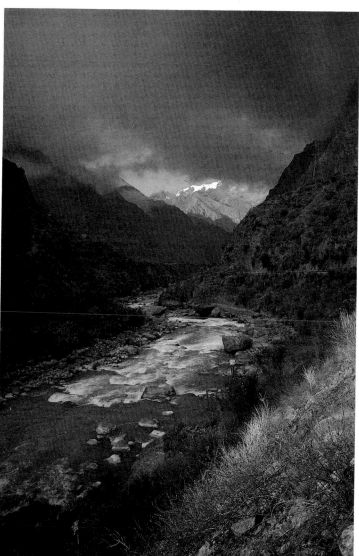

◁ This gorge in Norway looked best through a wide lens, but the overcast sky destroyed the sense of grandeur and of depth that were needed for a successful picture. Distant breaks in the cloud indicated that waiting for a chance shaft of light might be worthwhile – and it was. The bright foreground, lit by a fleeting splash of sun, arrests the eye and leads it deeper into the scene, towards the horizon.

*Pentax LX, 28 mm, Kodak Ektachrome 200, 1/125 sec, f16*

See also:
THE WIDE-ANGLE LENS pp20-21
COMPOSING THE SHOT pp52-53
VARIETIES OF LIGHT pp68-69
COLOUR INTENSITY pp70-71

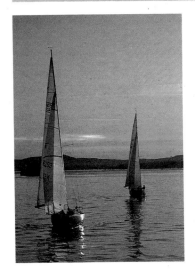

W ater is a mercurial reflector. At times it can be absolutely flat, like a lake at dawn, and reflect the land and sky as though it were a mirror. Then, with the slightest breeze, the reflection is broken into tiny fragments of shape and colour that form an endless sea of pictures. When it is an airborne mist or spray, water refracts light in displays of splendid colour that change by the second, providing a subject well worth exploring.

Light is reflected off the surface of water at the same angle that it is incident upon it. When the sun is low in the sky, its reflections are oblique and extended far from the observer. At midday the overhead sun makes a compact reflection that is close to the observer. At sunrise and sunset the surface of a lake or the sea is coloured with golds, reds, and yellows but at midday the predominant colours are those of the sky: blue, white, or grey. Bright days are ideal for photographing the reflections of objects by or on the water and you can easily spend several hours in a harbour making a range of totally different pictures of this one subject. It is best to underexpose by about half a stop to increase colour saturation, but perfectly good images can be made with up to one or two stops overexposure. The colours will be much diluted but, because the pictures are largely abstract, this result can be very agreeable.

△ A pair of yachts lies becalmed in a Norwegian fjord off Oslo. The setting sun, striking the hulls, adds a highlight to their broken reflections and tints the water with an amber sheen. No deviation from an averaged exposure reading was necessary.

*Pentax LX, 135 mm, Kodak Ektachrome 200, ¹/₂₅₀ sec, f8*

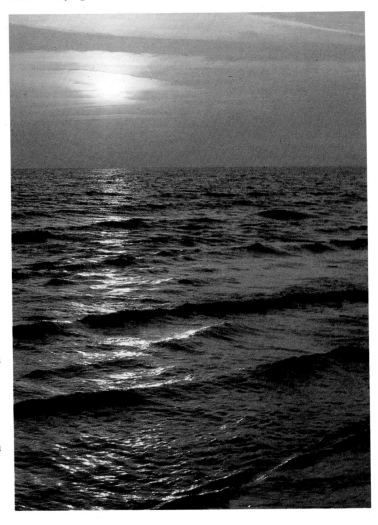

▷ A setting sun over a gilded sea – probably one of the most photographed scenes, but one that yields as many disappointments as it does delights. The prime cause of failure is gross underexposure, but this can be avoided by metering off the water and waiting for the sun to be obscured by cloud. This reduces flare and contrast, while deepening colour. Remember to compose the shot with the horizon away from the picture's midline.

*Pentax LX, 50 mm, Kodak Ektachrome 64, ¹/₁₂₅ sec, f16*

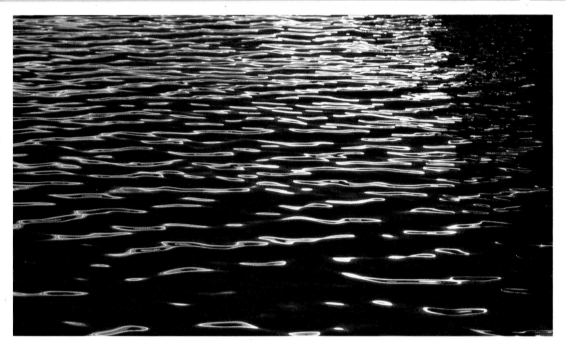

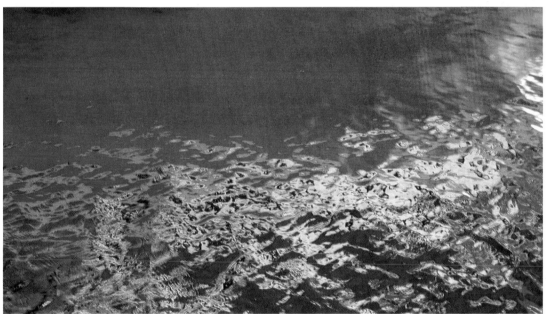

△ Close-ups of abstract reflections provide colourful and very varied images. In the picture at the top the rays of the setting sun just catch the rippled surface of the water. A relatively large area was selected in order to emphasize the pattern.

*Pentax LX, 50 mm, Kodak Ektachrome 64, ¹/₂₅₀ sec, f16*

△ Bright sun, an azure sky, and a gaudily painted boat are melted into one another by innumerable surface reflections to make a brightly coloured abstract.

*Pentax LX, 100 mm, Kodak Ektachrome 64, ¹/₂₅₀ sec, f11*

See also:
COMPOSING THE SHOT pp52-53
PATTERN AND DETAIL pp58-59
VARIETIES OF LIGHT pp68-69
COLOUR INTENSITY pp70-71

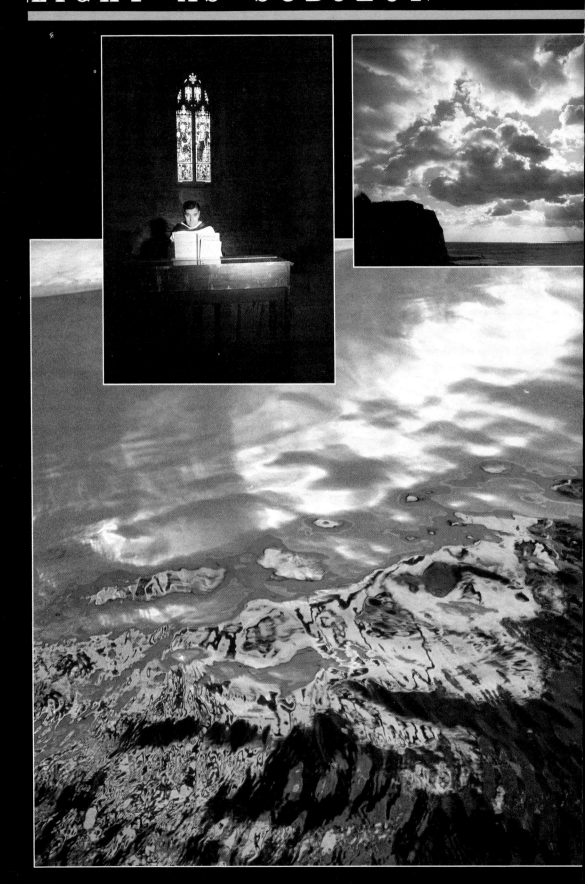

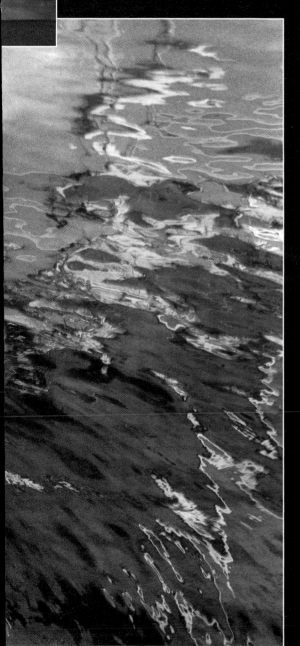

Photography is dependent upon light forming the image on film, but the photographer's understanding of light must go far deeper than that. Light has a fundamental influence on the character of a photographic image in ways that, at first, are not always obvious. It can bring surprising results which are quite different from what the eye may have seen. Learning to see light, experimenting with it, and making pictures of it should be the aim of every serious photographer. Light makes a fascinating subject, but it is not always easy to capture its essential qualities in a single image. Colour, brightness, the pattern of shadow and highlight, or the source itself need to dominate the scene, making light the pictorial theme and placing objects in a supporting role.

# EVENING LIGHT

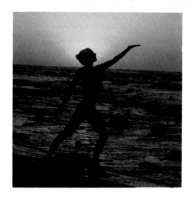

△ After a full day on the beach shooting swimwear in bright sunlight, the setting sun provided an opportunity to experiment a little. With the stunning sunset as her backdrop, the model was encouraged to play around, striking a series of dramatic poses. This is one of the last shots taken. Her body has blocked out the sun as it dips below the horizon. Its exclusion has reduced overall contrast, cut out any flare, and intensified the already crude colour. A straight exposure was made from an averaged reading of the scene.

*Canon AE-1, 50 mm, Kodak Ektachrome 64, semi-automatic exposure, 1/60 sec*

▷ A kilted piper and, in the background, Glamis Castle's 15th-century tower, bring together all the elements that are needed for a strong image of the Highlands of Scotland. Everything is bathed in the golden glow of a late winter afternoon's sunlight, which shares many of the characteristic effects of sunrise and sunset. Not least of these is the low lighting angle, which casts long, graphic shadows, throws small detail into relief, and emphasizes texture.

*Rolleiflex 6×6, 80 mm, Kodak Ektachrome 200, 1/125 sec, f8*

As sound is to music, so is light to photography. And just as there is a whole range of notes from which to compose a tune, so there are many different qualities of natural light with which a photograph can be made. Of these, evening light is probably the richest, as it envelops the landscape in a glow of colour that changes with each passing minute. Rich rewards await the photographer who is prepared to take advantage of the many different moods that this light can create. It is important not to concentrate on a favourite view, for doing so restricts picture possibilities at a time when small changes in viewpoint bring dramatic changes in colour and illumination. So, stay alert and alter your camera position as often as you can.

When the sun finally sets and disappears, the lighting is further softened, bringing more delicate hues to the sky. This is the moment when many photographers, suddenly deprived of sunlight, mistakenly pack their bags and leave. The colours that remain might appear pale and muted but the film will enrich them, while the concentration of a landscape on to a small piece of film further intensifies the results. Twilight, in the early morning or evening, presents a completely new set of possibilities, although the fading light of evening requires the use of faster film – ISO 200 or higher – and sometimes a tripod to steady the camera. A further problem can be the excessive brightness difference between sky and foreground, which is often too great for the film to record detail and colour in both. Some sacrifice has to be made in order to favour highlight or shadow, but there is no 'correct' exposure level – just different degrees of emphasis and a change of balance.

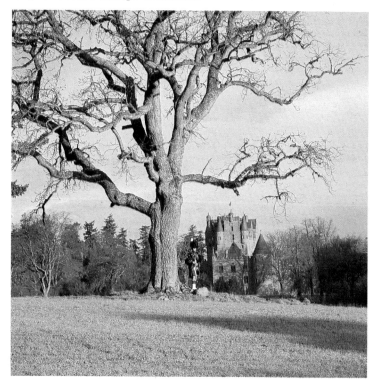

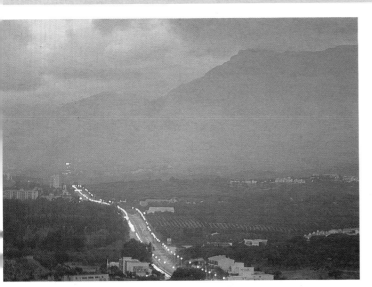

◁ Taken near Marbella, in Spain, this shot depends as much on the hazy atmosphere as on the colour and quality of the evening light. The strong aerial perspective that the haze created gives the photograph a feeling of depth, for we see pastel tones as being more distant. Bright streetlights arrest the attention, drawing the eye to the subtler detail in the scene. A camera with semi-automatic exposure was used and exposure was based on an overall reading with no modification.

*Canon AE-1, 90 mm, Kodak Ektachrome 200, $^1/_{250}$ sec, f8*

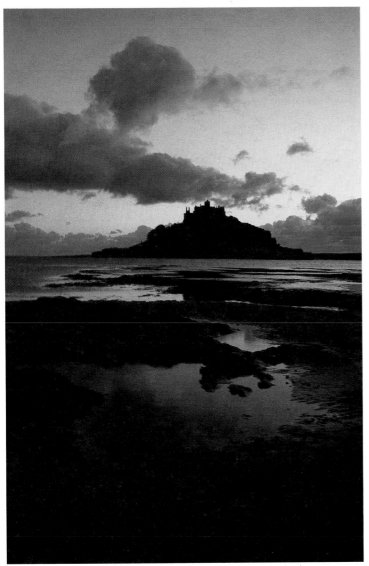

◁ A Cornish legend has it that the Archangel Michael visited local fishermen here and, as a consequence, a monastery was founded. The place is now known as St Michael's Mount. Twilight was chosen as fitting to picture this romantic castled isle, and served to enhance its mysterious beauty. After the sun set, the viewpoint was selected to take advantage of the mirror-like pools. An added bonus was the appearance of a brilliant full moon, which gave a subtle lift to shadow areas. Balancing the exposure to capture the island in silhouette has intensified the muted colour of the sky and its reflections in the bay.

*Hasselblad, 80 mm, Kodak Ektachrome 64, $^1/_{15}$ sec, f8*

See also:
USING BACKLIGHT pp34-35
SOFT AND HARD LIGHT pp36-39
VARIETIES OF LIGHT pp68-69
COLOUR FILTERS pp72-73

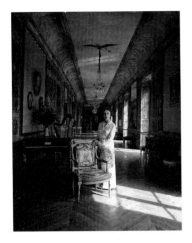

One of the first things that we learn when taking pictures is that photography depends on light. The word photography means 'writing with light' and has been in use since the early 19th century, when pioneers in the field recognized light as being the most important element in a photograph. Here we are concerned with one particular aspect of light – its impact on composition, when it catches the eye and demands attention. Strong light from a single source can create exciting, even magical effects. Shafts of sunlight, through trees, traceries of light on the ground beneath, brilliant and graphic patterns made by sunlight streaming into rooms, are sights enjoyed by us all. Here, nature is providing a light display that can only be duplicated in the studio after building elaborate contrivances of lamps, blinds, and shields. So, regardless of the subject matter illuminated, it is always worth taking advantage of such a situation when it arises. Often, a sudden beam of sunlight can transform a commonplace landscape into an enchanting picture, with the play of light and shadow becoming a dramatic theme in itself. Natural sunlight also produces nuances to exploit in portrait photography.

△ The long shaft of sunlight sweeping across the polished floor is the most arresting element in this portrait. It increases the sense of perspective and leads the eye straight to the figure, whose presence is emphasized by the light and shadow in the background. The exposure was balanced between highlight and shadow readings.

*Hasselblad, 120 mm, Kodak Ektachrome 64, 1/30 sec, f11*

▽ The rectangular patch of sunlight transformed what would have been a rather flat picture into an image of drama.

*Pentax LX, 85 mm, Kodak Ektachrome 400, 1/250 sec, f8*

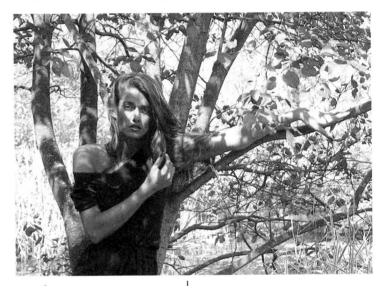

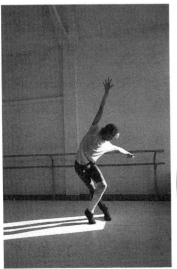

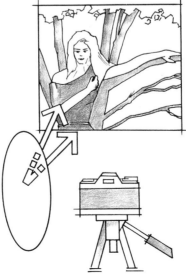

△ ◁ The pattern of bright sunlight, dappled shade, and the boldness of the girl's dress convey together the warmth of summer. This kind of lighting gives the photographer an opportunity to move the model around and experiment with different mixes of light and shade. The extreme contrast and harshness of the scene were softened with fill-in light from a silver reflector placed beside the camera, producing a much more flattering light.

*Pentax LX, 50 mm, Kodak Ektachrome 64, 1/125 sec, f16*

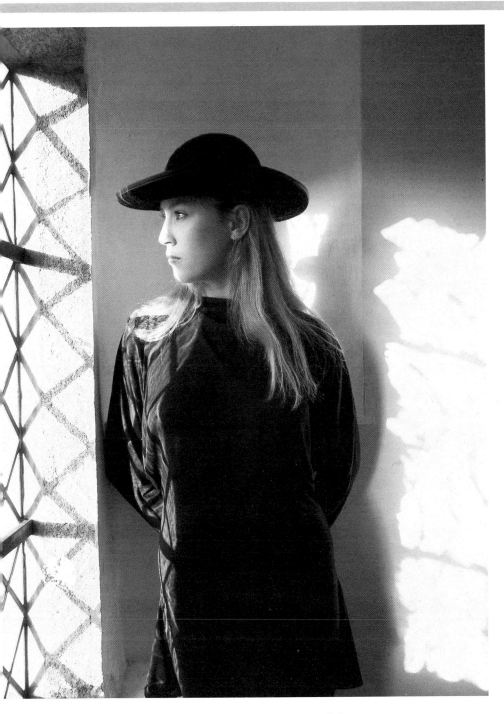

△ An oblique shaft of sunlight pours through a leaded window, painting a complex pattern of light and shadow. The cream-coloured walls softened the contrast of the harsh midday sun by providing a wash of light that compliments the girl's features. Careful positioning of her face resulted in the sun just catching her profile, as though a rim light had been used. The effect is an evocative one that would have been difficult to achieve in the studio.

*Hasselblad, 80 mm, Kodak Ektachrome 200, 1/125 sec, f8*

See also:
USING BACKLIGHT pp34-35
VARIETIES OF LIGHT pp68-69
SHADOW DESIGNS pp144-145
A TOUCH OF LIGHT pp148-149

# SHADOW DESIGNS

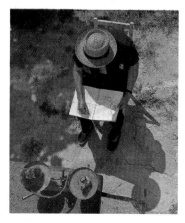

△ The shadows in this portrait of Graham Sutherland create intricate links in the picture's composition.

*Rolleiflex, 80 mm, Kodak Ektachrome 64, ¹/₂₅₀ sec, f8*

The shape of an object usually provides our first impression of it and is our primary means of identifying the things around us. Consequently, shape is a powerful design element in pictures. One of the richest sources of interesting shapes is shadows. All photographs are created by a combination of highlight and shadow, but compositional shadows must be much more than mere tonal variation. They need to be bold to create a strong visual impression and hold the viewer's attention. Shadows are particularly effective in providing strong picture elements. Not only do they form a design of their own, but they give vital clues about the object that cast them: its outline, where it is located, and its relationship to other elements in the scene. Sometimes shadows that are not linked to the object that cast them become abstracted. This strengthens the sense of mystery often associated with shadows, a feeling that is heightened if they become distorted by falling across an oblique or uneven surface and they can have a powerful influence on the mood and atmosphere created. Incorporating strong shadows into the composition of a picture can create striking visual impressions, and it is important for photographers to realize that shadows can have as powerful an influence in a photograph as light itself, and to accord them the same degree of care and attention.

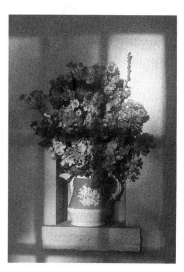

△ Late-evening sun casts the shadow of a lattice window across this vase of flowers. Trees outside soften the effect.

*Pentax LX, 100 mm macro, Scotch (3M) 1000, ¹/₆₀ sec, f16*

▷ The strong shadow thrown by the girl's body has created a double portrait – one in profile, the other full face.

*Pentax LX, 35 mm, Kodak Ektachrome 64, ¹/₂₅₀ sec, f11*

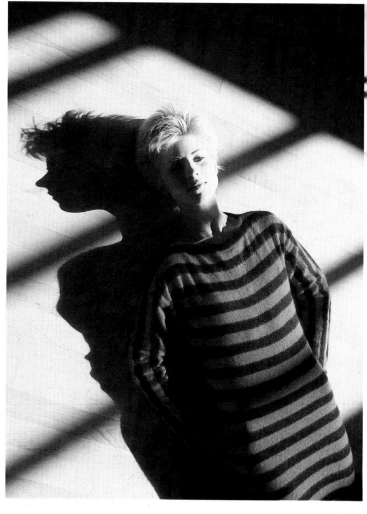

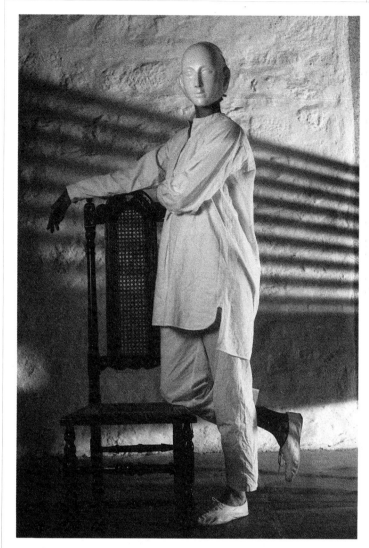

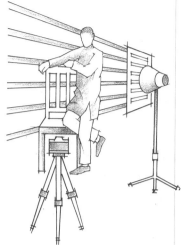

◁ A floodlight set up behind a screen with horizontal openings (see diagram above) was used to cast the shadows in this picture. The shadows themselves provide a strong compositional element and the sense of the melodramatic was heightened by the model's mask.

*Pentax LX, 50 mm, Scotch (3M) 640T, ¹/₆₀ sec, f8*

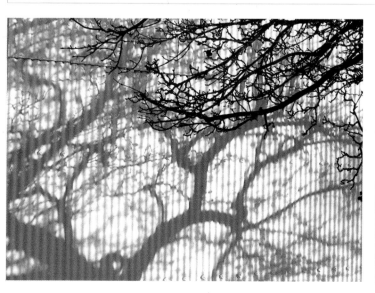

◁ This hideous corrugated-iron warehouse wall has been transformed into a fascinating design by shadows cast by an adjacent tree.

*Pentax LX, 28 mm, Kodak Ektachrome 64, ¹/₁₂₅ sec, f11*

See also:
USING BACKLIGHT pp34-35
VARIETIES OF LIGHT pp68-69
COMPOSING WITH LIGHT pp142-143
A TOUCH OF LIGHT pp148-149

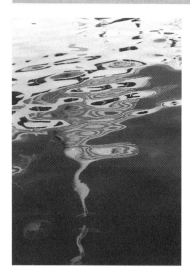

△ A tall, modern office block on Bergen's waterfront is transformed into a whimsical brush stroke. A near-perfect mirror image in the crystal clear water was instantly distorted by the wake of a passing row boat.

*Pentax LX, 150 mm, Kodak Ektachrome 200, ¹/₂₅₀ sec, f8*

▷ This picture of a 19th-century New York office block reflected in the glass of a modern skyscraper shows how it is hemmed in and dominated by new structures.

*Pentax LX, 150 mm, Kodak Ektachrome 200, ¹/₂₅₀ sec, f8*

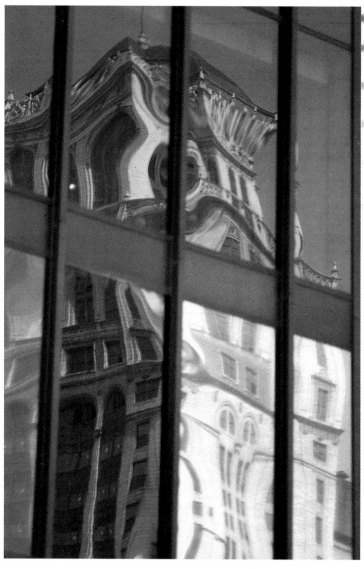

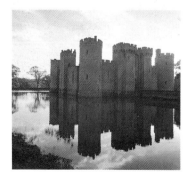

△ The darkened reflection dramatizes the formidable defences of Bodiam Castle, Sussex.

*Hasselblad, 80 mm, Kodak Ektachrome 200, ¹/₂₅₀ sec, f11*

Reflections place objects in unfamiliar relationships and unusual juxtapositions, sometimes portraying an old subject with added brilliance and at the least giving it a new interpretation. Reflections can also stretch a picture's horizons by providing us with an impression of something that would otherwise have been outside the picture area.

There are many readily available reflectors in our everyday surroundings. Water and glass are perhaps the most obvious, but polished metal, shiny paint, wet roads, eyes, and spectacles are also useful. Flexible reflectors, such as foils and chrome sheets, can be used both to reflect the subject and to turn it into bizarre, even unrecognizable shapes.

Less abstract, but sometimes amusing distortions can result from imaging a familiar subject in a shaped reflector such as a hubcap or a curved window. What is more, windows can do more than just reflect: they can be used to superimpose a reflection on top of a direct image transmitted through the glass, but the lens needs to be well stopped down to render both sharp.

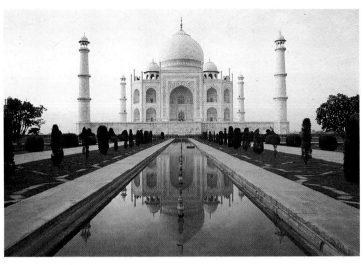

◁ Built by a Mogul emperor in memory of a favourite wife, the Taj Mahal and its ornamental lake were designed to create an image of reality and its reflection, of stability and change. This classic view is best captured at dawn's first light.

*Pentax LX, 150 mm, Kodak Ektachrome 200, ¹/₂₅₀ sec, f11*

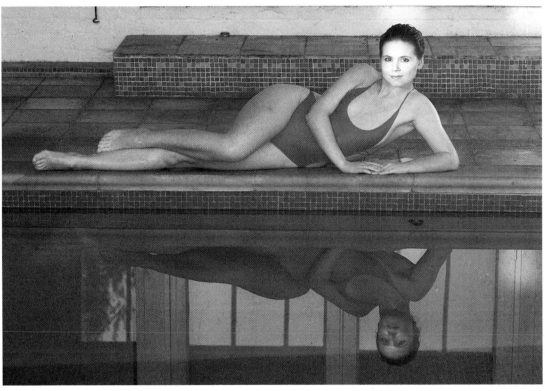

△ This is a familiar use of a reflection, particularly in poolside glamour shots. In this photograph, taken in the surroundings of an elegant indoor pool, the reflection reveals a slightly different view of the girl from the one seen normally, and adds another dimension to the image. Framing the girl at the top of the picture, with a large expanse of foreground, adds compositional interest to this simple image.

*Pentax LX, 100 mm, Kodak Ektachrome 200, ¹/₁₂₅ sec, f8*

See also:
COMPOSING THE SHOT pp52-53
PATTERN AND DETAIL pp58-59
VARIETIES OF LIGHT pp68-69
LIGHT ON WATER pp136-137

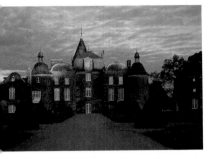

Daylight, when it is carefully controlled, is capable of producing richly coloured low-key images, without the harshness associated with normal, direct sunlight. Such light is readily available indoors, particularly at the end of the day, but outdoors it tends to be most available in autumn, winter, and spring. In these seasons low cloud layers often act as a mask, focusing the rays of the sun into a golden spotlight that produces magical lighting effects on whatever it touches. In these conditions bright patches of warm light form a rich contrast with the darker grey backdrop of clouds. Almost inevitably, these golden opportunities are fleeting, disappearing even as they present themselves, so it takes a prepared and alert photographer to make use of them. If possible, select your subject in advance, and then wait for the right quality of sunlight and shade to appear.

△ It was worth waiting for a shaft of sunlight briefly to highlight the top of this French château. What had been a sunless scene moments before was transformed into this atmospheric picture.

*Hasselblad, 80 mm, Kodak Ektachrome 200, 1/125 sec, f11*

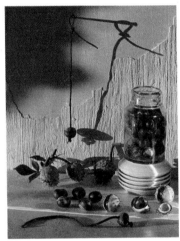

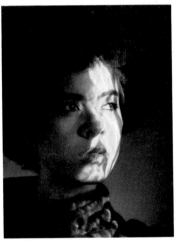

▽ Shafts of sunlight occasionally burst through broken cloud to cast patches of light on the sea, as in this picture taken off Flamborough Head in Yorkshire, but it was some time before a beam finally highlighted the cliffs. The shot was taken quickly, before it vanished.

*Pentax LX, 35 mm, Scotch (3M) 100, 1/500 sec, f16*

△ Following an afternoon storm, a sudden burst of sunlight caught this simple still life arrangement, which had been left out after use earlier in a session.

*Pentax LX, 100 mm macro, Kodak Ektachrome 64, 1/30 sec, f16*

△ Window frames act as very good filters when sunlight needs focusing. This portrait was made in the late afternoon. Rich, directional light enhanced the colour and texture of the skin.

*Hasselblad, 120 mm, Kodak Ektachrome 200, 1/60 sec, f11*

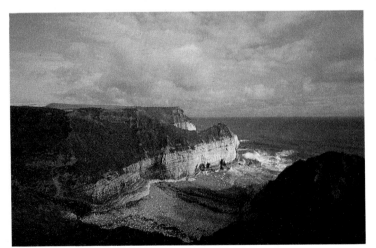

▷ After an autumn storm had passed, the setting sun appeared, casting a golden shaft of light across the field and church. It highlighted the corn stubble in the foreground and so led the eye to the tower and thence to the sky in the background.

*Pentax LX, 35 mm, Scotch (3M) 100, 1/500 sec, f16*

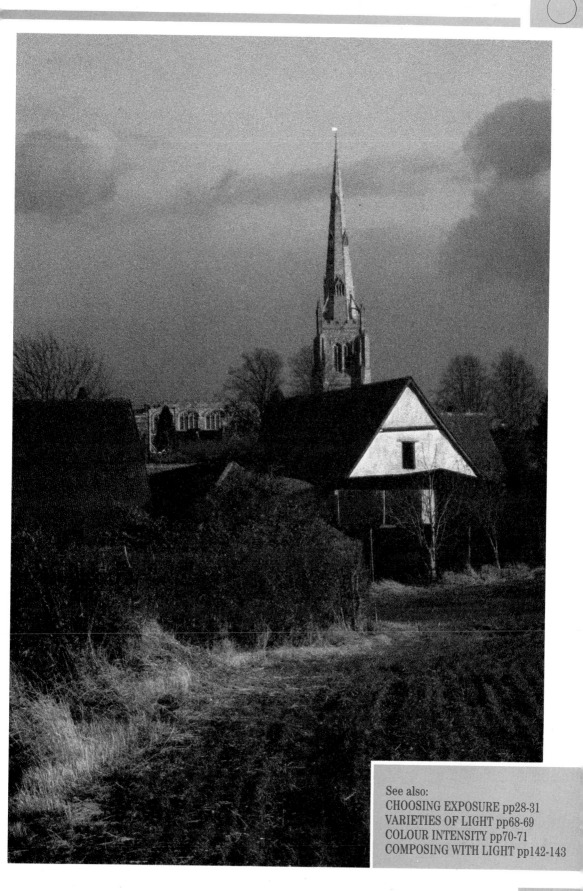

See also:
CHOOSING EXPOSURE pp28-31
VARIETIES OF LIGHT pp68-69
COLOUR INTENSITY pp70-71
COMPOSING WITH LIGHT pp142-143

# FLARE FOR EFFECT

Flare occurs when the camera is pointed towards a strong light source such as the sun and, in the normal course of photography, it is something to be avoided, just like unintentional under- or overexposure. But used creatively as a compositional element it can produce interesting effects and strengthen the atmosphere of a picture. With the light source just outside the edge of the frame, the flare light spills in to bathe the image in a diffuse glow, while if the light is within the frame, a bright, radiant star-like effect is achieved.

Flare 'spots' are created when the incoming light is reflected off the interior lens components, the size and shape of the spots depending on the lens aperture used. Compose them within the frame as carefully as you would any other major picture element. More than any other type of shot, those taken facing a light source depend upon correct exposure for success, so take a number of exposures to cover the shot if you can.

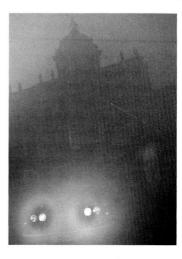

△ Haloed lights, a misted lens, and tungsten film create a twilight effect at Castle Howard.

*Hasselblad 80 mm, Kodak Ektachrome 160 Tungsten, 1/30 sec, f16*

◁ For this theatrical setting a broad swathe of flare has been used. Its source is a bare flash tube which radiates light in all directions. Notice how the effect is emphasized by its falling on to the black background of the model's cloak.

*Pentax LX, 28 mm, Kodak Ektachrome 64, 1/60 sec, f8*

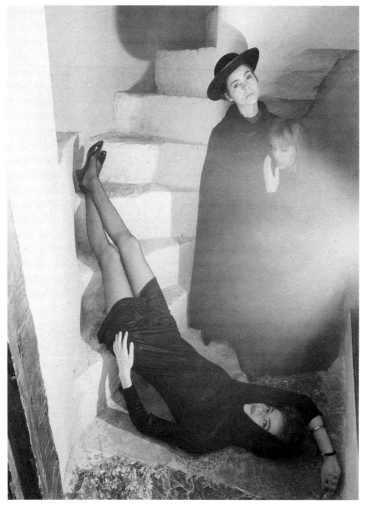

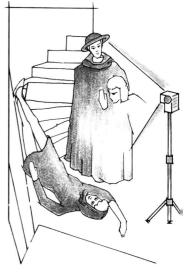

▷ The flash tube was placed just outside the frame, at a middle height to fall on the desired area of the shot.

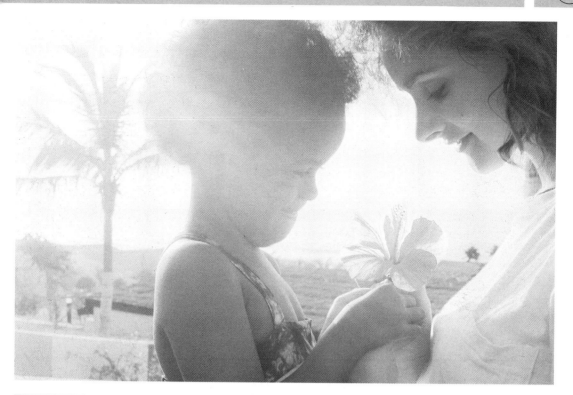

△ Here, an overall flare from outside the frame creates a warm, gentle light. The outlines of the two faces are highlighted, bringing them closer together, and the petals of the flower, lit from behind, form a natural focus for the image. Since atmosphere was important in the picture, the exposure was set to favour shadow – at about three stops over 'normal'.

*Pentax LX, 100 mm, macro, Kodak Ektachrome 64, ¹/₁₂₅ sec, f11*

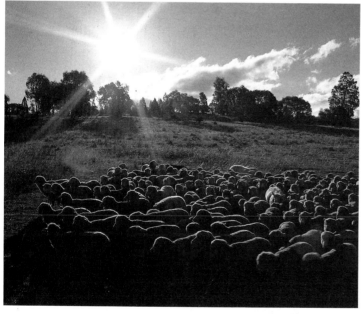

△ The intense heat and light of a Western Australian sheep farm is conveyed by the starburst effect of the sun. The flare is increased by using a small aperture. The scattered flare spots serve to enhance the diffused rimlight on the sheeps' backs.

*Pentax LX, 50 mm, Kodak Ektachrome 64, ¹/₂₅₀ sec, f16*

See also:
THE WIDE-ANGLE LENS pp20-21
LIGHT AND CONTRAST pp32-33
USING BACKLIGHT pp34-35
COLOUR INTENSITY pp70-71

Some of the very first photographs were silhouettes made by Thomas Wedgwood of leaves, insect wings, and the like. Today the silhouette is still the simplest image form and one of the best for creating evocative designs out of shape alone. Ordinarily, we read daily scenes from the most fleeting visual information and rely almost entirely on objects' outlines for our interpretation of what we see. A very effective way of exploring the impact of shape is through the two dimensions of a stark silhouette.

Many subjects make powerful silhouettes and it is a simple matter of using backlight and exposing for the highlights to make them stand out against the background. Appealing silhouettes of churches, castles, trees, people, and animals are easily made by choosing a viewpoint that places them against the sky or a particularly bright foreground. Bold subjects such as buildings make dramatic shapes, while complex ones – for example, trees – can create delicate traceries of black on white. The impact of focal length can easily be appreciated with silhouettes. The sides of tall buildings rapidly converge into pyramids when shot from below with a wide-angle lens. A long lens, by reducing steep perspective, will produce a normal-looking image.

▽ Brooklyn Bridge's suspension cables form a delicate pattern of parallels set against the skyscrapers in the distance. The misty air softens the severe rectilinear shapes of both.

*Pentax LX, 135 mm, Kodak Ektachrome 64, 1/250 sec, f8*

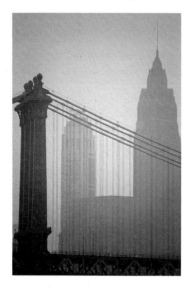

▷ A languid evening rest against the backdrop of an Indian dusk. A low viewpoint gave a clear silhouette and the exposure was set for the sky.

*Pentax LX, 135 mm, Kodak Ektachrome 64, 1/250 sec, f8*

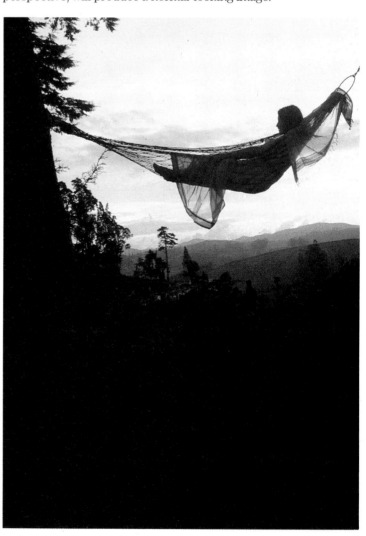

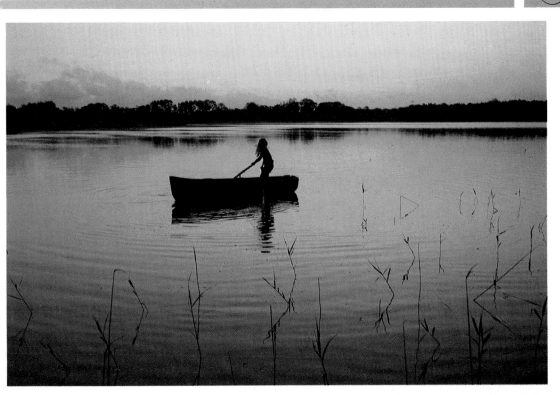

▽ Silhouettes can be effectively mixed with a more conventionally photographed subject. The fantastic outlines of these weeping ash trees have an eerie presence that envelops the distant monolith of Edinburgh Castle, hinting at its sinister past. It is an unusual, if gruesome, treatment of a subject that is more often depicted in summer sunlight.

*Leicaflex, 28 mm, Kodak Ektachrome 200, ¹/₃₀ sec, f11*

△ Normally the flatlands of the Norfolk Broads, lying by the exposed North Sea coast, are buffetted by stiff breezes, but here, in the quiet of a summer evening, a lake lies unruffled. The colours and placid atmosphere are heightened by the presence of a simple horizontal silhouette.

*Pentax LX, 50 mm, Kodak Ektachrome 200, ¹/₂₅₀ sec, f11*

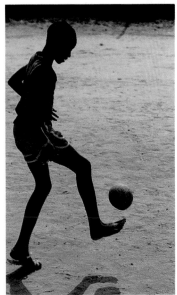

▷ A young boy in Guadeloupe displays his prowess with a ball. Almost in complete silhouette, his figure shows just a hint of colour and there is enough detail in the profile to convey his obvious pleasure.

*Pentax LX, 135 mm, Kodak Ektachrome 64, ¹/₂₅₀ sec, f8*

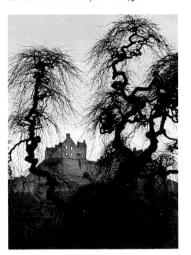

See also:
CHOOSING EXPOSURE pp28-31
LIGHT AND CONTRAST pp32-33
USING BACKLIGHT pp34-35
STUDIO SILHOUETTES pp248-249

# ARTIFICIAL LIGHT

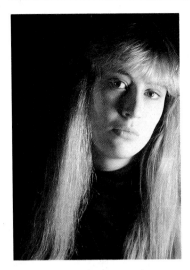

△ For this ethereal effect a small fluorescent torch was placed to the right and a little below the girl's face. The shadows thrown upward increase the sense of theatre produced by the pallid complexion.

*Pentax LX, 85 mm, Kodak Ektachrome 160 Tungsten, ¹/₁₅ sec, f5.6*

▷ Most of us associate candlelight with evocative, magical events such as childhood birthdays and romantic suppers. Typically, photographs of such events would include the light source, but a sense of atmosphere can still be retained by concentrating on the subject alone (here the candles have been included for reference). The equal balance between the two light sources has produced soft, even lighting for the portrait.

*Pentax LX, 28 mm, Scotch (3M) 640T, ¹/₁₅ sec, f5.6*

See also:
COLOUR FILM CHOICE pp66-67
COLOUR FILTERS pp72-73
TUNGSTEN LIGHTING pp78-79
LAMPLIGHT SCENES pp116-117

Today, with fast lenses and ultra-sensitive film emulsions, the photographer has no need to wait for strong sunlight or use flash or studio lighting to exercise his creative freedom. Low-level artificial light sources can be used to create striking images that are full of atmosphere. Naturally, longer exposure times will be required to make the shot successful.

Any type of light can be used – candles, firelight, small lamps and torches, even a single match. Naturally, the light should be focused on the prime point of interest in the composition, leaving the rest of the image to fall into shadow and so strengthen the sense of mood created.

Equipment can be kept to a minimum, which makes life easier for the photographer. A minimum of equipment can also make the session less of an ordeal for the sitter, who will probably feel more relaxed in the intimate atmosphere created by a small pool of light.

Experimenting with unusual light sources does not, of course, guarantee successful or innovative photographs, and there are just as many pitfalls as when using any other light source. The image may be simple, but it takes imagination on the part of the photographer to make it effective.

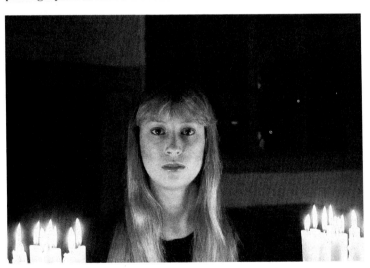

▷ The feeling of mystery and portent generated by the figures of the man and woman is heightened by the strong composition. The scene was lit with two desk lamps placed on tables behind the camera, one at either side. An unshaded standard lamp to the right produced the striking highlights in the woman's hair and face.

*Pentax LX, 28 mm, Scotch (3M) 640T, ¹/₁₅ sec, f8*

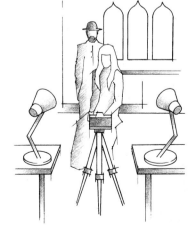

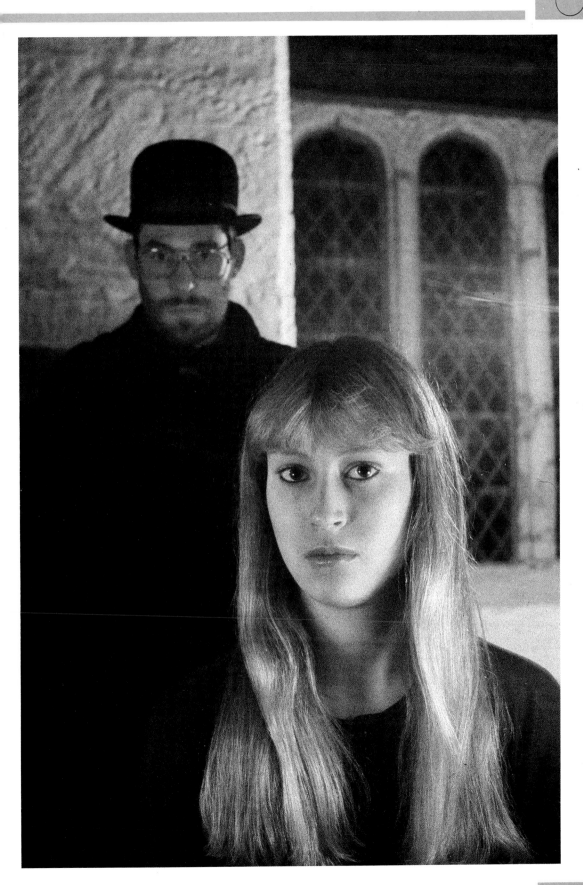

# THE DOCUMENTARY

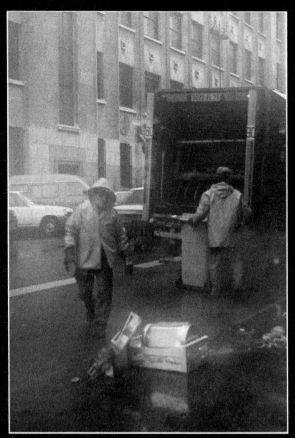

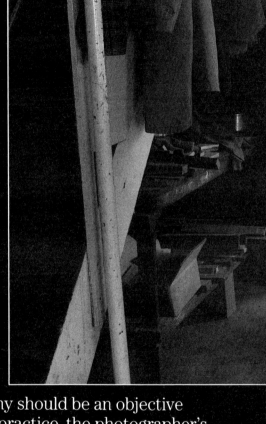

The importance of pictures in providing information in today's visually aware society is paramount. Documentary photography is largely responsible for the medium's pre-eminent role in factual communication. Many people hold the view that documentary photography should be an objective recording of people and events but, in practice, the photographer's approach is coloured by his reaction to the situation. This reaction springs from his own experience and views, and influences his choice of subject, viewpoint and emphasis. These factors, far from being detrimental, are key elements in developing a personal style that is the hallmark of great journalistic photography.

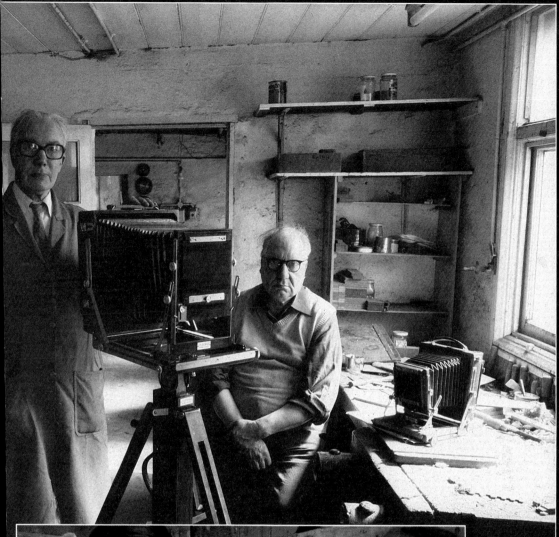

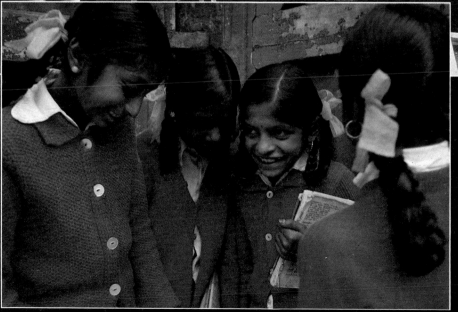

# THE WEDDING ALBUM

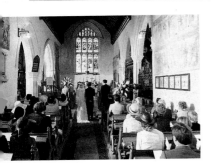

△ Check beforehand whether you are allowed to use flash inside the church. If not, you may have to switch to ISO 400 or 1000 film.

Successful wedding photography depends on careful planning and an ability to organize people. Shoot to a prearranged schedule so that nothing is missed out in a panic. In order to decide what pictures are wanted, make sure that you meet the families beforehand. In this way, you will know who is who and will be able to maintain the correct hierarchy in the traditional set pieces. Don't take it for granted that photography will be allowed in the church or in the grounds of the reception venue. Also, reconnoitre all locations to select suitable settings, remembering to allow for any special problems that space, backgrounds, and lighting might pose. Select the best viewpoints for each of your required shots at this stage. Check your equipment thoroughly, making sure that you have plenty of film and essential spares; weddings are not repeatable.

▷ If you are not the official photographer, you can concentrate on capturing those fleeting expressions that reflect the spirit of the occasion.

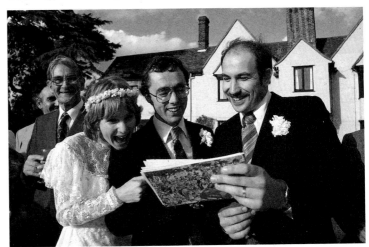

▽ The most effective way of posing a large group is in a half-circle. Make sure everyone gets a clear view of the camera, so that they will all be in the shot.

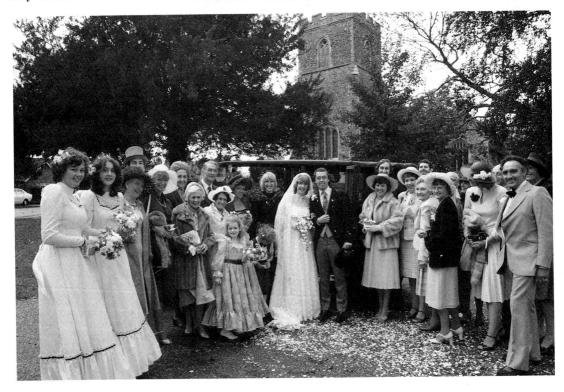

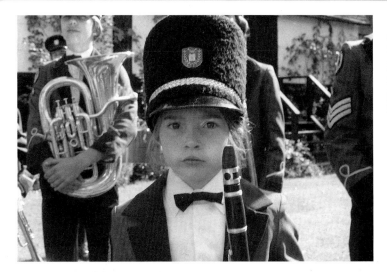

◁ Weddings often bring together a selection of people of all ages. Children make particularly fascinating portraits and are normally quite unconscious of the splendid clothes they have been dressed in for the occasion.

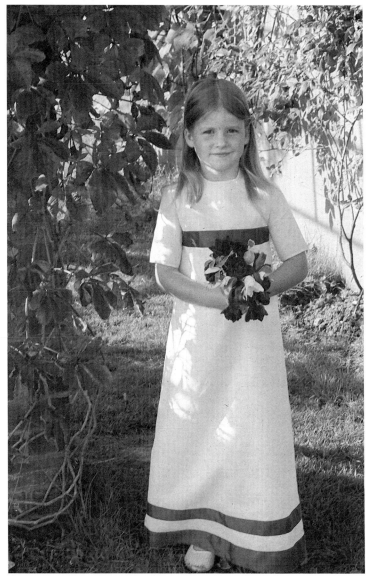

◁ Keep an eye out for opportunities to make individual portraits of important participants. A good setting, such as a large garden on a fine day, should be explored before the ceremony for possible backgrounds.

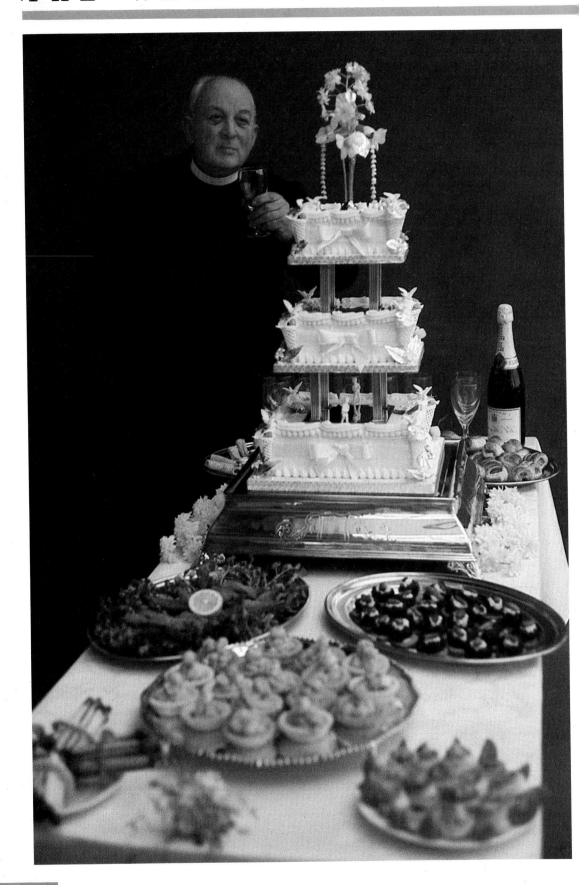

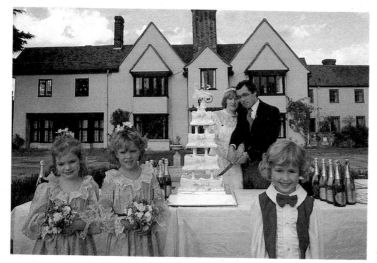

◁ Make sure you take the set shots: the bride, the bride and groom, the couple with their attendants, the couple with their families, all the guests, the couple cutting the cake, and their departure. Take a look at some wedding albums and make a list.

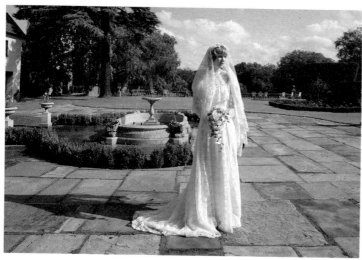

◁ Try to arrange an undisturbed photo session with the bride when she is in all her finery. A good half-hour or more in a beautiful setting will yield some of the best pictures of the day.

▷ Unusual shots like this overhead view of the reception help to give a set of wedding photographs an individual identity and make a change from the formal group shots.

◁ Indoor receptions nearly always lack sufficient ambient light for the use of normal (ISO 100) film, so take some high-speed stock to obtain candid shots without the need for flash.

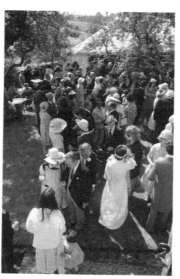

See also:
FRAMING THE SUBJECT pp50-51
COMPOSING THE SHOT pp52-53
PORTRAIT GROUPS pp96-97
GARDEN SETTINGS pp114-115

# WEDDING COUPLES

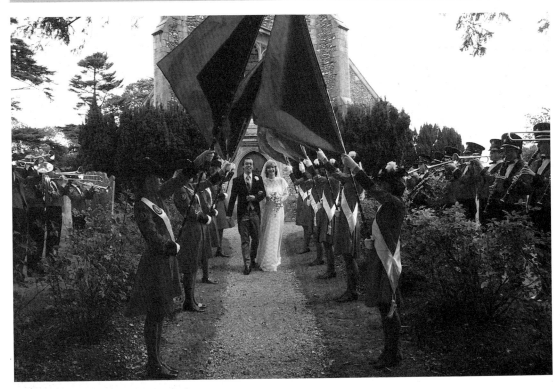

△ A shot of the couple leaving the church is traditional, but there is still plenty of scope for a creative approach. Try a high or low viewpoint, a long lens, or combining flash with ambient light for original results.

*Pentax LX, 28 mm, Kodak Ektachrome 200, ¹/₁₂₅ sec, f8*

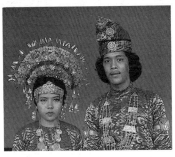

△ This Malayan couple have been posed so that groom's head is above the bride's, forming a triangular composition. Conventionally, it is the male who is made dominant, and this is achieved by his extra height and his direct gaze. The picture was taken with diffused flash.

*Pentax LX, 50 mm, Kodak Ektachrome 64, ¹/₆₀ sec, f8*

See also:
FILLING THE FRAME pp42-43
FRAMING THE SUBJECT pp50-51
COMPOSING THE SHOT pp52-53
CLOSE ENCOUNTERS pp92-93

The couple are at the centre of events on their wedding day and it is natural that the most attention, photographically and otherwise, should be paid to them. If you plan to photograph the event successfully, you should meet the bride and bridegroom beforehand to discuss how they would like to be portrayed, any special requests, and to rehearse them in response to your directions. This will at the very least put you on first-name terms, which helps to cement a closer and a more productive rapport.

Photographs of the couple together should capture the atmosphere of a close and loving relationship, and it is important that the setting should complement this. All proposed locations should be inspected before the event so that the lighting direction can be taken into your planned images.

An intimate photograph of the wedding couple, arranged in a pleasing and balanced composition, demands a special approach not necessarily applicable to other pairs or small groups. Keeping their heads close together and maintaining a close physical proximity can present you with problems. The trick is to keep the couple on slightly different planes. Heads at the same level create an over-symmetrical effect, so arrange them so that one's head is higher than the other's. For more interest, take some shots with one or both partners looking away from the camera, so that you will capture the lighter moments of the day as well as the more formal poses. Above all don't be too obtrusive – it is the couple's wedding day after all, not a photo-session!

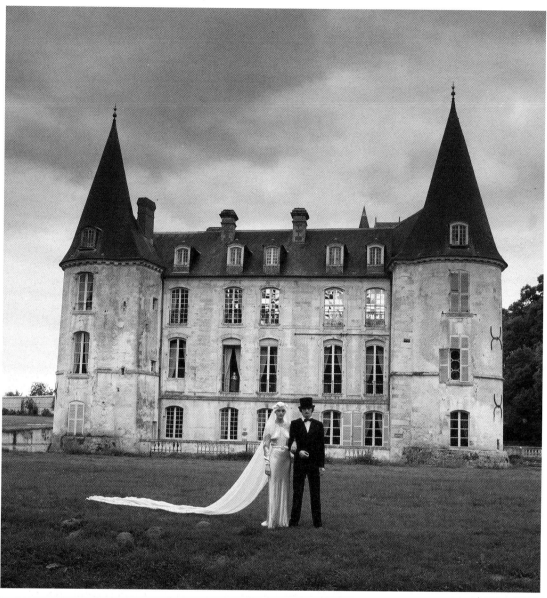

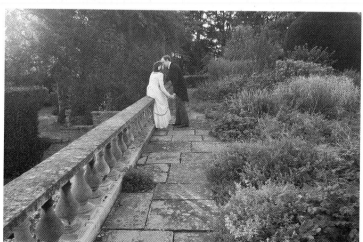

△ Unusual settings, such as this French château, are always worth using, especially if there is a location that allows you to separate the couple from a crowd of family and friends.

*Hasselblad, 80 mm, Kodak Ektachrome 200, 1/60 sec, f8*

◁ It is worth staying alert to the possibilities of taking candid shots at a wedding.

*Pentax LX, 28 mm, Kodak Ektachrome 200, 1/125 sec, f8*

# ART OF THE POSTER

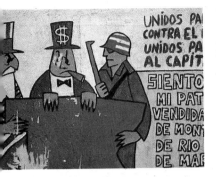

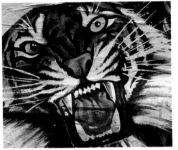

For the keen-eyed photographer, one of the most fruitful aspects of travel abroad is the opportunity to study the posters displayed on hoardings and walls in foreign cities. Whether they are derived from photographs or are hand-painted posters, they often reveal a great deal about the local culture and its artists and craftsmen. Some of these images are finely executed works of art by professionals working on a massive scale; others are simple scenes produced by local people with no artistic pretensions. But the aim of both is to provide information by eye-catching means. Sometimes the intention is purely decorative or an act of self-expression, as with graffiti, the best of which bears comparison with other contemporary art forms. For the photographer, poster art is a bright and colourful source of exciting imagery that is very accessible. The approach can be varied to suit the situation. It may be just part of a mural that catches the eye or reveals an amusing detail, but sometimes it is the relationship of the art to the surroundings, or the nostalgia generated by an old and faded poster, that provides the inspiration for a picture. Most of these photographs were made with either a 28 mm or an 85 mm lens, and with Kodak Ektachrome 200 film, which allows hand-held photography at wide apertures on all but the dullest of days.

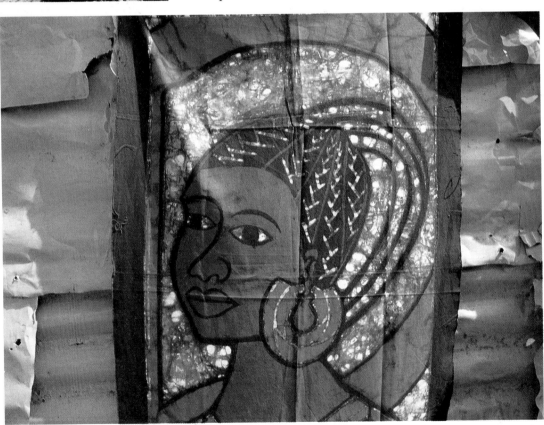

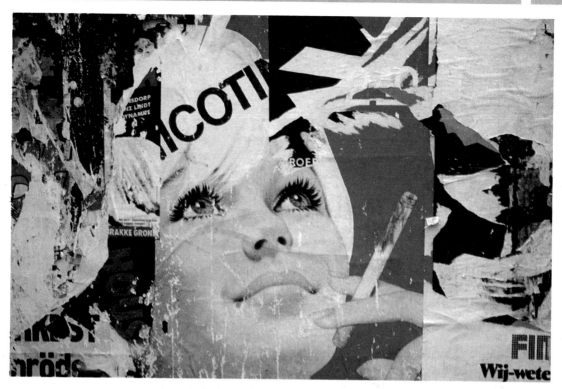

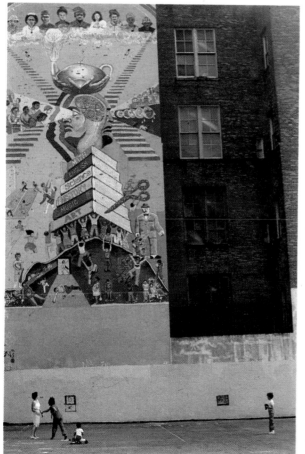

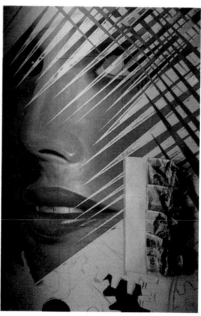

See also:
THE TELEPHOTO LENS pp22-23
COLOUR INTENSITY pp70-71
COLOUR FILTERS pp72-73

Old photographs depicting life in years past are almost always fascinating. We like to see what streets and cities looked like, what changes have been made, and how people lived. Everyday objects such as letterboxes, signs and posters become fascinating as historical references and illustrate the value of recording ordinary aspects of daily life as we see it.

Most old and valuable photographs were not commissioned by authorities or patrons interested in making documentary records for future generations but were made as 'snap shots' by keen amateurs. Today it is especially important that photographers continue to document modern life in its infinite variety because our world is changing more rapidly than ever. Although much of what can be photographed will automatically gain in interest and, possibly, value as time moves on, documentary pictures should always be made with the same creative input and thoughtful approach as any other photograph. By careful selection of subject matter and sensitive treatment, photographs can be much more than straightforward visual records, revealing a great deal about our lifestyles, attitudes, social organization and, in many cases, our sense of humour.

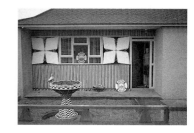

△ Most people who live in streets of identical houses decorate their homes to achieve a degree of individuality, painting the woodwork, replacing doors or windows, or using stone cladding. Sometimes decoration is more original. This family in Newcastle used old navy trophies in a bid to maintain an individual identity.

*Pentax LX, 50 mm, Kodak Ektachrome 64, $^1/_{125}$ sec, f8*

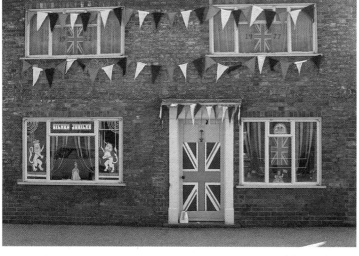

◁ Elaborate decorations such as this are a rare sight today, except for special occasions – when local football teams reach the Cup Final, for example, or during national celebrations. This modest home in Ely, Cambridgeshire, covered with patriotic emblems, shows the mood that swept Britain during the Queen's Silver Jubilee of 1977.

*Pentax LX, 50 mm, Kodak Ektachrome 64, $^1/_{125}$ sec, f8*

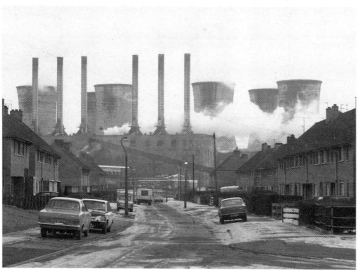

◁ The modern equivalent of those 'dark, satanic mills', this Manchester scene contains much information that may prove to be valuable as historical reference. The photograph is also an expressive image depicting the grim character of the modern industrial suburb.

*Pentax LX, 50 mm, Kodak Ektachrome 64, $^1/_{125}$ sec, f8*

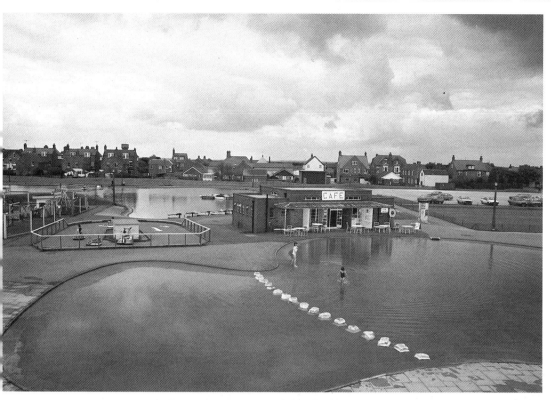

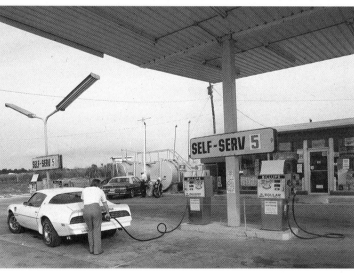

△ Rapid progress doesn't always lead to welcome change. This empty amenities park was part of open heathland that stretched to the sea. The heath was well used for picnics and had a flourishing community of wildlife. Now, the pool, playgrounds, car park, and café are seldom used, and the area is deserted for much of the time. The two lonely figures paddling in the empty expanse of water help portray the sense of change for the worse.

*Pentax LX, 24 mm, Kodak Ektachrome 64, ¹/125 sec, f8*

△ Some of the most telling images of the 20th century will show how our environment has been adapted to accommodate the car. Filling stations are a familiar sight everywhere, but look out for interesting regional variations.

*Pentax LX, 28 mm, Kodak Ektachrome 64, ¹/125 sec, f8*

See also:
FILLING THE FRAME pp42-43
VIEWPOINT AND SCALE pp48-49
COMPOSING THE SHOT pp52-53

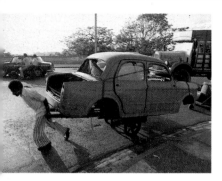

It is often said that, after the home, the car is a family's most treasured possession. The care and attention that most owners lavish on their cars suggest that they have become more than just a way of getting from A to B. Even the most-used and battered veterans seem to become almost family friends. And cars aren't the only vehicles to find their way into our hearts: taxis, trucks, and buses often do, too.

This peculiar relationship frequently suggests unusual pictures that a large proportion of viewers will identify with. The best images will both amuse the viewer and provide an insight into the way the relationship works. You'll find many interesting characters and machines, from the English gentleman in India with his prized 35-year-old Standard to the glamorous girl posing in the brand new Ferrari, and obtain glimpses of social conditions in foreign countries. Each picture shows a different attitude, but the owners are united by deep affection for their vehicles. Unusual modifications and accessories can also form the basis of successful pictures.

△ Sometimes an owner's relationship with his car results in humorous situations. This picture, taken in Bombay, was a grab shot taken as the man trotted by pulling his car. Strong backlighting needed compensation, and as there was little time to focus, a small aperture was chosen to give maximum depth of field.

*Pentax LX, 50 mm, Kodak Ektachrome 64, compensated autoexposure, f11*

▽ An image of affluence. The car is used to frame the portrait of the girl. If the whole car had been included, the picture would have become confused by the car's striking colour and shape.

*Pentax LX, 85 mm, Kodak Ektachrome 64, 1/60 sec, f8*

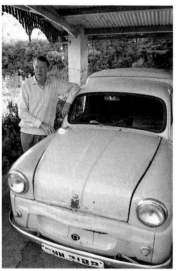

◁ Expatriates are often proud of their home country's products, especially when they are well served by them. This Standard and its owner had been together in India for more than 20 years and the man's relaxed pose against the car suggests that the partnership is a pleasurable one. Colour, tonal harmony, viewpoint, and the use of a wide lens to include all the important elements combine to make a composition that reflects this close association.

*Pentax LX, 28 mm, Kodak Ektachrome 64, 1/60 sec, f11*

▷ A sight typical of Third World countries is a crowded local bus – this one is full of schoolchildren. In order to capture the detail in their faces it was necessary to wait for the bus to stop and the dust to settle. One stop of extra exposure was given to lighten the very dark skin tones, which were shaded by the roof of the bus.

*Pentax LX, 85 mm, Kodak Ektachrome 64, 1/60 sec, f16*

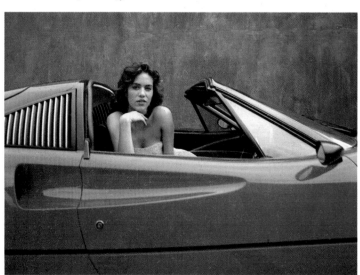

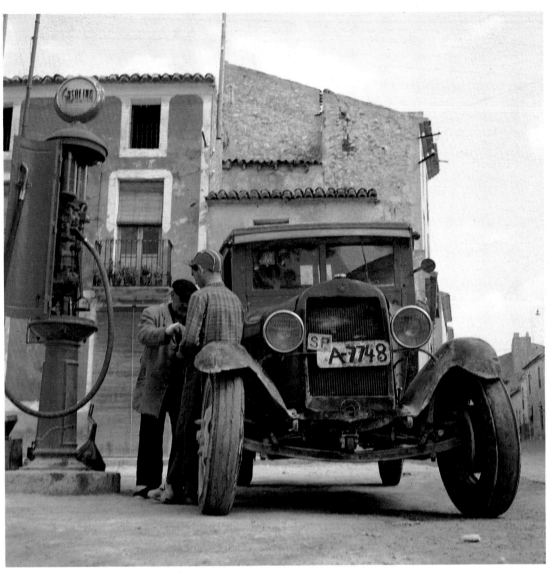

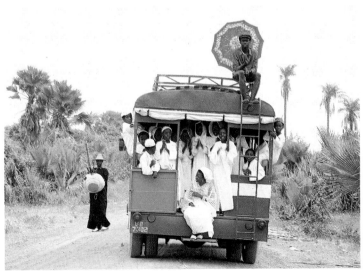

△ This farm truck had been in service for 50 years, and the farmer boasted that it would last for another half-century. The rakish angle of the wheels makes the shot.

*Rolleiflex, 80 mm, Kodak Ektachrome 64, $^1/_{125}$ sec, f11*

See also:
THE WIDE-ANGLE LENS pp20-21
CHOOSING EXPOSURE pp28-31
USING BACKLIGHT pp34-35
DEPTH OF FIELD pp40-41

# DOWN ON THE FARM

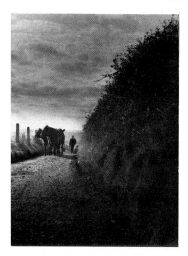

One of the most important tasks of a photographic essay, whether long or short, is to give the viewer a comprehensive picture of the subject. Although the narrative approach, with a beginning, middle, and end, is sometimes appropriate, it is not always the best, but, even so, each picture should support the series and give it a greater meaning. As a general guide, a picture essay will start with some 'establishing' shots that set the scene and introduce the viewer to the subject, followed by a selection of pictures showing different viewpoints, perspectives, and details to create variations in pace and style. Study the subject matter first and, if possible, visit the location and people involved to make yourself familiar with the features likely to make good picture material. Then list your proposed shots. This will be your 'storyboard', but do not stick to it too dogmatically. Adapt it as your knowledge of the subject develops during the course of the photography.

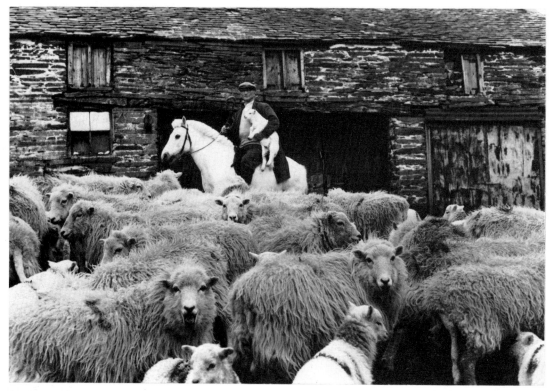

This small selection of photographs is taken from a series depicting the varying lifestyles and activities on some family-owned farms in England and Wales. When the documentary subject includes people, it is essential that you enlist their co-operation and support. It is their first impression of you and your work that counts, so take care to be polite and, if you promise prints, never forget to supply them. Farm life revolves around the seasons, so this series incorporates pictures made at different times throughout the year, mostly when important agricultural activities were taking place. To ensure that each shot was correctly used with the accompanying text, copious notes were made during each visit to the different farms and kept in the files with the contact sheets.

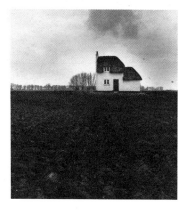

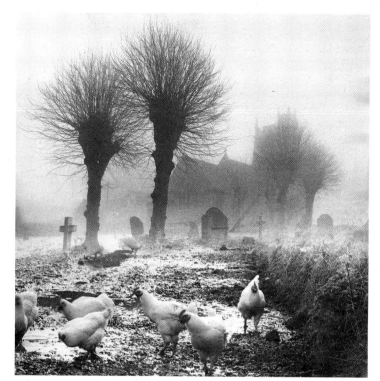

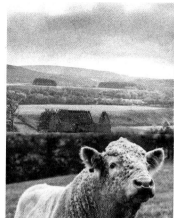

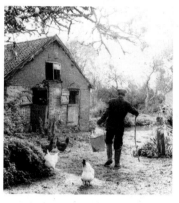

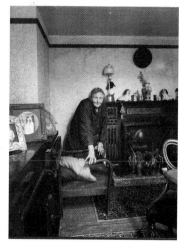

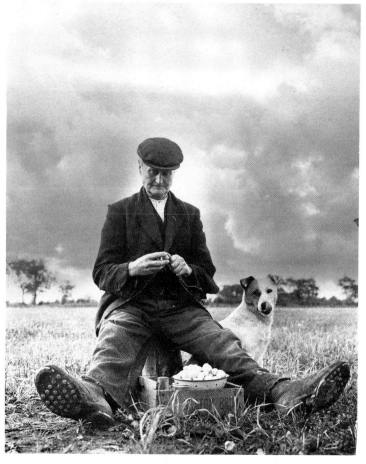

See also:
FILLING THE FRAME pp42-43
FRAMING THE SUBJECT pp50-51
COMPOSING THE SHOT pp52-53
BLACK AND WHITE pp54-57

171

# PORTRAIT STORY

Most of us make portrait photographs to be viewed on their own, as a single entity. But there are many occasions when a series of pictures will combine to make a far more telling portrait than an individual one. Portrait stories or essays are normally the domain of photojournalists but they can be tackled by any photographer wishing to enlarge his scope. In fact many familiar portraits proclaimed as outstanding examples of the art were taken for an essay and are the product of the close rapport between photographer and subject that is built up over the long time spent together. Magazine editors need a selection of different images that together can make an essay, often in the form of a story spiced with variety, changes in pace, and with a beginning, middle, and end. Prior knowledge of the subject's personality, occupation, and tastes, forms an essential part of the portrait photographer's approach. Not only does this demonstrate to the sitter a genuine interest in his or her life, it also helps the conversation to flow, preventing it from faltering to a strained silence which can make the session uneasy. In addition to researching the subject's background, the photographer must make sure that all the equipment is ready for immediate use.

▽ Here the printmaker Michael Rothenstein had been sketching pipes – one of the many everyday artefacts that catch his perceptive eye as being interesting subject matter for his prints. Shooting through the window with its bright reflections required care in estimating exposure balance, which was based on a close-up reading from the face. The shot was then reframed from a more suitable viewpoint to capture this image.

*Pentax LX, 85 mm, Scotch (3M) 1000, ¹/125 sec, f8*

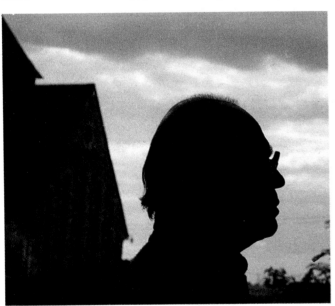

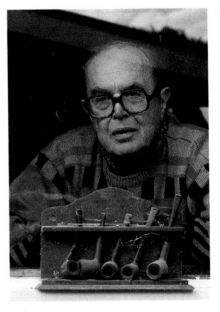

△ The silhouette is one of the strongest and yet simplest forms of portrait. A profile is capable of revealing a great deal about character and strength of personality, as this shot of the printmaker shows. A large, sloping forehead, deep eyebrows, a prominent nose and chin, all indicate a man of independent spirit. Each of these features would be evident whether the silhouette was big or small. A stark silhouette forms a striking visual counterpoint to other more colourful pictures. Exposure was for the sky.

*Pentax LX, 85 mm, Scotch (3M) 1000, ¹/500 sec, f5.6*

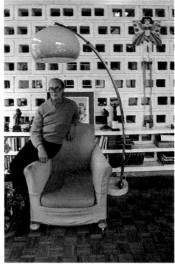

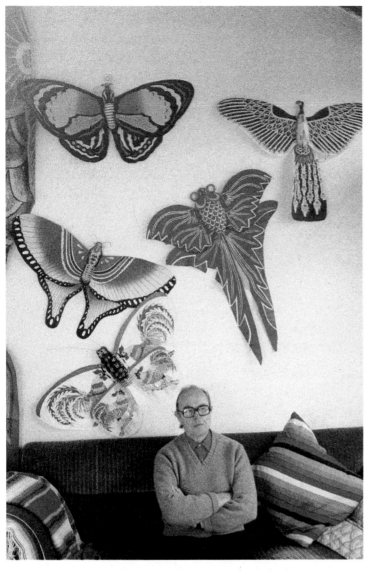

△ One of the most interesting features of Rothenstein's modern home was the use of utilitarian building materials for the interior finish. The white concrete lattice, normally seen in the garden, forms an effective contrasting backdrop.

◁ Influences are an important part of any portrait story, especially stories featuring creative personalities. Michael Rothenstein's new work had been inspired by these brightly-coloured Japanese kites and butterflies.

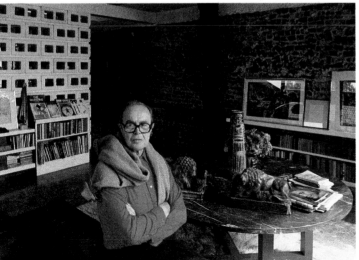

◁ For a more personal statement about Rothenstein's home, he was photographed in one of his favourite rooms. A wide-angle lens took in many intriguing objects.

*All three pictures taken with a Pentax LX, 28 mm, Scotch (3M) 1000*

# PORTRAIT STORY

Take only what is necessary when you go to shoot a portrait story. Most assignments of this kind can be handled with just a moderately wide lens, a standard lens, and a short telephoto. For lighting, a powerful hand-held flash and accompanying reflector will be adequate, and all that you need besides are a tripod, a cable release and film of different types and speeds. Never arrive late. When you arrive keep an eye out for suitable locations, always bearing in mind the editor's requirements. Prime among these are likely to be head and shoulders portraits; not one but several, including examples from the waist up and full length studies, with each shot showing the subject in a different setting. Other shots to include are some of the hands, which can reveal a great deal about the sitter. Readers can relate to the person more easily if they can see where he lives and works, what he likes to accumulate around him, whether he is tidy or lives in chaos, and what clothes he wears. Much time can be saved if natural and available light is used wherever possible. Superb results can be achieved with just window light and a large, white reflector for lightening the shadows. If artificial light is needed, try bouncing it off a neutral-coloured surface for a softer effect. Given time and a co-operative subject, most competent photographers can hope to make a success of a portrait session. It is important to stay relaxed under pressure. Diplomacy is of key importance during the whole of the session – while setting up, during shooting, and afterwards. It is particularly important to send prints if you have promised to supply them. You should, however, having expressed your gratitude, politely but firmly resist any request from the sitter that he or she approve the pictures before publication.

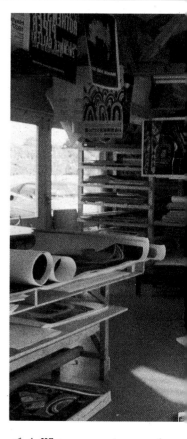

▽ To avoid repetition Rothenstein wore a different shirt and now blends in rather than contrasts with the surroundings. The strong foreground has been dramatized by making use of the exaggerated perspective of the wide-angle lens. Lighting was from a window.

*Pentax LX, 28 mm, Scotch (3M) 1000, ¹/₁₅ sec, f8*

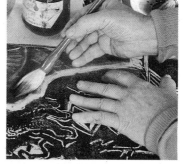

◁ △ When you meet anyone for the first time one of the first questions you will probably ask is what work he or she does. So it follows that few portrait stories are complete without a series depicting the person at work. Rothenstein's studio had many picture opportunities, most of them enlivened by bright colours, contrasts, comparison or scale, and varieties of form. To avoid any possibility of repetition, viewpoint, lenses, and poses were changed frequently and a good mix of vertical and horizontal shots was made both from close up and from a distance.

*Pentax LX, 50 mm, Scotch (3M) 1000, ¹/₁₅ sec, f8*

*Pentax LX, 28 mm, Scotch (3M) 1000, ¹/₃₀ sec, f5.6*

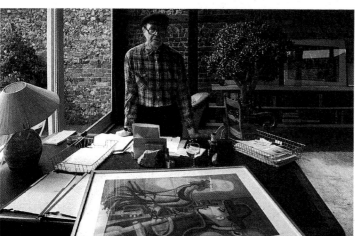

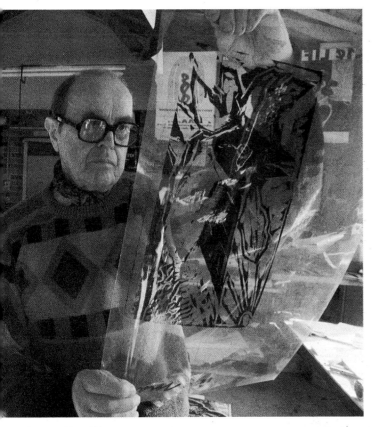

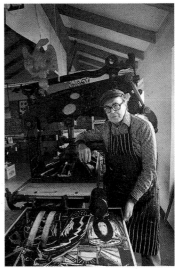

△ The artist with the printing press that is an indispensable tool of his craft.

*Pentax LX, 28 mm, Scotch (3M) 1000, 1/15 sec, f8*

◁ A further change of clothes keeps interest in the portrait series alive. The mass of plain tone in Rothenstein's jersey contrasts well with the intricately detailed background.

*Pentax LX, 28 mm, Scotch (3M) 1000, 1/15 sec, f8*

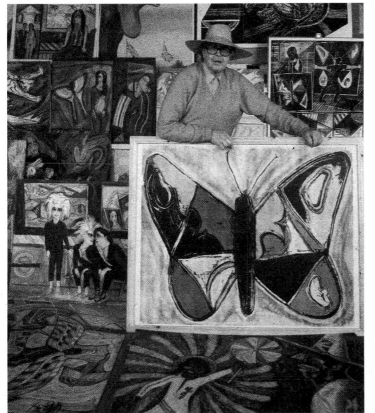

See also:
THE WIDE-ANGLE LENS pp20-21
SOFT AND HARD LIGHT pp36-39
COLOUR FILM CHOICE pp66-67
ELECTRONIC FLASH pp74-77

# THE AGE OF THE CAR

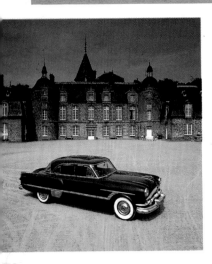

△ Those who can afford to indulge a love for classic cars are often only too pleased to show them off. Sometimes the inducement of some free high quality prints will ensure co-operation, but the owner of this 1950s Packard was very appreciative of any interest taken in his collection.

*Hasselblad, 80 mm, Kodak Ektachrome 200, ¹/₆₀ sec, f16, half-colour graduated ND filter*

This is the age of the car. Western society revolves around its ownership and use, and the rest of the world has been quick to follow suit. Almost everyone aspires to own a motor vehicle of some sort. Country dwellers need transport to get to town; pressured cityfolk need a car in which to escape and enjoy a sense of freedom. It is frequently this association with escape that the car advertisers play on. Cars are often portrayed as being a ticket to fantasy, and are often pictured in ideal and probably remote settings. Designers pay tremendous attention to every detail of styling to ensure that the vehicle is a highly desirable item. So it is not surprising that this, coupled with our own aspirations, makes the motor vehicle an emotive and fascinating subject for photography.

Isolating the car from its normal context and photographing it in the same way as we would a normal portrait will emphasize its 'personality', which is what we have a strong desire to give it anyway. Classic and beautiful vehicles can be placed in a complementary setting to suggest a certain type of ownership – a treatment frequently used in advertising – but technique has to be excellent and a precise atmosphere has to be created to carry it off well. But cars come in all shapes and sizes, reflecting the preferences of different types of owner, and it is often the case that a less specific, more casual approach can lead to some fine original and interesting pictures.

▽ The American love for extravagant automobiles is aptly portrayed in this photograph made in a parking lot in Atlanta, Georgia, which featured murals of country scenes. Juxtaposing the real tree and the car with the painted landscape has produced a dreamlike scene.

*Pentax LX, 28 mm, Kodak Ektachrome 200, ¹/₂₅₀ sec, f18*

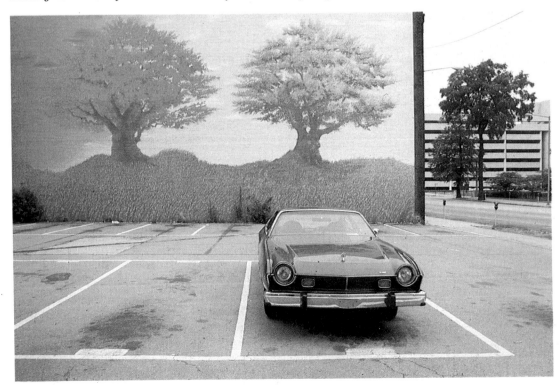

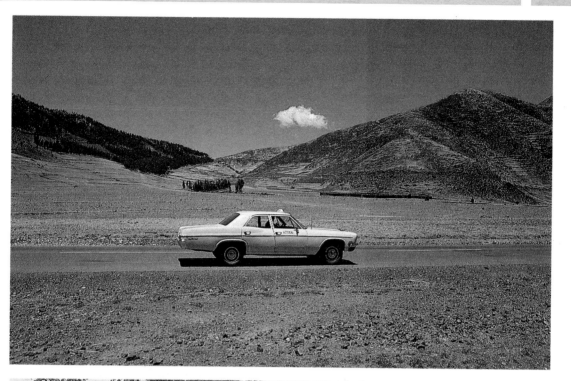

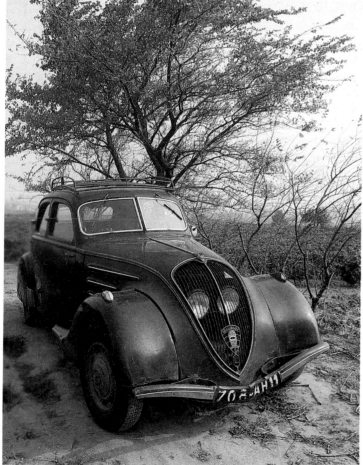

△ A lone motorist passes
by with what appears to be an
accompanying cloud. The odd
relationship of landscape, car, and
cloud is heightened by the colour
contrast and the emphasis on
space.

*Pentax LX, 85 mm, Kodak
Ektachrome 64, $^1\!/_{500}$ sec, f8*

◁ A French vintage Peugeot,
carefully parked for all to
appreciate as they drive by. The
owner and his family were some
distance away, enjoying a picnic,
but it was the car that enjoyed
the shade of the only tree.

*Rolleiflex, 80 mm, Kodak
Ektachrome 200, $^1\!/_{250}$ sec, f8*

See also:
VIEWPOINT AND SCALE pp48-49
FRAMING THE SUBJECT pp50-51
COMPOSING THE SHOT pp52-53
ON FOUR WHEELS pp168-169

# THE SIMPLE THEME

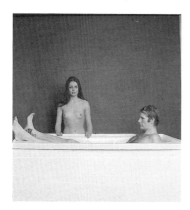

△ The original reason for making a thematic picture may have had nothing to do with the theme itself. This photograph was made for a German magazine to illustrate a feature on cleanliness but, on reflection, it adds a little variety to the bath-tub collection.

*Hasselblad, 80 mm, Kodak Ektachrome 200, 1/30 sec, f11*

One of the most rewarding aspects of photography is the way it develops your visual awareness, making you more perceptive of the intrinsic beauty of objects and places that most people fail to notice. As well as educating your eye, photography puts you into contact with people from all walks of life and with a vast range of differing subject matter. Within this wealth of experience, you will probably be drawn to shooting objects, people, and places that belong to one particular genre. This may only become apparent when you start sorting through a mass of photographs taken over a period of time but, once you realize that a subject invariably excites or intrigues you, then it is wise to exploit it and develop a theme.

Simple themes frequently reveal fascinating links and relationships that may be based on something as fundamental as shape – for example, ovals seen in mirrors, doors, flowers, and lakes – or on the different uses of one object – baskets used for plants, pets, shopping, and so on. Alternatively, the links might be a simple record of the variety of shape, size, colour, and location of, say, windows, fireplaces or, as here, bath-tubs. These photographs were taken over several years, developing into a theme gradually.

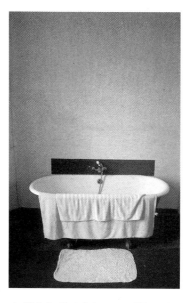

△ This bath-tub in a small hotel in a remote part of New England has a forlorn and rather sad appearance that is a common feature of little-used bathrooms in such places. The melancholy atmosphere has been emphasized by composing the picture with a considerable expanse of bare wall above the bath.

*Pentax LX, 28 mm, Kodak Ektachrome 200, 1/60 sec, f8*

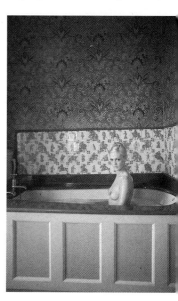

△ Old-style bathrooms have a rich elegance and an air of luxury that is rarely found in modern designs which often seem clinical by comparison. A polished-wood surround, old-fashioned decorative tiling, and a patterned wall covering are all set off by the presence of an attractive bather.

*Pentax LX, 50 mm, Kodak Ektachrome 200, 1/125 sec, f5.6*

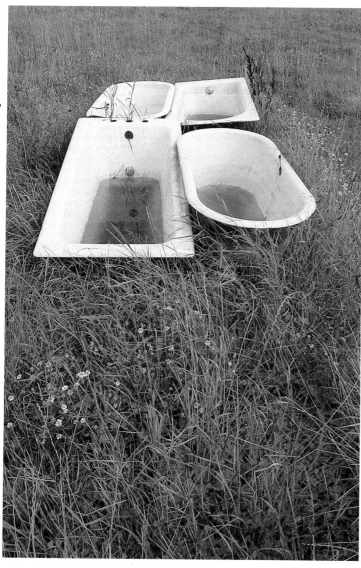

◁ Although hotel bath-tubs were the original inspiration for this series, examples of all shapes and sizes and in many locations caught the eye. These four discarded tubs rest in a pathetic group in a field in Shropshire.

*Pentax LX, 35 mm Kodak Ektachrome 200, ¹/₁₂₅ sec, f8*

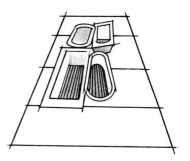

△ To achieve the extensive depth of field in this picture, the focus was set to the hyperfocal distance for a 35 mm lens at f8, which is 4.5 m (15 ft). The infinity symbol is set against 8 on the DoF lens scale.

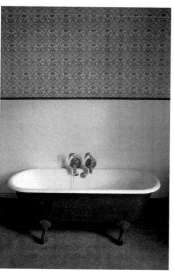

◁ The simple lines of the bathroom's decor counterpointed by the ornate, swan-necked taps and cast claw feet give this composition a quiet presence. The tub is just waiting for the rush of hot water, soapy bubbles, and enveloping clouds of steam. It was photographed in a hotel bathroom in Toronto, Canada.

*Pentax LX, 35 mm, Kodak Ektachrome 200, autoexposure, f8*

See also:
THE WIDE-ANGLE LENS pp20-21
DEPTH OF FIELD pp40-41
VIEWPOINT AND SCALE pp48-49

# OUT OF SEASON

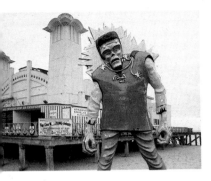

In temperate climates, any environment, whether natural or manmade, changes with the seasons. The touch of warm summer light affects the physical appearance of a scene as much as it does its atmosphere, and gives a sense of vitality and life when compared with the cold, grey light of an overcast day in the winter.

In seasonal holiday spots the difference is even more marked: the colourful crowds of summer are gone, the beaches are empty and storm-lashed, and entertainment places are empty. The whole ambience of a resort out of season is one of sadness and desertion. But for the photographer, such scenes can provide fruitful material. They form poignant and unusual settings for composed shots, or a rich vein of documentary material, showing the place and the lives of the people who live there all year round as they really are. Similar studies can be made of other subjects – the football stadium after the match, the deserted restaurant, or a city park on a cold weekday afternoon. When placed in context within a series, photographs such as these provide images of striking contrast.

△ Double exposure techniques are useful both for packing more information into one shot and evoking atmosphere. Effective composition of the elements from different scenes creates a powerful mood. The two scenes in this picture are of a pier and a painted backdrop from one of its features. The pier – shot first – was underexposed by one stop and the second shot (of the figure) was exposed normally.

*Pentax LX, 28 mm, Kodak Ektachrome 200, 1/125 sec, f11*

▷ Even in the depths of winter, British youth is determined to enjoy itself, despite the wind and cold. Often, when the holidaymakers have gone, the town shuts down, leaving the residents with little or nothing in the way of entertainment.

*Pentax LX, 28 mm, Kodak Ektachrome 200, 1/250 sec, f5.6*

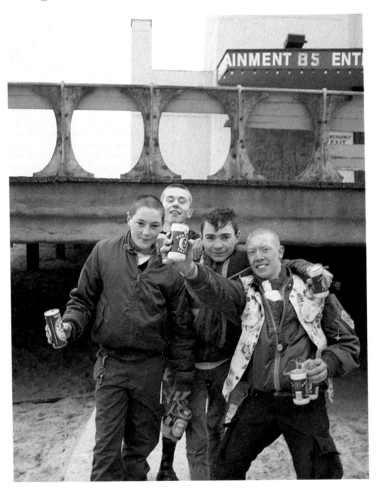

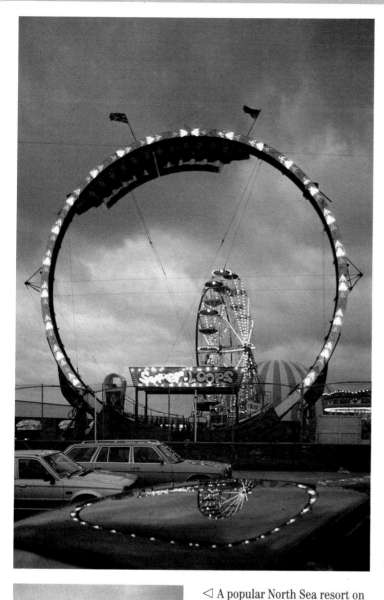

◁ Grey clouds in a rain-laden sky form an appropriate backdrop to this seaside funfair on the last evening of the season. Despite the absence of customers, the 'Super-Loop' is given an occasional twirl and the lights still sparkle. The composition includes the reflection of the lights in a car roof, framed as the foreground, to add more colour and interest. Night shots can often be enlivened by making use of lights reflected off water or wet pavements near to the camera.

*Pentax LX, 28 mm, Kodak Ektachrome 200, ¹/₂₅₀ sec, f5.6*

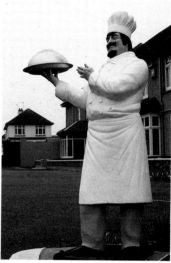

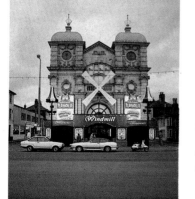

◁ A popular North Sea resort on the coast of Norfolk, Great Yarmouth is usually pictured teeming with people. This end-of-season shot, taken at twilight, features an amusement arcade still lit up in the vain hope of attracting custom. The nearly empty streets and grey skies suggest that the hope is illusory and evoke that sense of 'all dressed up with nowhere to go'.

*Pentax LX, 50 mm, Kodak Ektachrome 200, ¹/₃₀ sec, f5.6*

△ The happy expression of this figure of a chef inviting passers-by to enjoy his gastronomic delights is made incongruous by the wintry setting and a desolate scene devoid of people.

*Pentax LX, 28 mm, Kodak Ektachrome 64, ¹/₁₂₅ sec, f8*

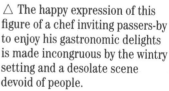

See also:
COMPOSING THE SHOT pp52-53
VARIETIES OF LIGHT pp68-69
MULTIPLE IMAGES pp86-87
REFLECTED IMAGES pp146-147

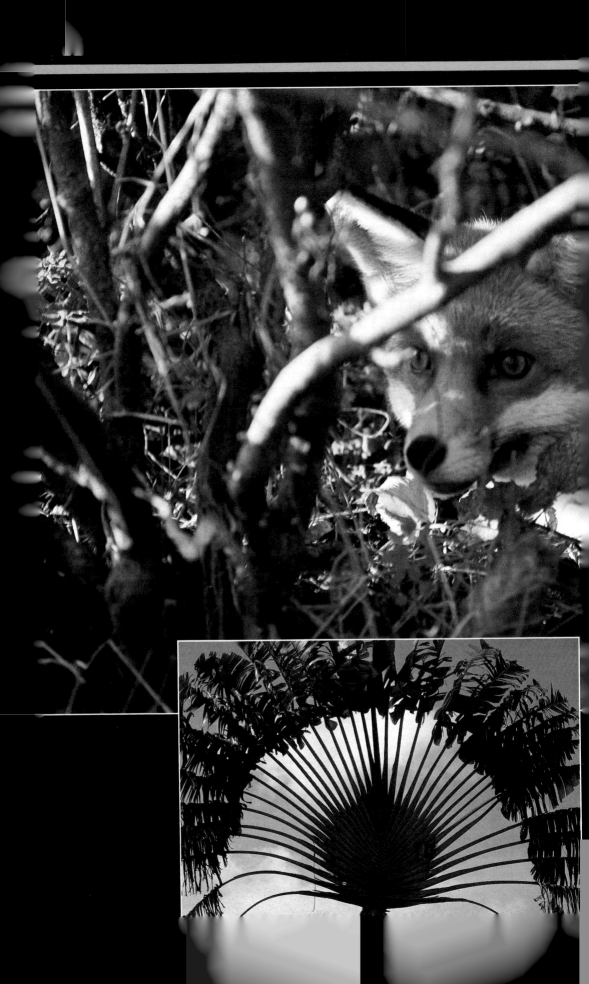

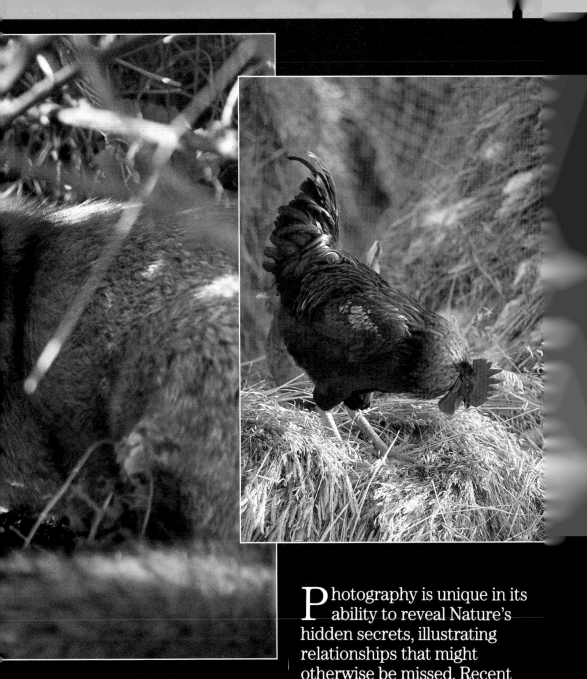

P hotography is unique in its ability to reveal Nature's hidden secrets, illustrating relationships that might otherwise be missed. Recent developments in camera and film technology have brought the diversity and splendour of nature and wildlife photography within the bounds of any competent photographer. From sweeping panoramas taken in African game reserves to minute details seen under the laboratory microscope, the technicalities of obtaining dramatic, high-quality images no longer depend on the ownership of expensive, specialized equipment. But nature photography cannot be undertaken casually. There is no place for the photographer who does not already have a keen interest in wildlife and a sound knowledge of the subject.

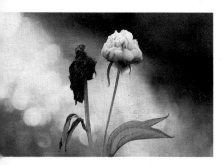

△ A crumpled peony shot against soft highlights produced by sunlight filtered through distant trees evokes a strong feeling of nature's beauty. A silver reflector positioned by the camera has lightened the shadows in the colourful flower.

*Pentax LX, 100 mm macro, Kodak Ektachrome 64, ¹/₅₀₀ sec, f6.3*

It is not easy to take a single shot that captures the overall atmosphere of any garden. The sheer quantity and diversity of the plants growing there and the great variety and range of garden designs only make the task more difficult. Since you cannot expect to photograph everything, you must be selective in your choice of subject. But the choice of subject is not the only consideration when you are trying to record the spirit of the garden and capture its quintessential feel. Probably the most compelling influence on a garden's atmosphere is light. Most people are familiar with the peace and serenity that are so typical of a still summer's evening when golden sunlight filters through the trees and long shadows stretch across the lawn. Light is a vital element in pictures that succeed in conveying the characteristic atmosphere of the garden, and it is the photographer's ability to recognize this essential ingredient and his sensitivity in appreciating the subtleties of natural light that leads to an expressive picture.

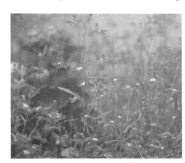

◁ Soft sunlight on a hazy day is best for flower photography. In this picture the light has been further subdued by the use of a soft-focus filter. The blurring of colour and tone adds to the romance of the image.

*Pentax LX, 50 mm macro, Kodak Ektachrome 200, ¹/₁₂₅ sec, f8*

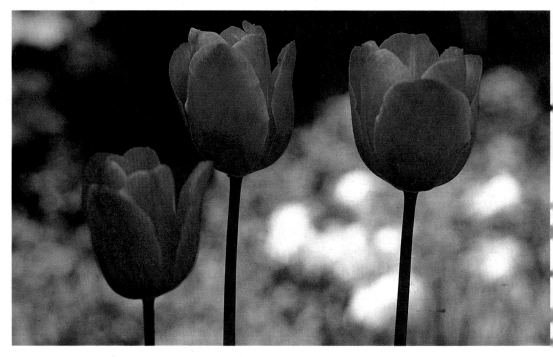

△ Extreme close-ups, such as this study of tulips, are very effective when you want to convey your strong impressions of a garden. The background was a confusing mass of colour, so a wide aperture was chosen to minimize depth of field and provide an unobtrusive backdrop.

*Pentax LX, 100 mm macro, Kodak Ektachrome 200, ¹/₂₅₀ sec, f5.6*

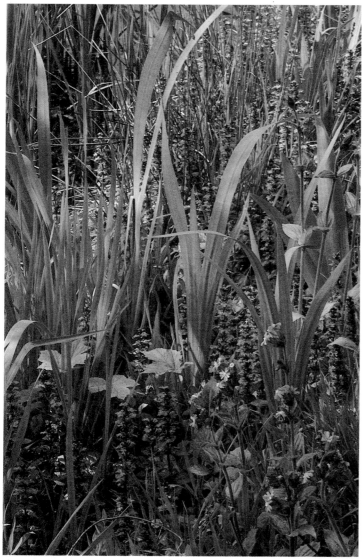

◁ Natural gardens have a special atmosphere of their own and enthusiasts often intermix wild flowers and garden varieties in an informal display. To capture the effect of this lakeside setting's luxuriant mass of plant life, an intimate view was chosen and the photograph was made when low light from late afternoon sun revealed shape and texture.

*Pentax LX, 28 mm, Kodak Ektachrome 200, ¹/₁₂₅ sec, f16*

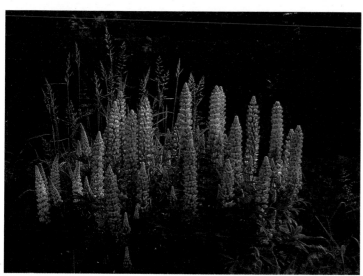

◁ These lupins were made more attractive towards evening, when a low-angled sun shone through an overhanging tree, illuminating them in a delicate oasis of warm golden sunlight.

*Pentax LX, 85 mm, Kodak Ektachrome 200, ¹/₁₂₅ sec, f16*

See also:
SPECIAL LENSES pp26-27
SOFT AND HARD LIGHT pp36-39
SOFT FOCUSING pp46-47
VARIETIES OF LIGHT pp68-69

# IMPACT OF FLOWERS

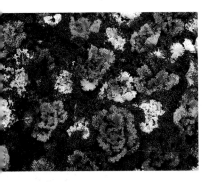

△ Although not, in fact, using flowers, this display of exotic, floral-looking cabbages illustrates how exciting images can be made with an arrangement in a tightly packed mass.

Flowers and shrubs are the most important element in any garden design, and deservedly attract attention. Special features of many British gardens are the luxuriant herbaceous borders and the wide variety of flower types, ranging from indigenous species to exotic imports. British gardens have exerted an influence all over the world.

There are many ways to photograph flowers. They can be shot as individual blooms in a manner similar to that of traditional portraiture, arranged in a display either formally or informally, in flower beds or borders, or in the wild. Naturally, if you are aiming for maximum impact in colour, shape and form, you should aim for perfect flowers in full bloom, but it's also worth photographing them when they are fading, dried, or even discarded – such images can be very striking and evocative.

Close-up flower photography is most successful with a macro lens – the short telephoto versions offering the best perspective rendition – and with the camera set on a tripod. A selection of white and silver reflectors help to control ambient light, while a collapsible windbreak will reduce subject movement. Concealed wires also help to keep the subject still.

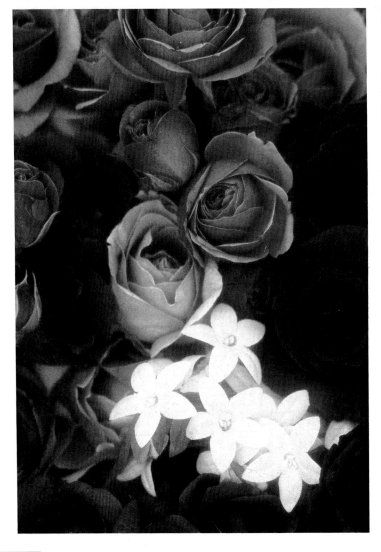

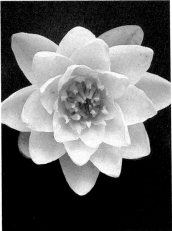

△ Damaged leaves in the background proved too distracting for this picture of a water-lily, so a card was placed underneath in order to hide them.

◁ These tightly packed rose blooms, with a mimosa as a counterpoint, have been made softer and more appealing and romantic by the use of a filter.

▷ These dried-up blooms still exhibit a subtle, if decayed, beauty. Soft, directional light from a north-facing window gives a richness to the faded flowers and reveals the texture of the fragile petals.

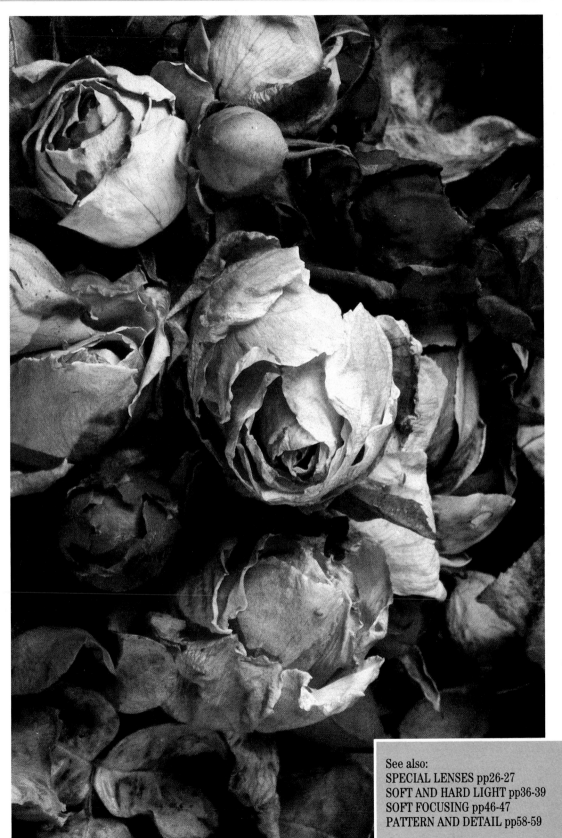

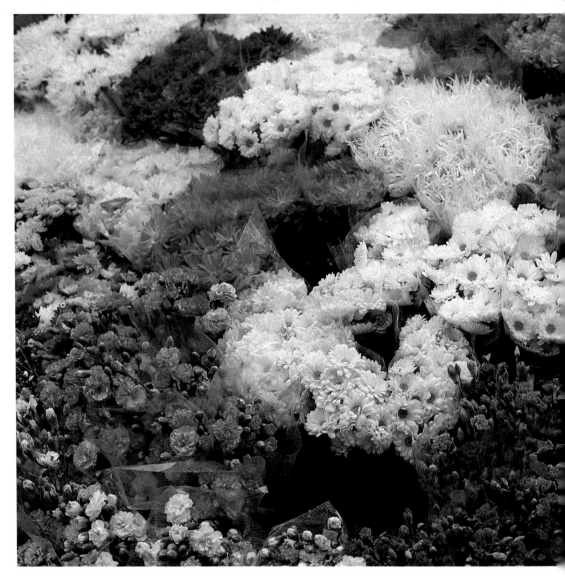

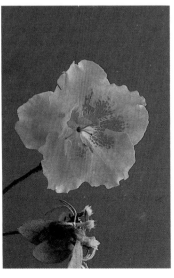

△ This mass of colour was displayed on a flower market stall. Such venues offer a wealth of picture opportunities, from perfect blooms carefully displayed to crushed flowers in the gutter.

◁ To isolate this hibiscus bloom from the surrounding greenhouse clutter it was framed against a blue door. This gave an appropriate hint of blue sky.

▷ Flowers look particularly delicate when covered in water droplets after a shower of rain. The effect can be imitated by using a garden sprayer.

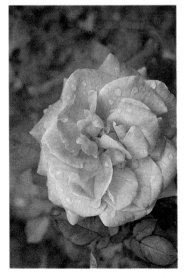

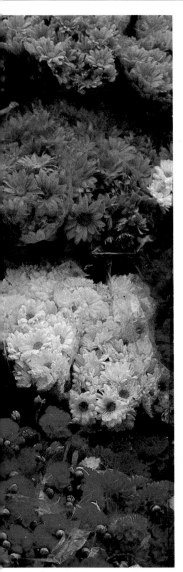

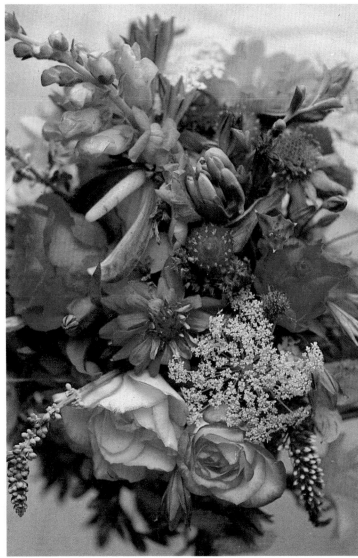

△ Beautiful flower arrangements are a feature of weddings and they frequently make attractive and intimate flower studies.

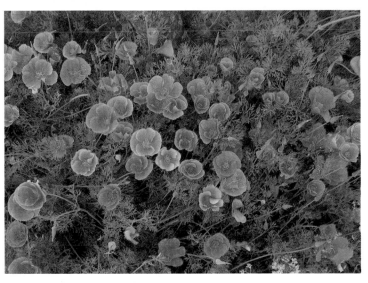

◁ Brightly coloured flowers framed against natural green foliage often make interesting patterns and rhythm.

# NATURAL REPETITION

We have a natural tendency to seek order in our lives, so it is not surprising that we discern pattern in the built environment and in nature, which is particularly rich in examples. Spiderwebs, leaf skeletons, tree branches and annual rings, rippling sand, are just a few examples from the many to be found.

Often patterns are not obvious from a normal viewpoint but reveal themselves only from a distance or from close up. The strongest patterns, easily spotted by the naked eye, are made up of a single shape repeated many times in a regular design, such as the cells in a beehive, but more subtle ones can be made up of less regular elements – the arrangement of leaves and branches in a shrub, for example. These patterns are often enhanced by the two-dimensional nature of photographs.

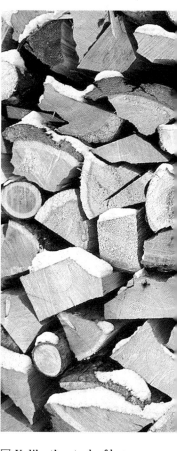

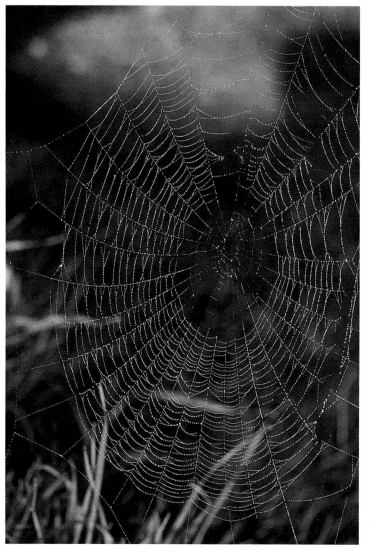

▽ Unlike the stack of logs, the delicately toned leaves of this succulent create a discordant pattern, given clarity because the third dimension has been subdued in the photograph.

*Pentax LX, 100 mm macro, Kodak Ektachrome 64, 1/60 sec, f11*

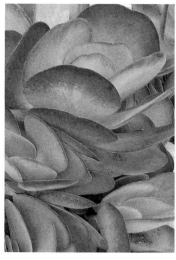

△ One of nature's most beautiful designs, the cobweb, is best photographed in the early morning, back-lit and moist with dew. It can be separated from the background by the use of a relatively wide aperture.

*Pentax LX, 100 mm macro, Kodak Ektachrome 64, 1/125 sec, f8*

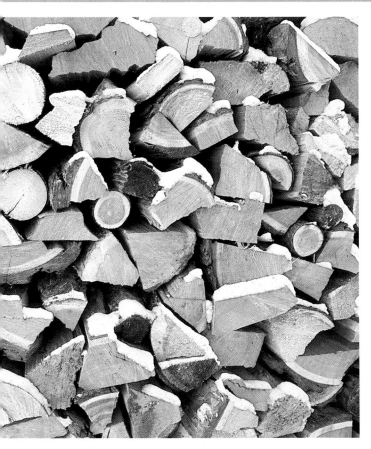

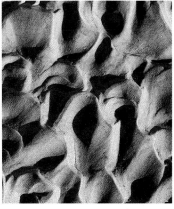

△ Just as the wind shapes snow into patterns, so the sea makes designs with sand. A gently sloping beach such as this is sculpted afresh with the ebb and flow of every tide.

*Pentax LX, 50 mm macro, Kodak Ektachrome 200, $^1/_{125}$ sec, f16*

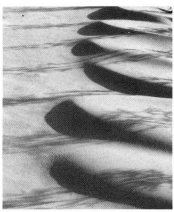

△ From across the farmyard this stack of logs appeared as a regular pattern, but, in fact, no two logs are the same shape. The pattern is created by repetition of elements of similar size and tone.

*Pentax LX, 50 mm, Kodak Ektachrome 64, $^1/_{125}$ sec, f16*

▽ The most prominent pattern in this picture of rice fields is that of the terrace walls. Then there are the broader bands of the terraces themselves and, on a smaller scale, the rice plants.

*Pentax LX, 150 mm, Kodak Ektachrome 64, $^1/_{125}$ sec, f16*

△ Wind-blown snow has eddied around these tree trunks, creating a pattern. Highlighted by weak winter sun, their shadows mingle with those cast by other trees.

*Pentax LX, 50 mm, Kodak Ektachrome 64, $^1/_{125}$ sec, f16*

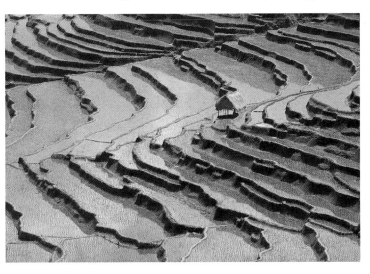

See also:
SPECIAL LENSES pp26-27
USING BACKLIGHT pp34-35
FILLING THE FRAME pp42-43
PATTERN AND DETAIL pp58-59

# ANIMAL STUDIES

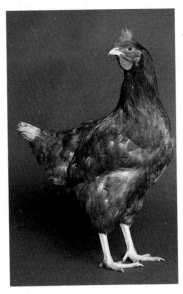

Animals, whether wild or domesticated, are notoriously difficult to photograph. They are unpredictable and often make unwilling subjects. In addition, wildlife photography involves a great deal more than simple photographic skills; you have to be something of a naturalist as well. Good wildlife pictures can rarely be made by an inexperienced photographer with a casual approach, as it is essential to have detailed knowledge of the subject's habitat and way of life. Under certain circumstances, such as on a photographic safari or field trip with a guide, exciting shots can be taken, but a large element of luck is involved and it may be days before a good chance is offered. Animal photography therefore requires patience as well as specialized knowledge or expert guidance.

Even in the comparatively controlled surroundings of a safari park or a zoo, good picture opportunities are both rare and fleeting. It often helps to seek the advice of a warden or keeper who may suggest the best times to photograph. Other sources of valuable information are local naturalist societies and clubs, who will welcome a photographer as a new member.

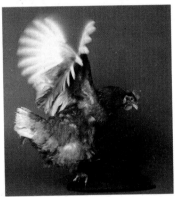

◁ An unusual subject for a studio portrait, this prized chicken – in reality, a family pet – proved to be more than a handful when it came to posing. It was most unwilling to stand still for the exposure, so the decision was made to use electronic flash to freeze movement (see top picture) and get one clear shot. After that had been achieved, a more experimental picture, capturing the bird's energy and vitality, was tried. An ambient light with flash exposure proved successful; the result is the picture at the bottom.

*Top picture: Hasselblad, 120 mm, Kodak Ektachrome 64, $^1/_{500}$ sec, f16*

*Bottom picture: Hasselblad, 120 mm, Kodak Ektachrome 64, $^1/_{30}$ sec, f16*

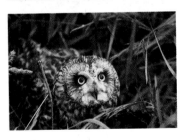

△ Close-up portraits of animals are much easier in controlled surroundings. This photograph was made in an owl-breeding sanctuary. The keeper's familiar presence calmed the bird, so that a relatively short lens could be used, giving a more natural perspective.

*Leicaflex, 90 mm macro, Kodak Ektachrome 200, $^1/_{125}$ sec, f8*

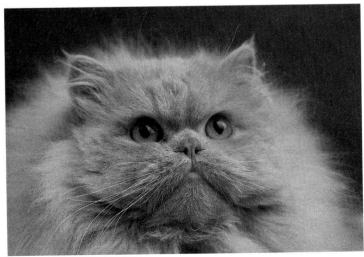

△ An affectionate cat, purring with pleasure from being stroked, needed no coercion to remain still. As with people, it is important to focus on the eyes and use a small aperture when shooting at close range.

*Hasselblad, 120 mm, Kodak Ektachrome 64, $^1/_{250}$ sec, f8*

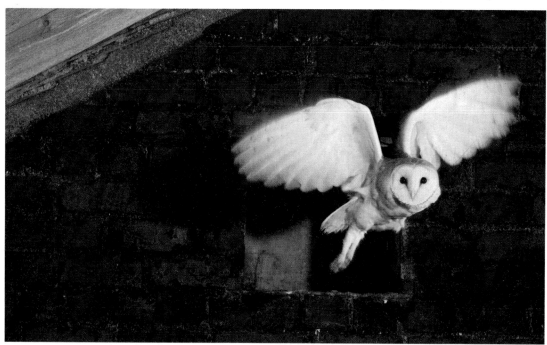

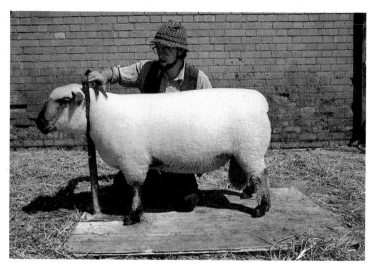

△ You need to know the runs or flight paths of nocturnal animals and to set up the equipment in daylight.

*Leicaflex, 135 mm, Kodak Ektachrome 200, $^1/_{125}$ sec, f8*

◁ Even in wildlife parks, where animals come quite close, a long lens can prove useful.

*Pentax LX, 350 mm, Kodak Ektachrome 200, $^1/_{250}$ sec, f8*

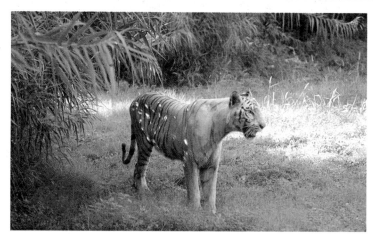

◁ When officially photographing show animals, it is important to maintain the correct perspective and proportions.

*Pentax LX, 135 mm, Kodak Ektachrome 64, $^1/_{250}$ sec, f8*

See also:
THE TELEPHOTO LENS pp22-23
SPECIAL LENSES pp26-27
CAPTURING MOVEMENT pp60-61
BLURRING MOVEMENT pp62-63

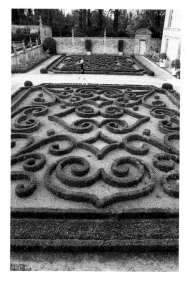

△ Formal gardens are composed of strong geometric designs which can make graphic images. The severe and rather barren landscape created by such formality is relieved here by including the girl's figure.

*Pentax LX, 24 mm, Kodak Ektachrome 64, ¹/₁₂₅ sec, f8*

▷ Garden pictures sometimes lack a centre of interest, so it can be a good idea to include statues, a seat, or a garden building such as a gazebo, to provide a counterpoint to the plants.

*Pentax LX, 28 mm, Kodak Ektachrome 64, ¹/₁₂₅ sec, f11*

▷ Popular gardens hold a special problem for the photographer – crowds of people. Although a scattering of people is sometimes appropriate, too many will spoil the shot. For this shot of a Baroque garden in Tuscany it was necessary to wait until lunchtime for the crowds to clear.

*Pentax LX, 24 mm, Kodak Ektachrome 64, ¹/₂₅₀ sec, f11*

Gardens are a wonderful subject to photograph; they come in an endless variety of shapes and sizes and are located the world over. Arguably, Britain has the finest selection, ranging from the small cottage garden with its colourful herbaceous borders to the landscaped vistas that surround the great country houses. Other European countries have a different tradition, often tending towards more formal creations along the lines of the magnificent Versailles. Whatever the scale and style of gardens, they are usually fascinating and offer the photographer both a wide range of subjects and scope for a broad deployment of photographic techniques.

Start by exploring the garden. Many are planned as a series of different elements, although only a few will be in their prime at any one time. A quick tour will enable you to absorb the garden's broad concept as well as its notable features. It is worth remembering, for example, that suburban gardens are frequently designed as a setting for the house, and good viewpoints are likely to be from a distance. Gardens that surround a grand manor are often best viewed from near the house, or even from inside. Many larger gardens are laid out with the surrounding landscape in mind, with broad vistas over parkland and local woods, so look for the landscape shot as well as for detail.

Spring, early summer, and autumn are generally the best times to photograph gardens, as many plants are then at their most beautiful. Gardens open to the public tend to be crowded at these times, so it is best to arrive early or wait until evening.

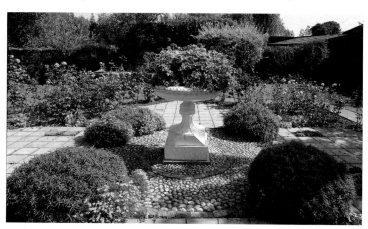

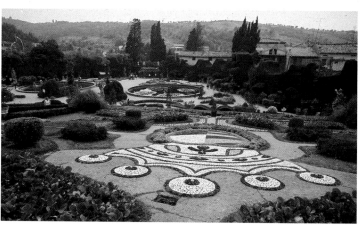

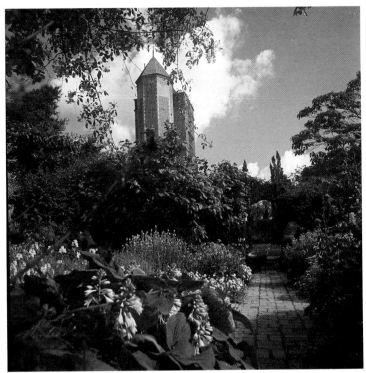

◁ Sissinghurst in Kent is one of the world's great gardens and typifies the English approach of combining a series of small, quite different gardens. The low viewpoint emphasizes the exuberant display of flowers and a feeling of depth is given by the relationship of the nearby plants and the distant tower.

*Rolleiflex, 80 mm, Kodak Ektachrome 64, 1/125 sec, f8*

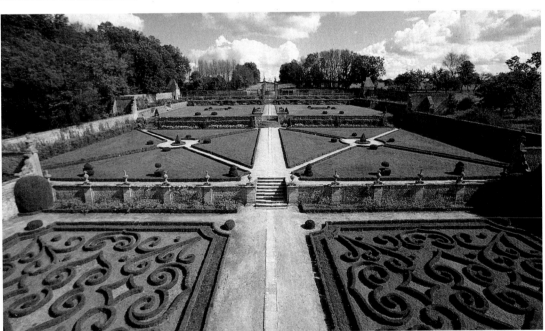

△ Many of the grander gardens of Europe, such as the one at Versailles, are based on the formal designs pioneered in the 17th and 18th centuries. The overall pattern is best seen from a high vantage point; in the case of this French garden the best view was from a room on the top floor of the château. A wide-angle lens was used to exaggerate perspective and make the most of the strong linear patterns.

*Pentax LX, 24 mm, Kodak Ektachrome 64, 1/250 sec, f8*

See also:
VIEWPOINT AND SCALE pp48-49
COMPOSING THE SHOT pp52-53
VARIETIES OF LIGHT pp68-69
EVENING LIGHT pp140-141

# THE VERSATILE LENS

The macro lens was first developed as a specialist optic, designed for medical and scientific photography. It was not long before wildlife photographers recognized its remarkable potential for revealing nature in new ways, but these lenses were not widely used by other photographers until new designs improved the optical performance at more usual focusing distances. Modern macros are multi-purpose, capable of focusing from infinity down to very close distances.

Macros are available in many focal lengths, from wide-angle to mid-range telephotos, but the most useful are the standard (50 mm) and short-telephoto versions (85-100 mm) for the 35 mm format. The short telephoto is the pictorial photographer's favourite. The short-telephoto macro has an extremely wide focusing range – from about 0.5 m to infinity – and enables you to fill the frame with images up to half life-sized. Close-up photography demands an extensive depth of field, so these lenses are designed to stop down to f32 or f45. These small apertures can also be useful at more normal focusing distances.

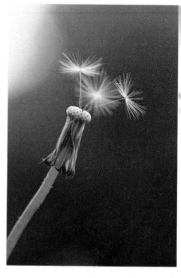

△ Photographing this dandelion's seed head against a dark background has accentuated the delicate rim light created by the last rays of a setting sun.

*Pentax LX, 100 mm macro, Kodak Ektachrome 64, 1/60 sec, f8*

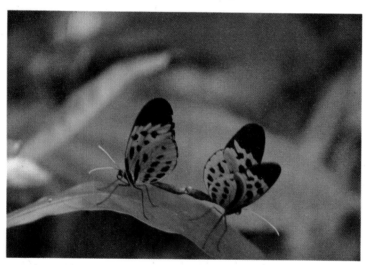

△ Insects are normally highly active, making them difficult to photograph in close-up. Choose a moment when they are still to maintain focus and framing.

*Pentax LX, 50 mm macro, Kodak Ektachrome 200, autoexposure, f8*

▷ Macro lenses are ideal for making selective images of subjects in the middle distance where surrounding detail would prove too distracting.

*Pentax LX, 50 mm macro, Kodak Ektachrome 64, 1/125 sec, f8*

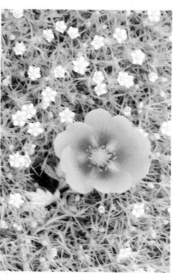

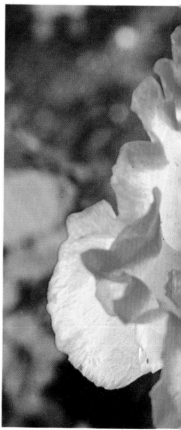

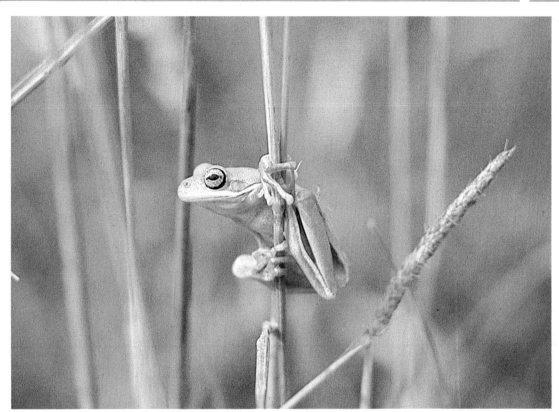

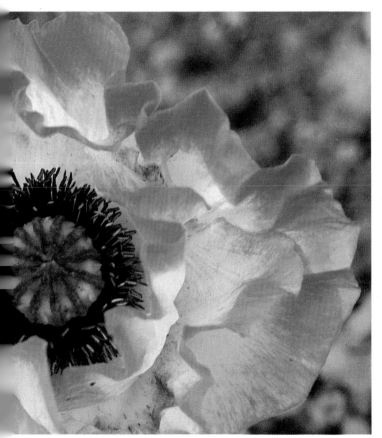

△ This well-camouflaged frog would have been lost against a background of sharply focused reeds. But, by using a wide aperture, they have been thrown out of focus to form a soft backdrop.

*Pentax LX, 100 mm macro, Kodak Ektachrome 200, 1/500 sec, f11*

◁ Even slight movement in macro photography will cause blurring so unstable subjects have to be supported. This flower was held steady by hidden wires.

*Pentax LX, 100 mm macro, Kodak Ektachrome 64, 1/30 sec, f16*

See also:
SPECIAL LENSES pp26-27
DEPTH OF FIELD pp40-41
PATTERN AND DETAIL pp58-59
IMPACT OF FLOWERS pp186-189

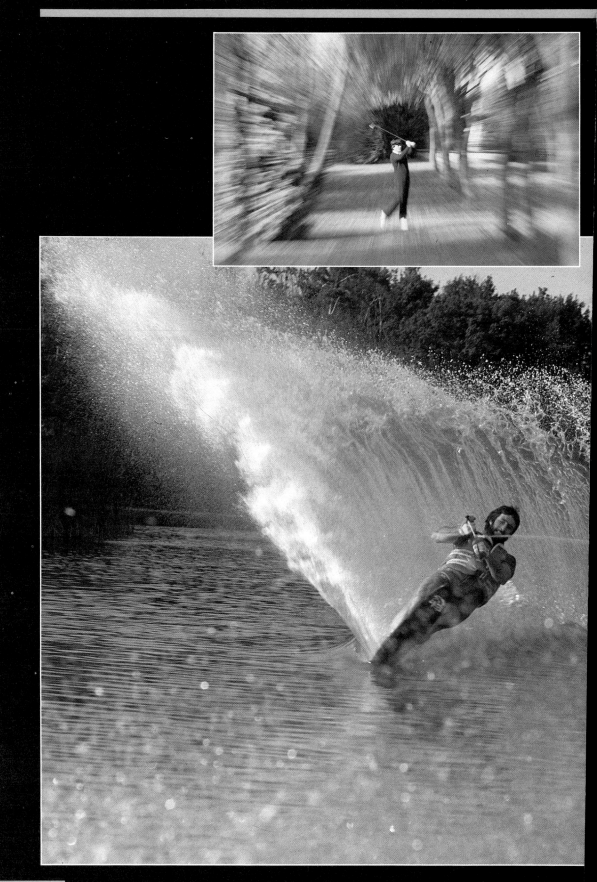

Sports are about people in action, spectators as well as competitors, and great sporting shots are as much portraits as they are photographs that capture the spirit of an event. The most photogenic moments are not always instances of high-speed action or the winner at the line; the creative sports photographer will look for situations arising out of conflict – the determined face of effort, joy at beating the odds, and the despair of failure. Good sports photography depends upon a thorough knowledge of the event, familiarity with the venue, and a flexible approach that enables you to exploit unforeseen incidents.

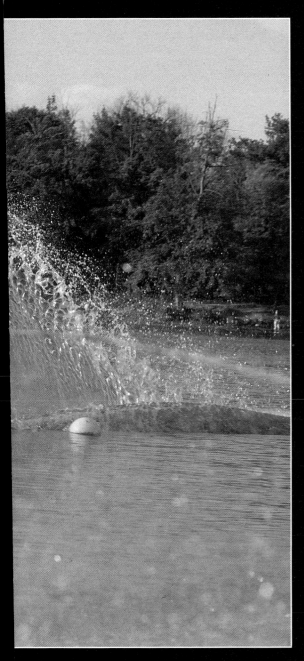

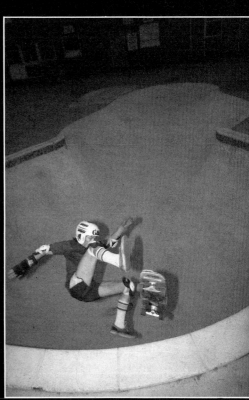

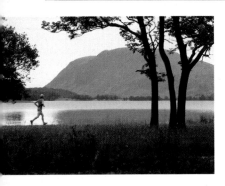

△ The viewpoint for this shot of a fell walker in the Lake District was carefully selected to silhouette the contestants as they passed. All camera controls were preset before the walkers arrived so it was just a question of waiting until they crossed the bright reflection on the lake.

*Pentax LX, 85 mm, Kodak Ektachrome 64, ¹/250 sec, f8*

Almost any sporting event, from a school sports day to the World Cup Final, offers enough picture-taking opportunities to stretch the skill and satisfy the appetite of the keenest photographer.

Sport is about competition, about people pitting their prowess, skill and determination against each other. Raw emotion – excitement, elation, aggression, defeat, dejection, misery – gives rise to intense drama that is seldom encountered elsewhere. A wealth of exciting pictures is there for the taking.

A professional photographer working for a newspaper or magazine must concentrate on capturing the winner or the height of the action, but as an amateur you can simply look for the best pictures. Excited spectators, exhausted competitors, tension at the start line, and a proud parent's praise are aspects of a sporting event that may not be newsworthy, but nevertheless provide opportunities to take excellent pictures.

Light and weather can be crucial in sports photography, where fast action can be frozen only with high shutter speeds, while typical viewpoints often dictate the use of long lenses. You need good light, even with fast film, so an overcast day is often restrictive, forcing the use of wide apertures, as well as affecting the general atmosphere. This in turn leads to limited depth of field and greater demands on your focusing abilities.

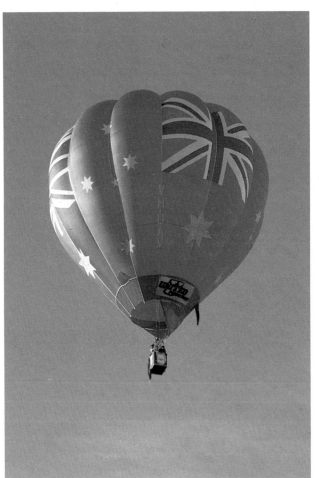

◁ Ballooning has its own special problems, especially if you are restricted to shooting from ground level. If you can hitch a ride, your chances of getting some really exciting images are greatly increased. Most events start in the early morning when rich, warm light and blue skies complement the bright colours of the envelopes. In competitions the balloons go up in quick succession, offering the chance of group pictures, but they soon disperse. This balloon was taking part in an international race.

*Pentax LX, 85 mm, Kodak Ektachrome 200, ¹/500 sec, f8*

▷ The supporters' club frequently puts as much effort, energy and enthusiasm into urging the team on as the team do in playing the game. Turning the camera away from the event can pay dividends – the resulting pictures are often very revealing.

*Pentax LX, 35 mm, Kodak Ektachrome 200, ¹/500 sec, f11*

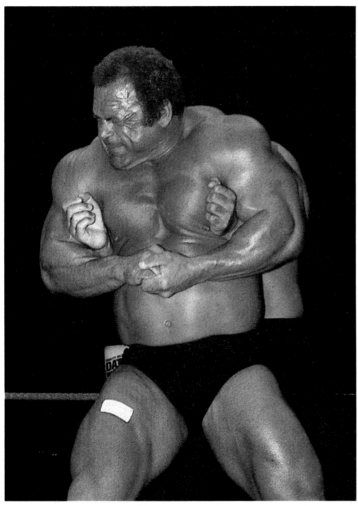

◁ Flash on camera is the best way to capture the rough and tumble of a wrestling match, but you should watch out for the ropes, as they can throw ugly shadows across the picture if they cross the flash beam. Hurtling bodies, animated expressions, and rowdy crowd scenes are all fair game for the photographer who is quick off the mark and is able to move around. Spectators at competition or exhibition matches may get annoyed if you take too much time for framing and composition, so more creative work is best left to training sessions at the local gym.

*Pentax LX, 85 mm, Kodak Ektachrome 200, X-sync, f16*

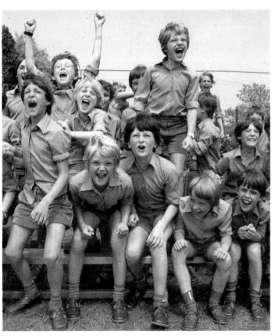

See also:
THE TELEPHOTO LENS pp22-23
FOCUSING METHODS pp44-45
CAPTURING MOVEMENT pp60-61
THE ESSENTIAL SHOT pp216-217

# THE HIGHPOINT

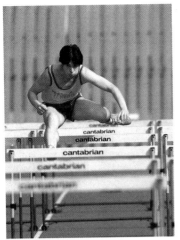

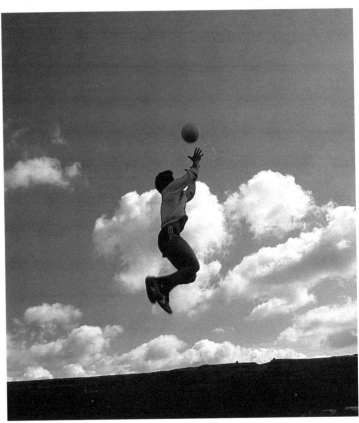

Whatever the sport, it is essential for the photographer to capture the winning moment and, if possible, to encapsulate the spirit of the event in the same shot. If you can add creative expression of movement, you have the ingredients for a truly dramatic sports picture. Despite the photographer's best endeavours, these elements rarely come together in one frame, but you should always aim to make a picture that records the vital moments and actions which decide the outcome of an event. In a horse-race, it might be the last part of the final straight, with the leaders running neck-and-neck, turf flying, a jockey throwing a quick glance at his rival, and the horses wide-eyed and with their necks straining for the winning post. Within a split second, it will all be gone. There is no need to frequent important national sporting events to capture such moments; local competitions and school sports events offer similar opportunities, the competitors showing the same elation or disappointment.

△ This telephoto shot of a hurdler does not give an accurate impression of the track, for the 'stacking' effect of the lens has brought the background forwards. However, this head-on camera position allows you to shoot several frames as the athlete approaches.

*Pentax LX, 800 mm, Kodak Ektachrome 200, ¹/₁₀₀₀ sec, f8*

▷ The highpoint is when action changes direction and slows momentarily – an ideal time to freeze movement. Here it happened at the top of the goalkeeper's leap.

*Pentax LX, 150 mm, Kodak Ektachrome 200, ¹/₂₀₀₀ sec, f8*

**Guide to minimum shutter speeds for freezing movement**

| | Medium shot | Long shot | Panning | Diagonal movement |
|---|---|---|---|---|
| Walking (3mph/5kph) | 1/250 sec | 1/125 sec | 1/30 sec | 1/125 sec |
| Running (13mph/20kph) | 1/500 sec | 1/250 sec | 1/125 sec | 1/250 sec |
| Kicking Ball | 1/1000 sec | 1/500 sec | 1/125 sec | 1/1000 sec |
| Car (50mph/80kph) | 1/4000 sec | 1/2000 sec | 1/125 sec | 1/1000 sec |

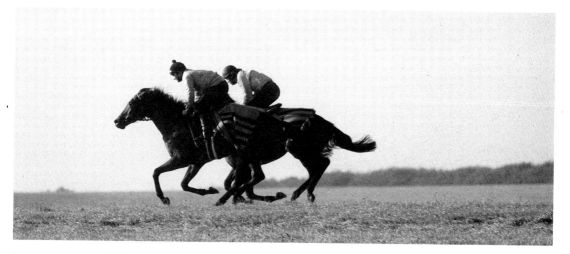

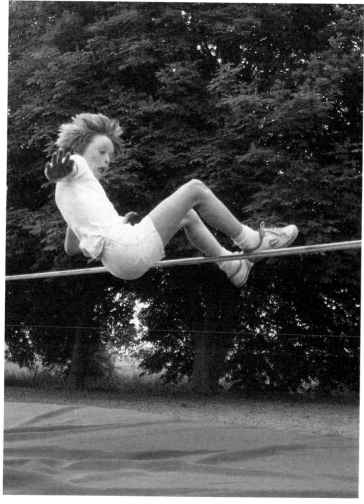

△ Training sessions are more relaxed than 'live' events and there are plenty of opportunities to take pictures that capture the spirit of a race. These two steeplechasers, galloping head-to-head during early morning exercise, are just as intent on beating each other to the end of the gallop as they would be in a race.

*Pentax LX, 85 mm, Kodak Ektachrome 200, 1/1000 sec, f8*

△ In this instant of time, frozen by the camera's fast shutter, a schoolboy achieves his ambition – a leap to clear the daunting barrier in a crucial high-jump final at the school's annual sports day.

*Pentax LX, 85 mm, Kodak Ektachrome 200, 1/500 sec, f8*

See also:
THE TELEPHOTO LENS pp22-23
FOCUSING METHODS pp44-45
VIEWPOINT AND SCALE pp48-49
CAPTURING MOVEMENT pp60-61

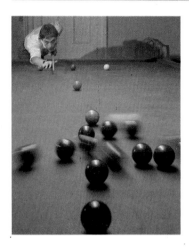

One approach to photographing fast action in sports is to attempt to freeze an instant of time by using a fast shutter speed. Results that are possibly even more exciting can be obtained by using a slow shutter speed and allowing the image to blur. You can either let the subject blur, or you can use panning, the result of which is that the subject is sharply focused but it is set against a streaked background. Make sure that you continue the pan after releasing the shutter. Stopping will cause camera jerk and spoil the image.

These techniques can be applied to almost any action in any sport. If you decide to use blur, make sure you use colour film, since successful shots rely on subject movement creating sweeps of tone across the frame, and their impact depends on contrast differences within the blurring.

Colour contrasts are commoner and have greater visual power than pure tonal contrasts that will need to be very marked to stop the picture tending towards a uniform grey tone. In the shot of the bike rider the blurred background created by panning is effective only because the bright highlights from light filtering through the trees contrasts against the dark trees.

△ Sometimes the speed of the action, in this case the moving snooker balls, is totally unpredictable and may move in many directions simultaneously. Selecting the correct shutter speed is largely down to experience – and a little luck! Try taking several shots at various speeds – for example, ¼, ⅛, 1/15 and 1/30 sec.

*Hasselblad, 80 mm, Kodak Ektachrome 200, 1/15 sec, f16*

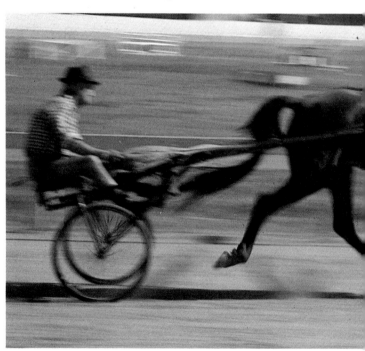

△ At track events a photographer can select a viewpoint, set up the camera, pre-focus on a section of the track and then wait for the competitors to approach before picking them up in the viewfinder to begin a pan. This shot made during a trotting race in Sydney, Australia, was taken when the horse passed directly in front of the camera. Note how its legs and the wheels are still very blurred and just some parts of the image are in fact sharp. This is because only those areas that travel in sympathy with the pan stay in one place relative to the film and are imaged sharply.

*Hasselblad, 135 mm, Kodak Ektachrome 64, 1/60 sec, f16*

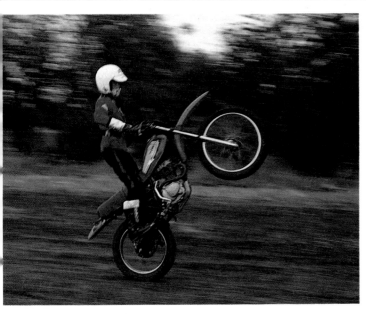

◁ Panning is the technique of following a subject with the camera and releasing the shutter as the subject passes in front of you. The smoothness and fluidity of the pan is a vital factor and it must continue for a short way after the shutter has fired. Sometimes a tripod with a panning head will help when the subject is travelling along a straight path such as a road. For this shot of a bike rider in a display team a telephoto lens was used and this had the effect of increasing the degree of blurring in the background.

*Pentax LX, 135 mm, Kodak Ektachrome 200, 1/30 sec, f22*

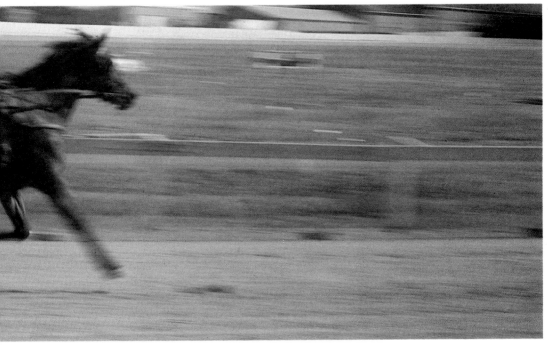

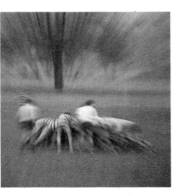

◁ Changing focal length during an exposure with a zoom lens also creates a dramatic blurring that suits some subjects. A tripod is usually necessary and zooming is most effective with a telephoto zoom lens and at shutter speeds of around 1/4-1/15 sec.

*Pentax LX, 70-210 mm, Kodak Ektachrome 200, 1/15 sec, f11*

See also:
THE TELEPHOTO LENS pp22-23
THE ZOOM LENS pp24-25
FOCUSING METHODS pp44-45
CAPTURING MOVEMENT pp60-61

# SPORT AND WATER

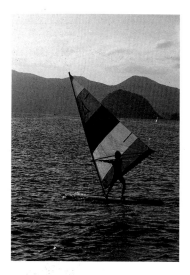

Water sports such as swimming, diving, powerboat racing, sailing, canoeing, and water skiing offer a continuous spectacle to the photographer. Stunning images can be taken during the drama of race and competition, but the nature of the events often makes exhibitions and practice sessions a better bet. There are relatively few climactic moments, so the more relaxed atmosphere away from competition will not lower the quality of your work. You may also be lucky enough to hitch a ride with a participant or use a marshal's boat as a floating camera platform. Shooting from a boat takes a degree of expertise to cope with being tossed about and still keep the camera steady and the horizons straight. You must also be careful that your equipment does not get wet, particularly when photographing saltwater events, as salt is particularly corrosive.

△ Not all sports pictures need to be dramatic action shots – there is plenty of scope to shoot images that set the scene and capture the spirit of the sport. Windsurfing conjures up images of exotic islands in the sun. This image contains the right evocative elements – sun, sparkling seas and bright light – to depict the sport as an exhilarating and pleasurable recreation.

*Pentax LX, 85 mm, Kodak Ektachrome 64, 1/250 sec, f8*

▽ The stern of the tow launch is the best place to capture images of the plumes of spray thrown up by water skiers. The most effective pictures are produced when the spray is back- or side-lit, especially by a low sun.

*Pentax LX, 75-150 mm, Kodak Ektachrome 200, 1/500 sec, f8*

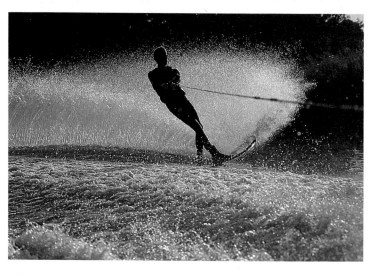

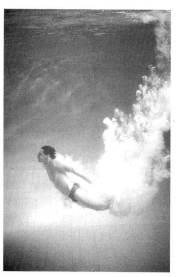

◁ Some international-standard pools have glass ports below the water level which provide a view that allows you to take shots of divers with a difference. This diver was one of a group practising at Crystal Palace, London, for a competition, so there were plenty of chances to get good pictures. Even so, it required split-second timing to capture the exact moment when the diver's body was curved upwards, followed by a trail of streaming bubbles.

*Pentax LX, 50 mm, Kodak Ektachrome 200, 1/125 sec, f5.6*

▷ Capturing dramatic action shots depends very much on viewpoint. For this shot, taken during a canoe slalom race in the turbulent waters of a Welsh river, a temporary bridge erected over the rushing water proved an excellent vantage point. From there, it was easy to see approaching competitors, anticipate their course, and isolate them from the confusion of tree-lined banks. Combined dull light and high-speed action called for a fast film.

*Pentax LX, 50 mm, Kodak Ektachrome 200, 1/250 sec, f5.6*

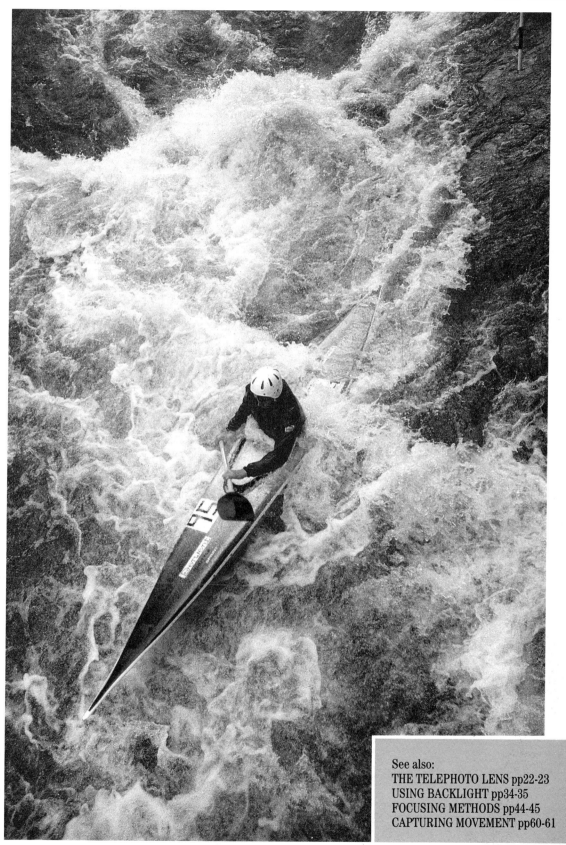

See also:
**THE TELEPHOTO LENS pp22-23**
**USING BACKLIGHT pp34-35**
**FOCUSING METHODS pp44-45**
**CAPTURING MOVEMENT pp60-61**

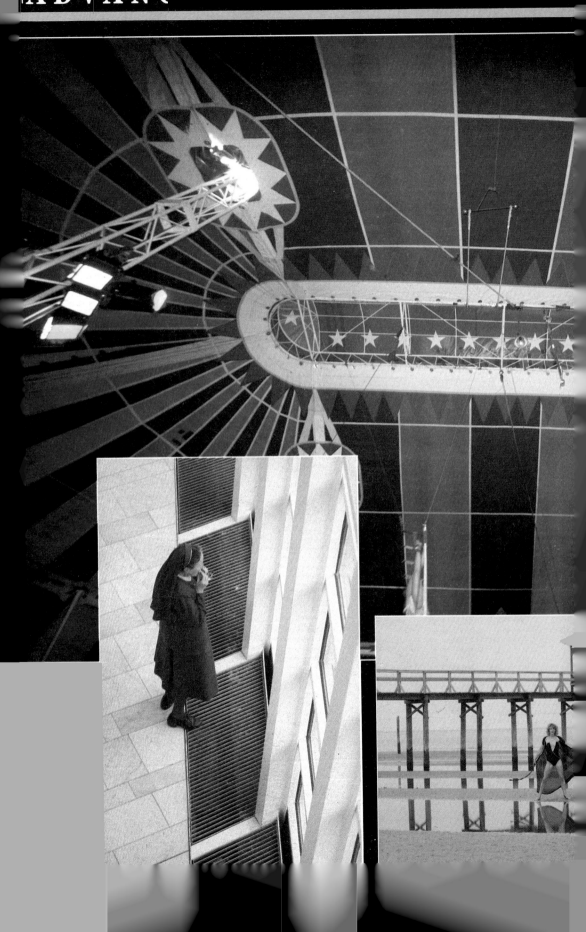

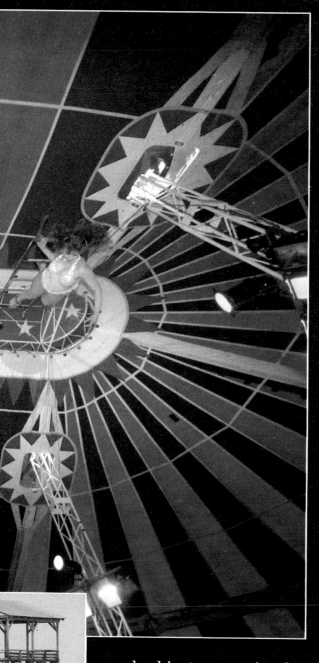

Composition is the organization of picture elements into a purposeful relationship to enrich the visual experience and simplify the understanding of an image. Attention to lighting quality, viewpoint and subject properties does not assure success. To be more than ordinary, a photograph needs compositional finesse. You can use perspective, line, or pattern to lead the eye and create balance within the frame. Mood and atmosphere may benefit from abstracting the image to a simple form of tone and line. Alternatively, you can exploit the medium with multiple images and montage.

# DIAGONAL DESIGNS

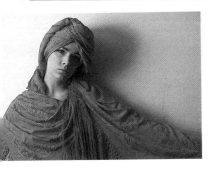

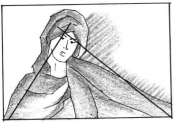

△ The framing in this picture was arranged in order that the model's pose should create three triangles. Intersecting diagonals lead the eye to the face, which is tilted to add emphasis.

*Pentax LX, 50 mm, Kodak Ektachrome 200, ¹/₃₀ sec, f11*

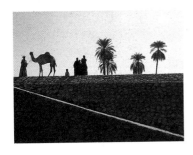

△ Early morning in Egypt. This composition in silhouette has had its graphic element dramatized by the highlighted diagonal. It cuts across and breaks up the dark mass of the wall, leading the eye to the figures.

*Pentax LX, 135 mm, Kodak Ektachrome 64, ¹/₂₅₀ sec, f8*

Most of the time we compose pictures to create a sense of order. They exhibit balance, have a single centre of interest, and make use of horizontal and vertical lines for framing and division. But there are times when a subject needs to be made more dynamic, to portray tension and imbalance. Using the diagonal is one of the simplest ways of achieving this.

Diagonals have to be emphatic. It is no use employing a slightly sloping line in an effort to enliven a classical composition; the line needs to be obvious. The most effective diagonals extend from corner to corner – a division which, of course, creates two triangles. In terms of composition, the triangle is among the strongest of shapes and evokes different emotional responses, depending on its orientation, from one of stability, when the apex is uppermost and the base is horizontal, to tottering imbalance when it is standing on a corner. It is possible to create a diagonal by angling the camera but there are many times when the result is unconvincing, for it is not simply a matter of tilting the camera. Often it is more productive to explore the subject more thoroughly and frame the shot in different ways.

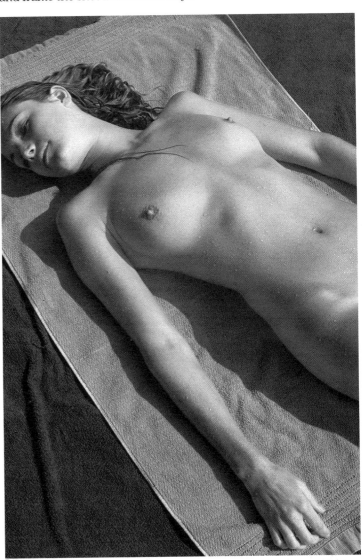

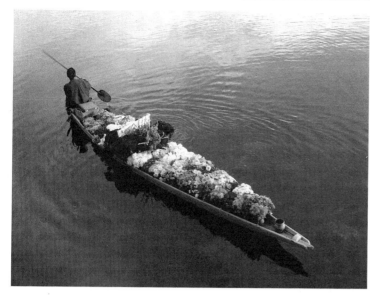

◁ Long, thin subjects such as this flowerseller's canoe on Lake Dal in Kashmir invariably benefit from diagonal framing. Conventionally framed from ground level, the boat would appear as a thin line, but a high viewpoint has isolated it and ensured that the flowers achieve maximum impact.

*Pentax LX, 85 mm, Kodak Ektachrome 64, 1/125 sec, f11*

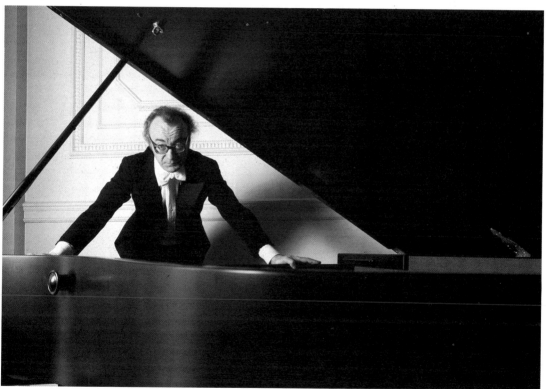

◁ The background tones contrast with the girl's tanned skin, to emphasize the diagonals and create the compositional interest. Had she been framed horizontally or vertically the result would have been much more pedestrian.

*Pentax LX, 50 mm, Kodak Ektachrome 64, 1/125 sec, f11*

△ Pianist Alfred Brendel's portrait was made in a very confined area. But the piano with its diagonals and triangles offered the perfect setting. The strong flash lighting and tonal contrast enhance the effect.

*Hasselblad, 80 mm, Kodak Ektachrome 64, 1/125 sec, f16*

See also:
LIGHT AND CONTRAST pp32-33
FILLING THE FRAME pp42-43
VIEWPOINT AND SCALE pp48-49
FRAMING THE SUBJECT pp50-51

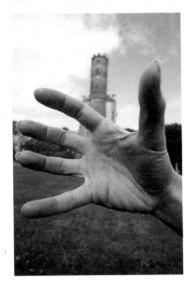

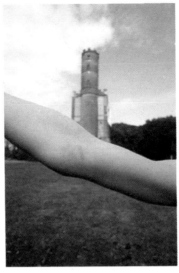

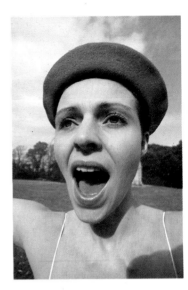

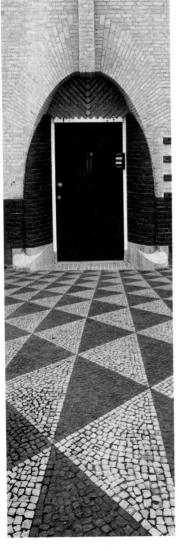

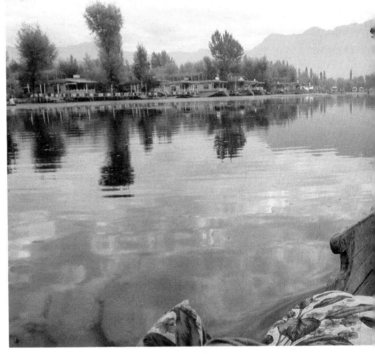

◁ Synthesis, rather than fragmentation, is another technique available to the creative photographer. This scene is created from two entirely separate images, taken at different times in two different places – the mosaic pavement in Rio de Janeiro and the doorway in Amsterdam. Together, they form a satisfying and convincing whole.

*Doorway: Pentax LX, 50 mm, Kodak Ektachrome 64, $^1/_{125}$ sec, f8*

*Pavement: Pentax LX, 28 mm, Kodak Ektachrome 64, $^1/_{125}$ sec, f11*

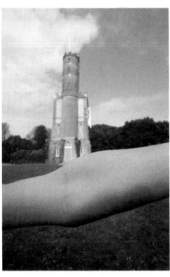 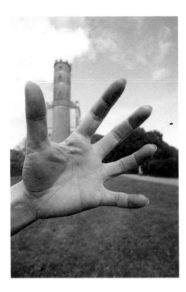

◁ When the subject is appropriate, loosely planned fragmented images can result in some amusing pictures. Here the distortion of the wide lens has been used to good effect by photographing a girl at very close range. The camera was moved between each exposure, describing a slight curve to increase the bow effect.

*Pentax LX, 18 mm, Kodak Ektachrome 64, autoexposure, f5.6*

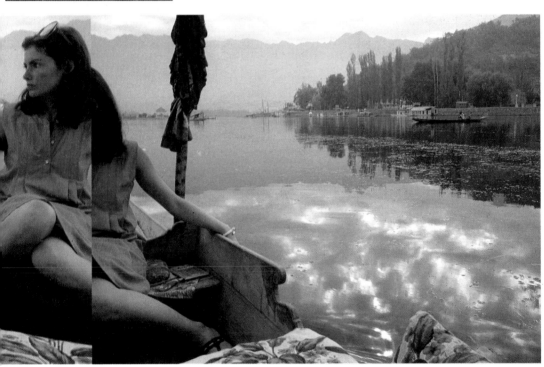

△ One of the commonest uses of joining a number of images together is to create a panoramic view, often to emphasize the expanse and tranquillity of a particular landscape. In many cases, there is no need to be ultra-precise when framing the shots, as long as some degree of overlap is allowed for. Using a wide lens, a broad vista can usually be included in just two shots. This picture was made on Lake Dal, Kashmir.

*Pentax LX, 28 mm, Kodak Ektachrome 64, 1/125 sec, f11*

# SPLITTING IMAGES

Fragmenting an image by means of multiple exposure can be a very fruitful method of making your images transcend the bounds of reality. The technique is very simple, needing no special equipment and no complex image manipulation, but the results can be fascinating, breaking up what would normally appear on a single frame into pieces and giving a unique view of the subject, like a dismantled jigsaw puzzle. The whole image can be composed of many parts – from two to hundreds – formed by moving the camera slightly between exposures. There is no need to use one subject or to keep the movements in the same plane. Different figures can be mixed together, or the same one can be rebuilt. Moving images can be mixed with static ones, backgrounds can be changed, and so can lenses. Even film edges can be trimmed to suit whatever effect the photographer is looking for. No special lighting is needed and no extra space is necessary. It is usually best to work with the camera on a tripod so that each change in viewpoint can be selected with accuracy. Tape markers can be placed at the corners of the viewed area to help align the next exposure in the series.

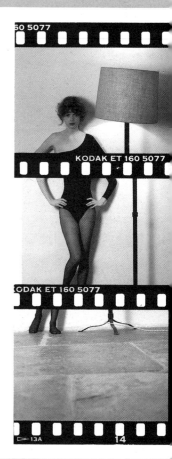

The three examples here were built up in a similar way, using just a camera and a tripod. The backgrounds have been kept plain in order to simplify the result. Complex backgrounds can create a confusing effect when split up and reassembled. Each picture was carefully planned, since one misplaced shot may ruin the whole image. A visualization can be done first in the form of a sketch.

*Pentax LX, 100 mm macro, Kodak Ektachrome 160 Tungsten*

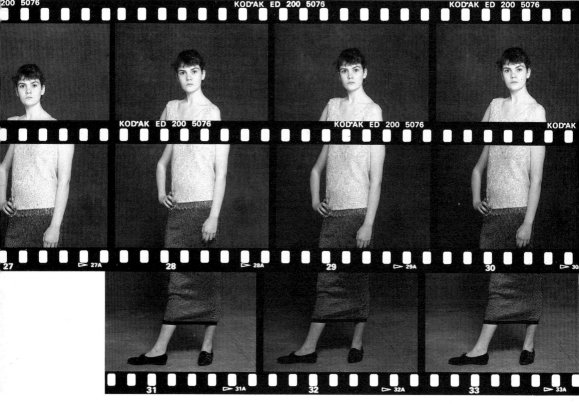

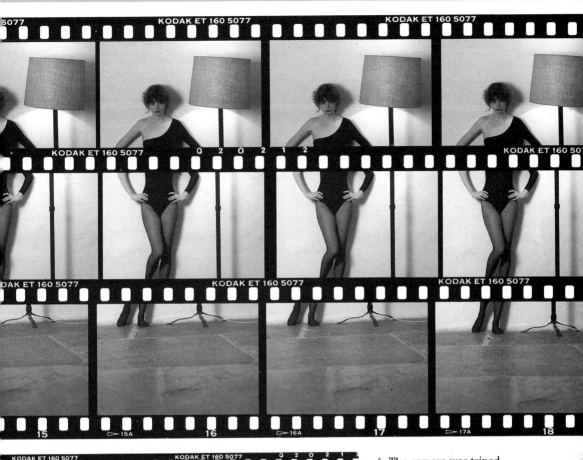

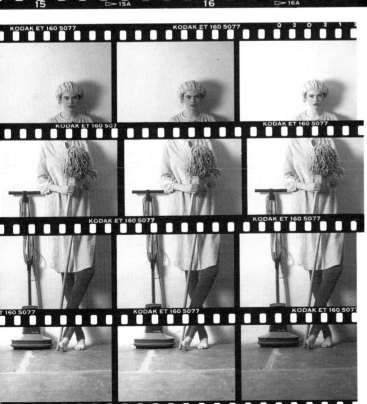

△ The camera was tripod-mounted and, starting from a height of about 2 m (6 ft), it was lowered for a fixed amount for each successive exposure sequence. Tape markers were used to assist in the repositioning of the camera.

See also:
FRAMING THE SUBJECT pp50-51
TUNGSTEN LIGHTING pp78-79
STUDY IN MOSAIC pp238-239

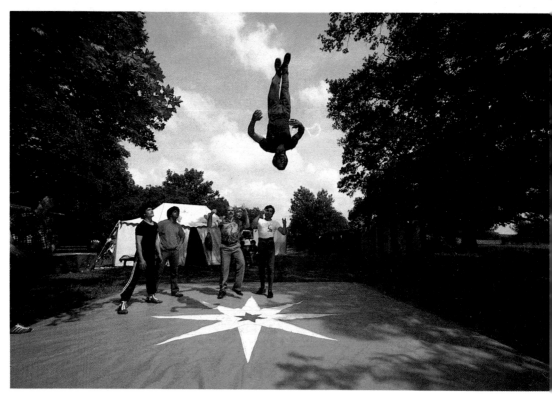

△ These acrobats were practising in a field without the benefit of a trampoline; one mistake in their split-second timing could have been fatal. Anticipating that the climax of their show would be when the acrobat was in mid-air, the picture was taken from ground level, with the acrobat framed dramatically against the sky.

*Pentax LX, 28 mm, Kodak Ektachrome 200, $^1/_{1000}$ sec, f8*

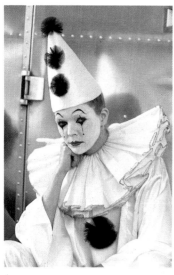

△ This poignant image of a melancholy clown is a portrait of the performer and gives considerable insight into his character. The soft light of open shadow and the muted tones ensure that there are no harsh contrasts to destroy the mood.

*Pentax LX, 135 mm, Kodak Ektachrome 200, $^1/_{125}$ sec, f8*

A photographer must, every time a subject is framed in the viewfinder, choose a moment in time and select a view from a multitude of possibilities. Even modest success depends on an ability to understand, either intuitively or consciously, what makes an image work. But to achieve excellence, to capture something of the precise moment, requires more.

With all subjects – active or passive – there are certain qualities that do more than just describe their physical state of colour, shape and form. These qualities include time, tension, balance, rhythm, atmosphere and attitude. A photograph that captures these more elusive elements – the taut muscles of an acrobat poised for action, an expression of anguish or loss, the subtlety of light on a landscape, the quiet of evening – is almost assured of capturing the essence of the subject. The most successful sports photography depicts not just the decisive moment and the peaks of the action, but the effort, fatigue, and even failure involved. Sometimes it may not be possible to combine all the desired elements into a single image to describe a subject fully, but it should always be the photographer's ambition to do so. Acute observation, anticipation, quick reflexes, and a sympathy with the subject are as important as technique.

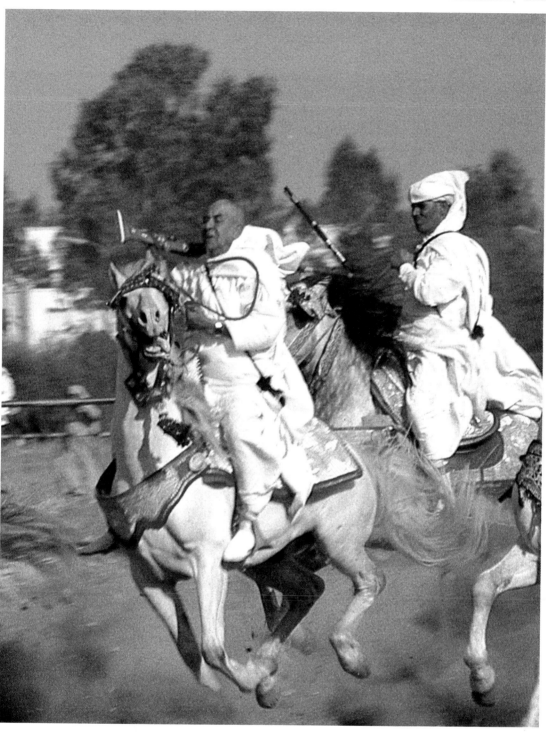

△ Events such as these races and displays of superb horsemanship in Morocco provide a continuous spectacle of skill and excitement. Precise moments that encapsulate the drama taking place amid the heat and frenzy of flying dust were numerous but fleeting, with the result that while many exciting moments were captured, many were lost.

*Pentax LX, 200 mm, Kodak Ektachrome 200, ¹/₁₀₀₀ sec, f8*

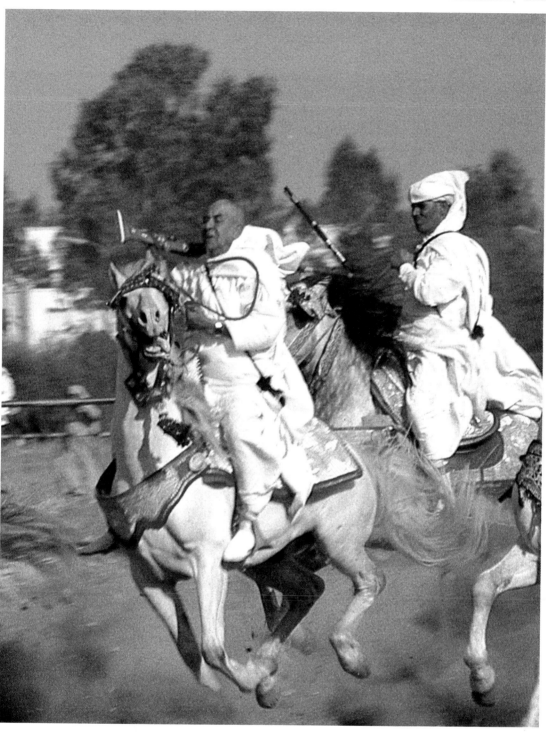

See also:
**SOFT AND HARD LIGHT pp36-39**
**CAPTURING MOVEMENT pp60-61**
**SPORT & ACTION pp198-207**

217

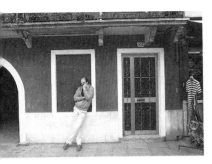

It is a fault of many photographers that they try to include too much in a picture, overloading it with superfluous detail. But this can be easily avoided by selective cropping. The simplest and most effective methods are to get closer to the subject or to use a longer lens. Moving in close simplifies the picture and makes the essential image area larger and so more significant. All too often, when the final print is viewed, you find that the key part of the image is lost, overshadowed by distracting detail. By cutting it out, you can reveal a much broader and deeper interpretation. The key to creative cropping is to experiment with framing and viewpoint. Ask yourself, for example, if a landscape is improved by using an 85 mm lens rather than a 28 mm. The final image may be distilled to just a fragment of the original view, but this can produce a far stronger visual statement.

△ A man relaxes against a wall in a Venice street. His pose, the textures of the wall, and the geometric backdrop were all strong elements. The first shot includes them all but there is much distracting detail and more than one focus of interest, so that the eye tends to wander aimlessly around the picture.

▷ The second picture was taken with the same lens a few seconds later. The extraneous detail has been discarded and the image reduced to its key elements: the man and his pose, and the strong lines of the background. An added bonus was his positive reaction to being photographed.

*Pentax LX, 28 mm, Kodak Ektachrome 64, 1/60 sec, f8*

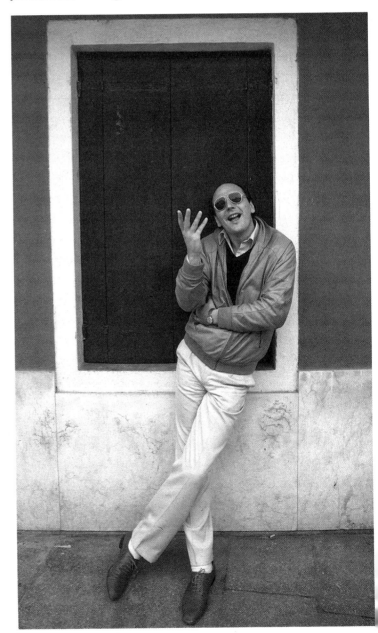

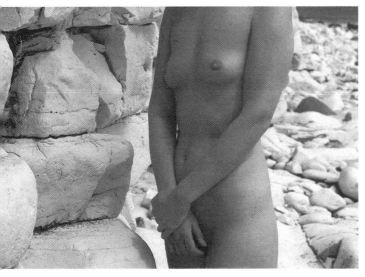

◁ Coastal areas offer many superb settings for pictures of the female form. While there is intentionally little actual information in the picture, there is enough to suggest sea, beach, and cliff. Tight cropping depersonalizes the model, so that her torso becomes more a part of the overall scene. This selective view is enriched by the skin tone, which contrasts with the textured rock and the sea and sky.

*Pentax LX, 50 mm, Kodak Ektachrome 64, ¹/₂₅₀ sec, f11*

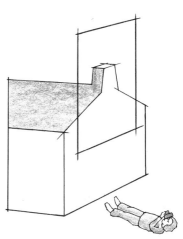

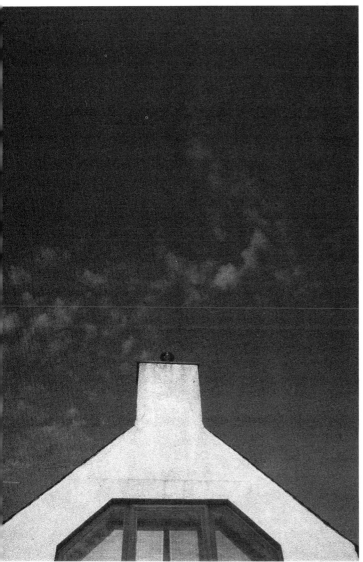

◁ △ An image of stark simplicity that is entirely the product of adopting a very low viewpoint. It is the top of an otherwise undistinguished building which was bathed in sunlight. Concentrating on a limited area creates an almost abstract image that is dramatized by the outlined shape.

*Pentax LX, 28 mm, Scotch (3M) 1000, ¹/₁₀₀₀ sec, f16*

See also:
THE TELEPHOTO LENS pp22-23
FILLING THE FRAME pp42-43
VIEWPOINT AND SCALE pp48-49
FRAMING THE SUBJECT pp50-51

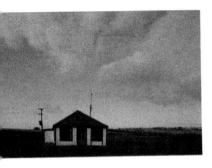

Any strong photographic image should contain mood and atmosphere, and the accomplished photographer should be able to recognize and exploit the picture elements that create them. Strength of mood does not necessarily mean drama, as in, say, a picture of dark brooding castle walls silhouetted against a stormy sky. Mood can encompass the whole spectrum of human emotions from lighthearted humour to the depths of misery. Mood is an elusive abstract quality that is difficult to define, and you will have to rely on your intuition to respond to it appropriately. In any case, you should aim to exclude elements that distract from or distort the mood.

These pictures have a strong mood of isolation. You can create such an impression in most environments by selecting elements that convey a sense of separateness. These might be compositional, such as the relative size of the subject in relation to the surroundings, or you might capture a gesture or expression that suggests sadness or loss. The crucial point is to recognize the mood and atmosphere and then tune the composition to underline them strongly but subtly.

△ The large expanse of sky and the use of a gritty fast film have heightened the bleak atmosphere of this picture of an isolated cottage on the Yorkshire coast.

*Pentax LX, 24 mm, Scotch (3M) 1000, 1/500 sec, f16*

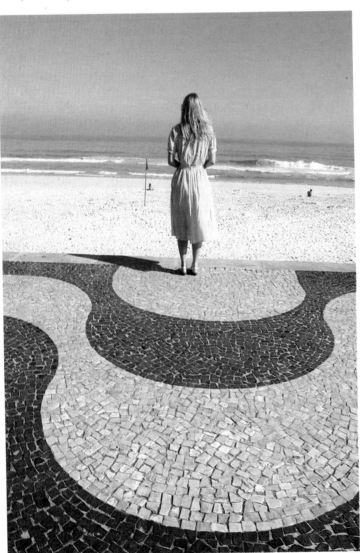

◁ In the early hours of a summer morning a wide beach is populated by just two people, sitting well apart and gazing out to sea. The girl, back to the camera and with hands clasped in front of her, is distanced both from the other figures and the viewer by careful arrangement of the composition. The atmosphere of isolation is tinged with one of sadness, largely as a result of the girl's pose.

*Pentax LX, 28 mm, Kodak Ektachrome 64, 1/250 sec, f8*

▷ The life of a travelling salesman is frequently a lonely one but that sense of isolation must be even more poignant for the man who travels the dry and dusty roads of Australia's remote outback, not seeing a soul for days at a time. Taken in the main street of Coober Pedy, this shot features the solitary shape of one such salesman. The atmosphere of remoteness has been accentuated by recording the subject as a small silhouette balanced against an expanse of dusty street.

*Leicaflex, 35 mm, Kodak Tri-X, 1/1000 sec, f16*

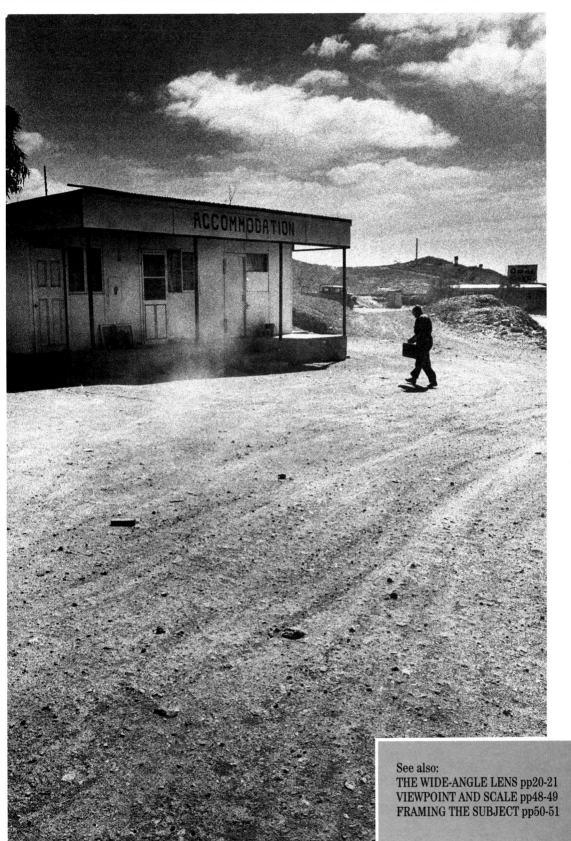

See also:
THE WIDE-ANGLE LENS pp20-21
VIEWPOINT AND SCALE pp48-49
FRAMING THE SUBJECT pp50-51

# UNUSUAL ANGLES

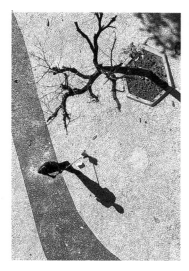

△ An overhead view, taken from a hotel balcony in Rio de Janeiro. The low, directional sunlight has cast strong shadows and highlighted textures. The viewpoint gives the composition a strong sense of design.

*Pentax LX, 85 mm, Kodak Ektachrome 64, 1/125 sec, f8*

It is easy for photographers to fall into the trap of always taking pictures from eye- or waist-level. The inevitable result is a stream of images that are predictably dull, unless the subjects are very strong in themselves. Selecting an alternative view is one of our basic options when we want to add life to a composition, and often it is just a matter of departing from the two commonest shooting levels. In everyday life the normal angles of view change horizontally and we are used to seeing everything this way, but pictures taken from worm's eye or bird's eye viewpoints have an unusual quality of their own. Familiar subjects such as people, statues, and buildings become more imposing and acquire a sense of strength, towering above the viewer. Seen from above, these same subjects are diminished in relation to their surroundings and the viewer experiences a sense of domination. But raised or lowered camera positions are not the only alternative angles of view. Looking up from eye-level is perhaps the simplest change of all and often provides a refreshing perspective, especially from close range. The exploration of different viewpoints broadens the photographer's repertoire, and the aim should be for it to become second nature once conventional methods are familiar.

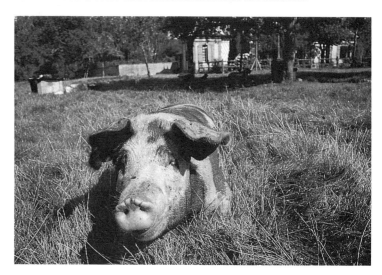

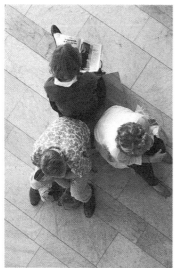

◁ Modern buildings often incorporate well-lit public spaces that can be viewed from a high vantage point such as a walkway or balcony. This picture comments on the planners' indifference to human scale and needs. Odd seats, uncomfortably spaced, enforced an awkward meeting of complete strangers. Naturally, people chose not to linger.

*Pentax LX, 85 mm, Kodak Ektachrome 200, 1/60 sec, f16*

△ A piglet's eye view of mother. The pig's snout is an unmistakable feature, and the most important and sensitive part of its anatomy, so that it is natural to give it prominence. This was done by lying on the grass and taking the shot using a wide-angle lens to exaggerate perspective.

*Pentax LX, 28 mm, Kodak Ektachrome 200, 1/60 sec, f16*

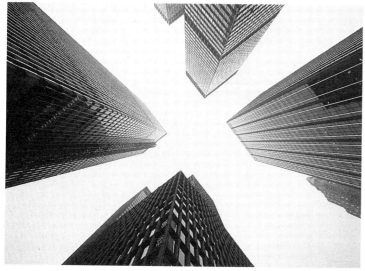

◁ An ultra-wide lens was used to capture this dizzy view of New York skyscrapers seen from the street, an almost compulsory view for the visitor. The perspective distortion characteristic of short-focal-length lenses emphasizes the towering dominance of the buildings. The best vantage point for these shots is usually the middle of the street, so the photographer needs to exercise great caution.

*Pentax LX, 18 mm, Kodak Ektachrome 64, 1/250 sec, f8*

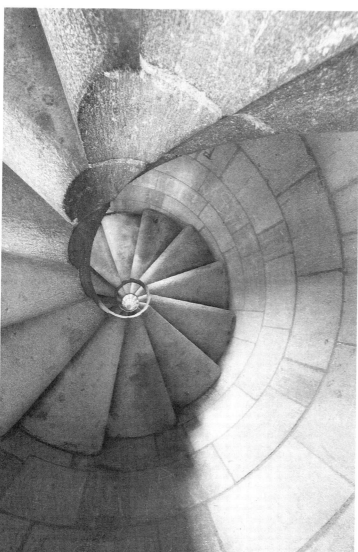

◁ Looking up a spiral stairway in the Catedral de la Sagrada Familia, in Barcelona, revealed a striking pattern and an attention to detail in an aspect of architecture that is often ignored. Searching out the alternative view helps to create good architectural photography and can yield exciting images.

*Pentax LX, 28 mm, Kodak Ektachrome 200, 1/8 sec, f22*

See also:
THE WIDE-ANGLE LENS pp20-21
LIGHT AND CONTRAST pp32-33
VIEWPOINT AND SCALE pp48-49
SHADOW DESIGNS pp144-145

# LINEAR PERSPECTIVE

Perspective is an illusion that we are accustomed to accepting without question. In photography, a three-dimensional image is convincingly represented on two-dimensional film by making distant parts of the scene appear smaller than the nearer parts of the scene. Linear perspective – where parallel lines such as railway tracks appear to converge as they recede into the distance – is one of the most convincing forms of the visual deception characteristic of perspective.

Unlike draughtsmen and painters, the photographer has no need to learn the skills of shaping perspective – the camera and its lenses see to that – but it is important to know how to use it. The convincing portrayal of three dimensions is, however, a most demanding aspect of photographic composition.

Linear perspective is greatly enhanced by using wide-angle rather than long lenses, as they tend to enlarge foreground detail in relation to distant objects. The result of this is that parallel lines are seen to converge very sharply, so creating a strong illusion of great depth.

You can further dramatize the effect by choosing scenes that contain obvious linear elements, both near and far, and by placing them so that they run obliquely from the edges of the frame. Planes and lines that feature regular patterns in texture, form or tone, will also give an added sense of realism through the device of linear perspective.

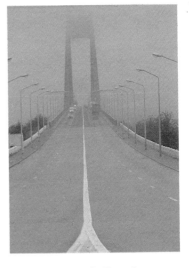

△ In this shot of a French suspension bridge, space and height are emphasized by the diminishing size and converging lines of the lamps. Use of tungsten-balanced film has added to the overall atmosphere.

*Pentax LX, 28 mm, Kodak Ektachrome 160 Tungsten, 1/125 sec, f8*

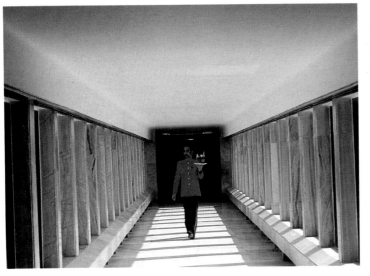

△ An advancing waiter in an Indian hotel hallway makes a simple picture taken on the spur of the moment. The linear elements leading to the one bright splash of colour were such a strong design that framing was entirely intuitive. The strong perspective depth is interrupted but enlivened by the repetitive pattern of sunlight and shade.

*Pentax LX, 50 mm, Kodak Ektachrome 64, 1/125 sec, f8*

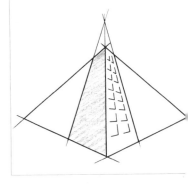

▽ Linear perspective applied to three dimensions, such as the sides of a building, creates three vanishing points at the ends of three sets of converging lines.

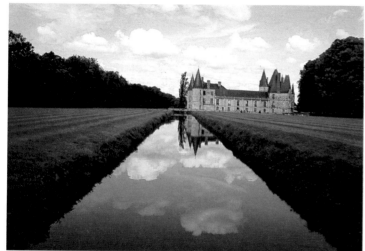

◁ The canal-moat has been dramatized by the effect of linear perspective, which has been heightened by the use of a wide-angle lens. The far château, which sits on the horizon, appears more distant than might be expected and the parallel banks of the canal widen sharply as they approach the foreground. The whole effect has been strengthened by adopting a landscape format.

*Pentax LX, 28 mm, Kodak Ektachrome 64, $^{1}/_{125}$ sec, f16*

◁ The original intention was to photograph the receding avenue of trees but this couple of Portuguese farmworkers entered stage left and posed, evidently wishing to be part of the picture. In fact their presence has enhanced the feeling of depth by introducing a strong foreground image to contrast with the diminishing line of trees.

*Pentax LX, 100 mm, Kodak Ektachrome 200, $^{1}/_{125}$ sec, f16*

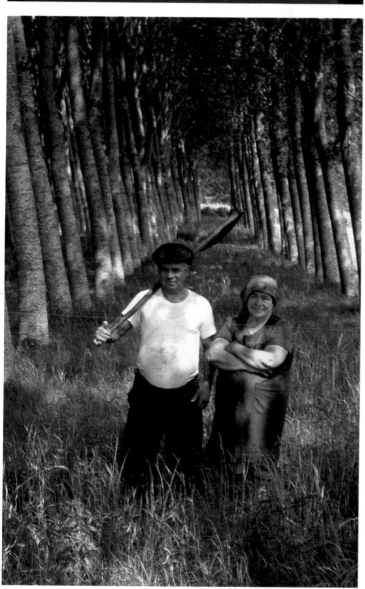

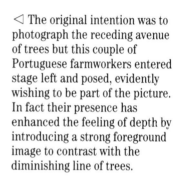

See also:
THE WIDE-ANGLE LENS pp20-21
VIEWPOINT AND SCALE pp48-49
DIAGONAL DESIGNS pp210-211

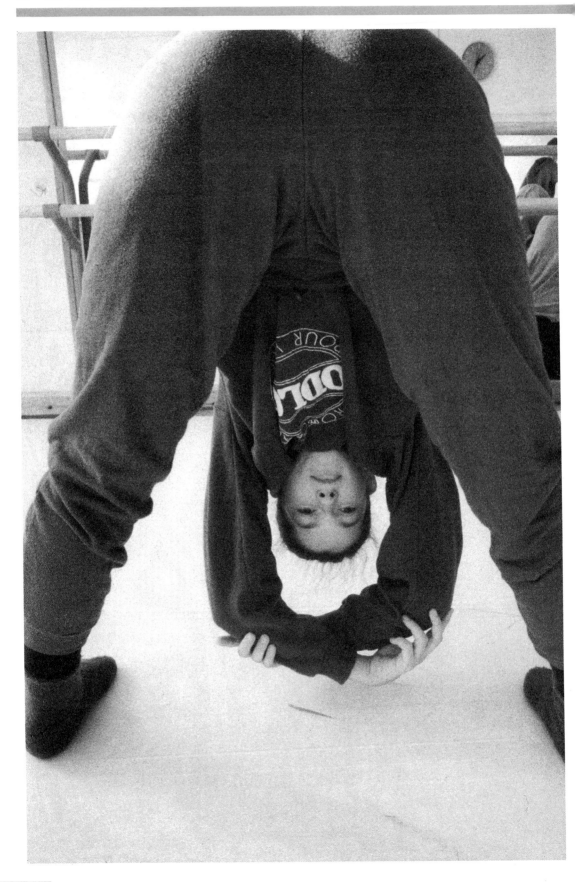

Very often, it is the way in which the photographer imposes the camera's framing on a scene that decides the outcome of the picture. The viewfinder is a cropping device, eliminating some shapes and detail while including others. What is included and how it is arranged within the picture are functions of the camera's format and the way the photographer uses the restrictions and division of its framing. But the borders of the viewfinder need not be the only way of framing a picture. It sometimes happens that part of the scene itself can echo the format, so that a picture within a picture is made. Although this frequently leads to a contrived image division, there are times when it can successfully draw the attention of the viewer to the more subtle qualities of the subject. Often-used examples are building details such as arches, windows, and doorways. They need an extra element – unusual shape, contrast, or colour – to make an arresting shot, but subjects that are not usually seen as a frame, such as hats, shafts of light, or people, may themselves supply impact. But shape is not the only compositional element that can be used as a frame. More subtle framing can be achieved by relying on colour or textural qualities.

▽ The stone archway frames and lends scale to this ancient tower in the Indian seaport of Madras, while the repetition of pointed forms strengthens the impression of soaring height.

*Pentax LX, 28 mm shift, Kodak Ektachrome 200, 1/250 sec, f11*

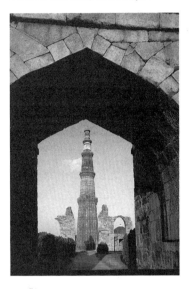

◁ The framing and the use of the shaving mirror accentuate the humour, with a hint of melancholy, characteristic of a clown's personality.

*Pentax LX, 100 mm macro, Kodak Ektachrome 200, 1/125 sec, f8*

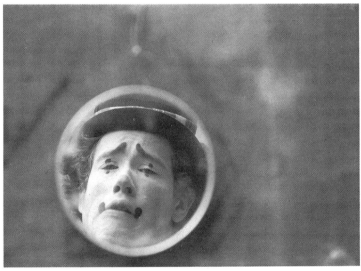

◁ It is not often that the subject provides its own frame, as this dancer has done. Her face clearly shows that she is unaware of the visual humour inherent in her pose, which has been emphasized by the choice of a wide-angle lens.

*Pentax LX, 28 mm, Kodak Ektachrome 200, 1/60 sec, f11*

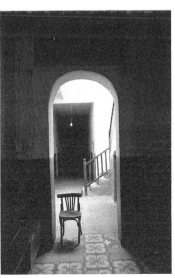

◁ Taken in a passageway in Luxor, Egypt, this picture's impact is entirely due to framing; the image is very simple and is in keeping with the style of dwelling.

*Pentax LX, 28 mm shift, Kodak Ektachrome 200, 1/30 sec, f16*

See also:
FILLING THE FRAME pp42-43
FRAMING THE SUBJECT pp50-51
COMPOSING THE SHOT pp52-53
FRAMING THE FIGURE pp262-263

227

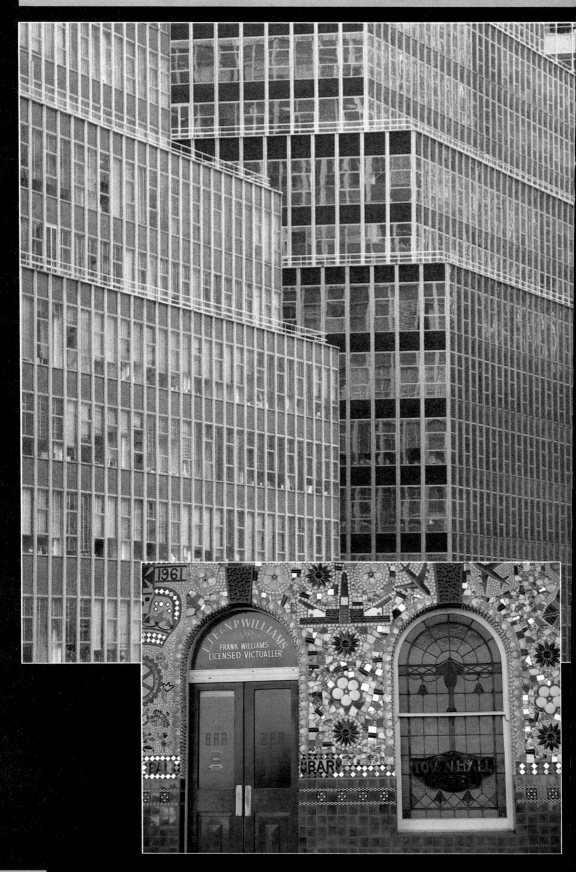

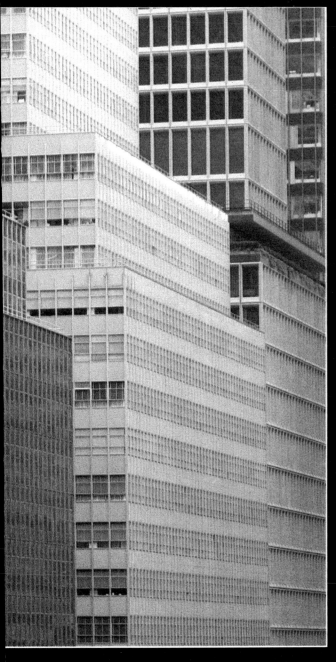

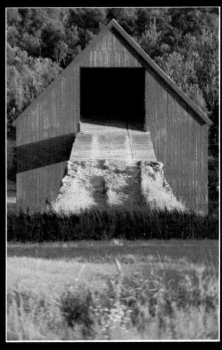

Architectural photography is fascinating and embraces a wide range of subject matter, from a straightforward record of an architect's creation in brick and stone to an abstract interpretation of a building's character. Buildings can be pictured singly or in groups, derelict and disused, or full of charm and vitality. This variety in subject matter, each aspect demanding a different kind of approach, is very challenging and it is easy to lose sight of what is really required of the image: it should display the essential character and form of a building through careful choice of viewpoint and the sympathetic use of light.

In architecture, interesting shapes and details abound and very often a photograph of a detail is more expressive than one of a whole building. Good architects pay attention to small details as well as to large, specifying furnishings and decor to fit in with their overall plan. It is in this way that individual parts can reflect the whole. To do justice to the architect's intentions, the photographer should select and frame carefully. The detail might show a good deal of the structure as a complete and coherent shape. Such pictures are best made in a sympathetic light. Rough stone or wood surfaces ought to appear textured; polished metal must gleam and reflect, and red brick or honey-coloured stone should have their warmth enriched. These qualities will be enhanced by the lighting conditions in different ways at different times of day, as the angle of the light and its colour change. This is particularly true of interiors, so it is a good idea to tour the building, making a note of where you should be and when.

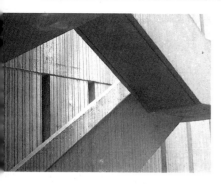

△ Reinforced concrete is a rather unfriendly material, but it has a certain graphic quality that is brought out in strong, textural light. Colour shots could be subtly altered by using weak colour-correction filters.

*Pentax LX, 28 mm shift, Kodak Ektachrome 64, 1/60 sec, f11*

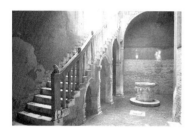

△ A corner of a courtyard in the Palazzo Fortuny in Venice encapsulates perfectly the warm and mellow atmosphere of the whole place.

*Pentax LX, 28 mm shift, Kodak Ektachrome 200, 1/250 sec, f11*

▷ Dappled light softens the impact of the strong geometric shapes in this picture of a convent school in Meknes, Morocco. The figure at the window brings the photograph to life.

*Pentax LX, 28 mm shift, Kodak Ektachrome 64, 1/125 sec, f8*

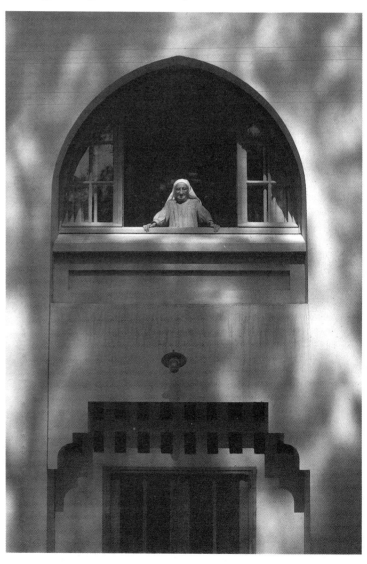

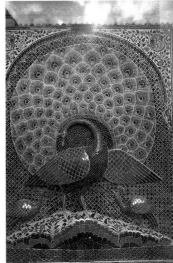

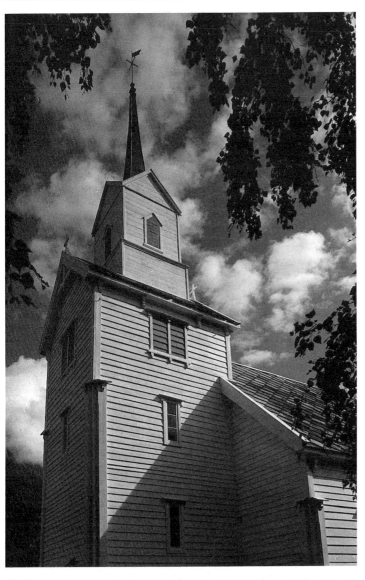

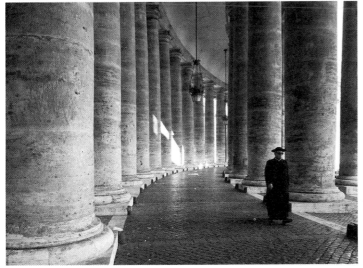

△ Islamic architecture abounds with intricate and detailed mosaic. This peacock motif had to be photographed through glass that was carefully cleaned. The lens was pressed against the surface to cut out reflections.

*Pentax LX, 35 mm Kodak Ektachrome 64, 1/250 sec, f8*

◁ A Norwegian timber-framed church built largely of rectangles set one upon the other. A low viewpoint was adopted to convey a feeling of power.

*Pentax LX, 28 mm shift, Kodak Ektachrome 64, 1/250 sec, f8*

◁ This colonnade at St Peters, Rome, is a mass of shapes that lead the eye into the picture. The lone priest is the only clue to the vast scale of the building.

*Pentax LX, 28 mm shift, Kodak Ektachrome 200, 1/250 sec, f11*

See also:
FRAMING THE SUBJECT pp50-51
PATTERN AND DETAIL pp58-59
THE VERSATILE LENS pp196-197
SELECTIVE VIEWS pp218-219

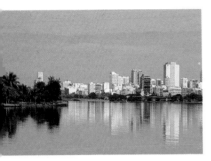

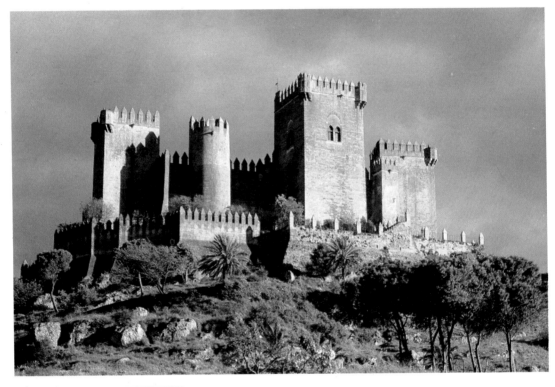

M aking pictures of distant buildings and cityscapes has many parallels with landscape photography. Instead of fields, trees, rocks, and sky, the picture elements are manmade structures such as suburban housing estates, office blocks, and bridges. But the quality of light is still of prime importance. Buildings can completely alter their appearance under changing weather conditions and this will affect the mood of the picture. Skyscrapers, especially when clustered together, as is so often the case in thriving commercial centres, may look forbidding and claustrophobic under heavy cloud and dull light, but in the bright sun of early morning they can be transformed into shimmering towers of reflective glass and steel. At such times the effect of a little sun on the building is often magical, seemingly out of proportion with what is, in fact, a common event.

Architects often plan their buildings with a 'front', the side which they present to the world, but buildings are also very often designed to look their best in a particular light. The most successful buildings are also sensitively placed within their surroundings, an aspect which can be best brought out by exploring the distant view.

△ Individual skyscrapers are not usually very beautiful. They need to be grouped for their full effect to be appreciated. These, in Brazil, are also much improved by their lakeside setting.

*Pentax LX, 50 mm, Kodak Ektachrome 64, ¹/₅₀₀ sec, f8*

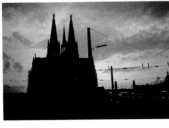

◁ Cologne's ancient cathedral is surrounded by a sea of ugly buildings which, because this picture was taken at dusk, are largely hidden.

*Pentax LX, 28 mm shift, Kodak Ektachrome 64, ¹/₃₀ sec, f8*

△ A shaft of evening sunlight breaks through summer storm clouds to spotlight this Spanish castle near Almería. As a result, colour, texture, and form are all enhanced in the near-perfect illumination.

*Pentax LX, 135 mm, Kodak Ektachrome 64, ¹/₂₅₀ sec, f11*

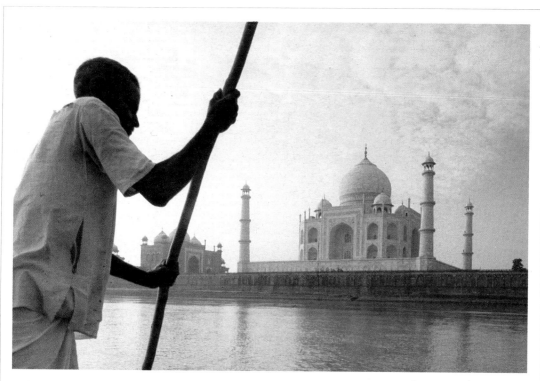

△ An unusual view of the Taj Mahal has been given a sense of scale and depth by framing it against this ferryman. A low viewpoint and the hazy lighting conditions heighten the impression of space.

*Pentax LX, 28 mm, Kodak Ektachrome 64, 1/60 sec, f22*

▷ The 'Rule of Thirds' is an aid to picture composition and recommends division of the picture area into thirds, creating an imaginary grid of lines with four off-centre intersections. These lines can act as a guide for dividing the picture up – note the Taj Mahal shot – and the intersections indicate balanced locations for the centres of interest within the composition.

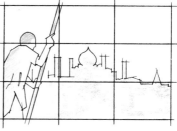

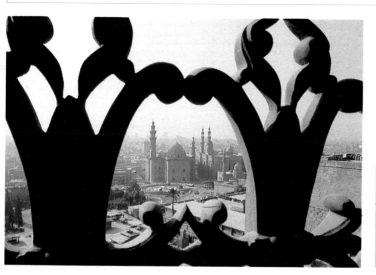

◁ Architectural features sometimes form excellent frames for distant scenes, hinting at detail in similar buildings.

*Pentax LX, 28 mm, Kodak Ektachrome 64, 1/125 sec, f22*

See also:
THE TELEPHOTO LENS pp22-23
VIEWPOINT AND SCALE pp48-49
VARIETIES OF LIGHT pp68-69

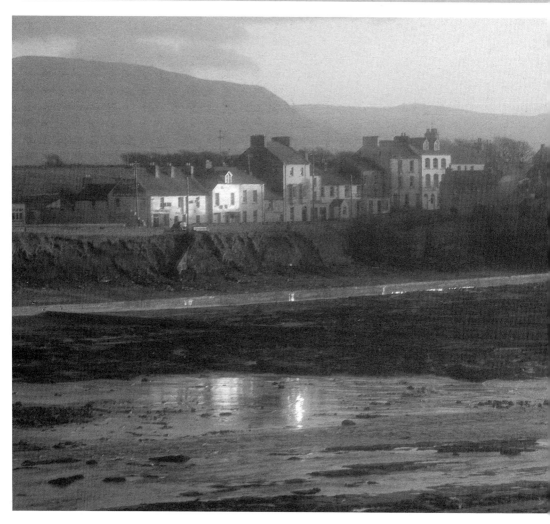

△ Early morning is one of the few times when a town is still enough for you to capture an atmosphere of tranquillity. In this photograph, taken on the outskirts of a town in Scotland, the light of the rising sun beautifies what later turned out to be an uninteresting scene. Lingering mists, rising from the river, add to the romantic mood.

*Hasselblad, 150 mm, Kodak Ektachrome 200, 1/30 sec, f11*

See also:
SPECIAL LENSES pp26-27
SOFT AND HARD LIGHT pp36-39
VARIETIES OF LIGHT pp68-69

Photography in the urban environment has many parallels with traditional landscape photography. The roles of light and weather, and the arrangement of elements within the composition, affect landscapes and cityscapes in similar ways. This is not so surprising when you remember that most urban areas were once rural and, indeed, in some towns and on the edges of cities this rural heritage is quite apparent.

Most photographers concentrate on the immediately striking and clearly attractive features of an urban scene. Remnants of the past, such as an old country house, now municipal offices, its gardens, now a public park, or an old inn or church, tend to be a main focus of attraction. So do the ultra-modern buildings that house business operations, but there are alternatives worth seeking out. In the right light, urban sprawl can provide a wealth of picture opportunities. Terraces, bridges, church spires, even lampposts in an urban environment can be portrayed in the same way as hills, rocks and trees in an open landscape. Factories, industrial plants, gasworks, and power stations all have their photogenic moments. Often it is a shaft of sunlight from a stormy sky, floodlighting at night, the warm glow of late twilight, or the atmosphere created by early morning mist that transforms a drab urban scene into an exciting image.

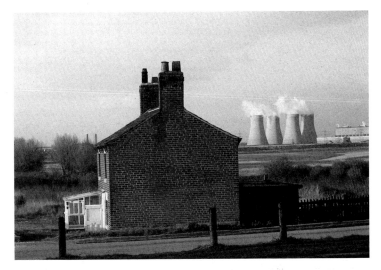

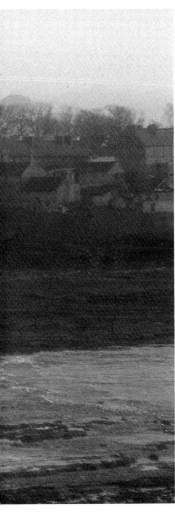

△ Late-afternoon sun brings out the shape and texture of the townscape. This type of low, directional light also emphasizes depth, increasing the sense of perspective, which is especially strong in the cottage. A long lens has brought the cottage into a closer relationship with the contrasting shapes of the cooling towers in the distance.

*Pentax LX, 200 mm, Kodak Ektachrome 64, ¹/₆₀ sec, f16*

▷ Occasionally, ordinary buildings are sufficiently striking to furnish a strong image. This apartment block in Morocco was photographed in the hard light of the midday sun. The strong shadows and bright highlights suit the regular geometric shapes. Converging verticals would have upset the composition, so a shift lens was used to keep them straight.

*Pentax LX, 28 mm shift, Kodak Ektachrome 64, ¹/₁₂₅ sec, f11*

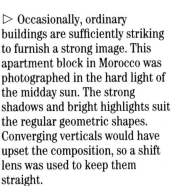

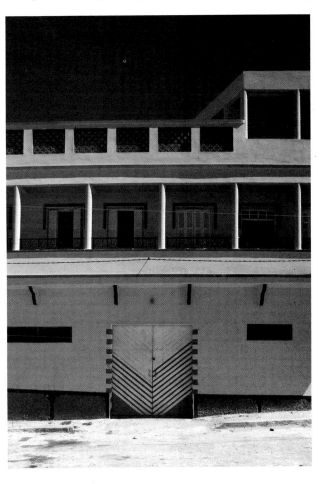

# MANMADE PATTERN

The manmade world reflects humankind's natural desire to see order in the environment and the perceptive photographer can often detect an underlying pattern, revealing it for the rest of us. Photographs of patterns alone can be intriguing, though they are rarely more than a design in themselves. However, pattern used as a compositional element is frequently a source of strength in an image. In black and white photography, patterns tend to be abstract because they usually obscure and confuse depth. Texture's role, which may appear to be similar, is in fact quite different, because it helps give the picture a sense of depth. Coloured patterns evoke an emotional response – we see bright, warm colours, for example, as being closer than dark, cool ones. In our urban environments patterns take many forms; some can be appreciated close-to, others only from a distance. They are always worth seeking out to add a further dimension to your cityscapes.

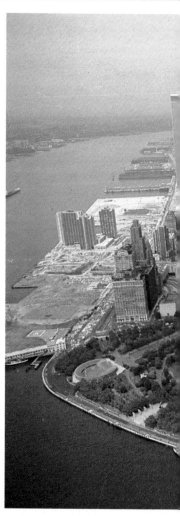

▽ There are many occasions, as with this exposed interior of a New York tenement, when a pattern is made up of organized but irregular elements. The broken plaster, open stairs, and peeling paint constitute intimate, telling detail.

*Pentax LX, 135 mm, Kodak Ektachrome 200, 1/250 sec, f8*

▷ A pattern is formed by the decaying spars of a pier silhouetted against a setting sun. The poignant atmosphere of this photograph derives from the slow but inevitable breakdown and collapse of a formerly ordered structure.

*Pentax LX, 50 mm, Kodak Ektachrome 64, 1/125 sec, f8*

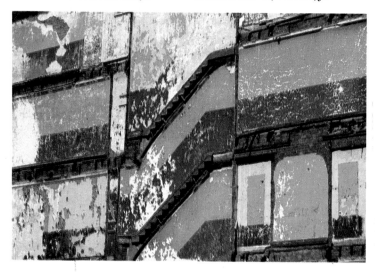

▷ The classic helicopter view of Manhattan illustrates human pattern-making on a grand scale. Flying presents useful opportunities to the photographer but you have to ask which side of the aircraft it is best to shoot from before boarding.

*Pentax LX, 28 mm, Kodak Ektachrome 64, 1/500 sec, f6.3*

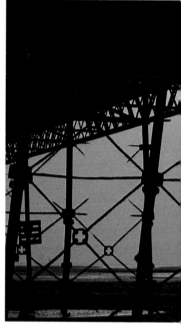

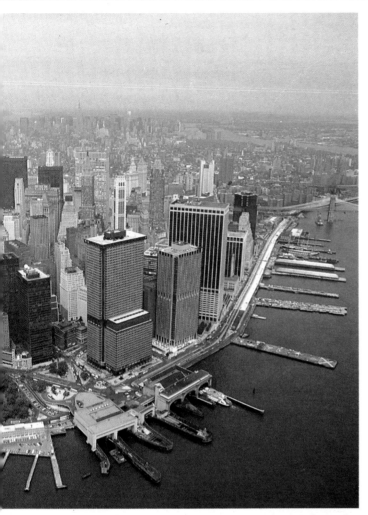

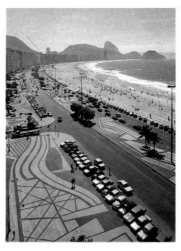

△ High viewpoints in cities frequently reveal pattern that is hard to see at ground level. These exotic pavements in Rio de Janeiro, designed by Robert Burle Marx, form part of an overall order when seen from the air.

*Pentax LX, 28 mm, Kodak Ektachrome 64, 1/500 sec, f16*

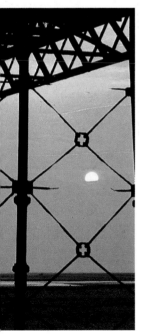

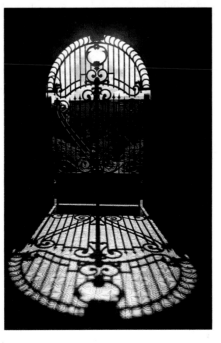

◁ Wrought iron work presents some of the most beautiful and intricate of manmade patterns. Often it is based on natural motifs. Here it is only the shadow that reveals the complete design.

*Pentax LX, 28 mm, Kodak Ektachrome 64, 1/250 sec, f16*

See also:
THE WIDE-ANGLE LENS pp20-21
VIEWPOINT AND SCALE pp48-49
FRAMING THE SUBJECT pp50-51

# STUDY IN MOSAIC

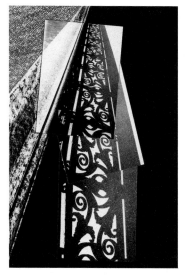

Taking interesting photographs of buildings is frequently made more difficult by the surroundings – for example, interesting buildings are often sandwiched between high-rise office blocks. It is difficult to exclude unwanted or distracting surroundings from conventional shots, but a novel approach can pay dividends and produce far more interesting pictures.

One approach is to marry up separate shots of selected areas, keeping verticals upright, so that the resulting image is a realistic view of the building. Alternatively, a more interpretative approach can be adopted, creating a mosaic that presents an impression of the building and emphasizes its impact on the senses. For this type of approach it is important to take time to walk round the building first, searching out interesting viewpoints and gaining a sense of the architect's design. The photographs may be taken from one position, or you can change viewpoint and/or lenses. Try to start out with a firm idea of the result you want, but be prepared to shoot plenty of film to ensure that you have lots of material to work from.

△ This image consists of a combination of photographs and crayon. The photographs were taken in Versailles, near Paris and show the intriguing shadows thrown by ornate railings that border a pathway.

*Olympus Pen-F, Fujicolor HR 100, autoexposure (Photo: Auberon Hedgecoe)*

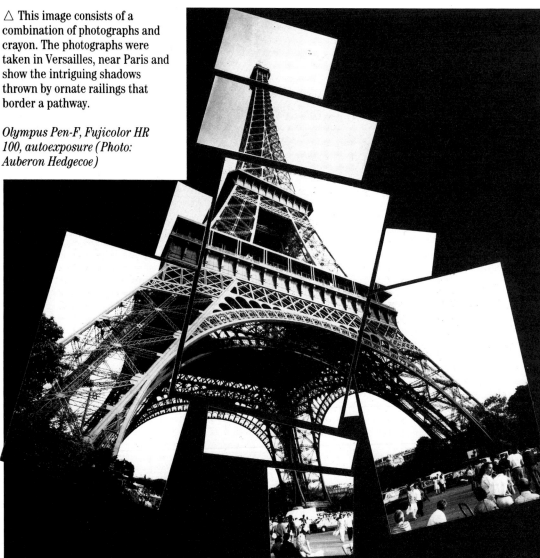

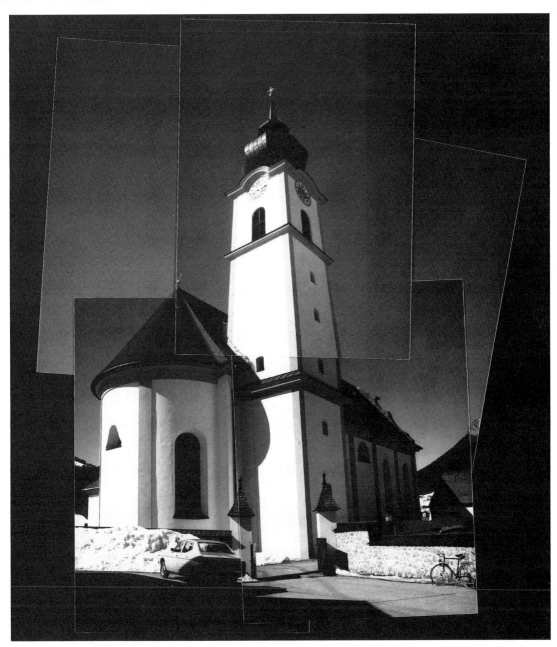

◁ This picture of the Eiffel Tower was made from over a dozen separate enprints, taken on a simple automatic camera. Despite the limitations of the equipment, the final image presents a radically different view from those taken by other visitors that day.

*Olympus Pen-F, Fujicolor HR 100, autoexposure (Photo: Auberon Hedgecoe)*

△ Few buildings conform to the rigid rectangular shapes of modern office blocks. Reflecting this fact, the mosaic here creates an irregular outline that furthermore refuses to conform to the rigid boundary of a single print. The varying print density enhances the effect of the mosaic.

*Olympus Pen-F, Fujicolour HR 100, autoexposure (Photo: Auberon Hedgecoe)*

See also:
COMPACT CAMERAS pp16-17
FRAMING THE SUBJECT pp50-51
SPLITTING IMAGES pp212-215

I n the confines of a studio, the photographer has full control over the picture and success is born of a creative mind, careful application of photographic techniques and, above all, a clear idea of what the final image is to be, at whom it is aimed, and what it has to say. Failure is entirely the photographer's fault. This is a

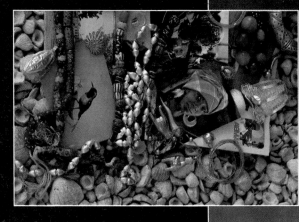

harsh reality, but it does benefit the photographer by highlighting his or her shortcomings. The studio is, therefore, an ideal learning environment, not only for acquiring new skills – and in the studio you have to be something of a Jack of all trades – but for exploiting creative catalysts and developing a personal photographic style that is uniquely your own.

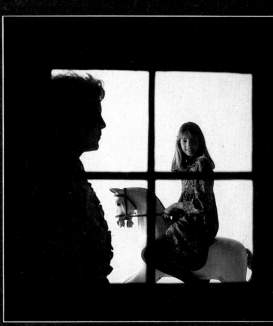

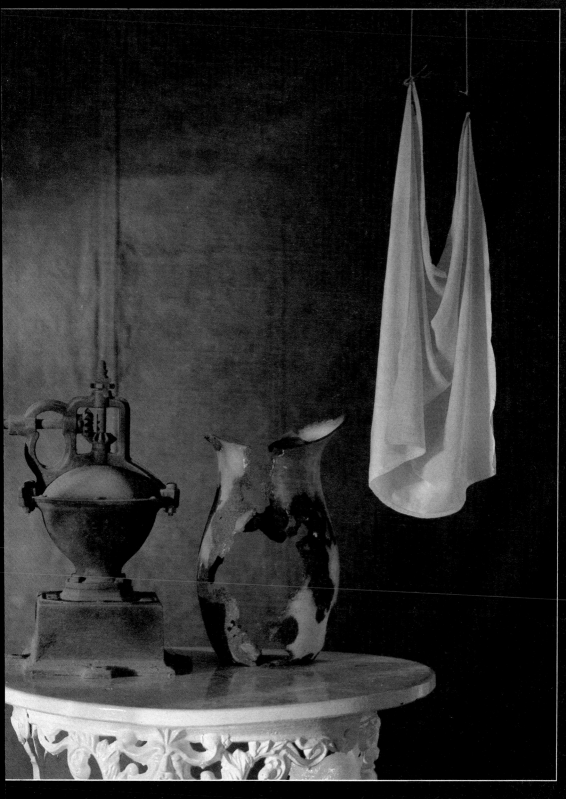

# THE STILL LIFE

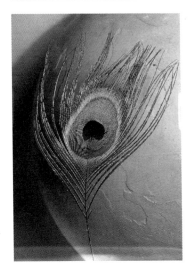

Lighting is one of the most important factors in still-life photography. Whether it is good or bad, lighting has a profound effect on the realism and mood of the picture, so it is very important to get it right. One of the commonest faults is to swamp a still life in bright light from a bank of lamps, thereby spoiling any hope of revealing form, texture and tone. Simplicity, both in arranging the composition and in deciding on the lighting required, is the key to success here.

In nature, illumination comes from one source – the sun, helped by reflected light from the surroundings. Its direction is usually from above or from one side, and only one set of shadows is cast. Imitating natural light and using one main light source is a good way to start. Having arranged your composition, decide on lighting that will be in keeping with the image. Hard, directional light from an oblique angle will reveal detail and texture, highlight smooth surfaces, and suggest energy and strength, but you must be careful that shadows do not confuse the effect. Diffused illumination from a large source is ideal for displaying form, emphasizing tone, and portraying a softer atmosphere. It is particularly suitable when you are using set-ups that contain a large number of items.

△ Only two lights were used for this picture. The white ball was placed on a white card and lit with soft, directional light from a large floodlight. A sheet of glass supported the feather above the ball and a spotlight was used to give a hard light that skimmed the surface to reveal texture and lighten tone. A large white reflector was placed over the whole set-up to provide soft fill-in light.

*Pentax 6×7, 80 mm, Kodak Ektachrome 160 Tungsten, 1 sec, f45, one tungsten flood and one tungsten spot.*

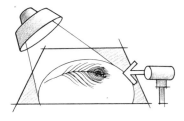

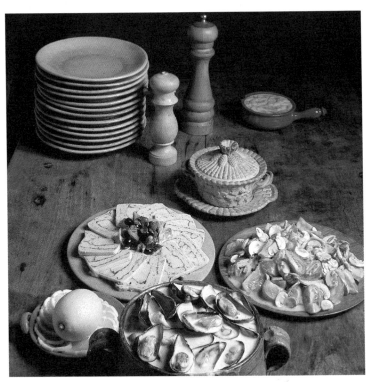

▷ Part of the brief for this shot was to evoke a rich mood. A suitable approach is to use a light soft enough to show a full range of tones, but hard enough to reveal detail and texture. A studio flash, relected off a silver umbrella, produced the diffuse light. The light was positioned close to the still life to act as a large source and shaded to give a ⅔ stop fall-off in brightness towards the back of the shot.

*Hasselblad, 60 mm, Kodak Ektachrome 64, ¹/₂₅₀ sec, f16*

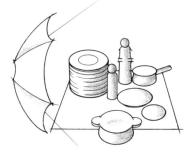

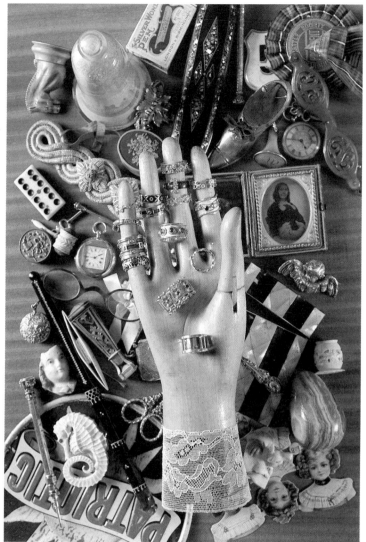

◁ Victorian rings were the main subject of this picture. The memorabilia were added to strengthen the atmosphere. The resulting complex jumble of shapes suggested an overall soft light as the best illumination. In this picture the objects were placed in front of a large north-facing window. White reflectors were placed opposite the window to lighten shadow areas. The hand is supported above the other items so that these could be recorded slightly defocused, giving additional contrast.

*Linhof 6×7, 90 mm, Kodak Ektachrome 64, ½ sec,f22*

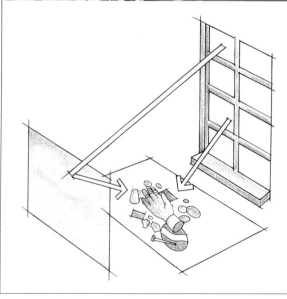

See also:
LIGHT AND CONTRAST pp32-33
SOFT AND HARD LIGHT pp36-39
ELECTRONIC FLASH pp74-77

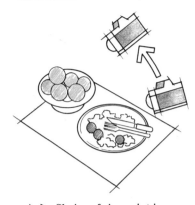

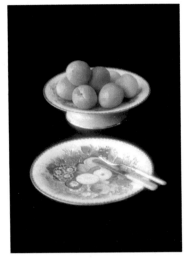

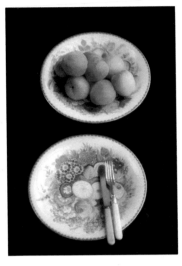

△ ▷ Choice of viewpoint is crucial to the final result. From certain angles, shape and form can be quite distorted, so care has to be taken that their appearance does not detract from the arrangement. Also, make sure that outlines are not confused and that the viewpoint selected places the emphasis correctly. The only difference between these two pictures is a change in camera position from 45° to the subject plane to nearly overhead, as illustrated in the diagram.

*Pentax LX, 100 mm macro, Kodak Ektachrome 64, 1/4 sec, f22*

Still life is one branch of photography where the results are entirely the product of the photographer's skill. The choice of subject, lighting, viewpoint, and arrangement is solely the photographer's responsibility, so that still life is an ideal subject area in which to develop photographic expertise.

Constructing a successful still life depends on having a clear vision of the idea or theme that is to be photographed, for starting out without a clear conception of your picture is usually fruitless. A still life does not have to be complex – frequently it is a simple arrangement given a sympathetic treatment that leads to the most striking and lasting images.

The key to a good picture is to build it up slowly, step by step, checking the effect of each additional element's contribution through the viewfinder, and paying attention to lighting, texture, tone, form and mood. Sometimes, one object, carefully positioned within a straightforward setting, makes a complete picture, but try a group of old clocks or kitchen tools – anything, in fact, that is easily accessible – for pleasing results.

▷ Although this arrangement of peaches might appear to be very simple it did take some time to complete. All blemishes had to be carefully hidden, and the colour and shape of each fruit had to be balanced with the others and positioned so that the eye is lead straight into the composition.

*Pentax LX, 100 mm macro, Kodak Ektachrome 64, 1/15 sec, f22*

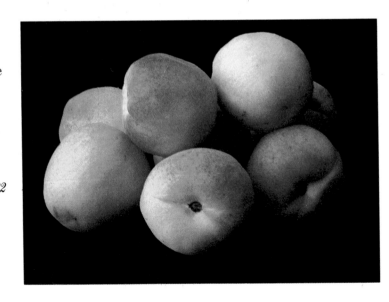

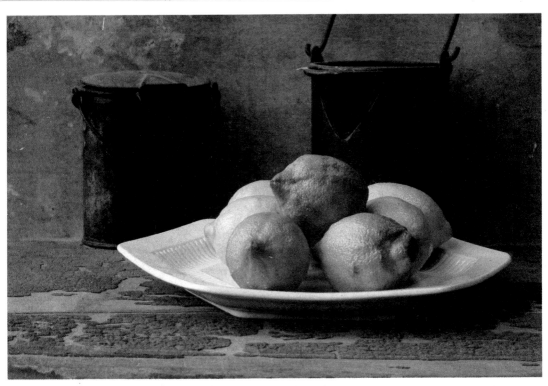

△ It is not only perfect specimens which make a successful still life. Strangely formed or blemished examples sometimes provide intriguing pictures. Under-ripe lemons with a greenish tinge were in keeping with the sombre mood created by the background. The lemons' colour also contrasts strongly with that of the plate.

*Pentax LX, 100 mm macro, Kodak Ektachrome 64, ¼ sec, f22*

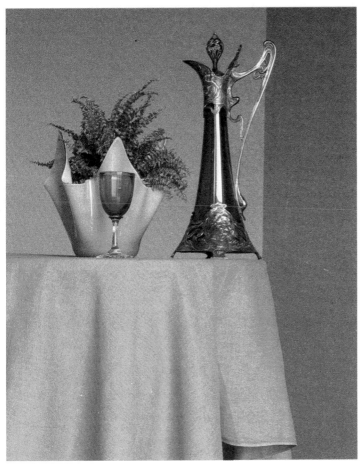

◁ The original intention was to concentrate on the objects on the table, but it was clear that the tablecloth and the walls made an attractive, contrasting setting.

*Pentax LX, 28 mm shift, Scotch (3M) 100, ¹/₃₀ sec, f16*

See also:
SPECIAL LENSES pp26-27
VIEWPOINT AND SCALE pp48-49
FRAMING THE SUBJECT pp50-51
COMPOSING THE SHOT pp52-53

# THE SIMPLE STILL LIFE

One of the basic aims of still-life photography is to make the subject of a picture appear real – so real that the viewer is given the impression that he could reach out and touch it, feeling texture, shape, weight, moisture and heat. Whatever tactile quality an object can be expected to possess should be made obvious to the viewer. This might seem difficult, but it can be achieved by using light and shadow to reveal form. Form is not shape. Shape is merely the outline of an object, but form is the way an object occupies a space, described by the tonal gradation from light to dark.

To begin with, select one or two objects with a straightforward geometric shape – a box, ball, pyramid, cylinder, or cone – and, using a simple light source, try to emphasize the essential qualities, such as shape, texture and weight. You will know you have the correct lighting when you can appreciate how the subject would feel if held in the hand.

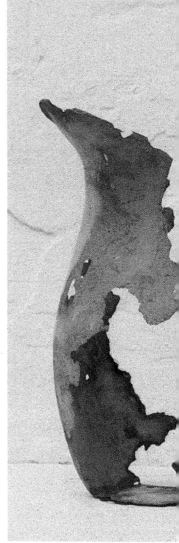

▽ Diffused light from a hazy sky has given these tomatoes good modelling and the subdued highlights hint at their smoothness. A white reflector was placed on their shadow side, as in the diagram, to provide some fill-in. The rich gradations of tone help give the impression of weight and solidity and the background of the rough wooden bench contrasts well with the smooth texture. Such contrasts between background and subject are often used to strengthen textural differences between objects in still-life pictures.

*Pentax LX, 100 mm macro, Kodak Ektachrome 64, ¹/₃₀ sec, f11*

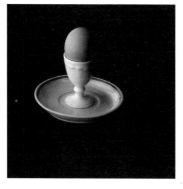

▽ Soft directional light from a nearby window reveals the curved outline of the egg. Slight underexposure has helped convey the solidity of the saucer.

*Hasselblad, 150 mm, Kodak Ektachrome 64, ¹/₃₀ sec, f16*

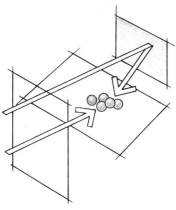

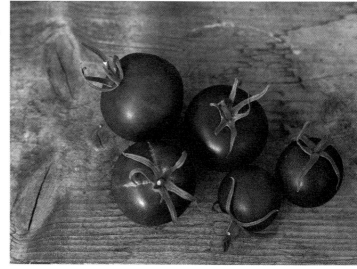

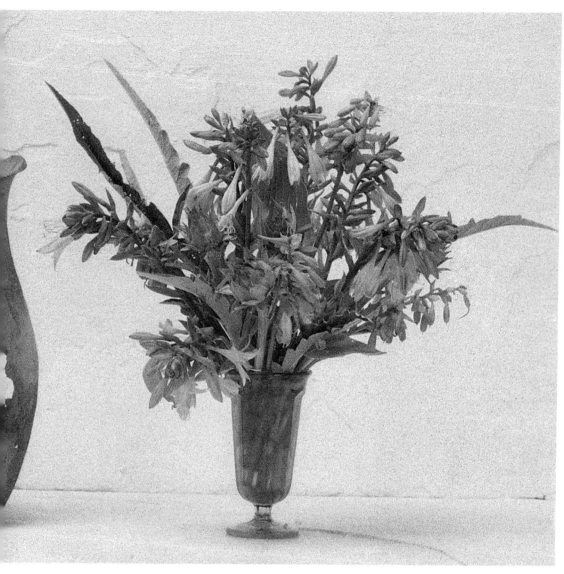

△ Diffused light is extremely soft and produces a nearly shadowless effect. It is ideal for emphasizing shape, rather than form and is, therefore, particularly well suited to photographing still life subjects that are light and delicate. The petals and foliage of plants and flowers have complex shapes and many different surfaces at a variety of different angles and planes. Soft lighting gives very delicate modelling that makes it the best choice for such subjects. This photograph was shot using light reflected from a north-facing window to capture the lightness, delicacy, and fragility of the jug and the flowers.

*Pentax LX, 100 mm, Scotch (3M) 1000, ¹/₆₀ sec, f16*

See also:
SOFT AND HARD LIGHT pp36-39
VIEWPOINT AND SCALE pp48-49
FRAMING THE SUBJECT pp50-51
COMPOSING THE SHOT pp52-53

# STUDIO SILHOUETTES

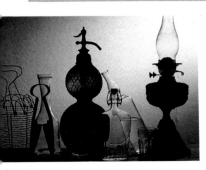

A silhouette is an image in which a dark shape is set against a bright background. The lighting is arranged so that detail is suppressed in the main subject and the shape is emphasized. Creating a silhouette in the studio is one of the easiest of photographs to set up; the only problem is in providing a sufficiently large area of bright and evenly lit background.

The best subjects for the silhouette treatment are ones with easily recognizable shapes, such as faces and figures, tools and implements, and animals and plants. To prevent specular reflections ruining the effect, it is sometimes possible to coat shiny objects with a dulling spray or with water-soluble black poster paint. Some translucent objects – bottles are the obvious example – also make intriguing silhouettes.

Having chosen the subjects, it is a matter of arranging them so that their identity is not confused by presenting an ambiguous and cluttered outline. The background need be nothing more elaborate than an indoor windowsill or a sheet of white paper. As with any still-life, working with a tripod frees the photographer to fine-tune the set-up and check the results through the viewfinder, before committing the image to film.

△ Straightforward still-life silhouettes can be made with no more equipment than a sheet of white paper, an Anglepoise lamp, a tripod, and a camera.

*Pentax LX, 100 mm macro, Kodak Ektachrome 160 Tungsten, 1/125 sec, f8*

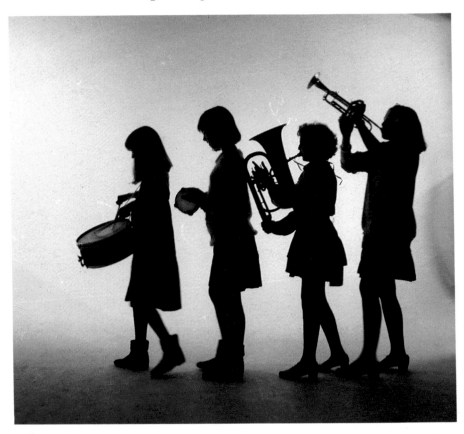

△ You need a good deal of studio space for a silhouette like this one. Outdoors, a wall or hill top are good alternatives so long as the background is at least three stops brighter than the subjects. A strong sense of movement is conveyed but the posing was exact, clearly defining the outlines.

*Pentax LX, 50 mm, Kodak Ektachrome 160 Tungsten, 1/125 sec, f8*

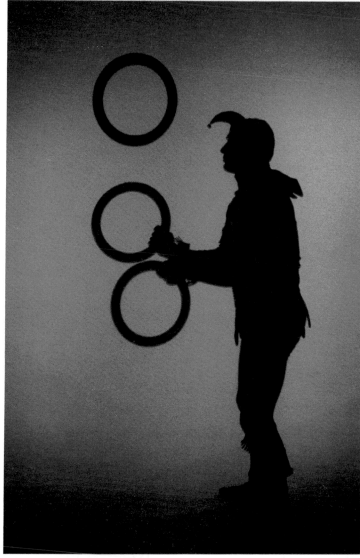

◁ It's fun to add colour to silhouettes. This shot was done by putting a ×3 red filter over the lens, but it can be done by covering the lights with colour gels or bulbs and by using coloured background paper.

*Pentax LX, 50 mm, Kodak Ektachrome 160 Tungsten, ¹⁄₃₀ sec, f8*

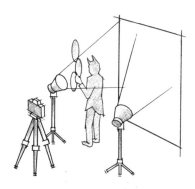

△ To create a good, even backdrop for silhouettes it is best to use plain, white background paper and light it from each side with tungsten floods or studio flash fitted with a standard or flood reflector. Place the lights about 2 m (6 ft) from the background and check for evenness of illumination with a meter – it should be 3 or 4 stops brighter than the subject.

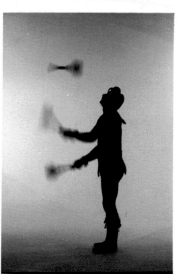

◁ An alternative approach to moving silhouettes is to use a slow shutter speed to create blur. The same lighting set-up was used here as for the children's band but with them dimmed; too bright a background might burn out the image of the clubs.

*Pentax LX, 50 mm, Kodak Ektachrome 160 Tungsten, ¹⁄₃₀ sec, f16*

See also:
CHOOSING EXPOSURE pp28-31
USING BACKLIGHT pp34-35
ELECTRONIC FLASH pp74-77
TUNGSTEN LIGHTING pp78-79

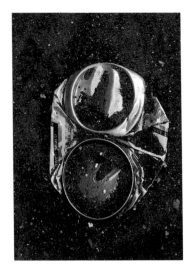

A still life is an arrangement of inanimate objects photographed as an image in their own right. Usually a still life is thought of as being constructed by the photographer who, through skilfully handling light, composition, and materials, creates a pleasing image. But this need not be the only approach, for you can photograph found objects that form an attractive arrangement themselves, without your intervention as the designer of the scene.

The skill in making fine still-life pictures from chanced-upon objects lies in selecting a small but significant area that makes a complete composition. Often, familiar everyday items are the substance of such photographs but they are seen with a fresh view that may highlight shape, design, function, spatial texture, tone, colour or relationships. Although it takes an observant eye and an imaginative mind to come up with strong pictures, the beauty of making still lifes from found objects is that it can be done with the simplest of cameras.

△ This flattened can's stark tones and sculptural qualities suggest eyes, a mask, or ominous reflective sunglasses.

*Pentax LX, 50 mm, Kodak Ektachrome 64, $^1/_{125}$ sec, f11*

▽ Windows facing the street are sometimes used to display prized possessions such as this classical figure. The figure may not have merited a photograph in its own right, but the additional interest in the picture comes from the presence of the toy robot opposite it, perhaps placed on the sill by a child in imitation of his parents' pride.

*Pentax LX, 50 mm, Kodak Ektachrome 64, autoexposure, f8*

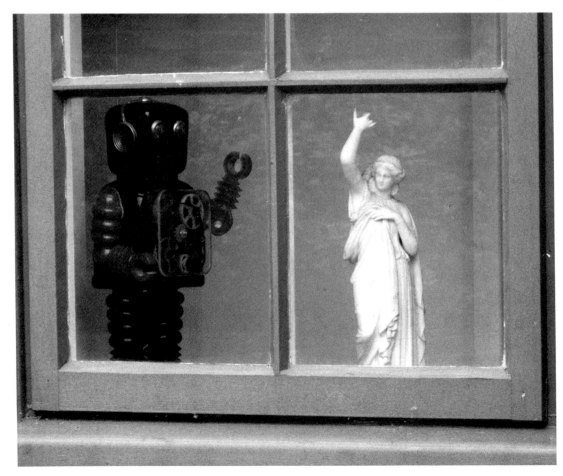

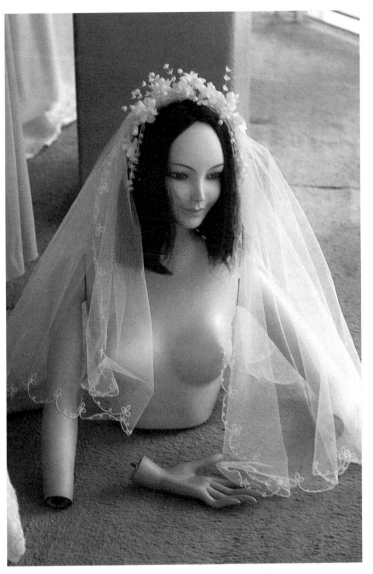

◁ The expression of this mannequin, pictured in a state of undress and dismemberment, conveys utter obliviousness of its state, which gives the picture a surrealistic quality. As the photographer has little or no control over light and arrangement in found still lifes, the successful image often depends on the ideas and associations that it gives rise to.

*Pentax LX, 50 mm, Kodak Ektachrome 64, 1/125 sec, f11*

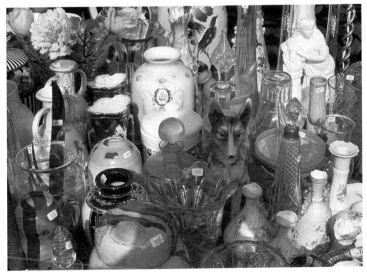

◁ Shop windows, especially those of antique shops, provide a never-ending stream of picture material. Here, an impression of a vast quantity of objects has been created by concentrating on a small part of the crowded display.

*Pentax LX, 35 mm, Kodak Ektachrome 64, 1/250 sec, f8*

See also:
SOFT AND HARD LIGHT pp36-39
VIEWPOINT AND SCALE pp48-49
FRAMING THE SUBJECT pp50-51
COMPOSING THE SHOT pp52-53

# COLOURED LIGHT

Coloured lighting is used frequently in theatres and discos, both to entertain and to highlight subjects. Theatrical effects can also be used in photography to add another dimension to pictures of simple forms. The most effective studio techniques use strongly-coloured light sources to re-colour the subject. White parts of the subject will take on the colour of the lighting, but the areas which are coloured in a tone complementary to that of the light source will appear as black. When using one colour, it is often a good idea to light part of the set with a simple white light to add contrast.

Lighting of mixed colours produces a whole range of results, often making unengaging subjects appear in striking hues. With two lights of complementary colours – red and cyan, for example – areas they both illuminate will appear as they would do under white light. Three or more lights make results harder to predict, but much of the enjoyment of using coloured lighting comes from the unexpected results achieved by experimentation.

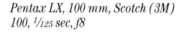

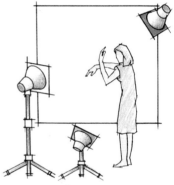

◁ ▷ Three lights produced the strange colouring here. The diagram shows the blue light at the model's feet, giving light from below, and the red light overhead. The green background – about 2 m (6 ft) distant – was lit by a white light.

*Pentax LX, 100 mm, Scotch (3M) 100, ¹/₁₂₅ sec, f8*

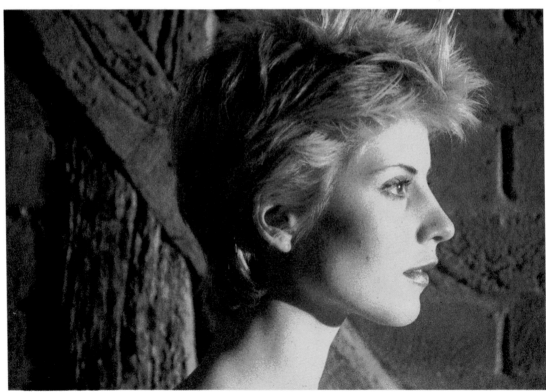

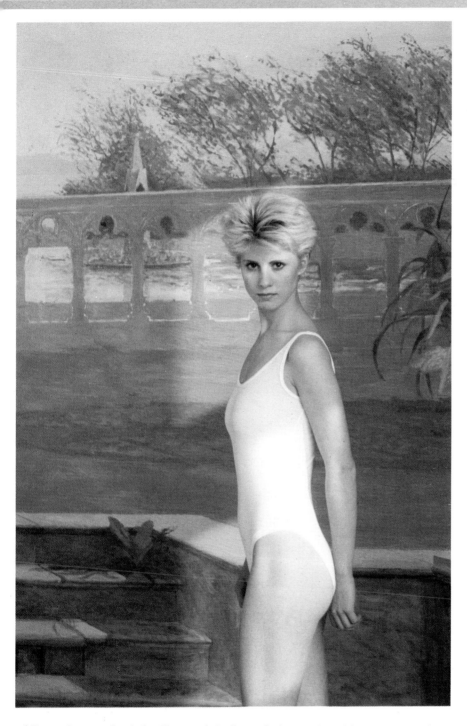

◁ Every photographer is familiar with the deep yellow colour of the setting sun. Light-tone subjects, such as this model's skin, are best for a strong tint. This portrait was made on a winter's evening.

*Pentax LX, 85 mm, Scotch (3M) 100, ¹/₆₀ sec, f8*

△ Delicate tinting can be achieved using natural light. Sunlight filtering through a tinted glass door has produced magenta highlights which contrast with the green of the mural.

*Pentax LX, 50 mm, Kodak Ektachrome 200, ¹/₃₀ sec, f8*

See also:
COLOUR INTENSITY pp70-71
COLOUR FILTERS pp72-73
TUNGSTEN LIGHTING pp78-79

# THE HUMAN FORM

The human form is one of the most demanding subjects, but it is also one of the most satisfying. It has enough inherent interest to gain a viewer's attention, but to keep it and gain his respect requires both taste and artistic ability. There is no denying the erotic nature of a nude figure – an aspect exploited in glamour work – but the subject is much more than that, and it can be said that if you can make outstanding images of the nude then you will be able to photograph anything.

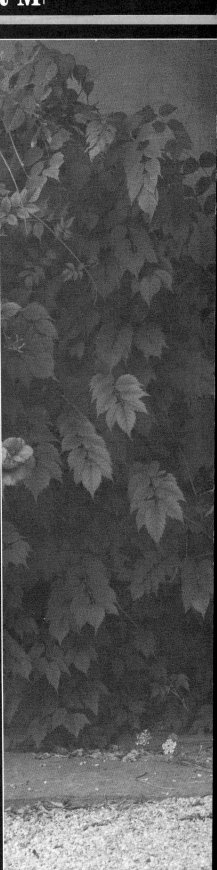

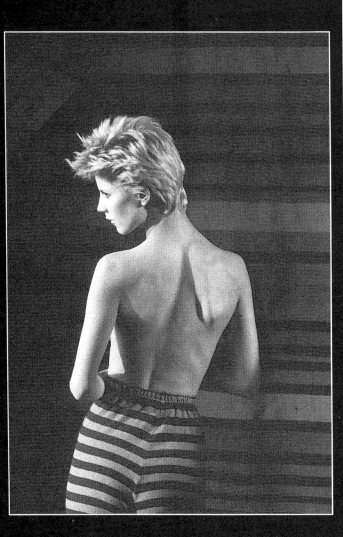

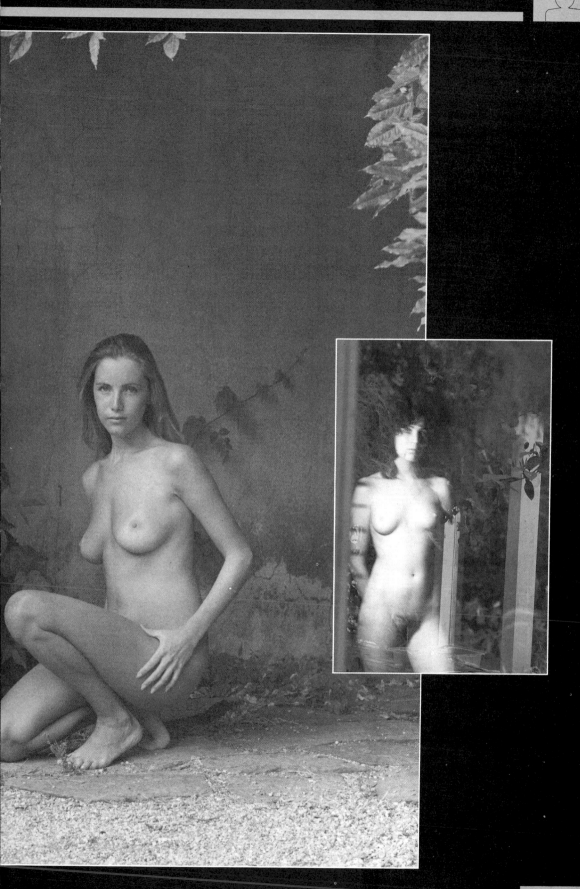

# THE HUMAN FORM

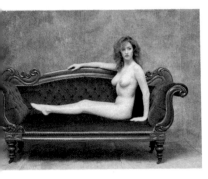

△ Fast film and soft light can highlight skin texture as well as form. The model was lit by a large, overhead window and white reflectors placed close to the camera ensured that shadow areas were well lit.

*Pentax LX, 50 mm, Scotch (3M) 1000, $^1/_{125}$ sec, f16*

Photographing the nude is always a challenge, whether you are an experienced professional or a hesitant amateur, but the subject need be no more daunting than landscapes. In fact, nude photography and landscape work have many pictorial and technical aspects in common, and photographers frequently move from one to the other or combine the two, using the landscape as a setting. Geological formations can be used to echo the human form and to counterpoint skin texture.

The selection of a good model and an appropriate location will depend on the ideas that you want to present. To start with, the best approach to nude photography is to make basic images of the human form, keeping props to an essential minimum and using daylight whenever possible. Concentrate on the poses and framing alone. Soft, directional light is ideal for revealing overall shape and form. Because shadows do not have a dramatic impact on composition, the model and photographer are free to exploit the pose and viewpoints.

For your first attempts at making nude studies, choose a model you know. Failing that, it would be an advantage to use an experienced model, perhaps from an art school, who is used to adopting relaxed and natural-looking poses without the more blatant sexuality prevalent in glamour photography.

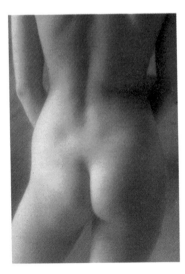

△ Often the simplest pictures are the strongest and first-time models will be more relaxed with semi-abstract shots like this.

*Pentax LX, 135 mm, Kodak Ektachrome 64, $^1/_{60}$ sec, f8*

▷ Props that add to the context of the picture or that help the model relax are useful. Beds and couches make a natural setting.

*Hasselblad, 80 mm, Kodak Ektachrome 200, $^1/_{30}$ sec, f16*

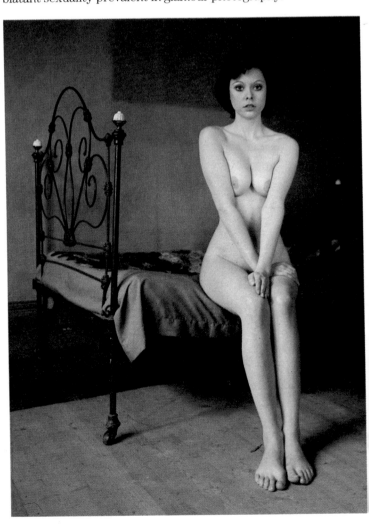

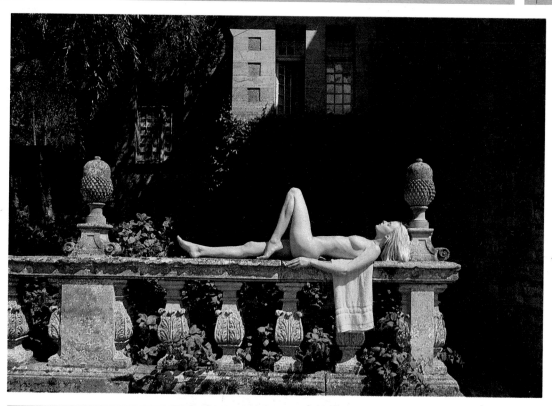

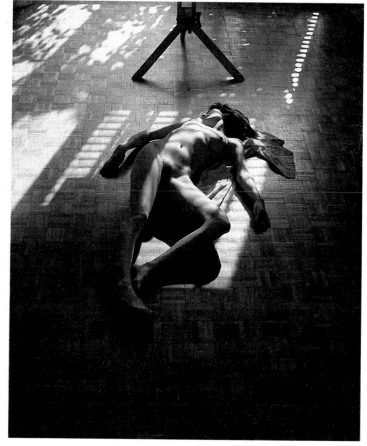

△ Outdoor locations can provide an ideal setting for nude pictures that contain a hint of innocence and sensuality. Simple settings are the most successful. Here the girl's languid form is set against a dark, contrasting background for added clarity.

*Pentax LX, 50 mm, Kodak Ektachrome 64, 1/125 sec, f8*

◁ The similarity between the colour of the wooden flooring and the model's golden skin tones make this an almost monochromatic picture where the emphasis is on light and form.

*Pentax LX 28 mm, Kodak Ektachrome 64, 1/60 sec, f8*

See also:
SOFT AND HARD LIGHT pp36-39
EXPLOITING FILM pp80-81
THE SIMPLE SETTING pp104-105

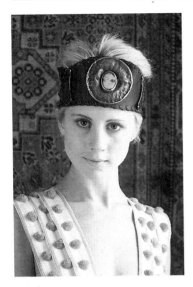

△ The ornate belt, when worn on the head, suggested an ancient Mediterranean outfit. This was provided by several feet of curtain braiding. The background is an Indian carpet and the light was from a north-facing window.

*Pentax LX, 50 mm, Kodak Ektachrome 200, 1/125 sec, f8*

▷ An upturned lampshade brought to mind an Egyptian priestess's headgear. To complete the outfit, all that was needed was a hastily-cut bin liner.

*Pentax LX, 85 mm, Kodak Ektachrome 200, 1/30 sec, f11*

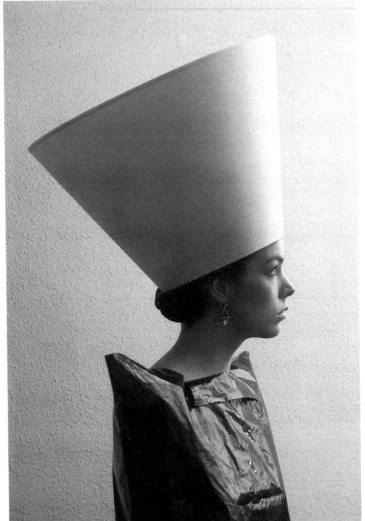

See also:
SOFT AND HARD LIGHT pp36-39
TUNGSTEN LIGHTING pp78-79
DOMESTIC CHORES pp272-273

Most people enjoy dressing up, and you can exploit this to produce unusual and interesting pictures. Traditionally, costumes are created with clothing cast-offs, but more surprising, shocking, and amusing pictures can result from using readily available household objects. Apart from obvious items, like curtains, you can use unusual objects like buckets and refuse sacks. Take every opportunity to exercise your imagination and present everyday items in a new light.

Once you start a dressing-up session, you'll find everybody involved will come up with a continuous stream of new ideas. Children, in particular, enjoy these sessions. The best costumes and pictures are those that relate to an overall idea or theme. This means selecting items that relate in colour, shape or function, and arranging them to compose a balanced design in much the same way as you would when deciding what goes with what when dressing for an evening out. Often one piece of furniture or household equipment will suggest a garment, and then it's a simple matter of finding other suitable props to complete the image.

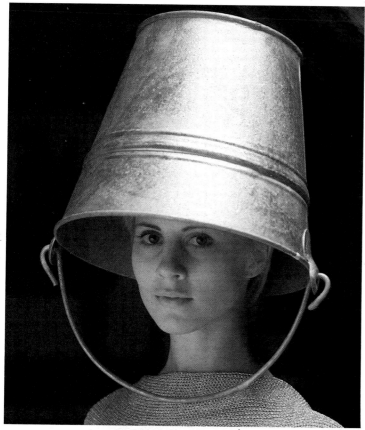

◁ The most unlikely objects can be pressed into service. A silver shawl has been draped over the model's shoulders to keep within the overall colour scheme suggested by the bucket. A reflector was used to give even lighting to the face.

*Pentax LX, 85 mm, Kodak Ektachrome 200, ¹/₃₀ sec, f11*

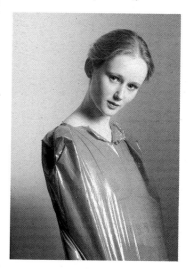

△ A plastic refuse sack as a dress. The simple composition and symmetrical shape of the sack have been enlivened by posing the model slightly diagonally and setting her head at an angle. Light from a large window provided the lighting and a silver reflector was used to fill in the shadows.

*Pentax LX, 85 mm, Kodak Ektachrome 200, ¹/₆₀ sec, f11*

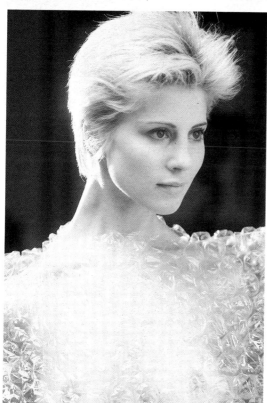

◁ The plastic bubble packing material used in this shot has a fascinating texture which reveals a new dimension as an article of clothing. The model's face was lit with sunlight – two reflectors were used to lighten shadows – and a 500 watt tungsten lamp provided the warm rimlight.

*Pentax LX, 85 mm, Kodak Ektachrome 200, ¹/₁₂₅ sec, f8*

# THE NAKED PRINT

The instant-picture camera is designed to provide an immediate visual record, but the medium has a magic all of its own which can be exploited to produce fascinating images. Every exposure is a finished result, and the print itself, with its attractive white border, has a pleasing format.

Professional photographers frequently use instant-picture cameras to check if a particular image works, for there is a real benefit in being able to show a model how she looks and in making sure that you will not have to hire her for a reshoot. The instant nature of the process will often inspire an easy rapport with the model that results in a large number of 'quick prints' being shot. The medium also lends itself to manipulation before the image becomes permanent.

With the development of the Polaroid SX-70 camera and film in the early 1970s and the later introduction of camera systems like the fully automated Polaroid Supercolor 600 series, instant photography has acquired a large number of devotees, both professional and amateur. The beauty of these systems lies in their ease of use and their unique scope for creative exploitation of the image.

▷ For this shot, the Polaroid emulsion was moved with a teaspoon that had been heated for five minutes under a hot tap. The manipulation took about the same time. You should be careful to finish moving the emulsion image before it hardens and so you need to start soon after the image appears.

▽ Polaroid film's immediacy encourages experimentation, every step in the exploration of viewpoint, colour, or composition yielding another result for comparison.

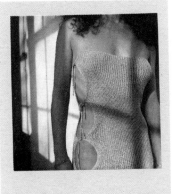

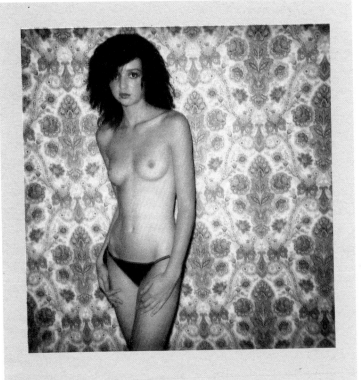

◁ Subtle and muted colours are the hallmark of the Polaroid 600 series print. Here it subdued the overpowering backdrop of brightly patterned wallpaper, producing a quieter mood. The picture was taken using the camera's built-in flash, which has helped retain the warm colour of the girl's glowing suntanned skin.

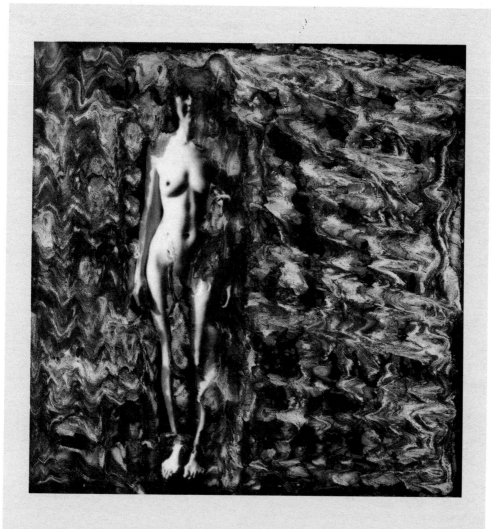

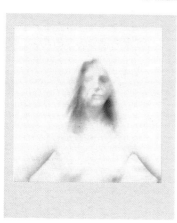

◁ It is possible to adjust the exposure balance on instant-picture cameras, so high- or low-key prints can be made. Pastel colours can also result from placing the print into a freezer before development is completed. The atmospheric blurring here was created by moving the SX-70 camera during the exposure.

See also:
EXPLOITING FILM pp80-81
SPECIAL FILTERS pp82-85
THE HUMAN FORM pp256-257

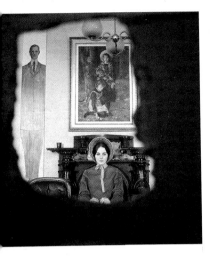

Framing is a strong compositional device that serves a distinct function in portrait pictures. It should not be confused with simply photographing a person in a setting. A setting may provide extra interest or provide more information about the subject, but a frame is used to contain a subject, add emphasis, and direct the viewer's attention.

The most important reason for using a frame is to isolate the figure and create impact, but there are other, slightly more subtle reasons for using a frame. If you use a frame in the foreground, you can increase the sense of three-dimensionality in a picture. Or visual ambiguities such as 'false attachment' may be played upon. In a complex scene, the figure may be given extra emphasis, or the frame used as a device to hide distracting or confusing elements. Whatever the function of the frame selected, remember that it must be in sympathy with the subject, and not obtrusive or distracting.

△ To direct the viewer's attention to the two sisters in the painting and the seated figure, a close foreground frame was used to hide the rest of the room. The asymmetrical shape of the frame adds interest and, because it is in shadow, its neutral tone does not detract from the main subject.

*Hasselblad, 150 mm, Kodak Ektachrome 200, 1/15 sec, f11*

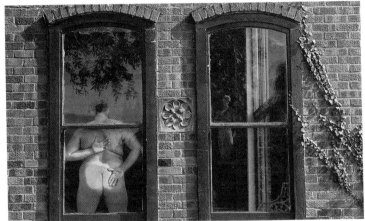

△ Warm, afternoon sun has brought out the texture of the brickwork which is punctuated by the two symmetrical windows. Two frames create a sense of ambiguity and the eye flicks from one to the other, comparing the nude in one with the sculpture glimpsed in the other.

*Hasselblad, 80 mm, Kodak Ektachrome 64, 1/125 sec, f11*

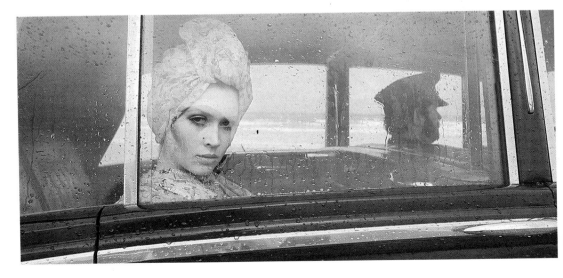

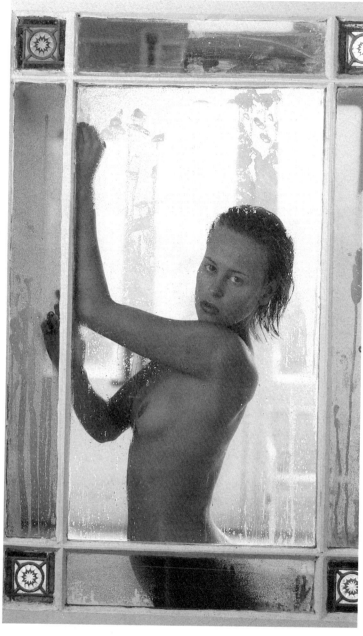

◁ A rich-toned rectangle of glass complements the paler tones of the girl's skin seen against the neutral background. Bright frames need to be used carefully, otherwise they dominate the subject, but here the girl's shapely outlines stand out in strong contrast and retain the viewer's attention. The shot was lit with a quartz-iodine lamp that was diffused through a wire scrim covered with a blue gel to give it daylight colour balance.

*Hasselblad, 150 mm, Kodak Ektachrome 64, $1/125$ sec, f8*

◁ This picture illustrates the use of a frame as a means of providing additional information about the subject. The girl's face is surrounded by the outlines of an expensive limousine, which suggests that she is used to living in style and comfort. The rain-splashed glass shows the protection afforded by the car and hints at the luxurious cocoon that wealth brings.

*Hasselblad, 80 mm, Kodak Ektachrome 200, $1/250$ sec, f8*

See also:
FRAMING THE SUBJECT pp50-51
COMPOSING THE SHOT pp52-53
VARIETIES OF LIGHT pp68-69

# FANTASY FIGURES

▽ The transparency of diaphanous materials is determined by the relative brightness of the illumination on each side. If the brightest light is on the viewing side then the material is relatively opaque and its colour and texture are clear. A bright light on the far side makes it more transparent, revealing more of the scene beyond. For this shot the front lighting from a window has been carefully balanced on the far side by a reflector (see diagram) so that the nude figure can just be seen through the damp cotton sheet. Where the sheet is in contact with her body the transparency is increased.

*Pentax LX, 50 mm, Kodak Ektachrome 160 Tungsten, 1/60 sec, f11*

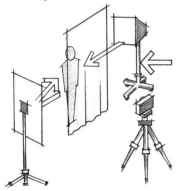

In the earliest days of photography the naked figure was often covered with soft diaphanous materials that revealed form but subdued intimate detail. The result was an idealized image of woman as a mysterious and romantic creature. The tradition has continued to this day, but with a different twist; the modern climate of overt sexuality has transformed the flowing cotton robes into the wet T-shirt look.

Harking back to the early pictorialist approach, but using modern colour materials, it is possible to produce strangely haunting images with an ethereal atmosphere. Subtle tints and colouring lend a strange kind of reality to the covered forms. Many types of material are suitable for covering your model, the best being neutral or white cotton, muslin, linings and gauze. Choose soft fabrics, as they drape naturally and cling when dampened. Lighting needs to be carefully balanced so that the covered figure is visible, and there should be sufficient light on the cloth to reveal its colour and texture.

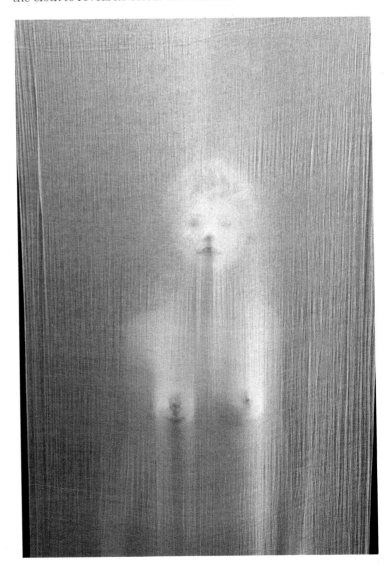

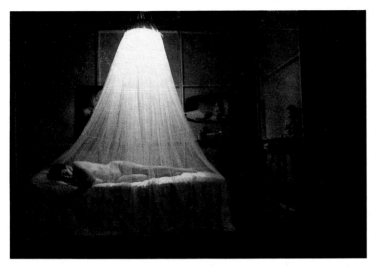

◁ Mosquito netting has formed a cone that channels the light down on to the sleeping figure, which is bathed in a soft, warm glow. Strong light behind netting will make it more transparent, especially if the area outside is in subdued light.

*Pentax LX, 50 mm, Scotch (3M) 640T, ¹/₁₅ sec, f8*

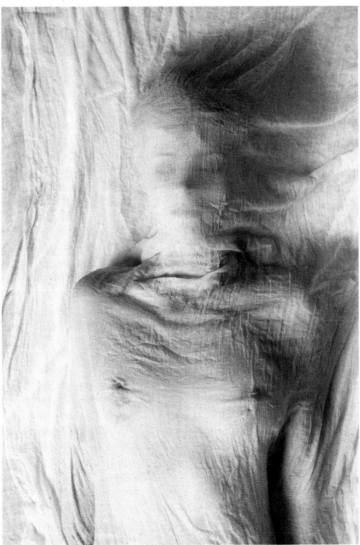

◁ To create this image of a shrouded nude the model was asked to lie down on a white board before being covered with a single layer of muslin. The cloth was dampened to make it cling to the model's body and reveal her outlines more clearly. Light came from a single window and a reflector was placed on the shadow side to lessen the contrast between bright and dark areas.

*Pentax LX, 100 mm macro, Kodak Ektachrome 200, ¹/₁₂₅ sec, f11*

See also:
SOFT AND HARD LIGHT pp36-39
SOFT FOCUSING pp46-47
TUNGSTEN LIGHTING pp78-79

# AN EYE FOR BEAUTY

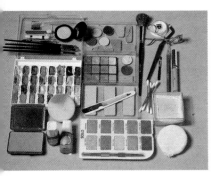

△ Many models carry their own kit of make-up and are expert at applying it. But, as beauty photography depends on the skilled use of make-up, it is wise to seek professional help.

Pictures of beautiful women often concentrate on the face: a frontal view, close-up and made in soft, diffuse light that throws little or no shadow and reveals a minimum amount of modelling. It is, therefore, essential that the model has extremely clear skin with a fine texture that will look attractive even in enlarged images. For professional work, such as advertisements for cosmetics or jewellery, a model with symmetrical features is preferred as her prime job is to enhance the product. For the less demanding requirements of an experimental or amateur session, a symmetrical face is not necessary and a touch of 'character' often adds interest. Hair styling and make-up in studio work are normally handled by professionals and their role is crucial to the success of high-quality beauty shots. Some models are trained to apply make-up, but very few can style hair as well as a professional. Therefore, even the amateur photographer, when taking beauty shots, is advised to seek the aid of the local salon or hairdressing school, where they will often help you in exchange for some useful publicity pictures.

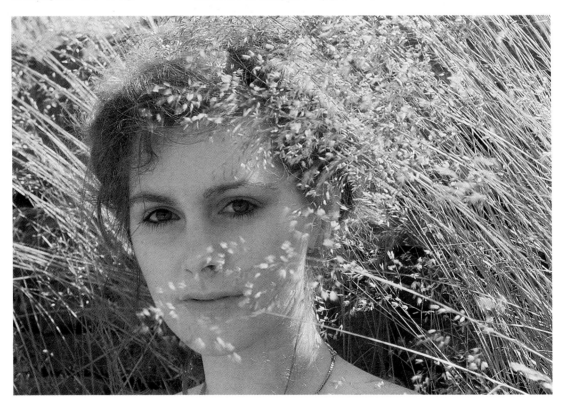

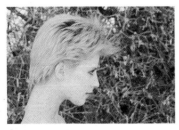

◁ Unusual and yet appropriate backgrounds are hard to find, so when you do, make use of them. In this picture, the hedge of heavily-frosted blackthorn provides a strong contrast in form and tone with the model's profile and complexion.

*Pentax LX, 85 mm, Kodak Ektachrome 64, 1/60 sec, f8*

△ Outdoor beauty pictures are ideal for shots that require a natural look. Choose a model with natural good looks and excellent skin. Settings that provide simple backgrounds in soft, delicate tones that will complement the subject are best.

*Pentax LX, 100 mm macro, Kodak Ektachrome 64, 1/125 sec, f11*

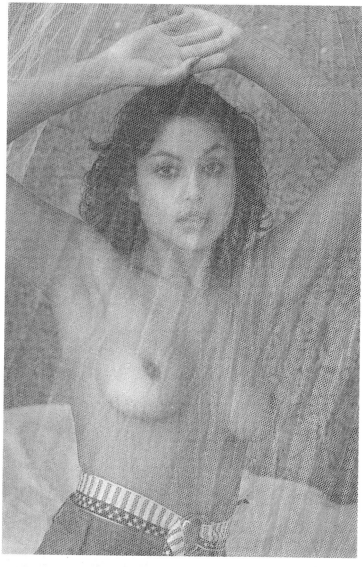

◁ On location, it is sometimes necessary to photograph in the hard light of direct sun which creates contrast that is too high to be flattering. One way to overcome this is to erect a cotton diffuser over the model, softening the light. Here, the spray of a convenient fountain was used as a soft-focus filter, diffusing the highlights and lowering the contrast.

*Pentax LX, 135 mm, Kodak Ektachrome 200, $1/125$ sec, f8*

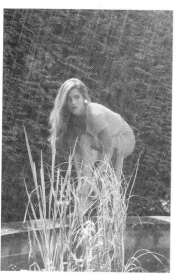

◁ A common practice for evoking a romantic atmosphere in beauty portraits is to shoot through a screen to diffuse the image. This photograph was made using a sheet of butter muslin as a diffuser, but other suitable materials include light netting, transparent plastic, and thin cotton. Emphasis should be on the model, not the screen, so make sure that there is ample light on her face.

*Pentax LX, 50 mm, Kodak Ektachrome 200, $1/30$ sec, f8*

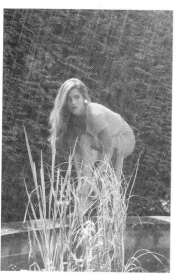

See also:
USING BACKLIGHT pp34-35
SOFT AND HARD LIGHT pp36-39
SOFT FOCUSING pp46-47
CLOSE ENCOUNTERS pp92-93

# BEAUTY ON THE BEACH

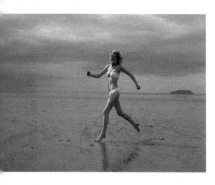

△ For a high success rate in capturing action shots of a model running along the beach, ask her to circle you at a preset distance and concentrate on her expression. An auto-winder lets you reset the shutter without taking your eye from the finder.

*Pentax LX, 50 mm, Kodak Ektachrome 200, autoexposure, f16*

The beach has long been a popular location for fashion and beauty shots for there sun, sea, sand, and beautiful girls combine to create the perfect environment. The bright, spacious atmosphere of the beach also has advantages for models and photographers. It encourages an experimental spirit and wide expanses of empty sand can be used as though they are huge stages where the model can move without restriction, expressing herself freely and without restraint. Fresh air, the smell of the sea, and warm sunshine are an intoxicating mixture to which many models respond positively, putting an extra element of vitality and dynamism into fashion and glamour pictures. The beach is also an ideal setting for more inspired studies of the nude. The textural qualities of sand, rock, and sea can be related to the delicate texture of naked skin in a variety of ways, and the coastline is often rich in geological features that can be used to counterpoint the human figure.

Where there are no shadows cast by buildings and trees, beach light is predictable and, if the sand is light-toned, shadows are less strident, reducing contrast in the subject. But overall contrast can be high. The difference in brightness between pale sand or reflections off the sea and dark areas can be extreme and it is best to balance the exposure for shadow skin tones. Auto-exposure cameras may be misled and you should use the override mechanism or manual exposure.

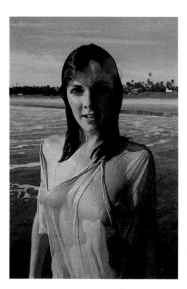

△ Although a cliché of glamour photography, the 'wet look' is often the best approach with an inexperienced model. Clarity has been given to the composition by setting the model against a background rendered unsharp by controlling the depth of field.

*Pentax LX, 50 mm, Kodak Kodachrome 64, ¹/₂₅₀ sec, f8*

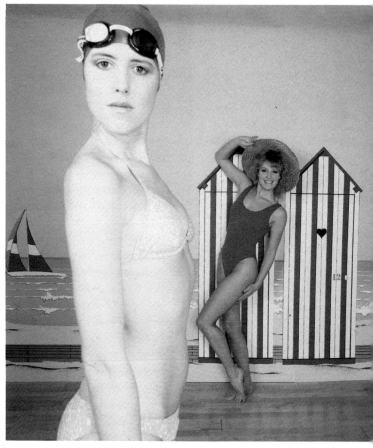

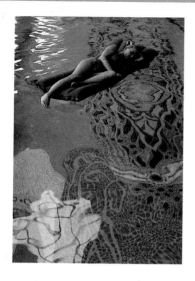

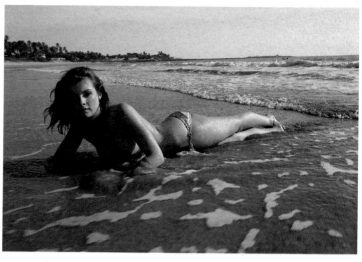

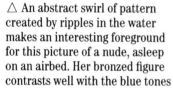

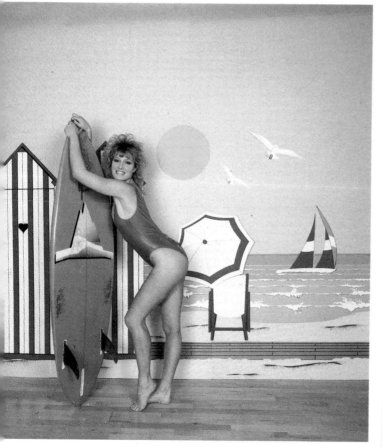

△ An abstract swirl of pattern created by ripples in the water makes an interesting foreground for this picture of a nude, asleep on an airbed. Her bronzed figure contrasts well with the blue tones of the surroundings, and soft, directional backlight has rim-lit her body's contours.

*Pentax LX, 28 mm, Kodak Ektachrome 200, ¹/₆₀ sec, f16*

△ Low-angled light from late-afternoon sun accentuates the texture of the model's water-splashed skin and gives her a warm glow that contrasts with the background. Background sets the scene and adds atmosphere, which is why this picture was taken from a low viewpoint.

*Pentax LX, 50 mm, Kodak Kodachrome 64, ¹/₂₅₀ sec, f8*

◁ To meet advertising schedules, fashion pictures for swimwear are invariably shot in the winter. One way of overcoming the problem of location is to use painted backdrops in the studio. These can be bought or you can construct them yourself. They are, in many ways, more successful than back-projecting real scenes.

*Hasselblad, 60 mm, Kodak Ektachrome 64, electronic flash, f16*

See also:
CAPTURING MOVEMENT pp60-61
VARIETIES OF LIGHT pp68-69
COLOUR INTENSITY pp70-71

# FASHIONABLE LEGS

Fashion photography is particularly enlivened by the photographer's willingness to experiment with techniques and composition, but, even so, some thought must be given to the approach. One solution is to simplify the image, concentrating on a single important element, such as the legs, to create a more abstract picture. Elegant legs are some of nature's most attractive shapes and consequently have a universal appeal. Even with a full-length shot of a figure, the placing of the legs is vital to the overall success of the image. Legs have to be lit, and then posed, with the same care and attention as given to any portrait or still life. They also have to be as near perfect as possible, especially when they become a semi-abstraction, because imperfections are greatly emphasized by this sort of treatment. They are no longer just a part of the model's figure; the photograph is about them alone. Concentrating solely on the legs may appear to be limiting, but it is often when the subject matter is restricted in this way that the photographer is challenged to create new and unusual images, avoiding fashion photography's commoner cliches. Naturally, using more than one model provides more picture opportunities and the possibility of more complex designs. Pairs of legs can be made to relate to each other in intriguing ways and, when odd numbers of limbs or unusual juxtapositions are involved, the results can be both stylish and humorous.

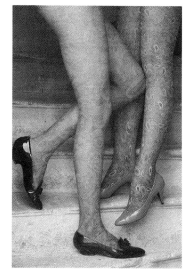

△ Steps are an ideal setting for showing off legs. These two pairs suggest a certain intimacy, particularly as they are posed in a casual and natural way. In fashion photography it is important that the shoes are in perfect condition.

*Pentax LX, 100 mm, Kodak Ektachrome 200, 1/250 sec, f11*

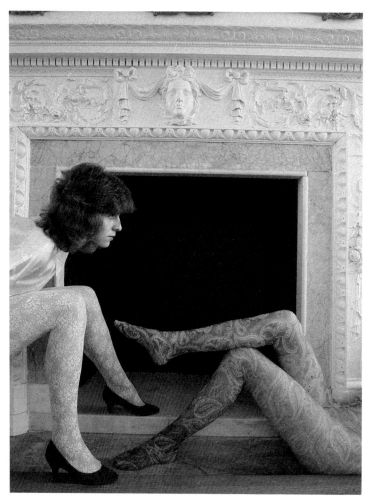

◁ The two girls were relaxing on the floor between shots and only needed to be moved slightly to make an elegant composition in front of the fireplace. The picture was taken with the available natural light.

*Pentax LX, 28 mm, Kodak Ektachrome 200, 1/60 sec, f8*

▷ The idea for this picture came from watching the model changing. Again, just a slight re-arrangement of the pose was all that was needed to create a more pleasing composition. Slight over-exposure was necessary to retain detail in the dark tights.

*Pentax LX, 28 mm, Kodak Ektachrome 200, 1/60 sec, f8*

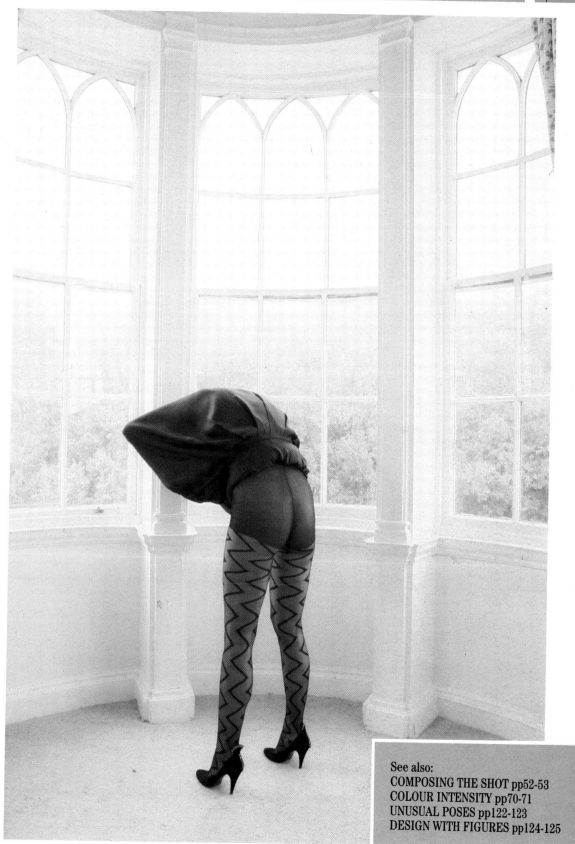

See also:
COMPOSING THE SHOT pp52-53
COLOUR INTENSITY pp70-71
UNUSUAL POSES pp122-123
DESIGN WITH FIGURES pp124-125

Photography tends to be about reality – its interpretation is usually purely representational – so when we see pictures that are obviously false, it can be unsettling. Optical distortions are blatant in their effect, but images that contain familiar objects presented in unusual relationships are more subtle in their effects and trigger off different emotional responses in the viewer, ranging from mild amusement to a sense of disquiet.

Perfectly commonplace items can be used to good effect and, in the most successful images, it is the very fact that everyday, mundane objects are presented in an alternative light that creates interest. Viewers are asked to re-evaluate the way they see things, perhaps seeing them in terms of shape, volume, and design rather than in terms of function or place. The idea is to give people a visual jolt, as well as some mental stimulation, which means selecting items that have strong graphic shapes and placing them out of context for symbolic or aesthetic effect. Including a human figure, particularly a beautiful female form, will make the image more disturbing. The final interpretation of the image's meaning can be left wide open.

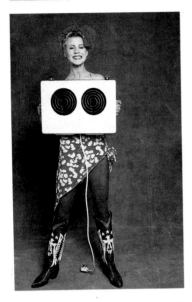

△ Humour, rather than the notion of 'false attachment', is the key to this visual pun.

*Pentax LX, 50 mm, Kodak Ektachrome 64, 1/60 sec, f11*

▷ Here it is the juxtaposition of elegant shapes and role-changing that creates interest. The visual message is presented in a clear and uncomplicated composition, but ultimately the viewer is left to make his or her own interpretation of the image.

*Pentax LX, 50 mm, Kodak Ektachrome 200, 1/60 sec, f8*

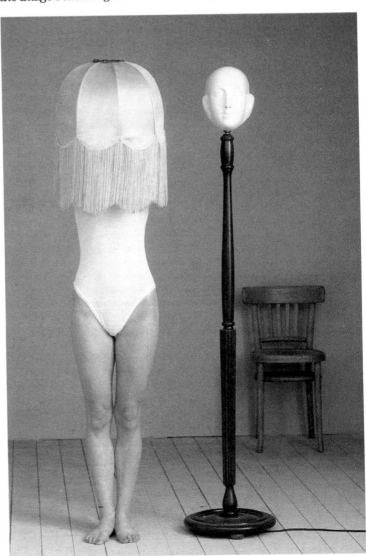

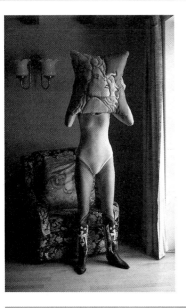

◁ The anonymous nature of beauty in modern society is the theme in this picture. The chosen form is a visual pun using the cushion as the trigger for the idea.

*Pentax LX, 50 mm, Kodak Ektachrome 200, 1/60 sec, f16*

▷ Another ambiguous message. But the replacement of the girl's body with a suitably shaped mirror reflecting an image of furniture perhaps suggests that the housewife is herself regarded almost as a piece of furniture.

*Pentax LX, 28 mm, Kodak Ektachrome 200, 1/30 sec, f11*

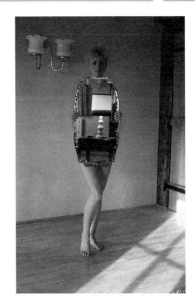

◁ This picture is built up around straight-sided geometric shapes and patterns, the model's shape acting as a counterpoint to the symmetry of the composition. There was no intention of producing an image with a message; it is simply the result of experimenting with unusual props – in this case an empty chocolate box tray.

*Pentax LX, 50 mm, Kodak Ektachrome 200, 1/30 sec, f8*

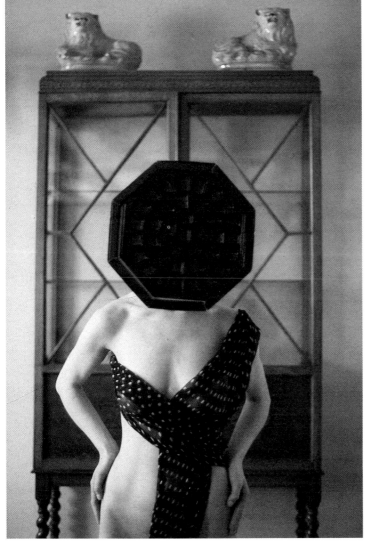

See also:
SOFT AND HARD LIGHT pp36-39
TUNGSTEN LIGHTING pp78-79
HOMEMADE FASHION pp276-277

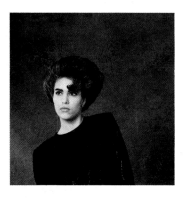

△ A soft, full light was needed to bring out the richness in this black dress.

*Hasselblad, 120 mm, Kodak Ektachrome 64, ¹/₆₀ sec, f11*

In fashion photography, the clothes are the most important element and it is usual to select the model and the setting to complement them. Occasionally, a striking model will inspire the photographer to find clothes to suit him or her and sometimes a setting will provoke ideas about the style of clothing that will look best in it, but normally the clothes come first.

A major problem for the young fashion photographer is finding stylish designs for his pictures. Two easily tapped sources are the fashion school of a local art college and local clothes shops and boutiques. Some chain stores are amenable, but this depends on the attitude of the manager of the individual branch. Photographers are not always familiar with the characteristics of textiles, so do not be shy about consulting experts on how the clothes should look, the type of figure that they are designed for, and even the right sort of setting. Pose is also crucial. Sometimes a static pose will display a garment's character to its best advantage, while at other times the cloth is best seen in a swirl of movement. Lighting quality, as in any photography, has a fundamental effect on the picture.

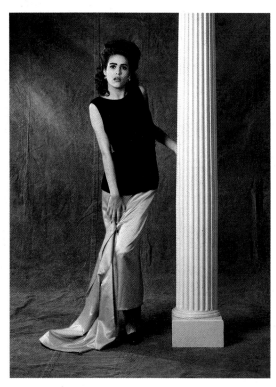

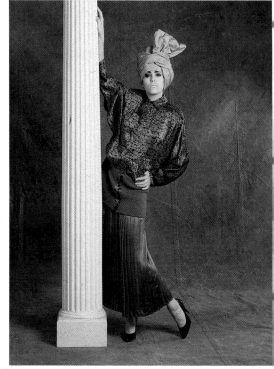

△ ▷ Working in the studio with electronic flash and a simple background is the best way to begin taking fashion photographs. The results are entirely of your own making and it is easy to look at them critically and to see where the strengths and weaknesses of the pictures lie. These two pictures were made with two flash heads fitted with reflective umbrellas, one placed to the side and a little behind the model and the other by the camera as a fill-in. In the picture on the right, the main light has been raised and directed down at a steeper angle to highlight the sheen of the fabric.

*Hasselblad, 80 mm, Kodak Ektachrome 64, ¹/₆₀ sec, f11*

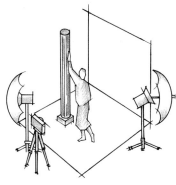

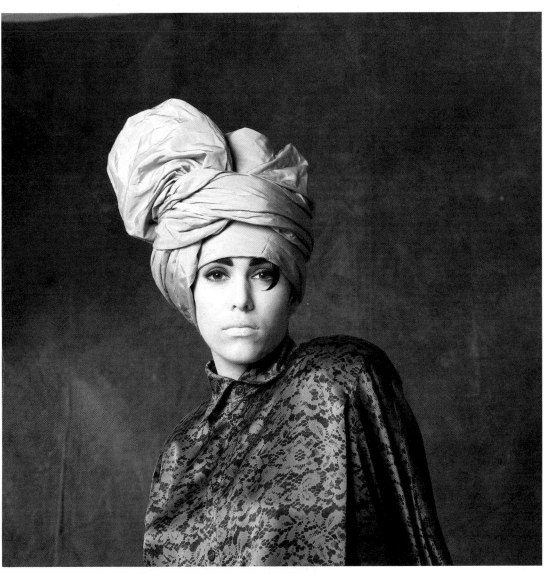

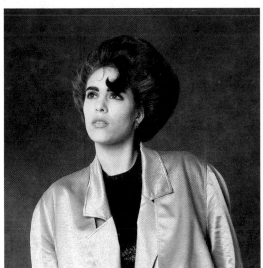

△ ◁A single reflective umbrella was used above and to the right of the model's head (above). The main light to the left of the model was lowered to near eye-level and a reflector placed on the shadow side (left).

*Hasselblad, 120 mm, Kodak Ektachrome 64, ¹/₆₀ sec, f11*

See also:
SOFT AND HARD LIGHT pp36-39
FRAMING THE SUBJECT pp50-51
ELECTRONIC FLASH pp74-77

# HOMEMADE FASHION

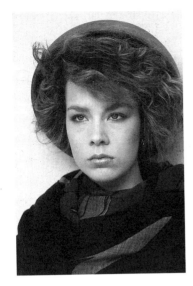

The aspiring fashion photographer has many problems to overcome, not least obtaining exciting, fashionable clothing without having to pay out large sums of money. One solution is to approach the local art college and offer to photograph students' designs. Alternatively, you can design your own clothes, making use of materials that are at hand, and perhaps enlisting the help of a talented assistant.

It is often the case that photographs in fashion magazines, featuring top models and the latest creations, hide the fact that the clothing is ill-fitting and has been crudely altered at the time of the shoot to look good in the picture. Behind the model and hidden from view there may well be a mass of pins and tape holding the dress together. Similar techniques can be applied to commonplace materials such as curtains, sheets, towels and rugs – anything, in fact, that catches your eye and can be woven, folded, or hung to look like a stylish item of clothing.

△ Elegant attire comprising nothing more exciting than a salad bowl for a hat and kitchen curtain draped over the model's shoulders to form the top of a dress. Lighting was subdued sunlight from an adjacent window, and there was a white reflector beside the camera for fill-in.

*Pentax LX, 85 mm, Kodak Ektachrome 200, 1/30 sec, f8*

▷ White toilet paper was put to unusual use for this shot. The outfit has been trimmed with a felt scarf and finished off with a cluster of Christmas decorations. The subdued background was provided by an Indian rug, and lighting was from a large window.

*Pentax LX, 85 mm, Kodak Ektachrome 200, 1/60 sec, f8*

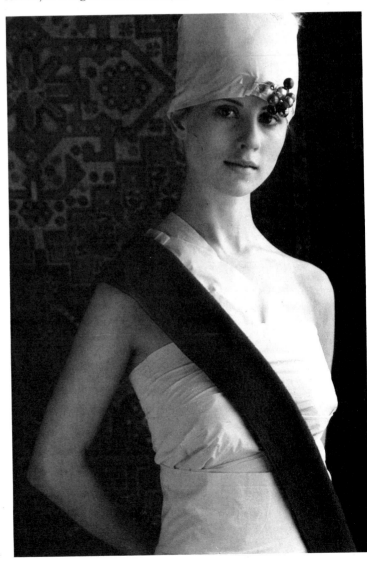

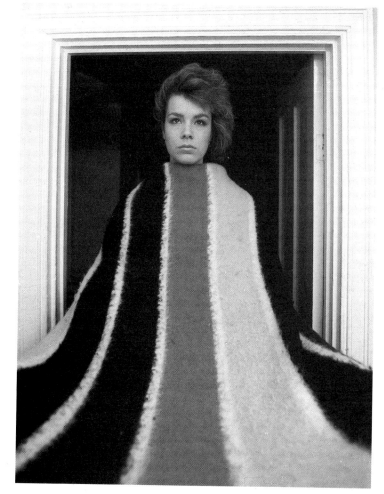

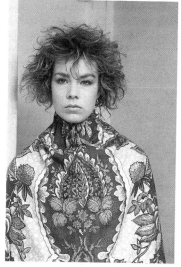

△ A stunning shawl created from a single curtain arranged so that its strong pattern dominated the picture. The elasticated pleating at the top of the curtain formed a convenient neck line.

*Pentax LX, 85 mm, Kodak Ektachrome 200, ¹/₁₅ sec, f8*

△ Vibrant stripes of colour in this blanket inspired a picture in which perspective and depth could be emphasized. The blanket was pinned behind the girl's shoulders and brought forward to within a foot of the camera. The shadowy doorway increases the sense of space with a void beyond. The use of a wide-angle shift lens with downwards shift has exaggerated perspective depth in the image while retaining normal verticals in the doorway. The picture was lit with bounced quartz-halogen lights.

*Pentax LX, 28 mm shift, Kodak Ektachrome 160 Tungsten, ¹/₆₀ sec, f16*

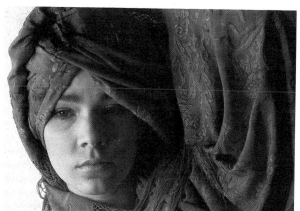

△ This picture required a small Victorian tablecloth, wrapped turban-like around the model's head and suspended to reveal the material's texture.

*Pentax LX, 85 mm, Kodak Ektachrome 200, ¹/₆₀ sec, f16*

See also:
SPECIAL LENSES pp26-27
SOFT AND HARD LIGHT pp36-39
TUNGSTEN LIGHTING pp78-79
KITCHEN GLAMOUR pp258-259

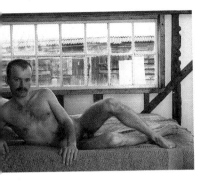

△ Sometimes it is possible to photograph models in their own homes where they are most likely to feel at ease. If you are lucky, as with this man's house, the rooms will be large enough to allow the use of a standard lens or a short telephoto for most shots.

*Hasselblad, 80 mm, Kodak Tri-X (400), 1/125 sec, f16*

The studio is not always the best place to photograph a model. He or she may find the atmosphere too sterile, or even intimidating, and would prefer to be photographed in a more natural setting. The setting may be indoors or out, but the main aim of abandoning the studio is to create a more relaxed atmosphere, particularly if your model is to be nude. Photographing nudes on location also has the benefit of solving the problem of what props to use, and how to obtain them.

Overall, soft directional light is best for photographing the nude, because it both reveals the form of the model and illuminates the setting without making it too dramatic or imposing. Outdoors, a sky with thin cloud gives the right kind of soft, directional light. Such light has a beautiful quality that reveals form and texture. If you wish to get the same kind of lighting in direct sun you can place a large screen of thin white cotton or gauze between the model and the sun to soften its direct rays, using reflectors to soften shadows and reveal details.

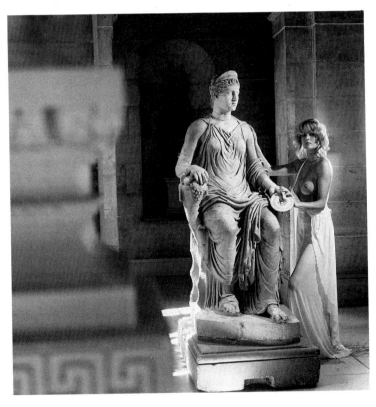

△ The best locations provide their own props and have an atmosphere that is creatively stimulating to both model and photographer. This picture was taken in an English stately home that revealed new and exciting settings at almost every turn. Here it was the classical figure with her flowing robes that inspired the dress and pose of the model. Lighting was carefully arranged so that the tonal values of the stone figure and the model's body matched each other.

*Hasselblad, 80 mm, Kodak Tri-X (400), 1/125 sec, f16*

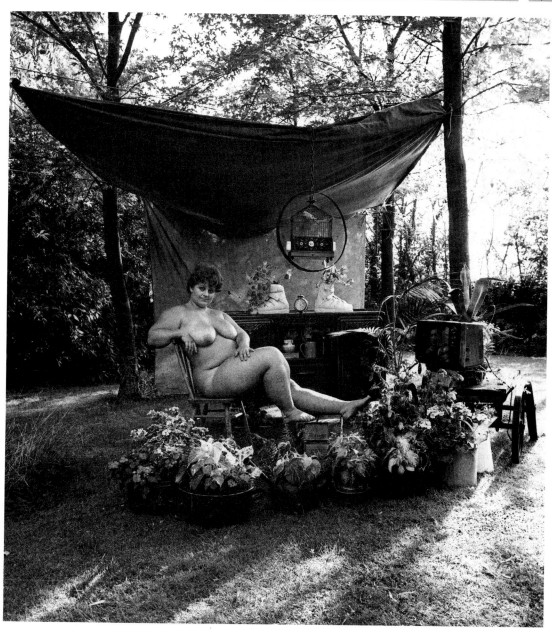

△ Naturist camps are not always as back-to-nature and spartan as their public image sometimes suggests. In true British tradition, all the trappings of civilized, even luxurious, life have been transported and set up as an exotic outdoor sitting room next to a caravan. The woman's naked form is ample in its proportions and in the Rubenesque tradition.

*Hasselblad, 60 mm, yellow filter, Kodak Tri-X (400), ¹/₃₀ sec, f16*

See also:
SOFT AND HARD LIGHT pp36-39
BLACK AND WHITE pp54-57
THE HUMAN FORM pp256-257

# MIRRORED IMAGES

▽ Mirrors make excellent frames for simple pictures, as well as contributing to the atmosphere of the image. The model was lit with a single spot lamp.

*Pentax LX, 100 mm macro, Kodak Ektachrome 160 Tungsten, 1/60 sec, f8*

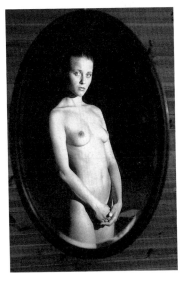

The conventional fixed viewpoint of a camera lens can be, in some circumstances, severely limiting. One of the most important things about a mirror image is that it is laterally reversed – right is left, and left is right. We are so used to seeing ourselves in a mirror that we are often surprised when we see ourselves in a photograph the right way round and as we appear to others.

The mirror's reversing effect has played on man's imagination for centuries, and has featured in legends, poems, plays and stories right up to the present day. So, too, has the way that, when a mirror is broken, the fragments each reflect a complete image, not part of it. In ancient times mystical properties were conferred on mirrors, and even today's mirrors' unusual properties make them an intriguing subject.

A single mirror can be used as a frame, reflecting one image; a pair of mirrors opposite each other will reflect a huge number of images, disappearing into infinity. Mirrors can be used to create bizarre double images, reflect a new foreground, or cover an obtrusive background and, used in conjunction with painted backdrops, they can create successful illusions.

▷ In this picture an aging 17th century Venetian mirror with a mottled surface has been used as a background to complement the young model. Soft, directional daylight from two opposing windows highlights the girl's form and a reflector, placed near the camera, lightens the shadows.

*Pentax LX, 85 mm, Kodak Ektachrome 200, 1/30 sec, f22*

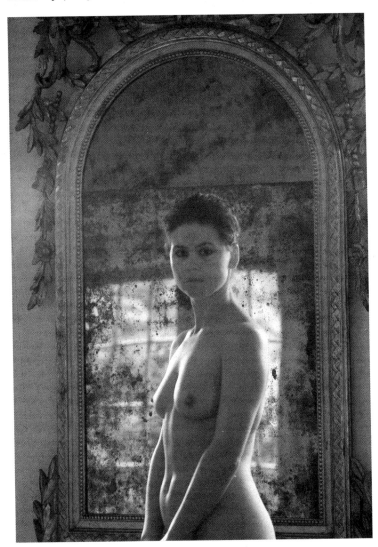

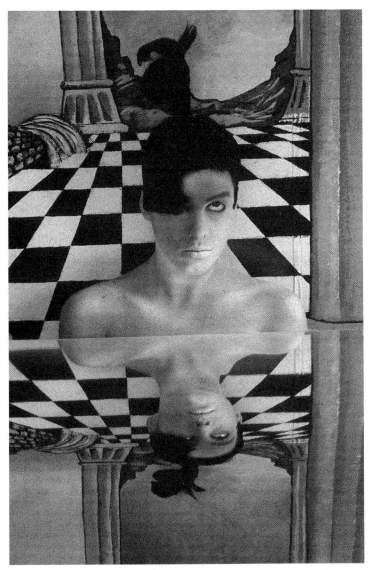

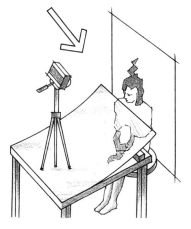

◁ △ Intriguing double images can be made when the background provides interesting shapes and illusions of perspective. The model was made up with theatrical paints and sat just in front of the mural, legs outstretched beneath a low table. A small, wooden block was placed on the table and a plastic mirror laid on top with an edge against the model's shoulders. The block bowed the mirror's surface, distorting the reflection.

*Pentax LX, 85 mm, Kodak Ektachrome 200, ¹/₆₀ sec, f16*

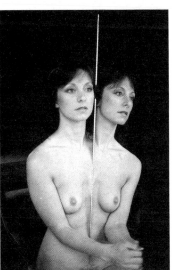

◁ An almost endless variety of views and shapes can be created by altering the relationship between the mirror and the subject. One of the most effective ways of using a mirror is in a double portrait like this one. If the edge of the mirror was blacked it would disappear, strengthening the image of a two-headed nude.

*Pentax LX, 28 mm, Kodak Ektachrome 200, ¹/₆₀ sec, f16*

See also:
DEPTH OF FIELD pp40-41
MULTIPLE IMAGES pp86-87
BENDING REALITY pp98-99
REFLECTED IMAGES pp146-147

# GLOSSARY

**Aberration**  A distortion of image quality, often at the edges of the lens field; caused by inherent optical errors that interfere with lens performance. Aberration can be reduced by using medium to small apertures.

**Absorption**  Materials partially absorb light falling on their surface. The selective absorption of light of different wavelengths, and the reflection of others, gives a subject its colour.

**Abstract**  A non-realistic image, frequently of shapes or patterns, in which the identity of the subject is obscured.

**Acutance**  The objective measurement of image sharpness.

**Aerial perspective**  An impression of three-dimensional depth created by the presence of atmospheric haze which causes a lightening of tone and loss of detail as distance is increased.

**Ambient light**  Light that is normally available in a scene. Can be natural (usually sunlight) or artificial light.

**Angle of incidence**  The angle formed between a light ray striking a surface and an imaginary line at right-angles to that surface.

**Angle of reflection**  The angle formed between a light ray reflected from a surface and an imaginary line at right-angles to that surface. Angles of incidence and reflection are equal.

**Angle of view**  The angle subtended at the lens between the outer limits of the image area seen by the lens.

**Aperture**  The opening, normally circular, that restricts the amount of light passing through a lens. On most cameras the size of the aperture can be varied.

**Aperture priority**  A semi-automatic exposure system in which the photographer selects the aperture and the camera meter sets shutter speed.

**Artificial light**  Any light that does not originate from a natural source, ultimately the sun.

**Artificial light film**  Colour film balanced for use with tungsten artificial light of 3200K; is usually marked 'Tungsten' on the pack.

**Autofocus**  An automatic focusing system featured on some SLR cameras, enlargers and projectors. The subject is electronically focused without manual adjustment.

**Autoexposure**  A system which uses a photoelectric cell for setting aperture and/or shutter speed automatically in response to subject brightness.

**Backlight**  Light originating from behind the subject. Also known as *contre-jour*.

**Barrel distortion**  A type of aberration which causes straight lines at image margins to curve out – like a barrel.

**B-setting**  A setting in which the shutter stays open when the release is kept depressed. Used to give longer exposures than those available on the camera settings.

**Bounced light**  Light that has been reflected from a matte surface. Gives softer light over a wider area and avoids harsh shadows.

**Bracketing**  A technique of taking a series of exposures at regular, stepped exposure levels, in order to obtain the 'best' one. Normally the steps are in ⅓ or ½ stops, over and under the estimated exposure level.

**Brightness range**  The difference in brightness – or luminance – between the lightest and darkest parts of a subject.

**Brilliance**  The intensity of light reflected from a surface.

**Catadioptric lens**  A telephoto lens that uses glass elements and mirrors in its construction to 'fold' the light path, and thereby fit a long focal length into a short barrel. Also called a mirror or reflex lens.

**CdS meter**  A light meter which uses the action of a photo-sensitive cadmium sulphide cell to measure the intensity of light.

**Chromogenic film**  Colour film that produces dyes during processing.

**Close-up**  A term used to describe an image made from a near distance, occupying most of the frame.

**Colour balance**  Colour balance is achieved when a neutral scale of grey tones is reproduced without a colour cast (see below).

**Colour cast**  An undesirable colour bias especially noticeable in neutral tones and skin colour.

**Colour circle**  The colour spectrum in the form of a circle, divided into segments with complementary colours (see below) opposing each other.

**Colour contrast**  The apparent difference in brilliance between two, adjacent colours.

**Colour filters**  Colour filters are of two basic types: colour balancing filters and colour correcting or compensating filters. The first are used to balance colour film with the colour temperature of the light source, to avoid a colour cast. For example, a blue balancing filter allows use of daylight film with tungsten lighting. Compensating filters are used to remove colour casts or induce them, to enhance mood. With black and white film, colour filters lighten or darken one tone relative to another, often increasing contrast.

**Colour saturation**   The purity and intensity of a colour.

**Colour temperature**   A method of describing a light source's colour quality in terms of a temperature scale, usually expressed in degrees Kelvin (K). Red light has a lower colour temperature (about 1800K) than blue (about 6000K). Normal sunlight has a value of 4500-5000K.

**Complementary colour**   A term which usually refers to the colours yellow, magenta and cyan which are complementary to blue, green and red.

**Contrast**   The difference between the brightest and darkest areas of a scene, subjectively assessed.

**Cropping**   The excluding of unwanted peripheral areas of an image or scene.

**Development**   The chemical process by which silver halides that have been exposed to light are converted to black, metallic silver, thus revealing a visible image.

**Diaphragm**   An adjustable aperture.

**Differential focusing**   A technique in which depth of field and sharpness are limited to the subject plane, isolating the subject against an unsharp background and/or foreground.

**Diffraction**   The effect of light scattering as it passes through a very small hole or close by the edge of an opaque surface. At very small apertures, diffraction can affect image quality.

**Diffraction filter**   A filter etched with a grid of fine lines which separates light into its constituent colours to give scattered rainbow coloured lines over the image. Also called a diffraction grating or diffractor.

**Diffuser**   A translucent material that scatters light. Used to soften hard illumination.

**Distortion**   Any alteration in the true representation of an image, changing the shape or proportions, often for special effects.

**Documentary photography** Photography intended to record social, environmental and/or political situations, to provide information and often, by implication, to make a comment.

**Emulsion**   The light-sensitive chemicals, such as silver halides, suspended in an inert medium, usually gelatin, that forms the active coat to film and photographic printing paper.

**Exposure**   The product of the light intensity reaching a film and the time during which the light acts on it. Aperture size and shutter speed, respectively, control these factors.

**Exposure latitude**   The range of over – or underexposure – over which a light-sensitive emulsion will still produce an acceptable result.

**Fast film**   Film that is very sensitive to light and has a high ISO rating (see below). Usually considered as ISO 400 or more.

**Fast lens**   A lens with a wider than normal maximum aperture for its type.

**Fill-in light**   Light used to illuminate shadow areas in a scene.

**Film plane**   The plane across which the film lies. Its position is denoted by a symbol on the top plate of some cameras.

**Film speed**   A term used to describe the sensitivity to light of film and denoted by ISO numbers (see below).

**Filter factor**   The factor by which an unfiltered exposure reading must be multiplied to compensate for the light held back by a filter.

**Flare**   Non-image-forming light that has been deflected from its true path to the film emulsion.

**Flash-factor**   See *Guide number*.

**Flash synchronization**   The coincidence of flash exposure with the period of maximum shutter opening.

**f-number**   The number that indicates the aperture setting in a scale common to all lenses. When focused to infinity, and set to a given f-number, all lenses transmit the same amount of light. Exposure is halved for each step to the next highest f-number.

**Focal plane shutter**   The shutter situated immediately in front of the film, consisting of a pair of moving blinds. Shutter speed is determined by the width of the gap between the blinds as they pass in front of the film.

**Graduated filter**   A toned filter which progressively reduces in density towards the centre line, leaving the second half clear.

**Grain**   Silver halide crystals that have been exposed and developed to form black, silver particles to produce the image.

# G L O S S A R Y

**Graininess** Clumps of silver grains and the qualitative assessment of their effect on image quality. Graininess is increased with fast film and/or developing techniques.

**Guide number** A figure given to an artificial light source, such as a flash, to indicate its power. When divided into the subject distance, it indicates the f-stop to set for correct flash exposure (in an environment equivalent to a medium-sized, light-toned room). The figure applies to ISO 100 film and to distances measured in feet or metres.

**High key** An image comprised of mostly pale tones.

**Highlights** The brightest parts of a scene or positive image. In a negative they are represented by the areas of highest density.

**Hot-shoe** An accessory shoe fitted on most modern cameras. Electrical contacts here form part of the flash/shutter synchronization circuit.

**Incident light** The light falling on a subject.

**Incident reading** A measurement of the intensity of light falling on a subject. Made with an incident light meter.

**Iris diaphragm** A set of interleaving blades that controls the size of the aperture.

**ISO** International Standards Organization. A film speed classification system that uses identical numbers to the now defunct ASA system. A doubling in the ISO number represents an increase in sensitivity of $\times 2$. Thus ISO 100 film requires twice the exposure under the same conditions as ISO 200 film.

**Kelvin (K)** The unit of temperature measurement used to describe the colour quality of a light source.

**Large format camera** A camera that has an image area of $5 \times 4$ in or more.

**Latitude** See *Exposure latitude*.

**Light box** A light source contained in a box and covered by a diffuser, used for viewing transparencies and negatives.

**Linear perspective** The apparent convergence with increased distance of parallel lines in a two-dimensional image, creating the illusion of depth.

**Low key** An image comprised of mostly dark tones.

**Macro lens** A lens designed to perform well at very close distances where image magnification is from $\times \frac{1}{2}$ to $\times 10$ life-size.

**Mirror lens** See *Catadioptric lens*.

**Mode** One of the operating programmes available in automated camera systems.

**Modelling light** A continuous light source built into studio electronic flash heads for visualizing lighting effects. Also refers to light used to create a three-dimensional effect through the play of light and shadow.

**Neutral density (ND)** Colourless tone.

**Neutral density filter** A grey filter used to reduce the amount of light reaching the film without affecting the overall colour balance of the final image.

**Normal lens** A lens with a focal length approximately equal to the diagonal of the film format used, and one which has an angle of view similar to that of human vision. Also called a standard lens.

**Open up** To select a lower f-number, thus increasing aperture size to admit more light.

**Panchromatic film** Film that is sensitive to all colours of the spectrum. Usually applied to black and white film.

**Parallax error** The difference between the image area recorded on the film and that seen through a direct vision viewfinder. It becomes exaggerated at close distances. Does not occur with SLRs.

**Pentaprism** A five-sided prism, located on the top of most SLR cameras, that gives a correctly-orientated image in the viewfinder.

**Perspective** A method of giving the illusion of three-dimensional depth in a two-dimensional image.

**Polarized light** A light ray travels in a straight line and is normally thought of as a wave motion vibrating in all planes at right-angles to that line. Polarized light vibrates in one plane only, brought about either by it being reflected off a non-metallic surface or by passing it through a polarizing filter.

**Polarizing filter** A filter that restricts the plane of vibration of light and is used to reduce specular reflections and increase colour saturation.

**Portrait lens** A lens with a focal length approximately twice that of a normal lens, used specifically for portrait photography. (Some portrait lenses also produce a slightly diffused effect.)

**Primary colours**   Blue, green and red are the primary colours in optics. These comprise roughly ⅓ each of the spectrum and when mixed in equal proportion make white light.

**Pulling**   Overexposing the film and then reducing development to produce an image of lower contrast.

**Pushing**   Underexposing the film and then increasing development to gain an increase in film speed and contrast. Also termed uprating the film.

**Reciprocity failure**   The effect of a normal film's progressive loss of sensitivity and shift in colour balance with long exposure times – 1 sec or more – and also with extremely brief exposure times.

**Recycling time**   The time taken for a freshly discharged electronic flash unit to recharge.

**Reflected light reading**   A measurement of subject brilliance. Made with a reflected light meter.

**Reflex lens** See *Catadioptric lens.*

**Reversal film**   Colour or black and white film that produces a positive image on exposure. Also called transparency film.

**Saturated colour**   Pure, undiluted colour tone.

**Selenium meter**   A type of exposure meter that uses a photo-electric selenium cell which generates electricity in proportion to the intensity of light acting on it.

**Sensitivity**   The capacity of a photographic emulsion to be affected by exposure to light. Also termed as the film's speed.

**Shadows**   The darkest areas of an image or scene.

**Shutter priority**   A semi-automatic exposure system in which the photographer selects the shutter speed and the camera then sets the aperture.

**Shutter speed**   The exposure duration, usually measured and set in seconds and fractions of a second. A halving or doubling of the shutter speed brings about a corresponding change in exposure.

**Silhouette**   An image that is filled with a dark tone and seen against a light background.

**Slave unit**   A light-sensitive device that triggers additional electronic flash units in response to light from the main unit connected to the camera.

**Slow film**   Film which has a low sensitivity to light. Usually reckoned to be ISO 50 or less.

**Slow lens**   A lens with a smaller than normal maximum aperture for its type.

**Soft-focus**   A technique used to produce diffused image detail with a slight loss in sharpness.

**Speed**   See *Sensitivity.*

**Spot-meter**   A light meter with a narrow angle of coverage – usually in the order of 10° or less – for taking reflected light readings, usually at some distance from the subject.

**Standard lens**   See *Normal lens.*

**Still life**   A static subject specially arranged to produce an aesthetically pleasing and self-contained image. Such a composition discovered by chance is called a found still life.

**Stopping down**   Selecting a smaller f-number to reduce the aperture and the amount of light reaching the film.

**Synchronized flash**   See *Flash synchronization.*

**Texture**   The degree of roughness or smoothness of a surface; its tactile quality.

**Textured lighting**   Light which falls at an oblique angle to a surface, highlighting its texture.

**Tonal range**   The various shades of grey distinguishable from each other between the lightest and darkest tones in an image.

**Tone**   An area of uniform density in an image that can be distinguished from lighter or darker areas.

**Transmitted light**   Light which has passed through a translucent material, as opposed to light direct from its source.

**Transparency film**   See *Reversal film.*

**TTL**   Through the lens. A TTL meter measures subject exposure through the taking lens.

**Tungsten light film**   Colour film that is balanced for use with tungsten illumination and other light sources with a colour temperature of 3200K.

**Uprating**   See *Pushing.*

**Vanishing point**   A distant point where parallel lines appear to meet.

**White light**   Light comprising of an equal mix of blue, green and red wavelengths. Also daylight with a colour temperature of 5500K.

# INDEX

# ACKNOWLEDGEMENTS

Mobius International Ltd would like to thank the following for their assistance in the production of this book:

Equipment suppliers: Chelsea Wharf Windsurfing, Fuji Film Co Ltd, Introphoto (UK) Ltd, Keigh Johnson Photographic Ltd, Minolta (UK) Ltd, Pelling & Cross Ltd, Vivitar (UK) Ltd

Photographers: Mike Dunning, Kim Sayer

Artists: Steve Braund, Gary Marsh, Jim Robins

Design assistance: Lisa Benzing, Michelle Cox, Patrizio Semproni

Editorial assistance: Mario Cecere, Jonathan Hilton, James McCarter, David Rosam

John Hedgecoe's assistant: Rosanna Wilson Stephens

Associate writer: Tim Woodcock

**Art editor** Jim Marks
**Assistant art editor** Mustafa Sami
**Editor** Linda Doeser
**Editorial director** Richard Dawes